MERCEDES-BENZ
Production Models Book
1946-1995

**Detailed descriptions, specifications, photos,
production data and prices of all
1946–95 passenger automobiles**

by W. Robert Nitske

Motorbooks International
Publishers & Wholesalers ®
Osceola, Wisconsin 54020, USA

Books by W. Robert Nitske

The Amazing Porsche and Volkswagen Story was published in 1958.

The Complete Mercedes Story was first published by the Macmillan Company in 1955.

Rudolf Diesel, Pioneer of the Age of Power (with Charles M. Wilson) was published by the University of Okalahoma Press in 1965.

The Life of Wilhelm Conrad Röntgen, Discoverer of the X-Ray, was published by the University of Arizona Press in 1971.

Travels in North America, 1822–1824, a translation of the important exploration diary of Duke Paul Wilhelm of Württemberg, was published by the University of Oklahoma Press in 1973.

Mercedes-Benz 300SL was published by Motorbooks International in 1974.

The Zeppelin Story was published by A. S. Barnes & Company in 1977.

Mercedes-Benz Production Models 1946–1975 was published by Motorbooks International in 1977.

Mercedes-Benz: A History was published by Motorbooks International in 1978.

Mercedes-Benz: Diesel Automobiles was published by Motorbooks International in 1981.

Mercedes-Benz Production Models 1946 – 1986 was published by Motorbooks International in 1986

Mercedes-Benz Production Models Book 1946–1990 was published by Motorbooks International in 1995.

Copyright © 1983, 1985, 1990, 1995
Printed and bound in the United States of America
Fourth Edition
First Printing

*All illustrations are from the archives of the
Daimler-Benz A.G.*

Printed by Fabe Litho, Ltd.
Tucson, Arizona 85705

Library of Congress Cataloging in Publication Data

Nitske, W. Robert.
Mercedes-Benz production models book, 1946-1983.

1. Mercedes automobile.   I. Title.
TL215.M4N518   1983   629.2'222   83-8041
ISBN 0-87938-190-6

World-wide distribution by:

Motorbooks International
Osceola, Wisconsin, U.S.A.

This edition first published in 1995 by W. Robert Nitske in association with Motorbooks International Publishers & Wholesalers, PO Box 2, Oscoela, WI 54020 USA.

All rights reserved. With the exception of quoting brief passages for the purpose of review no part of this publication may be reproduced without prior written permission from the publisher.

Motorbooks International is a certified trademark, registered with the United States Patent Office.

The information in this book is true and complete to the best of our knowledge. All recommendations are made without any guarantee on the part of the author or publisher, who also disclaim any liability incurred in connection with the use of this data or specific details.

We recognize that some words, model names and designations, for example, mentioned herein are the property of the the trademark holder. We use them for identification purposes only. This is not an official publication.

ISBN 0-7603-0245-6

Acknowledgments

Without the assistance of many fine people in the Daimler-Benz organization here and in Germany, these compilations of production details would, of course, have been impossible. I wish to express my most sincere thanks for all of the valuable help I received from Untertürkheim and Montvale, and especially to Herr Claus-Peter Schulze in the Archives department and Frau Ruth Witzel in the Press-Photo section.

Subsequent and vastly enlarged second anbd third editions were made possible with the invaluable assistance by other fine people as well. From this, A. B. Shuman at Montvale and from Stuttgart, Peter Viererbl and Thomas Hartman of the Presseabteilung and Herr Brommer and Karnowski of the Archives were some of the many who helped locate and furnish detailed authentic material for this book.

To all I am most grateful.

The final responsibility of the entire contents of this book is mine alone, however, and any seeming variations in the many detailed specifications, either inch or metric, are due often to the several documents used which did not always agree on every given model. Generally then, I have used what I felt was the most authentic information available.

This compilation of fifty years of Mercedes production is lovingly dedicated to Betty, my helpmate for over fifty-six years now.

When, thoroughly devastated, I was discharged from the military after a year of total paralysis with polyneuritis (Guillain-Barré syndrome) she presented me with a 3210-page Merriam-Webster dictionary I couldn't even lift and thus encouraged me to start a new career — writing.

So, if this book proves informative and useful to you, please direct your thanks to her. I have done so.

Table of Contents

Models Index

Production Eras

It is appropriate to begin this book on Mercedes Models with the year 1946. That year marked the beginning of the post-war production period and the Nallinger era, followed in 1963 by the Scherenberg era.

In the long and distinguished history of Daimler and Benz, there was always a definite engineering direction in their products, reflecting the personality of its then current Chef-Konstrukteur. It all began in 1900 when Wilhelm Maybach created the "New Daimler," developed from the 28-horsepower Phönix model built under the direction of Gottlieb Daimler in 1899. With the resounding success of this new 35-horsepower machine in Nice, the "Mercedes" era was first introduced.

Daimler received his basic patent number 28,022 for the fast-turning light gasoline engine on December 16, 1883. In October of that year, Karl Benz had established his Gas Engine Factory in Mannheim to build engines according to his own design.

On August 29, 1885, Daimler received patent number 36,423 for his vehicle and on January 29, 1886, Benz received patent number 37,435 from the Kaiserliche Patentamt for his motorwagon.

Wilhelm Maybach remained with Daimler until 1907 and was the creator of the powerful Mercedes racing car which in 1903 developed as much as 90 horsepower and in 1906 an astounding 120 horsepower.

Paul Daimler took over the responsibility of the Chief Constructor in 1907 to stay with the company until 1922. He made his debut with the 140-horsepower racing cars which astonished the automotive world with the decisive victories in the prestigious French Grand Prix. In 1910 the Knight patents for their engines was used, culminating in the 16/50-horsepower four-cylinder automobile in 1916 with that engine construction and a shaft drive, first used in 1905.

The 1914 racing cars — again to confound all expert observers — beat all competitors in the French Grand Prix. But Daimler's best remembered models were those using a supercharger. The 1921 models of 1.5 liter (6/25/40 horsepower) and 2.6 liter (10/40/65 horsepower) and the 2.0-liter racing car of 125 horsepower were truly exciting machines.

Ferdinand Porsche took over the leadership of the construction bureau in 1923 and remained there for five years. He was quick to capitalize on the victorious supercharged model and developed the four-cylinder engine into the six- and eight-cylinder types. In 1923 and 1924 the 2-, 4-, and 6-liter engines were used in passenger cars; and in 1928 the 2.6-, 3.5-, and 4.6-liter six- and eight-cylinder engines were used without superchargers in the sedan models Stuttgart, Mannheim, and Nürburg.

In 1924 it was decided to merge the interests of the Daimler and the Benz companies and to create a unified construction bureau.

As usual, however, the best-remembered Porsche creations were the powerful supercharged sports cars. Beginning with the K-model in 1927, with a 6.2-liter engine of 24/100/140 horsepower, and the S model with the 6.8-liter engine developing 26/120/180 horsepower, these six-cylinder cars were further developed to appear in 1928 as the 7.1-liter 170/225 horsepower touring models SS and SSK.

In 1929 Hans Nibel took over the position of Chief Construction Engineer of the recently formed Daimler-

Benz Vis-à-Vis 1894

Daimler Vis-à-Vis 1894

Daimler Phoenix racer 1899

Mercedes racer 1901

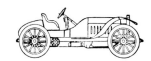

Mercedes racer 1906

Benz company. As early as 1908 he had startled everyone with his huge 200-horsepower Blitzen Benz, a fantastic car, which in 1909 established a world's record of 228.094 kilometers (141.7 miles) per hour in the United States to remain unbroken until 1924. With Max Wagner, Nibel was also responsible for the streamlined, rear-engined Benz Tropfenwagon of 1922. In the fall of 1926, Nibel joined the combined construction staff of the two merged firms, and was actively involved in the development details of the Porsche era models. (The SSK sports car of 1931 was a refinement of the touring car of 1928.)

In addition to the 1929 Nürburg and Mannheim sedans, Nibel created the "Grosser Mercedes," a 7.7-liter limousine, with or without supercharger. A 1.7-liter six-cylinder sedan, the first car with swing axles, appeared in 1931, followed by similar 2-liter 200 models the following year. In 1934 the first rear-engined Mercedes, the 130 model, was built, and the 1.7-liter sedans using an X-shaped oval tubular chassis, 170V front-, and 170H rear-engined, attracted considerable comment. A 150H model followed soon.

Along with these many new construction models, Nibel also created in 1934 the first racing car for the 750-kilogram formula, the 3.3-liter 280-horsepower eight-cylinder machine; and from the eight-cylinder 380 model sports car with a supercharger of 1932 the 5-liter 100/160 horsepower 500K model sports car was developed.

After the sudden death of Nibel in 1934, Max Sailer — with Fritz Nallinger as deputy — took over the duties of the engineering division. Sailer, even more than most of his predecessors or successors, had been a successful racing competitor. In 1914 he had auspiciously participated in the French Grand Prix; in 1921 he won the Coppa Florio; and in 1923 he raced in the Memorial Day Classic at Indianapolis. He came to Unterturkheim from the position of

manager of the Marienfelde plant. During the Sailer era, the first diesel-engined passenger car was marketed in 1935 — the 260D with the 2.6-liter 45-horsepower engine, utilizing the pre-chamber combustion system patented by Prosper L'Orange and developed originally at Mannheim in 1923. The advent of this diesel-engined sedan opened up an entirely new aspect in passenger automobile power.

But the racing cars developed by Sailer attracted the greatest admiration of automobile enthusiasts. These were: (1) in 1935 the 4- to 5.6-liter eight-cylinder cars to develop 600 horsepower, (2) the victorious 3-liter twelve-cylinder racing cars for the 1938-1939 formula, and (3) the spectacular 1.5-liter car of 1939 with the two-stage supercharger. There was also the 5.6-liter twelve-cylinder record car in 1936.

In addition, the six-cylinder sedans of 3.2 liters, developed from the 2.9-liter engines of 1932, were brought out in a 3.4-liter version as model 320. The 5.4-liter 115/180 horsepower eight-cylinder sports model 540K of 1937 was a further development of the 500K of 1934. And, of course, the 7.7-liter 155/230 horsepower eight-cylinder supercharged engine appeared in 1937 in a vastly improved Grosser Mercedes, using an oval tubular frame. In 1938 the 230 sedan model had the first all-steel body.

Throughout this brief resume of automobile development at Daimler-Benz, considerable emphasis has been given to the construction of racing cars. They were a most important part of the construction activity, and the valuable experience gathered in strong competition added immensely to the technical progress in automotive evolution. Especially in Mercedes automobiles was the influence of racing and sports engines and chassis noticable, perhaps more than in the products of any other passenger car manufacturer.

Wilhelm Maybach began this episode with the 30/35-

 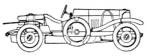 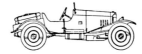 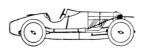 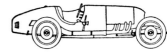

4.5-l. Mercedes racer 1914   Mercedes sports-and racing car 1921   1.5-l. Mercedes sports-and racing car 1922   1.5-l. Mercedes racer 1923   2-l Mercedes racer 1924

horsepower four-cylinder Mercedes of 1901 which two years later developed 60 and 90 horsepower and in 1905 an even 100 horsepower. In 1906 the huge six-cylinder engine developed 120 horsepower. The last Maybach racing car (1907) had only 80 horsepower, but with many improvements in construction the car actually outperformed the earlier models.

During the Paul Daimler era, Otto Schilling was especially concerned with the further development of racing car construction. The 130-horsepower Mercedes created tremendous admiration by the automotive public when in 1908 Christian Lautenschlager won the French race over twenty-three competitors at an average speed of 111.1 kilometers per hour and Otto Salzer drove the record lap at 126.5 kilometers (78.56 miles) per hour. The 1914 Mercedes made history by repeating the victorious feat. And the supercharged four-cylinder racing cars of 1921 and 1922 with the 1.5-, 2.6-, and 2-liter engines of 40, 65, and 125 horsepower were amazing machines, and way ahead of their times.

During the Ferdinand Porsche regime, the experience with the 2-liter eight-cylinder car of 1923 with supercharger led to that treatment for the 1914 model Grand Prix machines. The further developed 2-liter cars competed successfully in the Sicilian Targa and Coppa Florio, driven by Werner, Lautenschlager, and Neubauer. However, the construction of the fantasic sports models, K, S, SS, and SSK, with their huge 6- and 7-liter six-cylinder engines and whining superchargers are much better remembered by the general public.

But in 1934 Hans Nibel constructed for the new formula a racing car with an eight-cylinder engine of 3.3-liter displacement and 280 horsepower. Only twenty-eight years before the Maybach six-cylinder 11-liter engine (140 millimeter bore and 120 millimeter stroke) had developed 120 horsepower. (Prior to this time the S series of sports cars had participated in racing events during the difficult economic times of the post-war era.) The Nibel racing car engines had steel cylinders with four valves each with spark plugs located between them, and two overhead camshafts; the crankshaft had roller bearings. With this car the golden epoch of racing began for Mercedes. Rudolf Caracciola and this 750-kilogram car seemed invincible. The work of Hans Nibel remained in the capable hands of his assistants Max Sailer, Max Wagner, Albert Hees, and Fritz Nallinger.

Under the leadership of Max Sailer, the construction bureau developed the 4- and 5-liter eight-cylinder racing cars of 350 to 600 horsepower for the 1935-37 period along with a twelve-cylinder record car of 5.6-liters in 1936. Out of ten Grand Prix, Mercedes won nine events. In 1937, seven out of twelve Grandes Epreuves went to the Mercedes drivers. For the 1938 formula, the 3-liter twelve-cylinder racing car developing 450 horsepower was built. Even with less power the car reached the same average speeds of the earlier machines. Once again, the Mercedes drivers Caracciola, von Brauchitsch, and Lang were overwhelmingly successful in international competition — in fact so much so, that the Italians decided to allow only 1.5-liter cars in the prominent Tripoli race in 1939. Sailer and Wagner created, in record time and complete secrecy, the two-stage supercharged V-8 cylinder machine which gave Mercedes a double victory over twenty-eight other competitors. Lang averaged 197.8 kilometers (122.9 miles) per hour and Caracciola 191.9 km, a truly magnificent accomplishment of superb engineering and masterful driving of an excellent product.

The Fritz Nallinger era, officially begun late in 1940 after the Max Sailer reign, had its real beginning with the 170 gasoline vehicles of the Nibel period. Nallinger developed the 170V then to such a high level that it proved to

   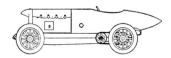 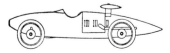

Benz racer 1900   Benz racer 1908   1.5-l. Benz sports car 1922   Blitzen Benz 1911   2-l. Benz Tropfen racer 1922

be the best-selling Mercedes model for ten years. The diesel engine was also further developed into the 1.76-liter unit by Max Wagner when Nallinger interruped his activity from the fall of 1945 to May 1948.

Since the various models constructed during this period will be presented in detail, it will be superfluous to summarize the Nallinger era in this section, except for a brief mention of the racing activities.

Greatly encouraged by the splendid successes with their 300SL sports car in international competition in 1952, Nallinger and his able assistants designed a new formula I car. The 196 made its debut in 1954 at the French Grand Prix with a startling double victory and won five Grands Prix that year and five in 1955, driven by Juan Manuel Fangio (eight), Karl Kling (one), and Sterling Moss (one). The 2.5-liter eight-cylinder engine of 76 millimeter bore and 68.8 millimeter stroke developed about 280 horsepower. A sports racing car, the 300SLR, based on the formula car, had a 3-liter engine of 300 horsepower at 7,500 rpm. It won the championship for Mercedes in 1955.

When Fritz Nallinger retired from his position in 1963, Hans Scherenberg took over the helm. The various models brought out at first were still those in the development stage of his predecessor, but the New Generation models showed the distinct imprint of the new head of the construction department and can unquestionably be considered as falling into the Scherenberg era. With the introduction in 1972 of the S-class of cars the change was complete.

One of the extra curricular constructions, the C-111, created much comment when first shown at the Frankfurt Auto Show in 1969. It was a highly sophisticated engineering exercise and a purely experimental car, but speculation — and hopes for the availability of such a vehicle to the buyer — ran high. The small coupe had a 3-chamber Wankel rotary engine of 1.8-liter displacement, developing 330 horsepower at 7,000 revolutions per minute. It reached 0-60 miles per hour in 4.9 seconds and had a maximum speed of 162 miles per hour. The rotary engine weighed only 275 pounds (against the 495 pounds of the V-8 of 230 horsepower) and had only 950 parts (the V-8 had 1,750). A year later, a 4-chamber rotary engine was installed and even better performance figures were achieved (0-60 in 4.7 seconds; maximum speed 186 mph). However, the Wankel rotary engine was not yet considered to be ready for installation in regular passenger cars.

The experimental C-111 was used in 1976 to establish several world speed records in slightly modified form with aerodynamic headlight fairing and solid wheel covers, and with a 5-cylinder diesel engine installed.

The basic power unit was that of the current 300D passenger car, but equipped with a Garrett Airesearch turbo charger. The engine developed over 200 horsepower at 4,200 to 4,700 revolutions per minute and had 275 ft/lb. (38 mkg) torque at 3,600 rpm. The final drive ratio in fifth gear was 2.7. The fastest average speed achieved was 158.368 miles per hour (254.856 kilometers per hour) for one hour. World records for 5,000 miles at 156.928 mph (252.540 kmph), for 10,000 kilometers at 156.748 mph (252.249 kmph), and for 10,000 miles at 156.467 mph (251.798 kmph), and thirteen class records were established in less than sixty-four hours of driving on the test track at Nardo, Italy, by four factory drivers/engineers (Moch, Liebold, Waxenberger, and Kadon). The event indicated the importance of this reliable, economical, and fast diesel engine and signified a trend to turbocharging of this well-established and still highly promising power plant by the imaginative Mercedes-Benz engineering department.

Another highly important project executed under the leadership of Hans Scherenberg, head of the Research and

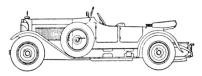
Mercedes-Benz Model K 1926

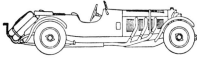
Mercedes-Benz Model S 1927

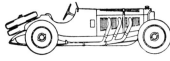
Mercedes-Benz Model SSK 1928

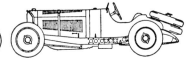
Mercedes-Benz Model SSKL 1931

Development Department, was the first of the special safety vehicles, the ESF (Experimentier-Sicherheits-Fahrzeug), constructed in 1971; even though passenger safety had always been a major consideration in the construction of Mercedes-Benz automobiles. This new safety vehicle included a vast number of outside and interior safety designs and devices and underwent extensive tests. Actually, more than a hundred safety elements had been developed and tested since 1946, and have been incorporated into the cars built. For instance, the cone type door lock was patented in 1949. In 1952 a patented body design, standard on all cars since 1959, was the safety body which upon impact would crush in front and rear but withstand exceptional forces in the extremely strong passenger compartment. Several ESF vehicles were built and exhaustively tested, and the ESF 24 looked startlingly similar to the production 450SE sedan.

Actually, the construction of safety cars was not new; in 1940 the experimental vehicle number 11 included the improved suspension system and such safety features as solid side protection and an extremely rigid floor and a three-part steering column. Design features over the years, adding to the safety of the cars built, were the complete independent wheel suspension in 1931, and the frame-floor construction and stressed chassis used since 1953. Engine features were the overhead camshaft design since 1952, the low-pivot single joint swing axle since 1954, power steering since 1959, air suspension system and automatic transmission since 1961, a dual circuit power braking with disc brakes for the entire passenger car line since 1963, a leveling adjustment device with coil springs available for all cars since 1965, the new diagonal-pivot swing axle from 1968 on, electronic fuel injection since 1969, and the antilock brake system, optional on the S-class cars since 1978.

With the appearance in 1977 of the 450SLC 5.0 coupe, the new light-alloy engines were introduced. A reduction of 7 percent in weight over the 450SLC was achieved by the use of lighter metals. The turbo-charged 5-cylinder diesel was also shown at that time, but that S-class sedan was intended for the United States market only. And the entirely new line of station wagons, the T-range, with a choice of five different engines, made its initial appearance at that Auto Show.

Another record attempt, using the C-111 vehicle, but then modified with a rear stabilizing fin and some alterations to reduce wind resistance even further, was made in April 1978. Again, the Nardo track was chosen, but a thick fog curtailed the planned speed event. Records were established for from 100 to 1,000 kilometers, and miles, and up to 12 hours. The fastest run was 199.995 miles per hour for the 500 kilometers, and for 12 hours the average speed was 195.398 mph. Fuel consumption was a remarkable 14.7 miles per gallon, with speeds of the 2,995 cc turbocharged diesel often exceeding 200 miles per hour.

Werner Breitschwerdt succeeded Hans Scherenberg as chief engineer, and introduced in 1979 the 380 and 500 lines of newly designed cars with the lighter engines. With less wind resistance than the previous models, these cars gave equal, or even superior, performance and used less fuel than those which they replaced — the 450s and 6.9.

That year, the cylinder cut-off system was demonstrated, promising a fuel saving of up to 32 percent. Work on that development had begun in 1974. Another innovation was the anti-knock control, whereby the compression could be raised to increase the thermal efficiency of the engine, thus allowing the use of a lower octane fuel.

With the introduction of the entirely new W-201 body style in late 1982, a small model automobile was again a vital part of the production program of Daimler-Benz.

(Continued on page 289)

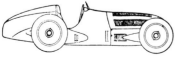

Mercedes-Benz racer 1936

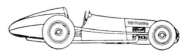

Mercedes-Benz racer 1938

Mercedes-Benz racer 1939

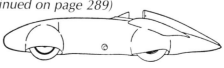

12-cyl. Mercedes-Benz record car 1936

From the dreary
wartime charcoal-
burning model (170) . . .

. . . to the elegant
stylish sedan of
fifty years later.

Model Details

In April 1945, the directors of the Daimler-Benz A.G. issued a statement to the effect that the company had "for all practical purposes ceased to exist." The devastation of their manufacturing facilities was appalling. The Untertürkheim automobile factory complex was 70 percent destroyed and the Sindelfingen plant about 85 percent. The truck facilities at Mannheim were 20 percent destroyed and those at Gaggenau about 80 percent. What remained of the Berlin Marienfelde factory was dismantled and shipped off by the victors.

Fortunately, the Untertürkheim, Sindelfingen, and Mannheim plants were in the same military occupational zone and they could be effectively managed after as many former employees and workers as possible were located. The slow and tedious task of cleaning up the rubble was begun and the reconstruction of manufacturing facilities made some progress.

Vehicle production could only be accomplished if the manufacture of previous models would be continued. It was the natural choice of the directors to put the 170 model into production as soon as possible. The other models, the larger 230 or the massive 540K or even the prestigious 770, were of course, never considered for manufacture at this critical time in 1945.

At first, repair maintenance work on existing cars and some assembly of the L 3500 model commercial vehicles occupied the small working force and cleared facilities. The first post-war four-cylinder engine for a 170V model was completed February 22, 1946, but entire cars were not produced until June; a total of 214 units were manufactured that year. In 1947 it was 1,045 inits, and the following year production reached 5,116 units. By that time the new currency reform had been instituted (on June 21, 1948) and the economy began to function properly. The financial paralysis ended with a sound governmental policy.

A Note on the U.S. Models

Prices quoted for the various models in the respective years are published merely as a matter of record. To compare those in Germany with their counterparts in the United States will only prove an exercise in frustration and drawing the obvious conclusions will be quite erroneous, at least for the models of recent years.

Because of the stricter emission and safety regulations, cars for the American market are equipped with many additional features. They also come furnished with many accessories generally available only optional at extra cost. For example, the United States 1976 price list enumerated 15 basic extra cost items for the 230 model and 6 for the 450SEL, while the German factory price list quoted actually 38 basic items for the 230.4 and 32 for the 450SEL as optional accessories. (A few were not available for U.S. cars.)

Nevertheless, despite the manifest futility, herewith are listed the exchange rates: In 1946 the U.S. dollar equalled about DM (German Mark) 2.50, but there was actually no official rate of exchange until 1948, when it was DM 3.33. In 1949 the rate was DM 4.20 which remained steady until 1961, when it was DM 3.98, and stayed that way until 1968. From 1969 the rate of exchange was slightly lower and dropped until it was in 1975 DM 2.49. The lowest point was reached in 1980 when it was DM 1.81. In 1981 the average exchange rate was DM 2.24, and in 1982 DM 2.51, to the U.S. dollar. (Pitfalls here are that the rate varied, sometimes hugely, during a given year.)

The 170V sedan, 1950

Prices and Production

The 170V four-door sedan sold for . . . . .DM 6,200
    from July 1948 . . . . .DM 8,180
    from May 1949 . . . . .DM 7,800
    from January 1950 . . . . .DM 7,380
The 170Va four-door sedan sold for . . . . .DM 7,400
The 170Vb four-door sedan sold for . . . . .DM 7,900
In New York the 170 sedan sold for . . . .$ 2,850

Production of the 170V, 170Va, and 170Vb [Manufacturing designation 136 I-V] (from June 1946 until August 1953)

was in	1946	214 units
	1947	1,045 units
	1948	5,116 units
	1949	13,101 units
	1950	11,876 units
	1951	12,867 units
	1952	3,692 units
	1953	1,636 units
	total	49,367 units

Model 170V (1946-1953)

V (Vorn) = front

The four-cylinder engined 170V and 170H sedans had first been shown at the Berlin Auto Show in February 1936. Priced at 3,750 Reichsmark, this outstanding vehicle was thereafter available as a two-door and four-door sedan, open touring car, and even two- and four-door convertible, or cabriolet-limousine. And as a commercial vehicle, the 170 also came as an open or closed delivery van, ambulance, or police car.

The chassis was of oval tubes, and the three-bearing crankshaft engine was mounted on two rubber blocks for vibrationless operation. The independent rear suspension had coil springs, the front leaf springs. The chassis weighed 650 kilograms (1,433 pounds). With the 38-horsepower engine, the sedan reached a maximum speed of 100 kilometers (62 miles) per hour and used about 10 liters of fuel. By 1942 more than 90,000 units had been manufactured, providing impressive proof of the popularity of this model. Production of passengar car models was 71,973 units.

Announced as "ein Wagen, der Ihnen Freude macht," a car which brings joy to you, the 170V was welcomed as a vehicle incorporating the tested — and by over 100,000 owners admired — qualities of the earlier construction.

The 170V production in 1946 consisted almost exclusively of delivery trucks, ambulances, and police cruisers. This model remained practically unchanged until May 1950.

The 170Va, built from May 1950 until April 1952, had a larger engine (1,767 cubic centimeters) and greater horsepower (45), softer springing, telescopic shock absorbers and larger brakes, as well as other improvements.

The 170Vb, built from May 1952 until September 1953, had a wider track, hypoid rear axle, a larger windshield, and smoother hoodline.

Specifications

	170V	170Va / 170Vb
Engine type	4 cyl (M 136)	4 cyl (M 136)
Bore and Stroke	73.5 x 100mm (2.89 x 3.94 in)	75 x 100mm (2.95 x 3.94 in)
Displacement	1697 cc	1767 cc
Power output	38 hp (DIN) @ 3600 rpm	45 hp (DIN) @ 3600 rpm
Compression ratio	6:1 (from 1949: 6.5:1)	6.5:1
Torque	10 mkg @ 1800 rpm (72.35 ft/lb)	11 mkg @ 1800 rpm (79.59 ft/lb)
Carburetion	1 updraft carburetor Solex 30 BFLVS	
Engine speed at 100 km/hr	3300 rpm	3300 rpm
Gear ratios	I. 4.025:1 II. 2.280:1 III. 1.420:1 IV. 1.000:1	I. 4.025:1 II. 2.280:1 III. 1.420:1 IV. 1.000:1
Rear axle ratio	4.125:1	4.125:1
Chassis	X-shaped oval tubular	X-shaped oval tubular
Suspension	independent front, swing axle rear, with coil springs	
Brakes and area	drum, 564 cm^2 (87.4 sq in)	drum, 736 cm^2 (114 sq in)
Wheelbase	2845mm (112 in)	2845mm (112 in)
Track, front/rear	1310/1296mm (51.6/51.0 in)	Va: 1310/1342mm (51.6/52.8 in) Vb: 1310/1360mm (51.6/53.5 in)
Length	4285mm (168.7 in)	4285mm (168.7 in)
Width	1580mm (62.2 in)	1630mm (64.2 in)
Height	1610mm (63.4 in)	1610mm (63.4 in)
Ground clearance	185mm (7.3 in)	185mm (7.3 in)
Tires	5.50 x 16	5.50 x 16
Turning circle	11.5 meters (37.7 ft)	11.5 meters (37.7 ft)
Steering type and ratio	worm, 14.4:1	worm, 14.4:1
Weight	1160 kg (2552 lbs)	1185 kg (2607 lbs)
Maximum speed	108 km/hr (67 mph)	116 km/hr (72 mph)
Acceleration	36 sec 0-100 km	36 sec 0-100 km
Fuel consumption	11 liters/100 km (21 mpg)	10 liters (23.5 mpg)
Fuel tank capacity	42 liters (11.1 gallons)	42 liters (11.1 gallons)

The chassis of the 170V, 1946

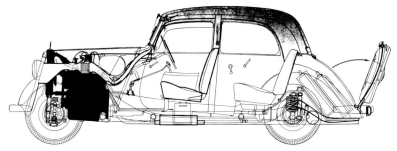

Drawing of the 170Vb, 1953

13

The 170S sedan, 1949

Prices and Production

The 170S four-door sedan sold from 1949-1953 for. . . .DM 10,100
   convertible B, two-door sedan – 1949-1951 . . . . . . .DM 12,850
   convertible A, 2-3 seats coupe – 1949-1951 . . . . . . .DM 15,800

The 170S-V four-door sedan sold from 1953-1955 for . .DM 8,300

Production of the 170S [136 IV] (from May 1949 until February 1952)

	was in	1949	3,370 units
		1950	14,735 units
		1951	10,333 units
		1952	326 units
		total	28,764 units

Production of the 170Sb [191] (from January 1952 until August 1953)

	was in	1952	4,580 units
		1953	3,514 units
		total	8,094 units

Production of the 170S [136 IV] convertible (from May 1949 until November 1951)

	was in	1949	39 units
		1950	1,686 units
		1951	708 units
		total	2,433 units

Production of the 170S-V [136 VIII] (from July 1953 until February 1955)

	was in	1953	2,102 units
		1954	880 units
		1955	140 units
		total	3,122 units

Model 170S (1949-1955)

S = Super

The 170S model, built from May 1949 to March 1952, was a further development of the V model sedan. The engine produced 52 horsepower. The valves were arranged side by side and a detachable light-alloy cylinder head was used. A downdraft Solex carburator was fitted with an air silencer and a wet-type air filter. The thermostat, set in the water circulation system, was so arranged that the heaviest work load in mountainous terrain would not cause any concern about water temperature. The drivability of the 170S showed a striking improvement, due to the more favorable weight distribution and center of gravity, with suitable track dimensions and the design of independent wheel suspension attached to the rigid cruciform frame of oval tube sections. Maximum speed was 120 kilometers (75 miles) per hour for this model which now had the larger body of the pre-war 230 model.

The car actually incorporated the newest scientific knowledge of modern automobile construction, coupled with the traditional qualities expected from the cars built by this company.

A convertible 170 model A was produced from May 1949 until February 1952, as was the model B, a convertible sedan.

The 170Sb, built from January 1952 until August 1953, had the gear shift lever attached to the steering wheel column, improved heating system, hypoid rear axle, wider track, and starting knob on the dashboard.

The 170S–V was to conclude the entire series. Built from July 1953 until February 1955, it incorporated the engine of the 170V, the chassis of the Sb with front axle of the V model, and the body of the S model.

Although no 170S models were sold in this country, an occasional one was brought back by tourists, and the editors of a magazine were able to test it. The 170S was found to be "one of the most interesting cars yet to pass through the hands of the test staff."

The 170S-V sedan, 1953

The 170S convertible A, 1949

The instrument panel of the 170S, 1949

Specifications

	170S / 170Sb	170S-V
Engine type	4 cyl (M 136)	4 cyl (M 136)
Bore and stroke	75 x 100mm (2.95 x 3.94 in)	75 x 100mm (2.95 x 3.94 in)
Displacement	1767 cc (107.7 cu in)	1767 cc (107.7 cu in)
Power output	52 hp (DIN) @ 4000 rpm	45 hp (DIN) @ 3600 rpm
Compression ratio	6.5:1	6.7:1
Torque	11.4mkg @1800rpm(82.5 ft/lb)	11mkg @ 1800 rpm (79.6 ft/lb)
Carburetion	1 downdraft carburetor Solex 32 PBJ	1 updraft carburetor Solex 30 BFLVS
Engine speed at 100 hm/hr	3330 rpm	3330 rpm
Gear ratio	I. 4.025:1 II. 2.280:1 III. 1.420:1 IV. 1.000:1	I. 4.025:1 II. 2.280:1 III. 1.420:1 IV. 1.000:1
Rear axle ratio	S: 4.375:1 Sb: 4.44:1	4.125:1
Chassis	X-shaped oval tubular	X-shaped oval tubular
Suspension	independent front, swing axle rear, with coil springs	
Brakes and area	drum, 736 cm² (114 sq in)	drum, 736 cm² (114 sq in)
Wheelbase	2845mm (112 in)	2845mm (112 in)
Track, front/rear	S: 1315/1420mm (51.57/55.89 in) Sb: 1315/1435mm (51.57/56.49 in)	1310/1435mm (51.6/56.5 in)
Length	4455mm (175.4 in)	4450mm (175.2 in)
Width	1684mm (66.3 in)	1685mm (66.3 in)
Height	1610mm (63.4 in)	1590mm (62.6 in)
Ground clearance	185mm (7.3 in)	185mm (7.3 in)
Tires	6.40 x 15	5.50 x 16
Turning circle	12 meters (39.37 ft)	12 meters (39.37 ft)
Steering type and ratio	worm, 13.9:1	worm, 14.1:1
Weight	S: 1220 kg (2684 lbs) Sb: 1250 kg (2750 lbs)	1220 kg (2684 lbs)
Maximum speed	122 km/hr (76 mph)	115 km/hr (71 mph)
Acceleration	32 sec 0-100 km	39 sec 0-100 km
Fuel consumption	12 liters/100 km (19.5 mpg)	11.5 liters (20.4 mpg)
Fuel tank capacity	47 liters (12.4 gallons)	47 liters (12.4 gallons)

The 170D sedan, 1950

Prices and Production

The 170D four-door sedan sold from May 1949 for . . . .DM 9,200
   and from January 1950 for . . . . .DM 8,620
The 170Da four-door sedan sold for . . . . .DM 8,900
The 170Db four-door sedan also sold for . . . . .DM 8,900
The 170DS four-door sedan sold for . . . . .DM 10,985
The 170S-D four-door sedan sold for. . . . . .DM 9,350

Production of the 170D, 170Da, and 170Db [136 I-VI] (from May 1949 to October 1953)

was in	1949	907 units
	1950	5,609 units
	1951	14,622 units
	1952	8,115 units
	1953	4,570 units
	total	33,823 untis

Production of the 170DS [191] (from January 1952 until August 1953)

was in	1952	6,734 units
	1953	6,251 units
	total	12,985 units

Production of the 170 S-D [136 VIII] (from July 1953 until September 1955)

was in	1953	6,494 units
	1954	5,992 units
	1955	2,401 units
	total	14,887 units

Model 170D (1949-1955)

D = Diesel

The introduction of the 170D in May 1949 indicated an increase in production facilities and further advancement in the passenger car program. This diesel-engined car was an even more economical automobile than the gasoline-powered model and was particularily well suited at that time of economic hardship in the country.

The experience gained in 1936 with the 2.6-liter diesel-engined passenger sedan (45 horsepower at 3,000 revolutions per minute) was utilized in the creation of this smaller displacement engine which had the good qualities and liveliness of a gasoline engine; in fact, in some respects was even superior. The pre-combustion chamber system engine developed 38 horsepower at 3,200 revolutions per minute. The torque curve was very steady over a wide range of engine speeds. Despite the unpleasant engine noise at idling speed, the exceptional qualities of this diesel model were readily recognized. Maximum speed was 100 kilometers (62 miles) per hour and climbing ability 29 percent in first gear. Fuel consumption was 6.4 liters for 100 kilometers of driving. And, as in all cars, the maximum speed was also the cruising speed of the vehicle.

Since there was no difference in the gasoline-engined 170 models and those equipped with the diesel engine, it was natural that the change-over in the two models coincided. The 170Da production was begun in May 1950, when the 170D model was discontinued, and ran until April 1952. At that time the 170Db appeared, to be built until October 1953.

The 170DS was built from January 1952 until August 1953 and the 170S-D from July 1953 until September 1955.

These inordinately sturdy and fantastically dependable diesel–engined cars were a most welcome addition to the previous gasoline models and represented the beginning of an unbelievable popularity of diesel models to come.

Specifications

	170D	170Da / 170Db	170DS	170S-D
Engine type	4 cyl diesel (OM 636)	4 cyl diesel (OM 636)	4 cyl diesel (OM 636)	4 cyl diesel (OM 636)
Bore and stroke	73.5 x 100mm (2.98 x 3.94 in)	75 x 100mm (2.95 x 3.94 in)	75 x 100mm (2.95 x 3.94 in)	75 x 100mm (2.95 x 3.94 in)
Displacement	1697 cc (103.5 cu in)	1767 cc (107.7 cu in)	1767 cc (107.7 cu in)	1767 cc (107.7 cu in)
Power output	38 hp (DIN) @ 3200 rpm	40 hp (DIN) @ 3200 rpm	40 hp (DIN) @ 3200 rpm	40 hp (DIN) @ 3200 rpm
Compression ratio	19:1	19:1	19:1	19:1
Torque	9.8 mkg @ 2000 rpm (70.9 ft/lb)	9.8 mkg @ 2000 rpm (70.9 ft/lb)	10.3 mkg @ 2000 rpm (74.5 ft/lb)	10.3 mkg @ 2000 rpm (74.5 ft/lb)
Carburetion	Bosch injection pump (pre-combustion chamber)		Bosch injection pump (pre-combustion chamber)	
Engine speed at 100 km/hr	3330 rpm	3330 rpm	3330 rpm	3330 rpm
Gear ratios	I. 4.025:1 II. 2.280:1 III. 1.420:1 IV. 1.000:1	I. 4.025:1 II. 2.280:1 III. 1.420:1 IV. 1.000:1	I. 4.025:1 II. 2.280:1 III. 1.420:1 IV. 1.000:1	I. 4.025:1 II. 2.280:1 III. 1.420:1 IV. 1.000:1
Rear axle ratio	4.125:1	4.125:1	4. 125:1	4.125:1
Chassis	X-shaped oval tubular	X-shaped oval tubular	X-shaped oval tubular	X-shaped oval tubular
Suspension	independent front and rear swing axle with coil springs		independent front and rear swing axle with coil springs	
Brakes and area	drum, 564 cm² (87.4 sq in)	drum, 736 cm² (114 sq in)	drum, 736 cm² (114 sq in)	drum, 736 cm² (114 sq in)
Wheelbase	2845mm (112 in)	2845mm (112 in)	2845mm (112 in)	2845mm (112 in)
Track, front/rear	1310/1296mm (51.6/51.0in)	Da: 1310/1342mm (51.6/52.8 in) Db: 1310/1360mm (51.6/53.5 in)	1315/1435mm (51.6/56.5 in)	1310/1435mm (51.6/56.5 in)
Length	4285mm (168.7 in)	4285mm (168.7 in)	4455mm (175.4 in)	4450mm (175.2 in)
Width	1580mm (62.2 in)	1630mm (64.2 in)	1684mm (66.3 in)	1685mm (66.3 in)
Height	1610mm (63.4 in)	1616mm (63.4 in)	1610mm (63.4 in)	1590mm (62.6 in)
Ground clearance	185mm (7.3 in)	185mm (7.3 in)	185mm (7.3 in)	185mm (7.3 in)
Tires	5.50 x 16	5.50 x 16	5.50 x 16	5.50 x 16
Turning circle	11.5 meters (37.7 ft)	11.5 meters (37.7 ft)	12 meters (39.37 ft)	12 meters (39.37 ft)
Steering type and ratio	worm, 14.4:1	worm, 14.4:1	worm, 13.9:1	worm, 14.1:1
Weight	1250 kg (2750 lbs)	1250 kg (2750 lbs)	1275 kg (2805 lbs)	1300 kg (2860 lbs)
Maximum speed	100 km/hr (62 mph)	105 km/hr (65 mph)	105 km/hr (65 mph)	105 km/hr (65 mph)
Acceleration	58 sec 0-100 km	50 sec 0-100 km	56 sec 0-100 km	56 sec 0-100 km
Fuel consumption	7.5 liters/100 km (32 mpg)	7.5 liters/100 km (32 mpg)	8.5 liters/100 km (27.75 mpg)	8.5 liters/100 km (27.75 mpg)
Fuel tank capacity	37 liters (9.8 gallons)	37 liters (9.8 gallons)	47 liters (12.4 gallons)	47 liters (12.4 gallons)

The 220 sedan, 1951

Prices and Production

The 220 four-door sedan sold for . . . . .DM 11,925
The 220 two-door convertible sedan sold for . . . . .DM 15,160
The 220 2-3 seater convertible sold for . . . . .DM 18,860
The 220 2-3 seater coupe sold for. . . . . .DM 20,850
The 220a four-door sedan sold for (in 1954). . . . . .DM 12,500
The 220 convertible sedan or coupe sold for. . . . . .DM 21,500
   (The 1954 and 1955 models did not get the "a")

Production of the 220 [187] (from July 1951 to May 1954)

was in	1951	3,453 units
	1952	9,165 units
	1953	3,322 units
	1954	214 units
total		16,154 units

Production of the 220 convertible models, B and A [187] (from July 1951 to August 1955)

was in	1951	368 units
	1952	1,178 units
	1953	403 units
	1954	259 units
	1955	152 units
total		2,360 units

Production of the 220a model [180 I] (from March 1954 to April 1956)

was in	1954	4,178 units
	1955	19,348 units
	1956	2,411 units
total		25,937 units

Model 220 (1951-1956)

The 220 sedan was introduced at the Frankfurt Auto Show in April 1951. Regular production began in July of that year. In appearance this model closely resembled the proven 170S model, but the headlights were mounted in the fenders and the interior furnishings were more elegant. The good road-holding, soft suspension, and road safety were technically refined and superior in this six-cylinder automobile. The 2.2-liter overhead camshaft engine developed 80 horsepower at 4,600 revolutions per minute. The extremely quiet running short stroke engine had a specially balanced crankshaft and long water jackets to the cylinder parting line. The fully synchronized gear box was provided with a gear shift lever on the steering column. Special tuning of the suspension and a certain resilience of the front wheel suspension in a horizontal direction improved the suspension and achieved exceptional road-holding characteristics. The power-to-weight ratio of 16.5 kilograms (36.4 pounds) per horsepower was a considerable improvement over the 22.9 kilograms (50.5 pounds) of the 170S.

The 220 achieved 0 to 100 kilometers per hour in just 21 seconds and had a maximum and cruising speed of 140 kilometers (87 miles) per hour. With its elegant lines and fine interior, especially in the convertible sedan and convertible coupe, the 220 combined the qualities of a comfortable family car with those of a lively sports model.

The 220 sedan models were built from July 1951 to May 1954 and the convertible sedan types (B and A) from July 1951 to August 1955. A coupe model became available in May 1954; from 1954 on it came equipped with a curved windshield.

An improved 220a sedan with the new style body and the 85-horsepower engine was built in 1954. Introduced in March and produced from July, the model was built until April 1956.

The 220 sedan, 1954

The 220 convertible B, 1951

The 220 convertible A, 1951

Specifications

	220	220a
Engine type	6 cyl overhead camshaft (M180)	6 cyl overhead camshaft (M 180)
Bore and stroke	80 x 72.8mm (3.15 x 2.87 in)	80 x 72.8mm (3.15 x 2.87 in)
Displacement	2195 cc (133.9 cu in)	2195 cc (133.9 cu in)
Power output	80 hp (DIN) @ 4850 rpm	85 hp (DIN) @ 4800 rpm (92 hp SAE)
Compression ratio	6.5:1	7.6:1
Torque	14.5 mkg @ 2500 rpm (104.9 ft/lb)	16 mkg @ 2400 rpm (116 ft/lb @ 2500 rpm)
Carburetion	1 dual downdraft carburetor Solex 30 PAAJ	1 dual downdraft carburetor Solex 32 PAATJ
Engine speed at 100 km/hr	3470 rpm	3470 rpm
Gear ratios	I. 3.68:1 II. 2.25:1 III. 1.42:1 IV. 1.00:1	I. 3.40:1 later 3.52 II. 2.32:1 III. 1.52:1 IV. 1.00:1
Rear axle ratio	4.44	4.11 (37:9) finally 4.10 (41:10)
Chassis	X-shaped oval tubular	unit frame and body
Suspension	independent front, swing axle rear, with coil springs	independent front, single swing axle rear, with coil springs
Brakes and area	drum, 736 cm² (114 sq in)	drum, 1064 cm² (164.9 sq in)
Wheelbase	2845mm (112 in)	2820mm (111 in) convertible: 2700mm (106 in)
Track, front/rear	1315/1435mm (51.6/56.5 in)	1430/1470mm (56.3/57.7 in)
Length	4507mm (177.4 in) convertible A:4538mm (178.7 in)	4715mm (185.6 in) convertible: 4670mm (183.9 in)
Width	1685mm (66.3 in)	1740mm (68.5 in) convertible: 1760mm (69.3 in)
Height	1610mm (63.4 in) convertible A:1560mm (61.4 in)	1560mm (61.42 in) convertible: 1530mm (60.2 in)
Ground clearance	185mm (7.3 in)	185mm (7.3 in)
Tires	6.40 x 15	6.70 x 13
Turning circle	12 meters (39.37 ft)	11.7 meters (38.39 ft) convertible:11.4 meters (37.4 ft)
Steering type and ratio	worm, 13.9:1 (2.75 turns)	recirculating ball, 21.4:1 (4 turns)
Weight	1350 kg (2970 lbs) convertible: 1440 kg (3168 lbs)	1300 kg (2860 lbs) convertible: 1300 kg (2860 lbs)
Maximum speed	141 km/hr (87.5 mph) convertible B:140 km/hr convertible A:145 km/hr	150 km/hr (93 mph) convertible: 155 km/hr
Acceleration	21 sec 0-100 km	19 sec 0-100 km
Fuel consumption	14 liters/100 km (16.75 mpg) convertible A&B: 14.5 liters	13.5 liters/100 km (17.4 mpg) convertible: 14 liters
Fuel tank capacity	65 liters (17.2 gallons)	64 liters (16.9 gallons)

The 300 sedan, 1951

Prices

The 300 four-door sedan sold for . . . . .DM 19,900
The 300 four-door convertible sedan D sold for. . . . . .DM 23,700
The 300b four-door sedan sold for . . . . .DM 22,000
The 300b four-door convertible sedan D sold for. . . . .DM 24,700
The 300c four-door sedan sold for . . . . .DM 22,000
The 300c four-door sedan "Automatic" sold for . . . . .DM 23,500
The 300c four-door convertible sedan D sold for . . . . .DM 24,700
The 300c four-door "Automatic" convertible sedan
    sold for . . . . .DM 26,200
The 300c four-door limousine with longer wheelbase
    was available at an additional. . . . . .DM   3,000
The 300d four-door sedan hardtop sold for . . . . .DM 27,000
    (available on special order only)
The 300d four-door sedan, hardtop "Automatic" . . . . .DM 28,500

The price of the 300 sedan in the United States was. . . .$ 6,980

Model 300 (1951-1962)

The 300 model was also introduced to the public at the 1951 Frankfurt Show. It signified the return to the old custom of producing a truly outstanding luxury limousine of utmost comfort and superb roadability, capable of sustained high speed. It had a maximum and cruising speed of 160 kilometers (100 miles) per hour. The six-passenger sedan, with conservative lines, had a six-cylinder 3-liter overhead camshaft engine developing 115 horsepower. The short stroke engine with a special valve arrangement and combustion chamber design and thermostatically controlled water circulation and oil temperature, was most durable and extremely quiet running. It had a seven-bearing crankshaft. The chassis incorporated all of the features of the 170S plus a number of additional refinements such as a new steering mechanism design, electrical control of the auxiliary rear suspension which was adjustable from the driver's seat according to the load carried, hypoid bevel final drive, and dynamically balanced wheels. The car represented the ultimate in safety and riding comfort.

The 300 sedan was built from November 1951 until March 1954. It was also available in cabriolet form (pre-series production in April 1951 with regular production from March 1952). The type 300b, built from March 1954 until August 1955, had a more powerful engine (125 horsepower) and large dimension brakes, but the same body style. The 300c had standard transmission, two compound carburetors, higher compression and better axle ratio, and was built from September 1955 until July 1957. The cabriolet D was available until July 1956, when a special model with a wheelbase of 3,150 millimeters and overall length of 5,165 millimeters was built on individual order. Then followed the 300d with a slightly modernized body style and fuel injection engine. It was available until March 1962.

Production

Production of the 300 and 300b sedans [186 II-III] (from November 1951 until August 1955)

	was in	1951	47 units
		1952	2,659 units
		1953	1,776 units
		1954	1,185 units
		1955	547 units
		total	6,214 units

Production of the 300 and 300b convertible sedans [186 II-III] (from April 1951/March 1952 until July 1955)*

	was in	1951	2 units
		1952	262 units
		1953	181 units
		1954	87 units
		1955	59 units
		total	591 units

Production of the 300c sedans [186 IV] (from September 1955 until June 1956)

	was in	1955	330 units
		1956	885 units
		1957	217 units
		total	1,432 units

Production of the 300c convertible sedans [186 IV] (from September/December 1955 until June 1956)

	was in	1955	3 units
		1956	48 units
		total	51 units

The 300d sedan, 1957

Production of the 300d sedans [189] (from August/November 1957 until March 1962)

	was in	1957	144 units
		1958	1,165 units
		1959	607 units
		1960	581 units
		1961	535 units
		1962	45 units
		total	3,077 units

Production of the 300d convertible sedans [189] (from July 1958 until February 1962)

	was in	1958	3 units
		1959	23 units
		1960	22 units
		1961	16 units
		1962	1 units
		total	65 units

*Note: *When two different months are given as production figures, as in* April 1951/March 1952, *the first indicates the pre-production and the second the start of regular series production of the model.*

The 300c sedan, 1955

Rear axle arrangement of 300 sedan, 1951

The 300c convertible D, 1955

Specifications

	300	300b	300c	300d
Engine type	6 cyl overhead camshaft (M 186)	6 cyl overhead camshaft (M 186)	6 cyl overhead camshaft (M 186)	6 cyl overhead camshaft (M 189)
Bore and stroke	85 x 88mm (3.35 x 3.46 in)	85 x 88mm (3.35 x 3.46 in)	85 x 88mm (3.35 x 3.46 in)	85 x 88mm (3.35 x 3.46 in)
Displacement	2996 cc (182.7 cu in)	2996 cc (182.7 cu in)	2996 cc (182.7 cu in)	2996 cc (182.7 cu in)
Power output	115 hp (DIN) @ 4600 rpm	125 hp (DIN) @ 4500 rpm (136 hp SAE)	125 hp (DIN) @ 4500 rpm (136 hp SAE)	160 hp (DIN) @ 5300 rpm (180 hp SAE)
Compression ratio	6.4:1	7.4-7.5:1	7.4-7.5:1	8.55:1
Torque	20 mkg @ 2500 rpm (114 ft/lb)	22.5 mkg @ 2600 rpm (163 ft/lb)	22.5 mkg @ 2600 rpm (163 ft/lb)	24.2 mkg @ 4200 rpm (175 ft/lb)
Carburetion	2 dual downdraft carburetors Solex 40 PBJC	2 dual downdraft carburetors Solex 32 PAJAT	2 dual downdraft carburetors	Bosch injection pump
Engine speed at 100 km/hr	3300 rpm	3300 rpm	3300 rpm (manual)	3300 rpm (automatic, 3-speed)
Gear ratios	I. 2.95:1 (later 3.30:1) II. 2.13:1 III. 1.46:1 IV. 1.00:1	I. 3.44:1 II. 2.30:1 III. 1.53:1 IV. 1.00:1	I. 3.44:1 II. 2.30:1 III. 1.53:1 IV. 1.00:1	I. 2.303:1 II. 1.435:1 III. 1.00:1
Rear axle ratio	4.44	4.67	4.67	4.67
Chassis	X-shaped oval tubular	X-shaped oval tubular	X-shaped oval tubular	X-shaped oval tubular
Suspension	independent front, swing axle rear, with coil springs		independent front, single swing axle rear, with coil springs	
Brakes and area	drum, 1270 cm² (197 sq in)	drum, 1470 cm² (228 sq in)	drum, 1470 cm² (227.9 sq in)	drum, 1470 cm² (227.9 sq in)
Wheelbase	3050mm (120 in)	3050mm (120 in)	3050mm (120 in)	3150mm (124 in)
Track, front/rear	1480/1525mm (58.2/60 in)	1480/1525mm (58.2/60 in)	1480/1525mm (58.3/60.0 in)	1480/1525mm (58.3/60.0 in)
Length	4950mm (194.9 in)	5065mm (199.4 in)	5065mm (199.4 in)	5190mm (204.3 in)
Width	1838mm (72.4 in)	1838 (72.4 in)	1838mm (72.4 in)	1860mm (73.2 in)
Height	1600mm (63.0 in)	1640mm (64.6 in)	1600mm (63.0 in)	1620mm (63.8 in)
Ground clearance	185mm (7.3 in)	185mm (7.3 in)	185mm (7.3 in)	185mm (7.3 in)
Tires	7.10 x 15 extra	7.10 x 15 extra	7.60 x 15 extra	7.60 x 15 extra
Turning circle	12.6-13.1 meters (41-43 ft)	12.6-13.1 meters (41-43 ft)	12.6-13.1 meters (41-43 ft)	12.8-13.3 meters (42-44 ft)
Steering type and ratio	worm, 17.9:1 (3.3 turns)	recirculating ball, 21.4:1 (3.75 turns)	recirculating ball, 21.4:1 (3.75 turns)	from Sept. '58 servo-assist, optional
Weight (automatic)	1780 kg (3916 lbs) convertible: 1830 kg (4026 lbs)		1860 kg (4092 lbs) convertible: 1910 kg (4202 lbs) 1910 kg (4202 lbs) convertible: 1960 kg (4312 lbs)	1950 kg (4290 lbs) 2000 kg (4400 lbs)
Maximum speed (automatic)	160 km/hr (99.5 mph)	163 km/hr (101 mph)	160 km/hr (99.5 mph) 155 km/hr (96.3 mph)	170 km/hr (105.6 mph) 165 km/hr (102.5 mph)
Acceleration (automatic)	18 sec 0-100 km	17 sec 0-100 km	17 sec 0-100 km 18 sec 0-100 km	17 sec 0-100 km 18 sec 0-100 km
Fuel consumption (automatic)	16.5 liters/100 km (14.2 mpg)	16 liters, super (14.7 mpg)	16 liters, super (14.7 mpg) 17 liters, super (13.7 mpg)	17 liters, super (13.7 mpg) 18 liters, super (13 mpg)
Fuel tank capacity	72 liters (19 gallons)	72 liters (19 gallons)	72 liters (19 gallons)	72 liters (19 gallons)

The 300Sc roadster, 1955

Prices and Production

The 300S coupe, convertible A, and roadster sold for DM 34,500. When in 1953 a new, modern showroom with excellent service facilities for Mercedes-Benz automobiles was opened at New York by the Hoffman Motor Company, importers for these cars in the United States, the 300S was priced at $12,500. The 300Sc coupe, convertible A, and open roadster sold for DM 36,500.

Production of the 300S model [188 I] (from September 1951/ July 1952 until August 1955)

was in	1951	2 units
	1952	113 units
	1953	353 units
	1954	37 units
	1955	55 units
	total	560 units

Production of the 300Sc model [188 II] (from September/December 1955 to April 1958)

was in	1955	5 units
	1956	140 units
	1957	52 units
	1958	3 units
	total	200 units

Model 300S (1951-1958)

S = Super

The 300S (super) model, first shown at the Paris Salon in October 1951 and produced in 1952, was created for the discriminating sports enthusiast driver. It was designed to carry on the tradition which had begun twenty-five years before with the 6-liter K model of 1927, followed by the superb S and SS models and finally the 540K model of 1936. With but half of the engine displacement, without supercharger, and weighing a ton less than its illustrious predecessor (and 450 pounds less than the 300 sedan), the 300S was actually faster, more responsive, safer, and more comfortable. (Karl Kling drove better times at the Nürburgring than with any other Mercedes since the SSK model.) The 540K had a 180-horsepower engine and weighed 5,735 pounds; the 300S had a 150 horsepower engine and weighed 3,880 pounds. Maximum speed was 109 miles per hour. The engine had a compression ratio of 7.5 to 1 and three downdraft carburetors. The wheelbase was 2,900 millimeters (114.2 inches) and overall length 4,700 millimeters (185 inches).

Two body styles were available, the coupe and convertible coupe or open roadster. The interior furnishings were of the finest material, real leather upholstery and rich wood matching the dash and the trim around the side and rear windows. The 300S was a joy to drive and to own, as this chronicler was fortunate to experience in ten years and a hundred thousand miles.

The 300Sc model was built from September 1955 until April 1958. That car had a fuel injection engine and single pivot swing axle, but was outwardly similar to the previous type, except that the rubber center piece in the bumpers was left off. A total of only 760 automobiles of both model types were produced.

The 300S line of cars was a truly "Super" range of models ever produced and was probably never exceeded in elegance. It was a joy to drive and for 10 years it was my pleasure and privilege to do so.

Specifications

	300S	300Sc
Engine type	6 cyl overhead camshaft (M188)	6 cyl overhead camshaft (M199)
Bore stroke	85 x 88mm (3.35 x 3.46 in)	85 x 88mm (3.35 x 3.46 in)
Displacement	2996 cc (182.7 cu in)	2996 cc (182.7 cu in)
Power output	150 hp (DIN) @ 5000 rpm	175 hp (DIN) @ 5400 rpm
Compression ratio	7.8:1	8.55:1
Torque	23.5 mkg @ 3800 rpm (170 ft/lb)	26 mkg @ 4300 rpm 188 ft/lb)
Carburetion	3 downdraft carburetors Solex 40 PBJC	Bosch injection pump
Engine speed at 100 km/hr	3260 rpm	3260 rpm
Gear ratios	I. 3.33:1 (later 3.68:1) II. 2.12:1 (later 2.25:1) III. 1.46:1 (later 1.42:1) IV. 1.00:1 (later 1.00:1)	I. 3.55:1 II. 2.30:1 III. 1.53:1 IV. 1.00:1
Rear axle ratio	4.125	4.44
Chassis	X-shaped oval tubular frame	X-shaped oval tubular frame
Suspension	independent front, swing axle rear, with coil springs	independent front, single pivot swing axle rear, with coil springs
Brakes and area	drum, 1270 cm² (197 sq in)	drum, 1470 cm² (228 sq in)
Wheelbase	2900mm (114.2 in)	2900mm (114.2 in)
Track, front/rear	1480/1525mm (58.2/60 in)	1480/1525mm (58.2/60 in)
Length	4700mm (185 in)	4700mm (185 in)
Width	1860mm (73.2 in)	1860mm (73.2 in)
Height	1510mm (59.4 in)	1510mm (59.4 in)
Ground clearance	180mm (7.1 in)	180mm (7.1 in)
Tires	6.70 x 15 extra	6.70 x 15 extra
Turning circle	12.2-12.7 meters (40-42 ft)	12.2-12.7 meters (40-42 ft)
Steering type and ratio	recirculating ball, 21.4:1 (3.75 turns)	recirculating ball, 21.4:1 (3.75 turns)
Weight	1760 kg (3880 lbs)	1780 kg (3924 lbs)
Maximum speed	176 km/hr (109 mph)	180 km/hr (112 mph)
Acceleration	15 sec 0-100 km	14 sec 0-100 km
Fuel consumption	17 liters, super/100 km (13.7 mpg)	
Fuel tank capacity	85 liters (22 gallons)	85 liters (22 gallons)

The 300S convertible, 1952

The 300S roadster, 1952

The 300S coupe, 1955; just like this writer owned for ten years

300S units built

	a,b	c
roadsters	141	53
convertibles	203	49
coupes	216	98

The 180 sedan, 1953

Prices

The 180 four-door sedan sold in 1953-1954 for. . . . . . .DM   9,950
(The U.S. price was $3,350 on the West coast)
in 1954-1956 . . . . .DM   9,450
in 1956-1961 . . . . .DM   8,700
from August 1961 . . . . .DM   8,950
from April 1962 . . . . .DM   9,350

For 180b and 180c power-assisted brakes were available at DM 300 extra cost.

The 180 sedan, 1953

Model 180 (1953-1962)

The 180 model, introduced in early 1953, featured a radically new type of chassis design, although the x-shaped oval tubular frame, used on the previous models, had proven thoroughly satisfactory. The most important element in this new design was that high sectional steel side members were united to the floor of the body to make a platform, greatly resistant to distortion. It actually doubled the rigidity of the assembly and considerably lessened noise.

The subframe which carried the entire power unit and transmission, as well as the steering and front wheel assembly, was anchored to the front part of the main chassis on rubber blocks on the three-point suspension system. This arrangement offered advantages in manufacture and maintenance. It was also the first example of a design where heavy components were readily detachable.

The double-joint swing axle was retained; and so was the four-cylinder, 1,767 cubic centimeter, 52-horsepower engine of the 170S model because of its ready availability and proven reliability. The external lines of the rather stubby-looking 180 model were in keeping with modern tendencies but retained the traditional radiator style. The radiator shell lifted up with the hood. The car was 22 percent roomier and more comfortable, more economical to operate, and allowed the driver an excellent view of the road. The window area was 40 percent greater than that of the 170S model. The smooth running and ideal road-holding properties were such that the driver was hardly aware of having reached its maximum speed of 125 kilometers (78 miles) per hour. The 180 model was built from September 1953 until August 1957. The 180a, built from September 1957 until July 1959, had the larger engine, 1,897 cubic centimeters and 65 horsepower. The 180b followed until August 1961. It had larger brakes, wider radiator, and no vertical bars on the bumpers. The 180c, with a changed valve gear was built from June 1961 until October 1962.

Production

Production of the 180 model [120 I] (from July 1953 until June 1957)

was in	1953	4,362 units
	1954	20,306 units
	1955	17,704 units
	1956	8,464 units
	1957	1,350 units
	total	52,186 units

Production of the 180a model [120 II] from June 1957 until July 1959)

was in	1957	4,656 units
	1958	15,967 units
	1959	6,730 units
	total	27,353 units

Production of the 180b model [120 III] (from July 1959 until August 1961)

was in	1959	7,314 units
	1960	14,384 units
	1961	7,717 units
	total	29,415 units

Production of the 180c model [120 IV] (from June 1961 until October 1962)

was in	1961	4,980 units
	1962	4,300 units
	total	9,280 units

The engine compartment of the 180 sedan, 1953

Specifications

	180	180a, b, c
Engine type	4 cyl (M 136)	4 cyl (M 121)
Bore and stroke	75 x 100mm (2.96 x 3.94 in)	85 x 83.6mm (3.35 x 3.29 in)
Displacement	1767 cc (107.7 cu in)	1897 cc (115.7 cu in)
Power output	52 hp (DIN) @ 4000 rpm	65 hp (DIN) @ 4500 rpm b: 68 hp (DIN) @ 4400 rpm
Compression ratio	6.8:1	6.8:1 b: 7:1
Torque	11.4 mkg @ 1800 rpm (82.5 ft/lb)	13 mkg @ 2200 rpm (94 ft/lb) b: 13.2 mkg @ 2500 rpm (96/4 ft/lb)
Carburetion	1 downdraft carburetor Solex 32 PICB	1 downdraft carburetor Solex 32 PICB b: Solex 34 PICB
Engine speed at 100 km/hr	3390 rpm	3390 rpm
Gear ratios	I. 4.05:1 II. 2.38:1 III. 1.53:1 IV. 1.00:1	I. 4.05:1 II. 2.38:1 III. 1.53:1 IV. 1.00:1
Rear axle ratio	3.89 (35:9)	3.90 (39:10)
Chassis	unit frame and body	unit frame and body
Suspension	independent front, swing axle rear, with coil springs from Sept '55: single swing axle	
Brakes and area	drum 816 cm² (126.5 sq in)	b: drum, 1064 cm² (164.9 sq in) servo optional
Wheelbase	2650mm (104.3 in)	2650mm (104.3 in)
Track, front/rear	1420/1475mm (55.9/58.1 in)	1420/1475mm (55.9/58.1 in)
Length	4480mm (176.4 in)	4480mm (176.4 in)
Width	1740mm (68.5 in)	1740mm (68.5 in)
Height	1560mm (61.4 in)	1560mm (61.4 in)
Ground clearance	185mm (7.3 in)	185mm (7.3 in)
Tires	6.40 x 13	6.40 x 13
Turning circle	11.5 meters (38 ft)	11.5 meters (38 ft)
Steering type and ratio	recirculating ball, 18.5:1	recirculating ball, 18.5:1
Weight	1180 kg (2596 lbs) from Sept: 1200 kg (2640 lbs)	1210 kg (2662 lbs)
Maximum speed	126 km/hr (78.4 mph)	136 km/hr (84 mph)
Acceleration	31 sec 0-100 km	21 sec 0-100 km
Fuel consumption	11.5 liters/100 km (20.4 mpg)	10.5 liters (22.4 mpg)
Fuel tank capacity	56 liters (14.8 gallons)	56 liters (14.8 gallons)

The 180D sedan, 1954

Prices and Production

The 180D four-door sedan sold in 1954-1955 for . . . . .DM 10,300
   in 1956 . . . . .DM 9,850
   in 1956-1958 . . . . .DM 9,480
   in 1958-1961 . . . . .DM 9,200
   from August 1961 . . . . .DM 9,450
   from April 1962 . . . . .DM 9,850

Production of the 180D model [120 I] (from October 1953/
February 1954 until July 1959)

was in	1953	11 units
	1954	15,532 units
	1955	20,345 units
	1956	21,013 units
	1957	22,910 units
	1958	26,693 units
	1959	9,981 units
	total	116,485 units

Production of the 180Db [120 II] (from July 1959 until August
1961)

was in	1959	8,076 units
	1960	11,151 units
	1961	5,449 units
	total	24,676 units

Production of the 180Dc [120 III] (from June 1961 until October
1962)

was in	1961	4,822 units
	1962	7,000 units
	total	11,822 units

Model 180D (1953-1962)

D = Diesel

The 180D was introduced after the 180 gasoline-engined sedan. Early production of this diesel-engined model was in October 1953 and regular production began in February 1954.

Again, in all respects, body and chassis of these two models were identical. The new unit frame construction and redesigned front end of this recently introduced four-door sedan was shared by both types. The 180D diesel engine was identical to that of the 170Db, but the rear axle ratio had been reduced and in September 1955 the engine output was raised to 43 horsepower. In April 1958 wind wings were placed on the front door windows, but otherwise the body remained the same as previously used.

The 180Db model production began in July 1959 and was to continue until August 1961. Larger diameter brakes, a wider radiator shell, and no vertical bumper bars were the only alterations.

The 180Dc, built from June 1961 until October 1962 had the larger engine. Displacing 1,988 cubic centimeters, it developed 48 horsepower at 3,800 revolutions per minute. Compression ratio was raised to 21 to 1.

Again, these diesel models proved to be considerably better sellers than the gasoline-powered versions which shared the body style and exterior and interior appointments.

To graphically illustrate the dependability of this diesel model, several 180Ds were entered in the rugged Mille Miglia race in 1955. Usually the exclusive field for fast and exotic sports cars, the rather austere and totally uncomplicated diesel-engined passenger models presented a most unusual sight to the inhabitants of the localities where this 922–mile-long race was held. Three 180D models won the first three places in their special diesel classification, averaging a quite respectable speed of over 60 miles per hour.

When the 180D became available in the United States, it sold for $3,394.

Specifications

	180D / 180Db	180Dc
Engine type	4 cyl diesel (OM 636)	4 cyl diesel (OM 621)
Bore and stroke	75 x 100mm (2.96 x 3.94 in)	87 x 83.6mm (3.43 x 3.29 in)
Displacement	1767 cc (107.7 cu in)	1988 cc (121 cu in)
Power output	40 hp (DIN) @ 3200 rpm 46 hp (SAE) @ 3500 rpm from Sept. '55: 43 hp @ 3500	48 hp (DIN) @ 3800 rpm
Compression ratio	19:1	21:1
Torque	10.3mgk @2000 rpm (75ft/lb)	11mkg @2200rpm (80ft/lb)
Fuel injection	Bosch injection pump (pre-combustion chamber)	
Engine speed at 100 km/hr	3330 rpm	3330 rpm
Gear ratios	I. 4.05:1 (15.0) II. 2.38:1 (8.81) III. 1.53:1 (5.66) IV. 1.00:1 (3.70)	I. 4.05:1 (15.0) II. 2.38:1 (8.81) III. 1.53:1 (5.66) IV. 1.00:1 (3.70)
Rear axle ratio	3.70 (37:10)	3.70 (37:10)
Chassis	unit frame and body	unit frame and body
Suspension	independent front, swing axle rear, with coil springs from Sept. '55: single swing axle	rear: single swing axle
Brakes and area	drum, 816 cm^2 (126.5 sq in)	drum, 1064 cm^2 (164.9 sq in)
Wheelbase	2650mm (104.3 in)	2650mm (104.3 in)
Track, front/rear	1430/1475mm (56.3/58.1 in)	1430/1475mm (56.3/58.1 in)
Length	4485mm (176.6 in)	4485mm (176.6 in)
Width	1740mm (68.5 in)	1740mm (68.5 in)
Height	1560mm (61.4 in)	1560mm (61.4 in)
Ground clearance	185mm (7.3 in)	185mm (7.3 in)
Tires	6.40 x 13	6.40 x 13
Turning circle	11.5 meters (38 ft)	11.5 meters (38 ft)
Steering type and ratio	recirculating ball, 18.5:1	recirculating ball, 18.5:1
Weight	1220 kg (2684 lbs)	1220 kg (2684 lbs)
Maximum speed	112 km/hr (70 mph) from Sept. '55: 115 km/hr	120 km/hr (75 mph)
Acceleration	39 sec 0-100 km from Sept. '55: 37 sec	36 sec 0-100 km
Fuel consumption	8 liters/100 km (29.3 mpg)	8 liters/100 km (29.3 mpg)
Fuel tank capacity	56 liters (14.8 gallons)	56 liters (14.8 gallons)

The frame–floor unit chassis of the 180, 1953

The OM 636 engine of the 180D, 1954

Model 300SL (1954-1963)

S = Sports, L (Leicht) = light

The 300SL sports car went into regular production in August 1954, but a more austere version had appeared on the international sports car racing scene in 1952. After an interval of many years, the company had decided to enter competition again and the 300SL was built. The designation SL (sport-light) described a new design in which the frame was replaced by a light but very stiff structure of a lattice pattern, made of thin welded steel tubing, and the outer cover was also very light since the lattice structure bears all stress.

The engine, developed from the 300S model, was mounted slanting 45 degrees for a lower hood line in order to allow the driver and passenger a better view ahead.

First tested in international competition in sports car races in Switzerland, at Le Mans, the Nürburgring, and the Panamericana in Mexico, the car earned its laurels. The magnificent victories, and the entire history of the 300SL, are related in another book by this author.

The production car incorporated many improvements gained from the racing experience. One of the striking features was the direct fuel injection which gave the 2,996 cubic centimeter six-cylinder engine 215 horsepower (240 SAE) at 5,800 revolutions per minute, and a maximum speed of 235 kilometers with the 3.64 rear axle and 260 kilometers (162 miles) per hour with the 3.25 axle fitted. The turbo brake drums were self-cooling and servo-assisted and were the same as on the 300S model. The speeds in the gears were 75 kilometers (47 miles) in first, 128 km (80 m) in second, 186 km (116 m) in third, and 240 kilometers (149 miles) in fourth at 6,000 revolutions per minute.

The 300SL roadster with conventional type doors was first shown at the Geneva Show in March 1957 and put into regular production in May. It was basically the same car as the gull-wing coupe, but the lower door line was closer to the ground and getting in and out was greatly facilitated. In many ways a superior sports car than the former, it never achieved the enthusiastic support of the

The 300SL coupe, 1956

original version, although actually more cars were produced during the seven years it was built.

The tubular frame was somewhat heavier because of the absence of the coupe body; the car weighed 1,330 kilograms to the 1,295 of the former, an increase of 77 pounds. The engine later had the competition camshaft installed with a higher compression ratio, 9.5 to 1, and was rated at 250 SAE horsepower at 6,200 revolutions per minute. The German specifications listed 215 horsepower at 5,800 revolutions per minute and the 8.55 compression ratio, as the earlier coupe model had. The U.S. cars also had the 3.89 rear axle ratio.

The various axle ratios gave the following maximum speeds: 3.25 at 155 miles per hour; 3.42 at 150, 3.64 at 146, 3.89 at 137, and 4.11 ratio at 129 miles per hour.

A hard top for the convertible roadster became available in September 1958 at extra cost, and in March 1961, four-wheel disc brakes were installed as a regular production item.

The 300SL roadster, 1957

Prices and Production

The 300SL coupe sold for . . . . .DM 29,000
Price in the United States was first . . . .$ 6,820
   then rose to (finally) . . . .$ 8,902
The 300SL roadster sold for . . . . . . .DM 32,500
   removable hardtop. . . . . .DM 1,500
Price in the United States was first . . . .$ 10,970
   then . . . .$ 11,099
   and. . . . .$ 11,573

Production of the 300 SL coupe [198 I] (from August 1954 until May 1957)

was in		
1954	146 units	
1955	867 units	
1956	311 units	
1957	76 units	
total	1,400 units	

Production of the 300SL roadster [198 II] (from February/May 1957 until February 1963)

was in		
1957	554 units	
1958	324 units	
1959	211 units	
1960	249 units	
1961	250 units	
1962	244 units	
1963	26 units	
total	1,858 units	

The 300SL coupe, 1956; just like this writer owned for two years

Specifications

	300SL (coupe)	300SL (roadster)
Engine type	6 cyl overhead camshaft (45° slanted to the left) (M 198)	
Bore and stroke	85 x 88mm (3.35 x 3.46 in)	85 x 88mm (3.35 x 3.46 in)
Displacement	2996 cc (182.7 cu in)	2996 cc (182.7 cu in)
Power output	215 hp (DIN) @ 5800 rpm (240 hp SAE) (for U.S.: 250 hp @ 6200 rpm)	
Compression ratio	8.55:1	9.5:1
Torque	28 mkg @ 4600 rpm (217 ft/lb @ 4800 rpm)	228 ft/lb
Fuel injection	Bosch injection pump	Bosch injection pump
Engine speed at 100 km/hr	3000 rpm	3000 rpm
Gear ratios	I. 3.34:1 (12.15) II. 1.97:1 (7.18) III. 1.385:1 (5.03) IV. 1.00:1 (3.64)	I. 3.34:1 (12.15) for U.S. (13.0) II. 1.97:1 (7.18) (7.66) III. 1.385:1 (5.03) (5.40) IV. 1.00:1 (3.64) (3.89)
Rear axle ratio	3.64; also 3.25; 3.42; 3.89; 4.11 upon request	
Chassis	tubular space frame with light alloy body	
Suspension	independent front, swing axle rear, with coil springs	
Brakes and area	drum, 1470 cm² (227.9 sq in) servo assisted; from Mar. '61 discs	
Wheelbase	2400mm (94.5 in)	2400mm (94.5 in)
Track, front/rear	1385/1435mm (54.5/56.5 in)	1398/1448mm (55.0/57.0 in)
Length	4520mm (178 in)	4570mm (180 in)
Width	1790mm (70.5 in)	1790mm (70.5 in)
Height	1300mm (51.2 in)	1300mm (51.2 in)
Ground clearance	130mm (5.1 in)	130mm (5.1 in)
Tires	6.50 x 15 super sport	6.70 x 15 super sport
Turning circle	11.4 meters (37 ft)	11.4 meters (37 ft)
Steering type and ratio	recirculating ball, 17.3:1 (3 turns)	recirculating ball, 17.3:1 (3 turns)
Weight	1295 kg (2849 lbs)	1330 kg (2926 lbs)
Maximum speed	3.64 axle: 235 km/hr (145 mph); 3.42-250 km/hr (155 mph); 3.25-260 km/hr (165 mph)	
Acceleration	8.7 sec 0-100 km/hr	8.1 sec 0-100 km/hr (for U.S. 7.2 sec)
Fuel consumption	17 liters, super / 100 km (13.7 mpg)	
Fuel tank capacity	130 liters (34 U.S. gallons)	100 liters (26 U.S. gallons)

The 190SL roadster, 1960

Prices and Production

The 190SL roadster, with cloth top, sold for . . . . .DM 16,500
   with removable hard top. . . . . .DM 17,100
   with both types top . . . . .DM 17,650
In the U.S. the 190SL roadster sold in 1958
   East coast . . . .$ 5,020
   West coast . . . .$ 5,129

Production of the 190SL [121 II] (from January/May 1955 until February 1963)

was in	1955	1,727 units
	1956	4,032 units
	1957	3,332 units
	1958	2,722 units
	1959	3,949 units
	1960	3,977 units
	1961	3,792 units
	1962	2,246 units
	1963	104 units
	total	25,881 units

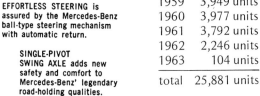

EFFORTLESS STEERING is assured by the Mercedes-Benz ball-type steering mechanism with automatic return.

SINGLE-PIVOT SWING AXLE adds new safety and comfort to Mercedes-Benz' legendary road-holding qualities.

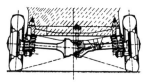

Model 190SL (1955-1963)

S = Sports, L (Leicht) = light

The 190SL model was announced early in 1954 as a smaller version of the 300SL, but initial production did not start until January 1955, when several important modifications had been made on the original design. This touring-sports car was based on the 180 model sedan and used the basic, but slightly altered, self-supporting frame-floor unit construction with the subframe assembly carrying the engine. The open roadster model needed greater support than the four-door sedan model.

The sporty body of the 190SL resembled that of the larger SL model but had regular fitted doors. A floor-located stick shift lever operated the four–speed synchro-meshed gear box. Speeds in gears were 46, 81, 128, and 190 kilometers (28, 50, 80, and 118 miles) per hour. Real leather bucket–type seats added greatly to the comfort and appearance of the silvery sports car.

The four-cylinder engine had a displacement of 1,897 cubic centimeters and a compression ratio of 8.5 to 1. The overhead camshaft engine, equipped with two Solex horizontal carburetors, developed 105 horsepower at 5,700 revolutions per minute (in the U.S. version 125 at 6,000). Maximum speed was given as 171 kilometers (106 miles) per hour. Torque was 101 ft/lbs.

The 190SL was advertised to sell in New York for $3,998 in 1955. The copy indicated a 125-horsepower engine and top speed of 118 miles per hour for this "blood brother" of the fabulous 300SL.

In September 1959 a new style hard top was designed with larger window area giving improved vision.

The 190SL was a popular selling car in this country, but owners hardly ever participated in competitive events, although the car proved fun to drive. It was not really an SL (sports, light) model. The car was too heavy for its particular class and was badly outperformed by the exotic sports cars available. However, in a 1958 Hong Kong rally, W. Sulke was the overall winner. Years later, the 190SL became a most desirable sports car and brought premium prices.

Specifications

	190SL
Engine type	4 cyl (M 121)
Bore and stroke	85 x 83.6mm (3.35 x 3.29 in)
Displacement	1897 cc (115.7 cu in)
Power output	105 hp (DIN) @ 5700 rpm (120 hp (SAE) @ 5700 rpm)
Compression ratio	8.5:1 from Sept. '59: 8.8:1
Torque	14.5 mkg @ 3200 rpm (105 ft/lb @ 3200 rpm)
Carburetion	2 dual downdraft carburetors Solex 44 PHH
Engine speed at 100 km/hr	3350 rpm
Gear ratios	I. 3.52:1 (13.7) II. 2.32:1 (9.02) III. 1.52:1 (5.92) IV. 1.00:1 (3.89)
Rear axle ratio	3.90 (39:10)
Chassis	unit frame and body
Suspension	independent front, single joint swing axle rear, with coil springs
Brakes and area	drum, 1064 cm^2 (164.9 sq in) servo optional
Wheelbase	2400mm (94.5 in)
Track, front/rear	1430/1475mm (56.2/58.1 in)
Length	4220mm (166.1 in)
Width	1740mm (68.5 in)
Height	1320mm (52 in)
Ground clearance	185mm (7.3 in)
Tires	6.40 x 13 sport
Turning circle	11 meters (36.1 ft)
Steering type and ratio	recirculating ball, 18.5:1
Weight	roadster: 1160 kg (2552 lbs) coupe: 1180 kg (2596 lbs)
Maximum speed	171 km/hr (106 mph)
Acceleration	14.5 sec 0-100 km
Fuel consumption	12.5 liters super/100 km (18.75 mpg)
Fuel tank capacity	65 liter (17 gallons)

The pre-production 190SL, 1954

The 190SL roadster with coupe top, 1955

The 190SL with the enlarged window, 1959

The 190 sedan, 1956

Prices and Production

The 190 four-door sedan in 1956-1961 sold for. . . . . . .DM 9,450
   Servo brakes available at additional. . . . . .DM   300
The 190c four-door sedan sold in 1961 for. . . . . .DM 9,950
   from April 1962 . . . . .DM 10,600
   Servo brakes available at additional. . . . . .DM   300
   (until August 1963)
   Power steering (from May 1964) . . . . .DM   550
   Automatic transmission (from August 1962) . . . . . .DM 1,400

Production of the 190 model [121 I] (from March 1956 until August 1959)

was in	1956	16,001 units
	1957	22,578 units
	1958	15,791 units
	1959	6,975 units
	total	61,345 units

Production of the 190b model [121 III] (from June 1959 until August 1961)

was in	1959	6,613 units
	1960	12,986 units
	1961	8,864 units
	total	28,463 units

Production of the 190c model [110] (from April 1961 until August 1965)

was in	1961	9,249 units
	1962	31,275 units
	1963	35,457 units
	1964	33,776 units
	1965	20,797 units
	total	130,554 units

Model 190 (1956-1965)

The 190 sedan, introduced at the Frankfurt Auto Show in 1956, was one of three new models shown to the public at that time. The body style was the same as that of the 180 sedan, but the new single overhead camshaft four-cylinder engine of 1,897 cubic centimeters (actually a detuned version of the 190SL power unit) developed 75 horsepower at 4,600 revolutions per minute. It was mounted on four points on the U-frame, resulting in greater quietness of operation. Interior furnishings of the 190 sedan were somewhat superior to those of the 180 model but outwardly the only distinguishing feature was a decorative chrome line around the body.

The 190b model, built from June 1959 on, had a wider radiator shell and the bumper had no vertical bumper guard bar.

The 190c model, produced from April 1961 until August 1965, was quite different from the preceding models of the same designation. It was longer, larger, and lower, and had the body style of the 220 models of that period, with the slight tail fins. But it had a slightly shorter hood line, round lights, and simple bumpers.

From August 1963 on, the model was equipped with disc brakes and a twin circuit hydraulic system. An automatic transmission was also available from August 1962 on at extra cost.

The 190 sedan, 1961

Specifications

	190	190b	190c
Engine type	4 cyl overhead camshaft (M 121)	4 cyl overhead camshaft (M 121)	4 cyl overhead camshaft (M 121)
Bore and stroke	85 x 83.6mm (3.35 x 3.29 in)	85 x 83.6mm (3.35 x 3.29 in)	85 x 83.6mm (3.34 x 3.29 in)
Displacement	1897 cc (115.7 cu in)	1897 cc (115.7 cu in)	1897 cc (115.7 cu in)
Power output	75 hp (DIN) @ 4600 rpm (84 SAE hp)	80 hp (DIN) @ 4800 rpm	80 hp (DIN) @ 5000 rpm (90 hp SAE @ 5200 rpm)
Compression ratio	7.5:1	8.5:1	8.7:1
Torque	13.9 mkg @ 2800 rpm (101 ft/lb)	14.2 mkg @ 2800 rpm (103 ft/lb)	14.5 mkg @ 2500 rpm (15.6 mkg @ 2700 rpm SAE 112.9 ft/lb)
Carburation	1 downdraft carburetor Solex 32 PAITA	1 downdraft carburetor Solex 32 PAITA	1 downdraft carburetor Solex 34 PJCB
Engine speed at 100 km/hr	3300 rpm	3300 rpm	3300 rpm
Gear ratios	I. 4.05:1 II. 2.38:1 III. 1.53:1 IV. 1.00:1	I. 4.05:1 II. 2.38:1 III. 1.53:1 IV. 1.00:1	I. 4.05:1 automatic 3.98:1 II. 2.28:1 2.52:1 III. 1.53:1 1.58:1 IV. 1.00:1 1.00:1
Rear axle ratio	4.10	4.10	4.08
Chassis	unit frame and body	unit frame and body	unit frame and body
Suspension	independent front, single joint swing axle rear, with coil springs (from 1963; air suspension, optional)		
Brakes and area	drum, 1064 cm^2 (164.9 sq in) servo optional		drum, 1064 cm^2 (164.9 sq in) servo assisted from Aug. '63; disc, front
Wheelbase	2650mm (104.3 in)	2650mm (104.3 in)	2700mm (106.3 in)
Track, front/rear	1430/1475mm (56.2/58.1 in)	1430/1475mm (56.2/58.1 in)	1468/1485mm (58/58.5in) from Aug.'63 1482/1465mm
Length	4485mm (176.6 in)	4500mm (177.2 in)	4730mm (186.5 in)
Width	1740mm (68.5 in)	1740mm (68.5 in)	1795mm (70.7 in)
Height	1560mm (61.4 in)	1560mm (61.4 in)	1495,mm (58.8 in)
Ground clearance	185mm (7.3 in)	185,mm (7.3 in)	185mm (7.3 in)
Tires	6.40 x 13	6.40 x 13	7.00 x 13
Turning circle	11.5 meters (38 ft)	11.5 meters (38 ft)	11.8-11.6 meters (38 ft)
Steering type and ratio	recirculating ball, 18.5:1 (3.75 turns)	recirculating ball, 18.5:1 (3.75 turns)	recirculating ball, 21.4:1 (3.75 turns) from May '64: servo assist 17.3:1 (3.2 turns)
Weight	1240 kg (2728 lbs)	1240 kg (2728 lbs)	1280 kg (2816 lbs)
Maximum speed	139 km/hr (86 mph)	144 km/hr (89 mph)	150 km/hr (93 mph) automatic: 145 km/hr (90 mph)
Acceleration	20.5 sec 0-100 km	19 sec 0-100 km	18 sec 0-100 km/hr automatic: 22 sec 0-100 km/hr
Fuel consumption	11.5 liters, super/100 km (20.4 mpg)		11.5 liters, super/100 km (20.4 mpg) automatic: 12.5 liters (18.75 mpg)
Fuel tank capacity	56 liters (14.8 gallons)	56 liters (14.8 gallons)	52 liters (13.5 gallons)

The 219 sedan, 1956

Model 219 (1956-1959)

The 219 sedan was the second model introduced at the Frankfurt Auto Show in 1956. The body style was identical to that of the 190 sedan, but the wheelbase was slightly larger, 2,750 millimeters to 2,650 millimeters for the 190 (3.937 inches longer). The six-cylinder engine was the same as that of the former 220 sedan, the proven 2,195 cubic centimeter unit developing 85 horsepower (92 SAE) at 4,800 revolutions per minute. Power output was increased in August 1957 to 90 horsepower (100 SAE), and the compression ratio from 7.6 to 8.7 to 1. With the increase in power, a slight increase in fuel consumption was also experienced, naturally, but only by one liter for 100 kilometers.

The 219 model was considered the middle range of the three newly developed sedans and the lowest priced six-cylinder one. The maximum speed, and cruising speed, was given as 148 kilometers (92 miles) per hour, with the 190 model doing 139 kilometers (86 miles) per hour and the 220S having a maximum speed of 99.4 miles, or 160 kilometers, per hour.

The 219 model was an economical car, yet quite powerful with the six-cylinder engine. It was available, as the other two similar models, with a sliding roof and in front a bench-type seat instead of the bucket seats.

As an optional extra, a hydraulic transmission was available. In this Hydrak system made by Fichtel and Sachs, a hydraulic coupling was used in connection with a conventional clutch automatically controlled. When the driver moved the gear lever, the clutch action was initiated. The system made for easier driving and provided engine braking at all times. It ensured smoothness of operation and saved the engine.

This Hydrak transmission, however, did not find too many enthusiastic supporters and, over the years, it seemed the one great handicap of these particular models whenever such a car became for sale as a used one. The operation was perhaps too tricky for the average driver — who usually held onto the lever — and a burned-out clutch seemed a regular occurrence. In retrospect, the Hydrak was an unfortunate choice.

Prices and Production

The 219 four-door sedan sold for . . . . .DM 10,500
    Servo brakes available at an additional. . . . . .DM   300
    Hydrak transmission . . . . .DM   450
Price in the U.S. was in 1956. . . . .$ 3,889

Production of the 219 model [105] (from March 1956 until July 1959)

was in	1956	5,474 units
	1957	8,505 units
	1958	9,296 units
	1959	4,570 units
	total	27,845 units

Specifications

	219
Engine type	6 cyl overhead camshaft (M 180)
Bore and stroke	80 x 72.8mm (3.15 x 2.87 in)
Displacement	2195 cc (133.9 cu in)
Power output	85 hp (DIN) @ 4800 rpm (92 hp SAE) from Aug. '57: 90 hp (DIN) (100 hp SAE)
Compression ratio	7.6:1 from Aug. '57: 8.7:1
Torque	16 mkg @ 2400 rpm (116 ft/lb) from Aug. '57: 17 mkg (123 ft/lb)
Carburetion	1 dual downdraft carburetor Solex 32 PAATJ
Engine speed at 100 km/hr	3320 rpm
Gear ratios	I. 3.52:1 (14.4) II. 2.32:1 (9.51) III. 1.52:1 (6.23) IV. 1.00:1 (4.10)
Rear axle ratio	4.10 from Aug. '57: 3.90
Chassis	unit frame and body
Suspension	independent front, single joint swing axle rear, with coil springs
Brakes and area	drum, 1064 cm^2 (164.9 sq in)
Wheelbase	2750mm (108.3 in)
Track, front/rear	1430/1470mm (56.2/57.9 in)
Length	4680mm (184.3 in)
Width	1740mm (68.5 in)
Height	1560mm (61.4 in)
Ground clearance	185mm (7.3 in)
Tires	6.40 x 13
Turning circle	11.5 meters (38 ft)
Steering type and ratio	recirculating ball, 21.4:1 (4 turns)
Weight	1290 kg (2838 lbs)
Maximum speed	148 km/hr (92 mph)
Acceleration	17 sec 0-100 km
Fuel consumption	14.5 liters/100 km (16.2 mpg) from Aug. '57 13.5 liters
Fuel tank capacity	56 liters (14.8 gallons)

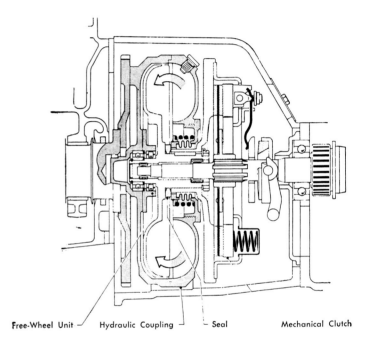

Free-Wheel Unit — Hydraulic Coupling — Seal   Mechanical Clutch

The Hydrak transmission, 1956

The 220S sedan, 1956

Prices and Production

The 220S four-door sedan sold for . . . . .DM 12,500
The 220S two-door convertible coupe sold for . . . . . . .DM 21,500
The 220S two-door hard top coupe sold for . . . . .DM 21,500
    Hydrak transmission . . . . .DM   450
Price in the United States was in 1956. . . . .$ 4,283

Production of the 220S [180 II] (from March 1956 until August
1959)

	was in	1956	10,525 units
		1957	15,459 units
		1958	20,181 units
		1959	9,114 units
		total	55,279 units

Production of the 220S convertible and coupe [180 II] (from July
1956 until October 1959)

	was in	1956	297 units
		1957	1,066 units
		1958	1,280 units
		1959	786 units
		total	3,429 units

Model 220S (1956-1959)

S = Super

The sedan was the third of the new models shown to the public at the Frankfurt Show in 1956. It was also the most powerful one of the trio and the most expensive one as well. The 2,195 cubic centimeter six-cylinder engine was of the same size as that of the 219, but it developed 100 horsepower (112 SAE) at 4,800 revolutions per minute. From August 1957 on, with the compression ratio increased from 7.6 to 8.7 to 1, it developed 106 horsepower at 5,200 revolutions per minute. In the United States the engine was rated at 120 SAE horsepower. The Hydrak automatic transmission was also available from August 1957 on at an additional cost of DM 450.

The 220S was considered the refined successor of the 220a model, but the body style had not undergone many changes. A convertible appeared in May 1956 and the hard top coupe in 1957.

The 220S convertible A, 1956

Specifications

	220S
Engine type	6 cyl overhead camshaft (M 180)
Bore and stroke	80 x 72.8mm (3.15 x 2.87 in)
Displacement	2195 cc (133.9 cu in)
Power output	100 hp (DIN) @ 4800 rpm (112 hp SAE) from Aug. '57: 106 @ 5200 (124 hp SAE)
Compression ratio	7.6:1 from Aug. '57: 8.7:1
Torque	16.5 mkg @ 3500 rpm (119 ft/lb) from Aug. '57: 17.5 mkg (127 ft/lb)
Carburetion	2 downdraft carburetors Solex 32 PAJTA
Engine speed at 100 km/hr	3320 rpm
Gear ratio	I. 3.52:1 II. 2.32:1 III. 1.52:1 IV. 1.00:1
Rear axle ratio	4.10
Chassis	unit frame and body
Suspension	independent front, single joint swing axle rear, with coil springs
Brakes and area	drum, 1064 cm^2 (164.9 sq in) servo assisted
Wheelbase	2820mm (111 in); coupe and convertible: 2,700mm (106.3 in)
Track, front/rear	1430/1470mm (56.2/57.9 in)
Length	4750mm (187 in); coupe and convertible: 4670mm (183.9 in)
Width	1740mm (68.5 in); coupe and convertible: 1765mm (69.5 in)
Height	1560mm (61.4 in); coupe and convertible: 1530mm (60.2 in)
Ground clearance	185mm (7.3 in)
Tires	6.70 x 13 sport
Turning circle	11.7 meters (38 ft); coupe and convertible: 11.4 meters (37 ft)
Steering type and ratio	recirculating ball, 21.4:1 (4 turns)
Weight	1350 kg (2970 lbs); coupe: 1410 kg (3102 lbs); convertible: 1450 kg (3219 lbs)
Maximum speed	160 km/hr (99.5 mph)
Acceleration	17 sec 0-100 km
Fuel consumption	13.5 liters super/100 km (17.4 mpg) coupe and convertible: 14 liters super
Fuel tank capacity	64 liters (16.9 gallons)

The 220S convertible A, 1956

The 220S sedan, 1956

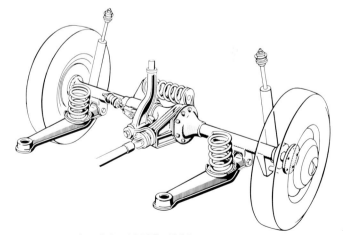

The joint swing axle of the 220SE, 1958

The 220SE sedan, 1958

Prices and Production

The 220SE four-door sedan sold for . . . . .DM 14,400
The 220SE two-door convertible sold for. . . . . .DM 23,400
The 220SE two-door coupe sold for . . . . .DM 23,400
    Hydrak transmission . . . . .DM   450
The 220SE convertible or coupe sold
    after August 1959 for. .DM 23,200

Production of the 220SE [128] (from April/October 1958 until August 1959)

was in	1958	201 units
	1959	1,773 units
	total	1,974 units

Production of the 220SE convertible and coupe [128] (from July/October 1958 until November 1960)

was in	1958	114 units
	1959	628 units
	1960	1,200 units
	total	1,942 units

Model 220SE (1958-1960)

S = Super, E (Einspritzung) = fuel injection

The 220SE was first introduced in September 1958. Early pre-production was actually begun in April of that year, but the regular production lines did not get underway until October. The sedan had the same body style and furnishing of the 220S and was only different in the fuel-injected engine. The regular carburetor engine was equipped with two Solex downdraft carburetors and developed 100 horsepower (112 SAE) for the 220S; while the injection engine, using a Bosch two-plunger injection pump, developed 120 horsepower (134 SAE). It was also considerably more flexible than the carburetor unit.

The manifold injection system cost about $400 more to produce than the regular carburetion system, but the engineers estimated that it resulted in 18 percent more power, 5 percent greater torque, and reduced fuel consumption by 8 percent.

The air collection chamber and six intake pipes fed the air to the individual ports and fuel was injected just ahead of the junction of the manifold and the cylinder head. A calibrated jet was used for each individual cylinder and the fuel was being fed from the two plunger pumps which operated at engine speed. Injection was also controlled by temperature and barometric pressure. It was not a direct injection, but a manifold injection system.

The 220SE two-door convertible and coupe models were also shown at the same time as the sedan model. When in August 1959 production of the sedan ceased, the convertible and coupe models remained in production until the end of 1960, but were equipped with the newer, 120-horsepower fuel injection engine of the 220SEb type.

Specifications

	220SE
Engine type	6 cyl overhead camshaft (M 127)
Bore and stroke	80 x 72.8mm (3.15 x 2.87 in)
Displacement	2195 cc (133.9 cu in)
Power output	115 hp (DIN) @ 4800 rpm (134 hp SAE @ 5000 rpm)
Compression ratio	8.7:1
Torque	19 mkg @ 3800 rpm (152 ft/lb @ 4100)
Fuel injection	Bosch two-plunger pump (into manifold)
Engine speed at 100 km/hr	3320 rpm
Gear ratios	I. 3.52:1 U.S. cars: I. 3.65:1 (14.9) II. 2.32:1 II. 2.36:1 (9.68) III. 1.52:1 III. 1.53:1 (6.27) IV. 1.00:1 IV. 1.00:1 (4.10)
Rear axle ratio	4.10
Chassis	unit frame and body
Suspension	independent front, single joint swing axle rear, with coil springs
Brakes and area	drum, 1064 cm² (164.9 sq in) servo assisted
Wheelbase	2820mm (111 in); coupe and convertible: 2700mm (106.3 in)
Track, front/rear	1430/1470mm (56.2/57.9 in)
Length	4750mm (187 in); coupe and convertible: 4670mm (183.9 in)
Width	1740mm (68.5 in); coupe and convertible: 1765mm (69.5 in)
Height	1560mm (61.4 in); coupe and convertible: 1530mm (60.2 in)
Ground clearance	185mm (7.3 in)
Tires	6.70 x 13 sport
Turning circle	11.7 meters (38 ft); coupe and convertible: 11.4 meters (37 ft)
Steering type and ratio	recirculating ball, 21.4:1 (4 turns)
Weight	1370 kg (3014 lbs); coupe: 1430 kg (3146 lbs); convertible: 1470 kg (3234 lbs)
Maximum speed	160 km/hr (99.5 mph)
Acceleration	15 sec 0-100 km
Fuel consumption	13 liters super/100 km (18 mpg); coupe and convertible: 13.5 liters (17.4 mpg)
Fuel tank capacity	62 liters (16.4 gallons)

The 220SE convertible, 1958

The 220SE coupe, 1958

The M 180 engine of the 220SE, 1958

The 190D sedan, 1958

Prices and Production

The 190D four-door sedan sold in 1958-1961 for . . . . .DM 9,950
The 190Dc four-door sedan in 1961 sold for. . . . . . . .DM 10,450
   from April 1962 for. . . . . .DM 11,100
   Power steering (from May 1964) . . . . .DM 550
   Automatic transmission (from September 1963) . . . .DM 1,400

Production of the 190D model [121 I] (from August 1958 until July 1959)

was in	1958	5,469 units
	1959	15,160 units
	total	20,629 units

Production of the 190Db [121 II] (from June 1959 until September 1961)

was in	1959	13,709 units
	1960	29,116 units
	1961	18,484 units
	total	61,309 units

Production of the 190Dc model [110] (from April/June 1961 until August 1965)

was in	1961	12,882 units
	1962	45,414 units
	1963	60,784 units
	1964	64,422 units
	1965	42,143 units
	total	225,645 units

Model 190D (1958-1965)

D = Diesel

The 190D model followed the gasoline-powered 190 model more than two years later. It was not put into production until August 1958. That year, the 180D was still being sold; in fact, over 26,000 units were produced and nearly 10,000 of them were sold the next year. Along with the new 190D model, the 180Db appeared in 1959 and the 180Dc in 1961. This smaller version (and older body style) was still a very popular car and in great demand. The 180D and 180Db had the 1,767 cubic centimeter displacement engine, while the 190D and 190Db had the larger 1,897 cubic centimeter diesel unit. The 180Dc had a 1,988 cubic centimeter engine and the 190Dc, as well as the 200D later, shared that same power plant.

The 190D model had the 1,897 cubic centimeter engine of 50 horsepower at 4,000 revolutions per minute. It was completely redesigned from the previous one, had a shorter stroke and single overhead camshaft instead of the older pushrod, long-stroke engine which was still being used in the 180D model. The maximum speed of the 190D was 126 kilometers (78 miles) per hour.

To dramatically introduce the new, larger, and more powerful diesel engine to the public, a car was entered to compete in the tortuous 8,727-mile African Rallye from Algiers to Capetown. Karl Kling drove the car to victory, averaging 55.5 miles per hour across the Dark Continent.

The 190Db, built from August 1959 to August 1961, shared the body with its gasoline engined counterpart, with the wider radiator grille and simpler bumper without guards.

The 190Dc, built until August 1965, was similar to the 190c. It had the same dimensions and shared that same newer body style with the tail fins, longer, larger, and lower than the previous one.

Specifications

	190D / 190Db	190Dc		
Engine type	4 cyl diesel, single overhead camshaft (OM 621)			
Bore and stroke	85 x 83.6mm (3.35 x 3.29 in)	87 x 83.6mm (3.43 x 3.29 in)		
Displacement	1897 cc (115.7 cu in)	1988 cc (121.27 cu in)		
Power output	50 hp (DIN) @ 4000 rpm (55 hp SAE)	55 hp (DIN) @ 4200 rpm (60 hp SAE)		
Compression ratio	21:1	21:1		
Torque	11mkg @2200 rpm(79.5 ft/lbs)	11.5 mkg 2400 rpm 12 mkg SAE 87 ft/lbs)		
Fuel injection	Bosch injection pump pre-combustion chamber	Bosch injection pump		
Engine speed at 100 km/hr	3300 rpm	3300 rpm		
Gear ratios	I. 4.05:1 II. 2.38:1 III. 1.53:1 IV. 1.00:1	I. 4.05:1 II. 2.28:1 III. 1.53:1 IV. 1.00:1	automatic	I. 3.98:1 II. 2.52:1 III. 1.58:1 IV. 1.00:1
Rear axle ratio	3.70	3.92		
Chassis	unit frame and body	unit frame and body		
Suspension	independent front, single joint swing axle rear, with coil springs from 1963: air suspension, optional			
Brakes and area	drum, 1064 cm² (164.9 sq in)	drum, 1064 cm² (164.9 sq in) servo assisted from Aug. '63: disc, front		
Wheelbase	2650mm (104.3 in)	2700mm (106.3 in)		
Track, front/rear	1430/1475mm (56.2/58.1 in)	1468/1485mm (58/58.5 in) from Aug.'63: 1482/1485mm (58.3/58.5 in)		
Length	4485mm (176.6 in) b: 4500mm (177.2 in)	4730mm (186.5 in)		
Width	1740mm (68.5 in)	1795mm (70.7 in)		
Height	1560mm (61.4 in)	1495mm (58.8 in)		
Ground clearance	185mm (7.3 in)	185mm (7.3 in)		
Tires	6.40 x 13	7.00 x 13		
Turning circle	11.5 meters (38 ft)	11.8-11.6 meters (38 ft)		
Steering type and ratio	recirculating ball, 18.5:1 (3.75 turns)	recirculating ball, 21.4:1; from May '64: servo assisted 17.3:1 (3.2 turns)		
Weight	1250 kg (2750 lbs)	1320 kg (2904 lbs)		
Maximum speed	126 km/hr (78 mph)	130 km/hr (81 mph); automatic 127 km/hr (79 mph)		
Acceleration	29 sec 0-100 km	29 sec 0-100 km/hr; automatic 30 sec 0-100 km/hr		
Fuel consumption	8.5 liters/100 km (27.75 mpg)	9 liters/100 km (26 mpg); automatic 10 liters/100 km (23.5 mpg)		
Fuel tank capacity	56 liters (14.8 gallons)	52 liters (13.5 gallons)		

The 190Db sedan, 1961

The 190D with sunroof and extra lights, 1963

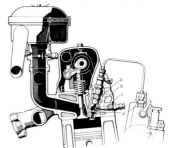

Drawing of the upper cylinder of M 621 engine, 1958

The 220S sedan, 1963

Prices and Production

The 220b four-door sedan sold for . . . . .DM 11,500
from April 1962 for. . . . . .DM 12,160
Power steering . . . . .DM   550
Hydrak transmission (until 1961). . . . .'. . . . .DM   450
Automatic transmission (from August 1962) . . . . . .DM   1,400
Price in the United States was . . . .$ 4,370

Production of the 220b [111/1] (from May/August 1959 until
August 1965)

was in	1959	3,375 units
	1960	13,127 units
	1961	14,842 units
	1962	11,618 units
	1963	10,492 units
	1964	11,327 units
	1965	4,910 units
	total	69,691 units

Prices and Production

The 220Sb four-door sedan sold for . . . . .DM 13,250
from April 1962 for. . . . . .DM 13,750
Power steering . . . . .DM   550
Hydrak transmission (until 1961). . . . . .DM   450
Automatic transmission (from August 1962) . . . . . .DM   1,400
Price in the United States was . . . .$ 5,120

Production of the 220Sb [111/2] (from May/August 1959 until
July 1965)

was in	1959	7,267 units
	1960	26,642 units
	1961	32,238 units
	1962	26,077 units
	1963	26,236 units
	1964	28,732 units
	1965	13,927 units
	total	161,119 units

Model 220 (1959-1965)

The 220b model sedan, shown to the public at the Frankfurt Auto Show in 1959, was one of four models which shared the new body style. The four-door sedans had a wider radiator shell, a longer body (4.875 millimeters, 191.9 inches, overall length) with slight rear fins, wrap-around windshield, and wide rear window, as well as dual vertically positioned headlights. Bumpers had a narrower one above the standard sized one.

The 220b model was the successor to the 219 sedan, which was then discontinued. The 2,195 cubic centimeter six-cylinder engine developed 95 horsepower (105 SAE) and had the higher compression ratio (8.7 to 1) of the later 219 production models. Maximum speed was also increased from 148 to 160 kilometers (99.4 miles) per hour.

The Hydrak transmission was available until 1961 and after August 1962 an automatic transmission became an optional extra item. A year later, in August 1963, the car was fitted with disc brakes on the front wheels and a hydraulic dual braking system. Power brakes were also available.

Model 220S (1959-1965)

S = Super

The 220S, first shown publicly in late 1959, was the second model which also shared the new body style of the sedans. All outside dimensions were the same as that of the other three models.

The six-cylinder engine developed 110 horsepower (124 SAE) and maximum speed was given as 165 kilometers (102.5 miles) per hour. Disc brakes on the front wheels were fitted from April 1962, and from August 1963 a hydraulic dual braking system was installed.

The 220 sedan, 1959

Specifications

	220	220S
Engine type	6 cyl overhead camshaft (M 180)	6 cyl overhead camshaft (M 180)
Bore and stroke	80 x 72.8mm (3.16 x 2.87 in)	80 x 72.8mm (3.16 x 2.87 in)
Displacement	2195 cc (133.9 cu in)	2195 cc (133.9 cu in)
Power output	95 hp (DIN) @ 4800 rpm (105 hp SAE @ 5000 rpm)	110 hp (DIN) @ 5000 rpm (124 hp SAE @ 5200 rpm)
Compression ratio	8.7:1	8.7:1
Torque	17.2 mkg @ 3200 rpm (18.4 mkg 133.2 ft/lb @ 3300)	17.5 mkg @ 3500 rpm (19.2 mkg 139 ft/lb @ 3700 rpm)
Carburetion	2 downdraft carburetors Solex 34 PJCB	2 dual downdraft carburetors Solex 34 PAJTA from July '63: 35/40 INAT
Engine speed at 100 km/hr	3300 rpm	3300 rpm
Gear ratios	I. 3.64:1 automatic I. 3.98:1 II. 2.36:1 (later 2.28:1) II. 2.52:1 III. 1.53:1 III. 1.58:1 IV. 1.00:1 IV. 1.00:1	I. 3.64:1 automatic I. 3.98:1 II. 2.36:1 (later 2.28:1) II. 2.52:1 III. 1.53:1 III. 1.58:1 IV. 1.00:1 IV. 1.00:1
Rear axle ratio	3.90 4.10	3.90 4.10
Chassis	unit frame and body	unit frame and body
Suspension	independent front, single joint swing axle rear, with coil springs	independent front, single joint swing axle rear, with coil springs
Brakes and area	drum, 1064 cm² (164.9 sq in), servo assisted, optional from Aug. '63 disc, front	drum, 1064 cm² (164.9 sq in), servo assisted, optional from Apr. '62 disc, front
Wheelbase	2750mm (108.3 in)	2750mm (108.3 in)
Track, front/rear	1470/1485mm (57.9/58.5 in) from Aug. '63: 1482/1485mm (58.3/58.5 in)	1470/1485mm (57.9/58.5 in) from Apr. '62: 1482/1485mm (58.3/58.5 in)
Length	4875mm (191.9 in)	4875mm (191.9 in)
Width	1795mm (70.7 in)	1795mm (70.7 in)
Height	1500mm (59.1 in)	1500mm (59.1 in)
Ground clearance	165mm (6.5 in)	165mm (6.5 in)
Tires	6.70 x 13; from 1960: 7.25 x 13	6.70 x 13 sport; from 1960: 7.25 x 13 sport
Turning circle	12.1-11.9 meters (39 ft)	12.1-11.9 meters (39 ft)
Steering type and ratio	recirculating ball, 21.4:1 (3.75 turns)	recirculating ball, 21.4:1 (3.75 turns)
Weight	1320 kg (2904 lbs)	1345 kg (2959 lbs)
Maximum speed	160 km/hr (99.5 mph)	165 km/hr (103 mph)
Acceleration	16 sec 0-100 km/hr	15 sec 0-100 km/hr
Fuel consumption	14 liters, super/100 km (16.75 mpg); automatic: 15 liters, super (15.6 mpg)	14 liters, super/100 km (16.75 mpg) automatic: 15 liters, super 100km/hr (15.6 mpg)
Fuel tank capacity	65 liters (17.2 gallons)	65 liters (17.2 gallons)

The 220SE convertible, 1961

Prices and Production

The 220SEb four-door sedan sold for . . . . .DM 14,950
   from April 1962 . . . . .DM 15,400
   Power steering . . . . .DM   550
   Hydrak transmission (until 1961) . . . . .DM   450
   Automatic transmission (from August 1961) . . . . .DM 1,400
The 220SEb two-door coupe sold for . . . . .DM 23,500
The 220SEb two-door convertible sold for . . . . .DM 25,500
The price in the United States for the sedan was . . . . . .$ 5,187
The price in the United States for the coupe was . . . . . .$ 8,895

Production of the 220SEb sedan [111/3] (from August 1959 until August 1965)

was in	1959	1,579 units
	1960	9,247 units
	1961	10,761 units
	1962	10,786 units
	1963	12,848 units
	1964	14,336 units
	1965	6,529 units
	total	66,086 units

Production of the 220SEb [111/3] coupe and convertible (from September 1960/February 1961 until October 1965)

was in	1960	2 units
	1961	2,537 units
	1962	4,287 units
	1963	3,755 units
	1964	3,528 units
	1965	2,793 units
	total	16,902 units

Model 220SE (1959-1965)

S = Super, E (Einspritzung) = fuel injection

The 220SEb, first shown also in late 1959, was the third of the models to share the identical body style with the others, but was more luxuriously outfitted in its interior.

The fuel-injection engine was essentially the same as that of the previous 220SE model, but now developed 120 horsepower (134 SAE) instead of 115. The maximum speed was 172 kilometers (107 miles) per hour. As in the carbureter engined model, this one had disc brakes on the front wheels fitted from April 1962 and the hydraulic dual braking system available from August 1963 on.

Production of the sedans got under way in August 1959, and in September 1960 a newly styled coupe became available, but it was not produced in quantity until February 1961. The convertible appeared in September 1961. All specifications were the same for the three body styles, except for the weights of the different models. Disc brakes were fitted for the two latter ones from the beginning, and at the same time the dual braking system was available in all three.

The body styles of the convertible and coupe were more modern — the rear fins were eliminated and the edge slightly rounded — and the cars were much more luxuriously equipped. Real leather upholstery was standard and a four-speed automatic transmission with floor-mounted shift lever, as well as a tachometer, were standard equipment of these truly elegant automobiles.

The 200SE coupe, 1961

Specifications

	220SEb	220SEb (coupe and convertible)		
Engine type	6 cyl overhead camshaft (M 127)	6 cyl overhead camshaft (M 127)		
Bore and stroke	80 x 72.8mm (3.16 x 2.87 in)	80 x 72.8mm (3.16 x 2.87 in)		
Displacement	2195 cc (133.9 cu in)	2195 cc (133.9 in)		
Power output	120 hp (DIN) @ 4800 rpm (134 hp SAE @ 5000 rpm)	120 hp (DIN) @ 4800 rpm (134 hp SAE @ 5000 rpm)		
Compression ratio	8.7:1	8.7:1		
Torque	19.3 mkg @ 3900 rpm; (21.0 mkg @ 4100 rpm SAE 151.9 ft/lb)			
Fuel injection	Bosch two plunger pump	Bosch two plunger pump		
Engine speed at 100 km/hr	3470 rpm	3470 rpm		
Gear ratios	I. 3.64:1 II. 2.36:1 (later 2.28:1) III. 1.53:1 IV. 1.00:1	I. 3.64:1 II. 2.36:1 (later 2.28:1) III. 1.53:1 IV. 1.00:1	automatic	I. 3.98:1 II. 2.52:1 III. 1.58:1 IV. 1.00:1
Rear axle ratio	4.10	4.10		
Chassis	unit frame and body	unit frame and body		
Suspension	independent front, single joint swing axle rear, with coil springs			
Brakes and area	drum, 1064 cm² (164.9 sq in) disc, front; drum, rear servo assisted, optional; from Aug. '63: two circuit hydraulic			
Wheelbase	2750mm (108.3 in)	2750mm (108.3 in)		
Track, front/rear	1470/1485mm (57.9/58.5 in)	1482/1485mm (58.3/58.4 in)		
Length	4875mm (191.9 in)	4880mm (192.1 in)		
Width	1795mm (70.7 in)	1845mm (72.7 in)		
Height	1500mm (59.1 in)	1440mm (57 in)		
Ground clearance	185mm (7.3 in)	185mm (7.3 in)		
Tires	6.70 x 13 sport from 1960: 7.25 x 13 sport	coupe: 7.25 x 13; conv: 750 x 13		
Turning circle	12.1-11.9 meters (39 ft)	12.1-11.9 meters (39 ft)		
Steering type and ratio	recirculating ball, 21.4:1 (3.75 turns) (with servo assistance: 17.3:1; 3.2 turns)	22.7:1 (4.1 turns)		
Weight	1380 kg (3036 lb)	coupe: 1410 kg (3102 lbs); conv: 1510 kg (3322 lbs)		
Maximum speed	172 km/hr (107 mph)	172 km/hr (107 mph)		
Acceleration	14 sec 0-100 km/hr	14 sec 0-100 km/hr		
Fuel consumption	14 liters, super/100 km (16.75 mpg); automatic: 15 liters (15.6 mpg) 14.5 liters/15.5 liters			
Fuel tank capacity	65 liters (17.2 gallons)	65 liter (17.2 gallons)		

The 220SE coupe, 1963

The instrument panel of the 220SE coupe, 1961

The 300SE sedan, 1961

Production

Production of the 300SE sedan [112/3] (from April 1961 until July 1965)

was in	1961	13 units
	1962	2,768 units
	1963	995 units
	1964	936 units
	1965	490 units
	total	5,202 units

Production of the 300SE convertible and coupe [112/3] (from February 1962 until December 1967)

was in	1962	331 units
	1963	630 units
	1964	706 units
	1965	710 units
	1966	497 units
	1967	253 units
	total	3,127 units

Production of the 300SE long sedan [112/3] (from December 1962/ March 1963 until August 1965)

was in	1962	1 unit
	1963	387 units
	1964	751 units
	1965	407 units
	total	1,546 units

Model 300SE (1961-1967)

S = Super, E (Einspritzung) = fuel injection

The 300SE was the fourth model to share the new basic body style first shown at the Frankfurt Auto Show in 1959. In appointments it was similar to the 220SE, but it had several important refinements, visible and hidden. The white-wall tires and wider use of chrome trim on the body made it look longer and more elegant than its lesser counterparts, but from afar it seemed the same. An air suspension system and disc brakes on all four wheels were standard. The hydraulic dual braking system was available from August 1963 on.

The 2,996 cubic centimeter light alloy engine with manifold fuel injection developed 160 horsepower at 5,000 revolutions per minute and from January 1964 on, 170 horsepower at 5,400 revolutions per minute. This was achieved by raising the compression ratio from 8.7 to 8.8 to 1; and instead of the two-plunger injection pump, a six-plunger Bosch pump was used. Maximum speeds varied according to rear axle ratios; the 160 horsepower engine with automatic transmission and 3.92 axle produced 175 kilometers per hour, while the 170 horsepower version with manual transmission and 3.75 axle gave the sedan a maximum speed of 200 kilometers (124 miles) per hour.

The 300SE coupe and convertible were added to the line in March 1962, and a longer (2,850 millimeter or 112.2 inch) wheelbase model sedan came out in March 1963.

Prices

The 330SE four-door sedan sold for . . . . .DM	23,100
The 300SE long four-door sedan sold for . . . . .DM	26,400
The 300SE two-door coupe sold for . . . . .DM	31,350
The 300SE two-door convertible sold for. . . . . .DM	33,350
Automatic transmission .DM	1,400
The price in the United States	
for the sedan in January 1966 was . . . .$	7,980
for the coupe in January 1966 was . . . .$	11,511
for the convertible in January 1966 was. . . . .$	12,295

Specifications

The 300SE coupe, 1962

300SE/ 300SE (long)/ 300SE (coupe and convertible)

Engine type	6 cyl overhead camshaft (M 189)
Bore and stroke	85 x 88mm (3.34 x 3.47 in)
Displacement	2996 cc (182.8 cu in)
Power output	160 hp (DIN) @ 5000 rpm; from Jan. '64: 170 hp (DIN) @ 5400 rpm (185 hp SAE @ 5200 rpm) (195 hp SAE @ 5500 rpm)
Compression ratio	8.7:1 from Jan. '64: 8.8:1
Torque	25.6 mkg @ 3800 rpm 25.4 mkg @ 4000 rpm (28.3 mkg @ 4000 rpm SAE 204.5 ft/lb)
Fuel injection	Bosch two plunger pump; from Jan. '64: six plunger pump
Engine speed at 100 km/hr	3310 rpm
Gear ratios	I. 4.05:1 automatic I. 3.98:1 (16.3) II. 2.28:1 II. 2.52:1 (10.3) III. 1.53:1 III. 1.58:1 (6.47) IV. 1.00:1 IV. 1.00:1 (4.10)
Rear axle ratio	3.92 or 3.75 4.10 from 1963: 3.92 or 3.75
Chassis	unit frame and body
Suspension	independent front and rear, with coil springs, single joint swing axle, air suspension
Brakes and area	disc, 253/255mm (99.6/100.4), servo assisted, two circuit hydraulic
Wheelbase	2750mm (108.3 in); SE long: 2850mm (112.2 in)
Track, front/rear	1482/1490mm (58.3/58.6)
Length	4875mm (191.9 in); long: 5875mm (231.2 in); coupe & convertible: 4880mm (192.1 in)
Width	1795mm (70.7 in) coupe & convertible: 1845mm (72.6 in)
Height	1455mm (58 in) coupe: 1395mm; conv: 1400mm (55.1 in)
Ground clearance	185mm (7.3 in)
Tires	7.50 x 13
Turning circle	12.1-11.9 meters (39 ft); long: 12.4-12.2 meters (40 ft)
Steering type and ratio	recirculating ball, 17.3:1 (3.2 turns), servo assisted
Weight	1580 kg (3476 lbs); long: 1630 kg (3586 lbs); coupe: 1600 kg (3520 lbs); conv: 1700 kg (3740 lbs)
Maximum speed	160 hp manual, 3.92 axle 180 km/hr (112 mph); autom. 175 km/hr 170 hp manual, 3.92 axle 190 km/hr (118 mph); autom. 185 km/hr 170 hp manual, 3.75 axle 200 km/hr (124 pmh); autom. 195 km/hr
Acceleration	160 hp: 13 sec 0-100 km/hr; 170 hp: 12 sec 0-100 km/hr
Fuel consumption	17 liters, super/100 km (13.7 mpg); automatic: 19 liters (12.3 mpg)
Fuel tank capacity	65 liters (17.2 gallons); from Jan. '63: 82 liters (21.6 gallons)

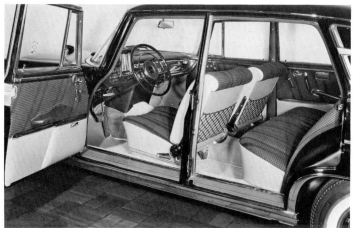

The interior of the 300SE sedan, 1961

The 230SL coupe, 1963

Model 230SL (1963-1967)

S = Sports, L (Leicht) = light

The 230SL sports car was first introduced at the Geneva Auto Show in March 1963. It was the successor to the 190SL which was phased out in February of that year. The engine for the 230SL was an enlarged version of the 220SE power unit, displacing 2,306 cubic centimeters and developing 150 horsepower (170 SAE) at 5,500 (5,600) revolutions per minute. Compression ratio was 9.3 to 1. The fuel was injected into the intake duct in the cylinder head instead of into the intake suction pipe as in the other models.

The four-speed transmission lever was placed on the floor and an automatic transmission was available. The rear axle ratio was 3.75 to 1. Maximum speeds were for the manual transmission 200 kilometers (124.2 miles) per hour and using the automatic transmission, 195 kilometers (121.2 miles) per hour.

A two-circuit servo brake system was installed as well as a vacuum operated brake booster. Disc brakes were fitted in front and drum brakes on the rear wheels. The coupe version had a slightly converse top, giving it the appearance of a pagoda top. The large glass area afforded an excellent view for the driver in all directions.

To start the introduction of the new model off with an impressive event, Eugen Böhringer won the tortuous Spa-Sofia-Liége Rally, driving the new 230SL. It was a spectacular performance for driver and car to win this initial test against strong international competition.

This victory proved, without a doubt, that this SL model was truly a light sports car and deserved that designation. In the United States the car was well received, but for many owners, performance was not its strongest asset. Perhaps compared with the really brutal power of the 300SL, this 230SL was a rather sedate, but quite adequately performing sports car model.

Prices and Production

The 230SL roadster sold in 1963 for	DM 20,600
from April 1966 for	DM 21,100
The 230SL coupe sold in 1963 for	DM 20,950
from April 1966 for	DM 21,450
Hard top (for the roadster)	DM 1,100
Power steering	DM 550
Automatic transmission	DM 1,400
Prices in the United States were, in April 1966,	
for the 230SL roadster (East coast)	$ 6,185
(West coast)	$ 6,262
for the 230SL coupe (East coast)	$ 6,343
(West coast)	$ 6,420
for the 230SL coupe/roadster (East coast)	$ 6,587
(West coast)	$ 6,665
Power steering (April 1966)	$ 171
Automatic transmission	$ 342
Prices previously were for the roadster	$ 6,144
for the coupe	$ 6,301
for the coupe/roadster	$ 6,543

Production of the 230SL [113] (from March/July 1963 until January 1967)

was in	1963	1,465 units
	1964	6,911 units
	1965	6,325 units
	1966	4,945 units
	1967	185 units
	total	19,831 units

Specifications

	230SL
Engine type	6 cyl overhead camshaft (M 127)
Bore and stroke	82 x 72.8mm (3.23 x 2.87 in)
Displacement	2,306 cc (140.7 cu in)
Power output	150 hp (DIN) @ 5500 rpm (170 hp SAE @ 5600 rpm)
Compression ratio	9.3:1
Torque	20 mkg @ 4200 rpm (22 mkg @ 4500 rpm 159 ft/lbs)
Fuel injection	Bosch six plunger pump
Engine speed at 100 km/hr	3145 rpm
Gear ratios	until 1965 automatic:

The 230SL roadster, 1963

Gear ratios detail:

	until 1965		automatic:	
I.	4.42:1 (later 4.05)	I.	3.98:1	(14.9)
II.	2.28:1 (later 2.23)	II.	2.52:1	(9.45)
III.	1.53:1 (later 1.42)	III.	1.58:1	(5.92)
IV.	1.00:1 (later 1.00)	IV.	1.00:1	(3.75)

Rear axle ratio	3.75; from Sept. '65: 3.69 or 3.92
Chassis	unit frame and body
Suspension	independent front, single joint swing axle rear, with coil springs
Brakes and area	disc, front; drum, rear, servo assist, two circuit hydraulic, 253/230mm (9.96/9.06 in)
Wheelbase	2400mm (94.5 in)
Track, front/rear	1486/1487mm (58.5/58.5 in)
Length	4285mm (168.8 in)
Width	1760mm (69.2 in)
Height	1305mm (51.4 in)
Ground clearance	139mm (5.5 in)
Tires	185 HR 14 radial
Turning circle	10.5 meters (34 ft)
Steering type and ratio	recirculating ball, 22.7:1 (4.1 turns); servo assisted 17.3:1 (3.2 turns)
Weight	roadster: 1300 kg (2860 lbs); coupe: 1380 kg (3036 lbs)
Maximum speed	200 km/hr (124 mph); automatic: 195 km/hr (121 mph)
Acceleration	11 sec 0-100 km/hr; automatic: 13 sec 0-100 km/hr
Fuel consumption	14 liter, super/100 km (16.75 mpg)
Fuel tank capacity	65 liters (17.2 gallons)

The instrument panel of the 230SL, 1963

The 250SL roadster, 1967

Prices and Production

The 250SL coupe sold in 1967 for . . . . .DM 22,800
    Power steering . . . . .DM   550
    Automatic transmission . . . . .DM 1,400
The 250SL roadster sold in the U.S. in September 1967
    (East coast) for . . . .$ 6,485
    (West coast) for. . . . .$ 6,568
The 250SL coupe sold (East coast) for . . . .$ 6,647
The 250SL coupe/roadster sold (East coast) for . . . . . .$ 6,897

Production of the 250SL [113 A] (from November/December 1966 until January 1968)

	was in	1966	17 units
		1967	5,177 units
		1968	2 units
		total	5,196 units

Model 250SL (1966-1968)

S = Sports, L (Leicht) = light

The 250SL model made its brief appearance toward the end of 1966. The first few cars (seventeen units) were built in late November and in December of that year. The body was the same as that of the former 230SL which it replaced. Minor improvements had been made in the interior furnishings and outfitting, such as a pressure-absorbing steering wheel, better seat belts, and modified lighting of some instruments, but basically it was the same.

With the larger engine of 2,496 cubic centimeter (152.3 cubic inch) displacement and 150 horsepower (DIN) and 170 SAE, and especially vastly increased torque from the former 159 ft/lbs. to 173.6 ft/lbs. (both at 4,500 revolutions per minute), this new model showed an appreciable improvement in performance. Fitted with the four- or five-speed transmission and a rear axle ratio of 3.69, the car reached 19.7 miles at 1,000 revolutions per minute in top gear — the same as that of the 230SL model, but it was much more responsive. The gear ratios of the later production of the former model were maintained. Along with the engine of the 250SE line, the sports car also got the disc brakes, front and rear, resulting in some improvement in stopping the car; power assist was standard.

While this newer SL model was superior to the one it replaced, its actual performance was only slightly better than that of its predecessor. The somewhat larger displacement engine produced the same horsepower, but had a 10 percent increase in torque. Yet, the acceleration figures and maximum speed remained the same as before.

The 250SL was actually a one–year production car. It was soon to be replaced by a yet larger engined model and was produced in any quantity only during the year 1967. Only two cars were built in 1968.

The next version, in fact the third of this body style, was to be a most satisfactory car in every respect. It sold better than the previous ones and became a much desired sports car practically everywhere. Here, it indeed commanded premium prices, and 15 years later double the original cost was the going rate.

Specifications

	250SL
Engine type	6 cyl overhead camshaft (M 129)
Bore and stroke	82 x 78.8mm (3.23 x 3.1 in)
Displacement	2496 cc (152.3 cu in)
Power output	150 hp (DIN) @ 5500 rpm (170 hp SAE @ 5600 rpm)
Compression ratio	9.3:1
Torque	22 mkg @ 4200 rpm (24 mkg SAE @ 4500 rpm 173.6 ft/lb)
Fuel injection	Bosch six plunger pump
Engine speed at 100 km/hr	3245 rpm
Gear ratios	I. 4.05:1 automatic I. 3.98:1 II. 2.23:1 II. 2.52:1 III. 1.42:1 III. 1.58:1 IV. 1.00:1 IV. 1.00:1
Rear axle ratio	3.69
Chassis	unit frame and body
Suspension	independent front and rear, with coil springs, single joint swing axle
Brakes and area	disc, servo assist, two circuit hydraulic, 273/279mm (10.75/10.99 in)
Wheelbase	2400mm (94.5 in)
Track, front/rear	1486/1487mm (58.5/58.5 in)
Length	4285mm (168.8 in)
Width	1760mm (69.2 in)
Height	1305mm (51.4 in)
Ground clearance	139mm (5.5 in)
Tires	185 H 14 radial
Turning circle	10.5 meters (34 ft)
Steering type and ratio	recirculating ball, 22.7:1 (4.1 turns); servo assisted, 17. 3:1 (3.2 turns)
Weight	roadster: 1300 kg (2860 lbs); coupe: 1380 kg (3036 lbs)
Maximum speed	200 km/hr (124 mph); automatic: 195 km/hr (121 mph)
Acceleration	11 sec 0-100 km/hr; automatic: 13 sec 0-100 km/hr
Fuel consumption	14 liters, super/100 km (16.75 mpg)
Fuel tank capacity	82 liters (21.7 gallons)

The 250SL coupe, 1967

The 250SL on the test track, 1967

The 250SL on the rain track, 1967

The 280SL coupe, 1968

Prices

The 280SL sports coupe/roadster sold for . . . . .DM 23,793
    Power steering . . . . .DM   550
    Automatic Transmission . . . . .DM 1,400
Prices were in March 1968 (East coast)
    for the 280SL roadster . . . .$ 6,485
    coupe . . . .$ 6,647
    roadster/coupe . . . .$ 6,897
Prices were in March 1968 (West coast)
    for the 280SL roadster . . . .$ 6,585
    coupe . . . .$ 6,731
    roadster/coupe . . . .$ 6,981
Prices were in September 1968 (East coast)
    for the 280SL roadster . . . .$ 6,638
    coupe . . . .$ 6,800
    roadster/coupe . . . .$ 7,050
Prices were in October 1969 (East coast)
    for the 280SL roadster . . . .$ 6,952
    coupe . . . .$ 7,118
    roadster/coupe . . . .$ 7,374
Prices were in October 1970 (East coast)
    for the 280SL roadster . . . .$ 7,444
    coupe . . . .$ 7,617
    roadster/coupe . . . .$ 7,884
Prices were in March 1971 (East coast)
    for the 280SL roadster . . . .$ 7,469
    coupe . . . .$ 7,642
    roadster/coupe . . . .$ 7,909
    Power steering (October 1970). . . . .$ 198
    Automatic transmission . . . .$ 392

Model 280SL (1967-1971)

S = Sports, L (Leicht) = light

The 280SL sports car was the next, and last, graduation in the development of the particular model line. Begun in March 1963 as the 230SL, it had succeeded the popular 190SL of which nearly 26,000 units were produced. Yet in the three variations (230SL, 250SL, and 280SL) this model sold almost twice as many cars. It was not a competitive, but luxurious, fast touring sports car.

The six-cylinder 2,778 cubic centimeter displacement engine for the 280SL was entirely new. It retained the same design characteristics as the 250 engine, with single overhead camshaft and a seven main bearing crankshaft. An air cooler for the lubricating oil, similar to that employed on racing cars, replaced the oil-water heat exchanger of the previous engine design. Developing 180 SAE horsepower (up from 170) and 193 ft/lbs. torque (up from 174), the performance of this newest model sports car was tremendously enhanced, despite the restricting stricter emission controls. (The horsepower per liter ratio was for the 230SL/74, 250SL/68, and 280SL/65.)

For the American market a rear axle ratio of 4.08 was furnished, but the other two ratios, 3.92 and 3.69, were available upon special request. As on the two previous models, the five-speed manual gearbox was also available, while the four-speed one was standard. Power steering was not yet a standard item on the car. The 280SL was offered as a coupe, roadster, or combination roadster-coupe model.

Production

Production of the 280SL [113 E28] (from November 1967/January 1968 until March 1971)

was in	1967	143 units
	1968	6,930 units
	1969	8,047 units
	1970	7,935 units
	1971	830 units
	total	23,885 units

Specifications

	280SL
Engine type	6 cyl overhead camshaft (M 130)
Bore and stroke	86.5 x 78.8mm (3.41 x 3.10 in)
Displacement	2778 cc (169.5 cu in)
Power output	170 hp (DIN) @ 5700 rpm (180 SAE hp @ 5700 rpm) or 180 hp (DIN) @ 5900 rpm, but not for U.S.
Compression ratio	9.5:1
Torque	24.5 mkg @ 4250 rpm (26.7 mkg SAE @ 4500 rpm 193 ft/lb)
Fuel injection	Bosch six plunger pump
Engine speed at 100 km/hr	3500 rpm
Gear ratios	I. 4.05:1 automatic I. 3.98:1 (16.21) II. 2.23:1 II. 2.52:1 (10.27) III. 1.42:1 III. 1.58:1 (6.44) IV. 1.00:1 IV. 1.00:1 (4.08)
Rear axle ratio	4.08 upon request: 3.92, 3.69
Chassis	unit frame and body
Suspension	independent front and rear, with coil springs, single joint swing axle
Brakes and area	disc, servo assist, two circuit hydraulic, 273/279mm (10.75/10.99 in)
Wheelbase	2400mm (94.5 in)
Track, front/rear	1486/1487mm (58.5/58.5 in)
Length	4285mm (168.8 in)
Width	1760mm (69.2 in)
Height	1305mm (51.4 in)
Ground clearance	139mm (5.5 in)
Tires	185 H 14 radial
Turning circle	10.5 meters (34 ft)
Steering type	recirculating ball, servo assisted 17.2:1 (3.2 turns)
Weight	roadster: 1340 kg (2948 lbs); coupe: 1420 kg (3124 lbs)
Maximum speed	195 km/hr (121 mph); automatic: 190 km/hr (118 pmh)
Acceleration	10 sec 0-100 km/hr; automatic: 11 sec 0-100 km/hr
Fuel consumption	14 liters, super/100 km (16.75 mpg)
Fuel tank capacity	82 liters (21.7 gallons)

The 280SL coupe, 1968, U.S. version

The 280SL roadster, 1968

The 280SL roadster, 1968

Prices

The 600 four-door limousine sold for . . . . .DM 56,500
The 600 four-door pullman sold for . . . . .DM 63,500
In the United States, advertised in May 1964,
   prices were for the limousine (called
   5-passenger sedan) . . . .$ 19,500
   and for the pullman (called
   7-passenger sedan) . . . .$ 24,000
The price list of October 1965 offered the
   limousine (East coast) for . . . .$ 20,143
   (West coast) for. . . . .$ 20,291
   pullman (East coast) for . . . .$ 23,098
   (West coast)for . . . .$ 23,245
The price list of October 1970 (registration 1971 vehicles)
   offered the limousine (East coast) for . . . .$ 25,707
   (West coast) for. . . . .$ 25,920
   pullman (East coast) for . . . .$ 29,385
   (West coast) for. . . . .$ 29,617
The price list of December 1971 (registration 1972 vehicles)
   offered the limousine (East coast) for . . . .$ 32,695
   pullman (East coast) for . . . .$ 37,928
Other prices were, in September 1966 (East coast)
   limousine. . . . .$ 22,299
   pullman. . . . .$ 25,582
in September 1968 (East coast)
   limousine. . . . .$ 23,007
   pullman. . . . .$ 26,290
in October 1969 (East coast)
   limousine. . . . .$ 23,580
   pullman. . . . .$ 26,953

Model 600 (1963-1981)

The 600 model — the Grosser Mercedes — was introduced at the Frankfurt Auto Show in 1963. It restored the tradition of sumptuous luxury and ultimate prestige of Mercedes-Benz.

A new V-type eight-cylinder engine of 6.3 liters (6,329 cubic centimeters) developing 250 horsepower (300 SAE) powered this newest edition of the great Mercedes to a maximum speed of 205 kilometers (127 miles) per hour. The 600 model was available in two body styles: a 5/6-seat limousine or 7/8-passenger pullman with wheelbases of 3,200 millimeters (126 inches) and 3,900 millimeters (153.5 inches), respectively. Overall length was 218 and 246 inches. From 1965 on, a landaulet also became available.

This fine automobile incorporated all modern design elements: fuel injection, overhead camshaft engine, air suspension and shock absorbers adjustment, disc brakes on all four wheels, automatic four-speed transmission and power steering, central vacuum locking system for the doors and luggage compartment, adjustable steering wheel, and two separate heating and ventilating systems. It was truly a majestic car of the highest order and an honorable descendant of the distinctive Great Mercedes automobiles of former years.

That year, 1963, the company offered fourteen passenger car models for sale. However, not all of them were made available to the American public, and most of them were naturally not entirely new models.

The M 100 V–8 engine of the 600, 1963

The 600 limousine, 1963

Production

Production of the 600 and 600 long model [100]
(from August 1963/September 1964 until June 1981)

		Limousine	Pullman
was in	1963	2 units	1 unit
	1964	99 units	8 units
	1965	345 units	63 units
	1966	293 units	30 units
	1967	138 units	21 units
	1968	184 units	39 units
	1969	279 units	57 units
	1970	198 units	38 units
	1971	186 units	51 units
	1972	172 units	38 units
	1973	64 units	18 units
	1974	24 units	28 units
	1975	25 units	17 units
	1976	33 units	14 units
	1977	36 units	19 units
	1978	28 units	12 units
	1979	36 units	17 units
	1980	33 units	11 units
	1981	15 units	5 units
	total	2,190 units	487 units

The 600 pullman, 1964

The 600 landaulet, 1965

Specifications

	600	Pullman
Engine type	V-8 cyl overhead camshaft, one for each bank (M 100)	
Bore and stroke	103 x 95mm (4.06 x 3.74 in)	103 x 95mm (4.06 x 3.74 in)
Displacement	6332 cc (386.3 cu in)	6332 cc (386.3 cu in)
Power output	250 hp (DIN) @ 4000 rpm (300 hp SAE @ 4100 rpm)	
Compression ratio	9.0:1	9.0:1
Torque	51 mkg @ 2800 rpm (434 ft/lbs @ 3000 rpm)	
Fuel injection	Bosch eight plunger pump	Bosch eight plunger pump
Engine speed at 100 km/hr	2475 rpm	2475 rpm
Gear ratios	I. 3.98:1 (12.86) II. 2.52:1 (8.14) III. 1.58:1 (5.10) IV. 1.00:1 (3.23)	I. 3.98:1 (12.86) II. 2.52:1 (8.14) (later 2.46:1) III. 1.58:1 (5.10) IV. 1.00:1 (3.23)
Rear axle ratio	3.23	3.23
Chassis	unit frame and body	unit frame and body
Suspension	independent front, single joint swing axle rear, air suspension	
Brakes and area	discs, 291/294.5mm (114.6/115.9 in), servo assisted, two circuit hydraulic	
Wheelbase	3200mm (126 in)	3900mm (153.5 in)
Track, front/rear	1587/1581mm (62.5/62 in)	1587/1581mm (62.5/62 in)
Length	5540mm (218 in)	6240mm (246 in)
Width	1950mm (76.8 in)	1950mm (76.8 in)
Height	1500mm (59.5 in)	1510mm (59.5 in)
Ground clearance	200mm (7.9 in) (later: 152mm (6.0 in)	
Tires	9.00 x 15 super sport	9.00 x 15 super sport
Turning circle	12.4 meters (40.7 ft) (later: 12.7m)	14.6 meters (47.8 ft) (later: 15.0m)
Steering type and ratio	recirculating ball, servo assisted, 17.3:1 (3.3 turns)	
Weight	2470 kg (5434 lbs) (later: 2475 kg)	2640 kg (5808 lbs) (later: 2660 kg)
Maximum speed	205 km/hr (127 mph)	200 km/hr (124 mph)
Acceleration	10 sec 0-100 km/hr (later: 9.7 sec)	12 sec 0-100 km/hr
Fuel consumption	24 liters, super/100 km (10.2 mpg)	26 liters, super/100 km (9 mpg)
Fuel tank capacity	112 liters (30 gallons)	112 liters (30 gallons)

The 200 sedan, 1965

Prices and Production

The 200 four-door sedan sold for . . . . .DM 10,800
    from April 1966 for. . . . . .DM 11,000
    Power steering . . . . .DM   500
    Automatic transmission . . . . .DM 1,400
The price in the United States was in 1965
    (East coast) . . . .$ 3,929
      (West coast) . . . .$ 4,039
    in September 1966 (East coast) . . . .$ 4,084
    in September 1967 (East coast) . . . .$ 4,179
    Power steering (1965) . . . .$ 171
    Automatic transmission . . . .$ 342

Production of the 200 model [110] (from July 1965 until February 1968)

	was in	1965	16,864 units
		1966	26,842 units
		1967	26,169 units
		1968	332 units
		total	70,207 units

Model 200 (1965-1968)

The 200 model was first shown, together with four other new models, at the Frankfurt Auto Show in 1965. It used the same body as the former 190c sedan which it replaced. Outwardly the change was a relocation of the indicator lights from the cowl to the front, just below the headlights, a redesigned cluster of rear lights, and a narrow chrome strip at the rear window for the air ventilation exit.

The four-cylinder engine had been increased from 1.9 liters to 2 liters (1,988 cubic centimeters) and developed 95 horsepower (105 SAE) instead of the former 80 horsepower (90 SAE). A five-bearing crankshaft gave it smoother and quieter operation. With the same weight as previously, performance was improved by some 20 percent. Acceleration figures from 0 to 100 kilometers (62 miles) were 15 seconds and maximum speed was 161 kilometers (100 miles) per hour. The 200 sedan was the smallest of the seventeen different models of passenger cars the company offered that year.

The M 121 engine of the 200, 1965

Specifications

	200
Engine type	4 cyl overhead camshaft (M 121)
Bore and stroke	87 x 83.6mm (3.43 x 3.29 in)
Displacement	1988 cc (121.27 cu in)
Power output	95 hp (DIN) @ 5200 rpm (105 hp SAE @ 5400 rpm)
Compression ratio	9.0:1
Torque	15.7 mkg @ 3600 rpm (16.9 mkg @ 3800 rpm 122.3 ft/lb)
Carburetion	2 downdraft carburetors Solex 38 PDSJ
Engine speed at 100 km/hr	3310 rpm
Gear ratios	I. 4.09:1 automatic I. 3.98:1 II. 2.25:1 II. 2.52:1 III. 1.42:1 III. 1.58:1 IV. 1.00:1 IV. 1.00:1
Rear axle ratio	4.08
Chassis	unit frame and body
Suspension	independent front, single joint swing axle rear, with coil springs
Brakes and area	disc, front; drum, rear; servo assist, two circuit hydraulic, 253/230mm (9.96/9.06 in)
Wheelbase	2700mm (106.3 in)
Track, front/rear	1482/1485mm (58.3/58.5 in)
Length	4730mm (186.5 in)
Width	1795mm (70.7 in)
Height	1495mm (58.8 in)
Ground clearance	185mm (7.3 in)
Tires	7.00 x 13
Turning circle	11.8-11.6 meters (39 ft)
Steering type and ratio	recirculating ball, 22.7:1 (4.1 turns); servo assisted 17.3:1 (3.2 turns)
Weight	1275 kg (2805 lbs)
Maximum speed	161 km/hr (100 mph); automatic: 158 km/hr (98 mph)
Acceleration	15 sec 0-100 km/hr; automatic: 16 sec 0-100 km/hr
Fuel consumption	12.5 liters, super/100 km (18.75 mpg); automatic: 13.5 liters, super (17.4 mpg)
Fuel tank capacity	65 liters (17.2 gallons)

Front view of the 200 sedan, 1965

The 200D sedan, 1965

Prices and Production

The 200D four-door sedan sold for . . . . .DM 11,300
    from April 1966 for. . . . . .DM 11,500
Power steering . . . . .DM   500
Automatic transmission .DM 1,400
The price in the United States was in 1965
    (East coast) . . . .$ 4,142
    (West coast) . . . .$ 4,252
    in September 1966 (East coast) . . . .$ 4,305
    in September 1967 (East coast) . . . .$ 4,380
    Power steering (1965) . . . .$ 171
    Automatic transmission . . . .$ 342

Production of the 200D model [110] (from July 1965 until
February 1968)

was in	1965	30,937 units
	1966	61,707 units
	1967	68,399 units
	1968	575 units
	total	161,618 units

Model 200D (1965-1968)

D = Diesel

The 200D was another new car, introduced at the time of the Frankfurt Show in 1965. As always, this diesel-engined model shared all of the appointments with the gasoline-engined model in its category. The body was exactly the same, and it, too, replaced the former 190Dc. Unlike its companion car, the engine of the 200D was of the same displacement as the previous one which already had displaced 1,988 cubic centimeters.

A five-bearing crankshaft, along with other noise attenuating measures, were built into the engine for quieter and smoother operation and less fatigue to the driver. These design features released greater power and increased the maximum speed of the car to 130 kilometers (80.8 miles) per hour. Fuel consumption remained extremely moderate, averaging between 7 to 9 liters (31 to 40 gallons) at regular cruising speeds. The standard consumption, according to DIN, was 35 miles per gallon (8.1 liters per 100 kilometers) at 60 miles per hour.

Since 1936, some 500,000 diesel-engined Mercedes-Benz cars had been built, attesting to the popularity of these economic and robust automobiles.

The instrument panel of the 200D sedan,

Specifications

	200D
Engine type	4 cyl diesel, overhead camshaft (OM 621)
Bore and stroke	87 x 83.6mm (3.43 x 3.29 in)
Displacement	1988 cc (121.27 cu in)
Power output	55 hp (DIN) @ 4200 rpm (60 hp SAE)
Compression ratio	21:1
Torque	11.5 mkg @ 2400 rpm (12 mkg SAE 87 ft/lbs)
Fuel injection	Bosch injection pump
Engine speed at 100 km/hr	3300 rpm
Gear ratios	I. 4.09:1 automatic I. 3.98:1 II. 2.25:1 II. 2.52:1 III. 1.42:1 III. 1.58:1 IV. 1.00:1 IV. 1.00:1
Rear axle ratio	3.92
Chassis	unit frame and body
Suspension	independent front, single joint swing axle rear, with coil springs air suspension, optional
Brakes and area	disc front; drum, rear, servo assist, 253/230mm (9.96/9.06 in) two circuit hydraulic
Wheelbase	2700mm (106.3 in)
Track, front/rear	1482/1485mm (58.3/58.5 in)
Length	4730mm (186.5 in)
Width	1795mm (70.7 in)
Height	1495mm (58.8 in)
Ground clearance	185mm (7.3 in)
Tires	7.00 x 13
Turning circle	11.8-11.6 meters (39 ft)
Steering type and ratio	recirculating ball, 22.7:1 (4.1 turns); servo assisted 17.3:1 (3.2 turns)
Weight	1325 kg (2915 lbs)
Maximum speed	130 km/hr (81 mph)
Acceleration	29 sec 0-100 km/hr; automatic: 30 sec 0-100 km/hr
Fuel consumption	9 liters/100 km (26 mpg); automatic: 10 liter/100 km (23 mpg)
Fuel tank capacity	65 liters (17.2 gallons)

The 200D sedan, 1965

The 200D sedan, 1965

The 230 sedan, 1965

Model 230 (1965-1968)

The 230 model, also first shown at the Frankfurt Show in 1965, was the successer to the 220 model. The body style was the same as that of the 200 line introduced at the same time. However, with the six-cylinder engine this model combined the compact dimensions with the performance and efficiency of a modern six-cylinder car.

The new engine had a bore of 82 millimeters, instead of the 80 millimeters of the former 2,195 cubic centimeter engine, resulting in an increase to 2,281 cubic centimeters (139.2 cubic inches). With a compression ratio of 9 to 1 and the new camshaft, the engine developed 105 horsepower at 5,200 revolutions per minute or 118 SAE horsepower at 5,400 revolutions per minute. The weight of this six-cylinder engine, now with a seven main bearing crankshaft for greater smoothness, was but slightly more than that of the four-cylinder unit and resulted in greatly improved performance over that model. Maximum speed was increased to 168 kilometers (104 miles) per hour. Automatic transmission and power steering were optional items for this model, of course.

Special attention was placed on internal safety in these cars. The passenger compartment was of extremely sturdy construction while the front and rear ends were deformable and yielded on impact in crash tests. The instrument panel was made of shock-absorbing material and the operating knobs were recessed. In the event of a collision, the inside mirror would become detached, and the steering wheel had the well–known padded center plate.

The unitized body system with strong side and cross members combined the four-door body and frame into a jointly supported torsionally stiff, welded unit. And the dual circuit power brake system was another safety feature of this new line of the New Medium Class of cars.

Prices and Production

The 230 four-door sedan sold for . . . . .DM 11,700
from April 1966 for . . . . .DM 11,950
Power steering . . . . .DM   500
Automatic transmission . . . . .DM 1,400
The price in the United States was in 1965
(East coast) . . . .$ 4,113
(West coast) . . . .$ 4,223
in September 1966 (East coast) . . . .$ 4,280
in September 1967 (East coast) . . . .$ 4,405
Power steering (1956) . . . .$ 171
Automatic transmission . . . .$ 342

Production of the 230 model [110] (from July 1965 until February 1968)

	was in	1965	8,548 units
		1966	14,951 units
		1967	16,441 units
		1968	318 units
		total	40,258 units

Specifications

	230
Engine type	6 cyl overhead camshaft (M 180)
Bore and stroke	82 x 72.8mm (3.23 x 2.87 in)
Displacement	2281 cc (139.2 cu in)
Power output	105 hp (DIN) @ 5200 rpm (118 hp SAE @ 5400 rpm)
Compression ratio	9:1
Torque	17.7 mkg @ 3600 rpm (19 mkg SAE @ 3800 rpm 137.4 ft/lb)
Carburetion	2 downdraft carburetors Solex 38 PDSJ
Engine speed at 100 km/hr	3470 rpm
Gear ratios	I. 4.09:1 automatic I. 3.98:1 II. 2.25:1 II. 2.52:1 III. 1.42:1 III. 1.58:1 IV. 1.00:1 IV. 1.00:1
Rear axle ratio	4.08
Chassis	unit frame and body
Suspension	independent front, single joint swing axle rear, with coil springs air suspension, optional
Brakes and area	disc front; drum rear, servo assist, two circuit hydraulic, 253/230mm (9.96/9.06 in)
Wheelbase	2700mm (106.3 in)
Track, front/rear	1482/1485mm (58.3/58.5 in)
Length	4730mm (186.5 in)
Width	1795mm (70.7 in)
Height	1495mm (58.8 in)
Ground clearance	185mm (7.3 in)
Tires	7.00 S 13
Turning circle	11.8-11.6 meters (39 ft)
Steering type and ratio	recirculating ball, 22.7:1 (4.1 turns); servo assisted 17.3:1 (3.2 turns)
Weight	1305 kg (2871 lbs)
Maximum speed	168 km/hr (104 mph); automatic: 165 km/hr (103 mph)
Acceleration	14 sec 0-100 km/hr; automatic: 16 sec 0-100 km/hr
Fuel consumption	15 liters, super/100 km (15.6 mpg); automatic: 16 liters, super (14.7 mpg)
Fuel tank capacity	65 liters (17.2 gallons)

The 230 sedan, 1965

The 230 sedan, 1965

63

The 230S sedan, 1965

Prices and Production

The 230S four-door sedan sold for . . . . .DM	13,750
from April 1966 for. . . . . .DM	14,000
Power steering . . . . .DM	500
Automatic transmission .DM	1,400

The price in the United States was in 1965

(East coast) . . . .$	4,754
(West coast) . . . .$	4,869
in September 1966 (East coast) . . . .$	4,910
in September 1967 (East coast) . . . .$	5,035
Power steering (1965) . . . .$	171
Automatic transmission . . . .$	342

Production of the 230S model [111/1A] (from July 1965 until January 1968)

was in	1965	12,621 units
	1966	17,230 units
	1967	11,176 units
	1968	80 units
	total	41,107 units

Model 230S (1965-1968)

S = Super

The 230S model differed only slightly from the 230 model with which it was first shown at the Frankfurt Show in 1965. The body was practically identical except in the arrangement of the headlights which were combined into one large covered unit. The car replaced the former 220S model and was now the top model of the new class series of passenger cars.

The six-cylinder engine with overhead camshaft had two two-phase downdraft carburetors with automatic starting device. The valve timing permitted a maxium engine speed of 6,250 revolutions per minute without any risk. The horsepower output of the 2,281 cubic centimeter displacement engine was 120 horsepower at 5,400 revolutions per minute (or 135 SAE at 5,600), the same as that of the former 220S model. Compression ratio was 9 to 1. Maximum speed was given at 176 kilometers (110 miles) per hour, and in third gear a top speed of 125 kilometers (78 miles) per hour could be achieved.

Here, again as before, the S–model was indeed the Super version of the regular 230 model. The dual carburetors gave the engine more power, increased the torque, and improved the all–around performance.

The interior of the 230S sedan, 1965

64

Specifications

	230S
Engine type	6 cyl overhead camshaft (M 180)
Bore and stroke	82 x 72.8mm (3.23 x 2.87 in)
Displacement	2281 cc (139.2 cu in)
Power output	120 hp (DIN) @ 5400 rpm (135 hp SAE @ 5600 rpm)
Compression ratio	9:1
Torque	18.2 mkg @ 4200 rpm (20 mkg SAE 144.7 ft/lb)
Carburetion	2 dual downdraft carburetors Zenith 35/40 INAT
Engine speed at 100 km/hr	3415 rpm
Gear ratios	I. 4.05:1 automatic I. 3.98:1 II. 2.23:1 II. 2.52:1 III. 1.42:1 III. 1.58:1 IV. 1.00:1 IV. 1.00:1
Rear axle ratio	4.08
Chassis	unit frame and body
Suspension	independent front, single joint swing axle rear, with coil springs, air suspension
Brakes and area	disc front; drum rear, servo assist, two circuit hydraulic, 253/230mm (9.96/9.06 in)
Wheelbase	2750mm (108.2 in)
Track, front/rear	1482/1485mm (58.3/58.5 in)
Length	4730mm (186.5 in)
Width	1795mm (70.7 in)
Height	1495mm (58.8 in)
Ground clearance	185mm (7.3 in)
Tires	7.25 x 13
Turning circle	12.0-11.8 meters (39 ft)
Steering type and ratio	recirculating ball, 22.7:1 (4.1 turns); servo assisted, 17.3:1 (3.2 turns)
Weight	1350 kg (2970 lbs)
Maximum speed	176 km/hr (109 mph); automatic: 174 km/hr (108 mph)
Acceleration	13 sec 0-100 km/hr; automatic: 15 sec 0-100 km/hr
Fuel consumption	15 liters, super/100 km (15.6 mpg); automatic: 16 liters, super (14.7 mpg)
Fuel tank capacity	65 liters (17.2 gallons)

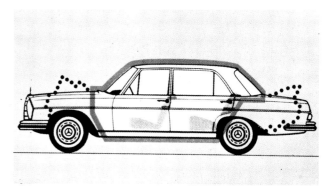

Impact-absorbing front and rear sections, 1967

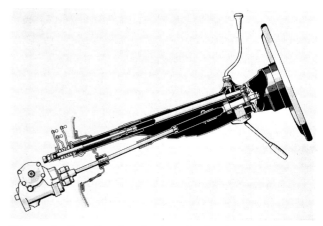

Telescopically collapsing steering wheel column, 1967

The 250S sedan, 1965

Prices and Production

The 250S four-door sedan sold for . . . . .DM 15,300
    from April 1966 for. . . . . .DM 15,800
    Power steering . . . . .DM 550
    Automatic transmission . . . . .DM 1,400
The price in the United States was in 1965
    (East coast) . . . .$ 5,696
    (West coast) . . . .$ 5,806
    in September 1966 (East coast) . . . .$ 5,747
    in September 1967 (East coast) . . . .$ 5,897
    Power steering (1965) . . . .$ 171
    Automatic transmission . . . .$ 342

Production of the 250S model [108 II] (from July/September 1965 until March 1969)

was in	1965	2,844 units
	1966	31,564 units
	1967	37,866 units
	1968	2,014 units
	1969	389 units
	total	74,677 units

Model 250S (1965-1969)

S = Super

The 250S model, also first shown at Frankfurt in 1965, had a brand new body style. The tail fins had been entirely eliminated and the overall appearance was similar to that of the coupe models. The body waist line was lowered and window area increased, with the windshield being 17 percent larger than that of the 220S model. The flat roof made it look wider, but width had increased by only 15 millimeters (0.59 inches). Height was reduced by 60 millimeters (2.36 inches).

The 2,496 cubic centimeter (152.3 cubic inch) engine was developed from the 2.2-liter power unit, but it had a larger bore and stroke and a seven-bearing crankshaft. A higher compression ratio and larger valves and induction passages were other changes. A double exhaust pipe was standard. The engine developed 130 horsepower at 5,400 revolutions per minute or 146 SAE horsepower at 5,600 revolutions.

Maximum speed of the 250S sedan was given as 180 kilometers (112 miles) per hour, and maximum allowable engine speed was 6,300 revolutions per minute.

Front view of the 250S sedan, 1965

Specifications

	250S
Engine type	6 cyl overhead camshaft (M180)
Bore and stroke	82 x 78.8mm (3.23 x 3.1 in)
Displacement	2496 cc (152.3 cu in)
Power output	130 hp (DIN) @ 5400 rpm (146 hp SAE @ 5600 rpm)
Compression ratio	9:1
Torque	19.8 mkg @ 4000 rpm (21.75 mkg SAE @ 4200 rpm 157.3 ft/lb)
Carburetion	2 dual downdraft carburetors Zenith 35/40 INAT
Engine speed at 100 km/hr	3245 rpm
Gear ratios	I. 4.05:1 automatic I. 3.98:1 (15.6) II. 2.23:1 II. 2.52:1 (9.88) III. 1.42:1 III. 1.58:1 (6.19) IV. 1.00:1 IV. 1.00:1 (3.92)
Rear axle ratio	3.92
Chassis	unit frame and body
Suspension	independent front, single joint swing axle rear, with coil springs, air suspension standard
Brakes and area	disc, servo assist, two circuit hydraulic, 273/279mm (10.75/10.99 in)
Wheelbase	2750mm (108.3 in)
Track, front/rear	1482/1485mm (58.3/58.5 in)
Length	4900mm (192.9 in)
Width	1810mm (71.3 in)
Height	1440mm (56.7 in)
Ground clearance	145mm (5.7 in)
Tires	7.35 H 14 or 185 H 14
Turning circle	12.1-11.9 meters (39 ft)
Steering type and ratio	recirculating ball, 22.7:1 (4.1 turns); servo assisted 17.3:1 (3.2 turns)
Weight	1440 kg (3168 lbs)
Maximum speed	182 km/hr (113 mph); automatic: 177 km/hr (110 mph)
Acceleration	13 sec 0-100 km/hr; automatic: 14 sec 0-100 km/hr
Fuel consumption	16 liters, super/100 km (14.7 mpg); automatic: 17 liters, super (13.7 mpg)
Fuel tank capacity	82 liters (21.7 gallons)

The M 108 engine of the 250S, 1965

The M 129 engine of the 250SE, 1965

The 250SE sedan, 1965

The 250SE coupe, 1965

Prices

The 250SE four-door sedan sold for . . . . .DM	16,850
from April 1966 for. . . . . .DM	17,350
The two-door coupe sold for . . . . .DM	24,350
from April 1966 for. . . . . .DM	24,950
The two-door convertible sold for . . . . .DM	26,350
from April 1966 for. . . . . .DM	26,950
Power steering . . . . .DM	550
Automatic transmission . . . . .DM	1,400
In the United States the sedan sold for in 1965	
(East coast) . . . .$	6,331
(West coast) . . . .$	6,445
in September 1966 (East coast) . . . .$	6,385
in September 1967 (East coast) . . . .$	6,222
The 250SE coupe sold for in 1965 (East coast) . . . .$	8,890
in September 1966 (East coast) . . . .$	9,099
in September 1967 (East coast) . . . .$	9,099
The 250SE convertible sold for in 1965 (East coast) . . .$	9,673
in September 1966 (East coast) . . . .$	9,892
in September 1967 (East coast) . . . .$	9,892
Power steering (1965) . . . .$	171
Automatic transmission . . . .$	342

Model 250SE (1965-1968)

S = Super, E (Einspritzung) = fuel injection

The 250SE model, introduced first at the Frankfurt Auto Show, was the fuel injected version of the 250S model. Both cars appeared identical. They shared the same body and running gear. The suspension system had been improved and the reinforced rear axle was equipped with the new hydro-pneumatic compensating spring. Larger wheels (14") and disc brakes all around were fitted.

The engine had a six-plunger fuel injection pump, with the fuel being injected intermittently into the suction pipe. Power output was rated at 150 horsepower at 5,500 revolutions per minute or 170 horsepower (SAE) at 5,600 revolutions per minute. As in the carburetor engine, maximum engine speed allowed was 6,300 revolutions per minute and the top speed of the 250SE sedan was 193 kilometers (120 miles) per hour.

In addition to the sedan, the elegant coupe and convertible were also available with the fuel-injection engine. The 220SE coupe and convertible — with identical bodies — were still being manufactured, but the more powerful version of the 250SE had, of course, better acceleration and higher maximum and cruising speed.

Production

Production of the 250SE model [108 III] (from August/September 1965 until January 1968)

was in	1965	1,334 units
	1966	26,555 units
	1967	27,242 units
	1968	50 units
	total	55,181 units

Production of the 250SE coupe and convertible model [111 III] (from August/September 1965 until December 1967)

was in	1965	1,205 units
	1966	3,601 units
	1967	1,407 units
	total	6,213 units

Specifications

250SE / 250SE (coupe and convertible)

Engine type	6 cyl overhead camshaft (M 129)
Bore and stroke	82 x 78.8mm (3.23 x 3.1 in)
Displacement	2496 cc (152.3 cu in)
Power output	150 hp (DIN) @ 5500 rpm (170 hp SAE @ 5600 rpm)
Compression ratio	9.3:1
Torque	22 mkg @ 4200 rpm (24 mkg SAE @ 4500 rpm 173.6 ft/lb)
Fuel injection	Bosch six plunger pump
Engine speed at 100 km/hr	3245 rpm
Gear ratios	I. 4.05:1 automatic I. 3.98:1 (15.6)
	II. 2.23:1 II. 2.52:1 (9.88)
	III. 1.42:1 III. 1.58:1 (6.19)
	IV. 1.00:1 IV. 1.00:1 (3.92)
Rear axle ratio	3.92
Chassis	unit frame and body
Suspension	independent front and rear, with coil springs, single joint swing axle
Brakes and area	disc, servo assist, two circuit hydraulic, 273/279mm (10.75/10.99 in)
Wheelbase	2750mm (108.3 in)
Track, front/rear	1482/1485mm (58.3/58.5 in)
Length	4900mm (192.9 in) coupe: 4880mm (192.1 in) conv: 4880mm (192.1 in)
Width	1810mm (71.3 in) coupe: 1845mm (72.6 in) conv: 1845mm (72.6 in)
Height	1440mm (56.7 in) coupe: 1420mm (55.9 in) conv: 1435mm (56.5 in)
Ground clearance	152mm (5.9 in)
Tires	7.35 H 14 or 185 H 14 7.75 H 14 or 195 H 14
Turning circle	12.1-11.9 meters (39 ft)
Steering type and ratio	recirculating ball, 22.7:1 (4.1 turns); servo assisted 17.3:1 (3.2 turns)
Weight	1510 kg (3322 lbs) coupe: 1490 kg (3278 lbs) conv: 1575 kg (3465 lbs)
Maximum speed	193 km/hr (120 mph); automatic: 188 km/hr (117 mph)
Acceleration	12 sec 0-100 km/hr; automatic 13 sec 0-100 km/hr
Fuel consumption	16 liters, super/100 km (14.7 mpg); automatic: 17 liters, super (13.7 mpg)
Fuel tank capacity	82 liters (21.7 gallons)

The instrument panel of the 250SE, 1965

The 300SE sedan, 1965

Prices

The 300SE four-door sedan sold for . . . . .DM 21,500
    from April 1966 for. . . . . .DM 22,100
The 300SEL four-door sedan sold for . . . . .DM 28,000
    from April 1966 for. . . . . .DM 28,600
The 300SE two-door coupe sold for . . . . .DM 31,350
    from April 1966 for. . . . . .DM 31,950
The 300SE two-door convertible sold for. . . . . .DM 33,350
    from April 1966 for. . . . . .DM 35,350
    Automatic transmission . . . . .DM 1,400
In the U.S. the price of the 300SE sedan was in 1965
    (East coast) . . . .$ 7,980
    (West coast) . . . .$ 9,980
    in September 1966 (East coast) . . . .$ 8,283
The price for the 300SEL sedan was in 1965
    (East coast) . . . .$ 9,863
    (West coast) . . . .$ 9,980
    in September 1966 (East coast) . . . .$ 10,144
The price for the 300SE coupe was in 1965
    (East coast) . . . .$ 11,511
    (West coast) . . . .$ 11,657
    in September 1966 (East coast) . . . .$ 11,807
The price for the 300SE convertible was in 1965
    (East coast) . . . .$ 12,295
    (West coast) . . . .$ 12,440
    in September 1966 (East coast) . . . .$ 12,591
    Power steering (1965) . . . .$ 171
    Automatic transmission (but standard equipment on the
      coupe and convertible models sold in the U.S.) . . .$ 342

Model 300SE/SEL (1965-1967)

S = Super, E (Einspritzung) = fuel injection

SE L (Lang) = long wheelbase chassis

The new 300SE, as well as the 300SEL, were also introduced to the public at the Frankfurt Auto Show in 1965. Both had the newly styled body. The longer car had a wheelbase of 2,850 millimeters (112.2 inches) just 100 millimeters (3.9 inches) longer than the regular sedan.

The six-cylinder light alloy fuel injection engine was equipped with the six-plunger pump which adjusted automatically to accelerator pedal pressure, engine speed, atmospheric pressure, and cooling water temperature, thus giving the best possible mixture for all driving conditions. Maximum power output was 170 horsepower at 5,400 revolutions per minute, or 190 horsepower (SAE) at 5,500 revolutions. With the regular 3.92 rear axle ratio and automatic transmission the car was capable of a maximum speed of 185 kilometers (115 miles) per hour. The faster ratio of 3.69 to 1 gave it 200 kilometer (124 miles) top speed (with manual transmission).

The elegant coupe and convertible models were also fitted with the 300SE engine and power train. These models had, however, the air suspension system, as did the 300SEL now.

Production

Production of the 300SE sedan [108 IV] (from August 1965 until December 1967)

was in 1965	214 units	
1966	1,989 units	
1967	534 units	
total	2,737 units	

Production of the 300SEL sedan [109 III] (from September 1965/ March 1966 until December 1967)

was in 1965	1 unit	
1966	1,404 units	
1967	964 units	
total	2,369 units	

Specifications

300SE / 300SEL / 300SE (coupe and convertible)

Engine type	6 cyl overhead camshaft (M 189)		
Bore and stroke	85 x 88mm (3.34 x 3.47 in)		
Displacement	2996 cc (182.8 cu in)		
Power output	170 hp (DIN) @ 5400 rpm (195 hp SAE @ 5500 rpm)		
Compression ratio	8.8:1		
Torque	25.4 mkg @ 4000 rpm (28.1 mkg @ 4100 rpm 203.3 ft/lb)		
Fuel injection	Bosch six plunger pump		
Engine speed at 100 km/hr	3245 rpm		

The 300SE convertible, 1966

Gear ratios	I. 4.05:1	automatic I. 3.98:1 (16.3)
	II. 2.23:1	II. 2.52:1 (10.3)
	III. 1.42:1	III. 1.58:1 (6.47)
	IV. 1.00:1	IV. 1.00:1 (4.10)

Rear axle ratio	3.92 or 3.69		
Chassis	unit frame and body		
Suspension	independent front and rear, with coil springs, single joint swing axle		
Brakes and area	disc, servo assist, two circuit hydraulic, 273/279mm (10.75/10.99 in)		
Wheelbase	2750mm (108.3 in)	SEL: 2850mm (112.2 in)	
Track, front/rear	1482/1485mm (58.3/58.6 in)	SEL: rear 1490mm (58.7 in)	
Length	4900mm (192.9 in)	SEL: 5000mm (196.9 in)	coupe & conv: 4880mm (192in)
Width	1810mm (71.3 in)		coupe & conv: 1845mm (72.6 in)
Height	1440mm (56.7 in)	SEL: 1415mm (55.7 in)	coupe: 1395mm (54.9 in)
			conv: 1400mm (55.1 in)
Ground clearance	152mm (5.9 in)		
Tires	7.35 H 14 or 185 H 14		conv: 7.75 H 14 or 195 H 14
Turning circle	12.1-11.9 meters (39 ft)	SEL: 12.4-12.2 meters (40 ft)	coupe & conv: 12.1-11.9 meters (39 ft)
Steering type and ratio	recirculating ball, 17.3:1 (3.2 turns) servo assisted		
Weight	1575 kg (3465 lbs)	SEL: 1655 kg (3641 lbs)	coupe: 1650 kg (3630 lbs)
			conv: 1715 kg (3773 lbs)
Maximum speed	manual, 3.92 axle 190 km/hr (118 mph)		
	automatic, 3.92 axle 185 km/hr (115 mph)		
	manual, 3.69 axle 200 km/hr (124 mph)		
	automatic, 369 axle 195 km/hr (121 mph)		
Acceleration	12 sec 0-100 km/hr		
Fuel consumption	17-19 liters, super/100 km (13.7 to 12.3 mpg)		
Fuel tank capacity	82 liters (21.7 gallons)		

The 300SEL 6.3 sedan, 1968

Model 300SEL 6.3 (1968-1972)

SE L (Lang) = long wheelbase chassis

The 300SEL 6.3 model was introduced in the United States in June 1968, quite appropriately at the Laguna Seca race course, with Rudolf Uhlenhaut in attendance. He pointed out that the car had better road-holding ability, braking potential, suspension stability, and maneuverability than any comparable automobile in the world. It had first been shown in Europe in March 1968.

With the 6,332 cubic centimeter fuel-injected 300-horsepower (SAE) V-8 engine installed in the slightly modified but outwardly regular sedan body of the New Generation type, the car weighed 3,835 pounds and had a power-to-weight ratio of 12.8 pounds per horsepower. Performance was truly fantastic, especially when Uhlenhaut demonstrated to us the car's abilities. Zero to 60 miles acceleration took 6.5 seconds and the maximum speed of the 6.3 was 137 miles (220 kilometers) per hour.

The sedan had the air suspension system of the 600 series and many extra features were included as standard items, such as air conditioning, radio, leather upholstery, power steering, and power windows. Except for the numbers 6.3 on the trunk lid, the car was not distinguishable from the regular 300SEL model.

After exhaustively testing the car, *Road & Track* magazine called it "the greatest sedan in the world" and summarized the test, stating that the 6.3 was "truly the executive road racer . . . does more different things well than any other single car." This author concurred. The 300SEL 6.3 was certainly an outstanding automobile in every way.

Prices and Production

The 300SEL 6.3 four-door sedan sold in 1968 for	. . . . .DM	39,160
in 1969	. . . . .DM	39,500
in 1970	. . . . .DM	43,180
in 1971	. . . . .DM	45,400
The 300SEL 6.3 sedan sold in the U.S. (when introduced) for	. . . .$	13,998
The price was in September 1968 (East coast)	. . . .$	14,065
in October 1969 (East coast)	. . . .$	14,530
in October 1970 (East coast)	. . . .$	15,875
in March 1971 (East coast)	. . . .$	16,275

Production of the 300SEL 6.3 sedan [109 E63] (from December 1967 until September 1972)

was in	1967	1 unit
	1968	1,094 units
	1969	2,578 units
	1970	1,797 units
	1971	670 units
	1972	386 units
total		6,526 units

Sales of the 300SEL 6.3 sedan in this country were

in 1968	98 cars
1969	601 cars
1970	642 cars
1971	487 cars
1972	9 cars
1973	2 cars
	1,839 cars

Specifications

300SEL 6.3

Engine type	V-8 cyl overhead camshaft for each cylinder bank (M 100)
Bore and stroke	103 x 95mm (4.06 x 3.74 in)
Displacement	6332 cc (386.3 cu in)
Power output	250 hp (DIN) @ 4000 rpm (300 hp SAE @ 4100 rpm)
Compression ratio	9.0:1
Torque	51 mkg @ 2800 rpm 369 ft/lb (60 mkg SAE @ 3000 rpm 434 ft/lb)
Fuel injection	Bosch eight plunger pump
Engine speed at 100 km/hr	2510 rpm
Gear ratios	I. 3.98:1 (11.34)
	II. 2.46:1 (7.00)
	III. 1.58:1 (4.50)
	IV. 1.00:1 (2.85)
Rear axle ratio	2.85
Chassis	unit frame and body
Suspension	independent front and rear, air springs, self leveling and air suspension, single joint swing axle
Brakes and area	disc, ventilated, servo assist, two circuit hydraulic, 273/279mm (107.5/109.9 in)
Wheelbase	2865 mm (112.8 in)
Track, front/rear	1482/1490mm (58.3/58.7 in)
Length	5000mm (196.9 in)
Width	1810mm (71.3 in)
Height	1410mm (55.5 in)
Ground clearance	160mm (6.3 in)
Tires	FR 70 VR 14 (Dunlop) or 7.75/195 H14 (Conti)
Turning circle	12.2 meters (40.4 ft)
Steering type and ratio	recirculating ball, 15.7:1 (3.0 turns)
Weight	1740 kg (3828 lbs)
Maximum speed	220 km/hr (137 mph)
Acceleration	6.5 sec 0-100 km/hr
Fuel consumption	15.5 liters, super/100 km (15.2 mpg)
Fuel tank capacity	105 liters (27.7 gallons)

	300 SEL-6.3 No. 1	300 SEL-6.3 No. 2
ENGINE CAPACITY	6.3	6.3
FINAL DRIVE RATIO	2.85	2.85
CURB WEIGHT LBS	4070	4070
TIME FOR 1/4 MILE SEC	14.4	14.25
TERMINAL SPEED AFTER 1/4 MILE MPH	93.8	97
TIME 0-60 MILES SEC	5.8	5.7
TIME 0-100 MILES SEC	15.9	15.0
TOP SPEED MPH	141 OBSERVED	144 OBSERVED
ENGINE SPEED AT TOP CAR SPEED RPM	5410	5530

Performance chart of the 300SEL 6.3, 1968

The M 100 V-8 engine of the 6.3, 1968

The 200 sedan, 1967

Prices and Production

The 200 four-door sedan sold in 1968 for . . . . .DM 11,500
    in 1970 for. . . . . .DM 12,745
    in 1972 for. . . . . .DM 13,390
    in 1974 for. . . . . .DM 15,140
    in 1975 for. . . . . .DM 16,710
    Power steering . . . . .DM 515
    Automatic transmission . . . . .DM 1,440

Production of the 200 model [115 V20] (from October 1967/
January 1968 until December 1976)

was in	1967	67 units
	1968	20,954 units
	1969	26,138 units
	1970	29,733 units
	1971	35,122 units
	1972	40,562 units
	1973	37,337 units
	1974	37,640 units
	1975	48,214 units
	1976	13,018 units
	total	288,785 units

Model 200 (1967-1976)

The new 200 sedan was the least expensive car of the fifteen models of the New Generation class, introduced to the public in January 1968. All of the four- and smaller six-cylinder models shared the same body and basic construction. At the Frankfurt Auto Show in 1967 the main emphasis was placed on safety rather than on speed. Such safety features as collapsible steering column, padded instrument panel with softer knobs and soft ignition key, breakaway rear mirror, and seatback locks activated by the doors were standard equipment. The body was designed for maximum crash resistance and the front and rear ends for easier crushing in collisions to protect the passengers in the vehicle. A new rear axle was designed for improved roadability. Fourteen-inch wheels were again used on these new models and they had a slightly longer (50 mm = 2 inch) wheelbase and a narrower track. The entire instrument panel was also redesigned for improved legibility.

These new body styles of the Lower Range of models were quite similar to those of the Intermediate Line of cars earlier, as the 250S of 1965. In fact, there was practically only the arrangement of the headlights to quickly differentiate these cars from each other. Despite the smaller overall size, the interior space was nearly the same as previously.

The engine for the 200 model was of the proven type and only minor improvements were made in it. The 1,988 cubic centimeter four-cylinder powerplant developed 95 DIN horsepower and 122.2 ft/lbs. torque, as it had in the former model. All performance figures were identical.

In 1972 all of the smaller models were equipped with the new, safer four-spoke steering wheel. In 1973, because of the fuel crisis, the compression of the engine was lowered to 8 to 1, so that normal octane gasoline could be used. That engine developed 85 DIN horsepower instead of the former 95.

Specifications

	200
Engine type	4 cyl overhead camshaft (M 115)
Bore and stroke	87 x 83.6mm (3.43 x 3.29 in)
Displacement	1988 cc (121.27 cu in)
Power output	95 hp (DIN) @ 5200 rpm (105 hp SAE @ 5400 rpm)
Compression ratio	9.0:1
Torque	15.7 mkg @ 3600 rpm (16.9 mkg @ 3800 rpm 122.2 ft/lb)
Carburetion	2 downdraft carburetors Solex 38 PCSJ
Engine speed at 100 km/hr	3310 rpm

The 200 sedan, 1973

Gear ratios			automatic	
	I. 4.09:1	3.90:1	I. 3.98:1	
	II. 2.25:1	2.30:1	II. 2.52:1	
	III. 1.42:1	1.41:1	III. 1.58:1	
	IV. 1.00:1	1.00:1	IV. 1.00:1	

Rear axle ratio	3.92 (4.08 for U.S.)
Chassis	unit frame and body
Suspension	independent front and rear, with coil springs, diagonal-pivot swing axle, anti-sway bars
Brakes and area	disc, power assisted standard, 273/279mm (10.75/10.99 in)
Wheelbase	2750mm (108.3 in)
Track, front/rear	1440/1434mm (56.7/56.5 in)
Length	4680mm (184.3 in)
Width	1770mm (69.7 in)
Height	1440mm (56.7 in)
Ground clearance	175mm (6.9 in)
Tires	6.95 x 14 or 175 x 14
Turning circle	11.7 meters (38.4 ft)
Steering type and ratio	recirculating ball (4.6 turns); servo assisted (4.0 turns)
Weight	1275 kg (2805 lbs)
Maximum speed	161 km/hr (100 mph); automatic: 158 km/hr (98 mph)
Acceleration	15 sec 0-100 km/hr; automatic: 16 sec 0-100 km/hr
Fuel consumption	12.5 liters, super/100 km (18.75 mpg); automatic: 13.5 liters, super (17.4 mpg)
Fuel tank capacity	65 liters (17.2 gallons)

Front view of the 200 sedan, 1968, U.S. version

The 200D sedan, 1974

Prices and Production

The 200D four-door sedan sold in 1968 for . . . . .DM 12,000
  in 1970 for. . . . . .DM 13,265
  in 1972 for. . . . . .DM 14,430
  in 1974 for. . . . . .DM 15,585
  in 1975 for. . . . . .DM 17,185
  Power steering . . . . .DM   515
  Automatic transmission .DM 1,440

Production of the 200D model [115 D20] (from October 1967/ January 1968 until December 1976)

was in	1967	106 units
	1968	23,293 units
	1969	27,663 units
	1970	32,841 units
	1971	35,000 units
	1972	41,065 units
	1973	45,287 units
	1974	50,613 units
	1975	62,978 units
	1976	21,081 units
	total	339,927 units

Model 200D (1967-1976)

D = Diesel

The 200D model was, as previously, the same as the gasoline-engined sedan of that size. One of the fifteen New Generation models, it shared the body style along with all of the new safety features and construction changes made for the 1968 model year. The body was nearly the same as that of the 250S line of 1966, which had a lower silhouette, lower center of gravity, and wider radiator design in the traditional manner, of course.

The engine of the 200D was the same as that of the earlier model. Displacing 1,988 cubic centimeters and developing 55 DIN (60 SAE) horsepower and 87 ft/lb. torque, it gave this economical diesel-engined model a most satisfactory performance. Power steering and power brakes were optional items, as was automatic transmission.

As before, the diesel version of the smaller model marketed by Daimler-Benz was again a best-seller and more of these 200D sedans were sold than those of the gasoline-powered version. The diesel cars offered actually the same comforts as the others and had in addition the tremendous cost advantages inherent only not in the simpler maintenance of the diesel engine, but also the economy of fuel, both in lower initial cost and in increased mileage achieved.

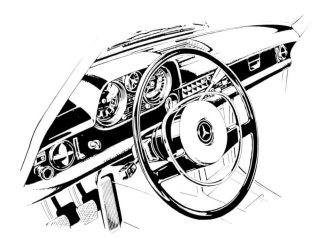

The instrument panel of the 200D, 1973

Specifications

	200D
Engine type	4 cyl diesel, overhead camshaft (OM 615)
Bore and stroke	87 x 83.6mm (3.43 x 3.29 in)
Displacement	1988 cc (121.27 cu in)
Power output	55 hp (DIN) @ 4200 rpm (61 hp SAE @ 4200 rpm)
Compression ratio	21:1
Torque	11.5 mkg @ 2400 rpm (83.2 ft/lb)
Fuel injection	Bosch four plunger pump
Engine speed at 100 km/hr	3375 rpm
Gear ratios	I. 3.90:1 II. 2.30:1 III. 1.41:1 IV. 1.00:1
Rear axle ratio	3.92 (for U.S. 4.08)
Chassis	unit frame and body
Suspension	independent front and rear, with coil springs, diagonal-pivot swing axle, anti-sway bars
Brakes and area	disc, power assisted standard, 273/279mm (10.75/10.99 in)
Wheelbase	2750mm (108.3 in)
Track, front/rear	1440/1434mm (56.7/56.5 in)
Length	4680mm (184.3 in)
Width	1770mm (69.7 in)
Height	1440mm (56.7 in)
Ground clearance	175mm (6.9 in)
Tires	6.95 x 14 or 175 x 14
Turning circle	11.7 meters (38.4 ft)
Steering type and ratio	recirculating ball, (4.6 turns), servo assisted (4.0 turns)
Weight	1350 kg (2970 lbs)
Maximum speed	130 km/hr (81 mph)
Acceleration	30 sec 0-100 km/hr
Fuel consumption	8.1 liters/100 km (29 mpg)
Fuel tank capacity	65 liters (17.2 gallons)

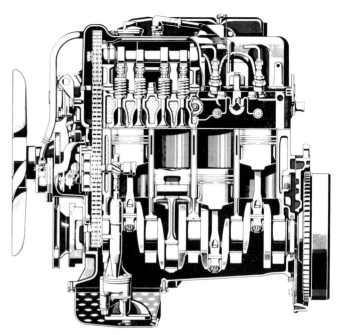

Longitudinal section of the OM 615 engine, 1967

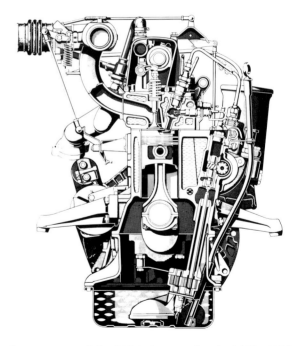

Cross section of the OM 615 engine for the 200D, 1967

The 220 sedan, 1968

Prices and Production

The 220 four-door sedan sold in 1968 for ....DM	12,000
in 1970 for...........................DM	13,165
in 1972 for...........................DM	14,375
in 1973 for...........................DM	14,985
Power steering ....DM	515
Automatic transmission ....DM	1,440
The 220 sedan sold in the United States in January 1968 for	
(East coast) ....$	4,360
(West coast) ....$	4,446
in September 1971, including automatic transmission	
(East coast) ....$	6,206
in September 1972, including automatic transmission	
(East coast) ....$	6,560
in March 1973, including automatic transmission	
(East coast) ....$	6,889
Power steering (1970) ....$	198
Power steering (1973) ....$	251
Automatic transmission (1970) ....$	392

Production of the 220 model [115 V22] (from October 1967/
February 1968 until August 1973)

was in	1967	131 units
	1968	23,486 units
	1969	22,493 units
	1970	22,652 units
	1971	24,140 units
	1972	23,691 units
	1973	12,146 units
	total	128,739 units

Model 220 (1967-1973)

The 220 model was basically the same car as the smaller-engined one. It was the third of the New Generation models to share the same body style, including all of the new safety features. It was meant to replace the 200 sedan in the United States market.

Over the previous model, this new style featured the lower silhouette, an increased wheelbase and narrower track, offered increased visibility, a new headlight treatment with the lower half of the unit having amber color, and protective strips with rubber inserts all around the body. The single front and rear bumpers also had a rubber insert for added scratch protection. New larger rear light clusters had been designed for brighter, improved visibility.

The engine had two single throat Solex carburetors and developed 116 SAE horsepower at 5,200 revolutions per minute and torque of 142 ft/lbs. at 3,000 revolutions. Maximum speed was 100 miles per hour.

Optional equipment was the power assisted steering, air conditioning, sliding sun roof, leather upholstery, power windows, and other features. The base price of the 220 sedan was $4,360 on the East coast in 1968.

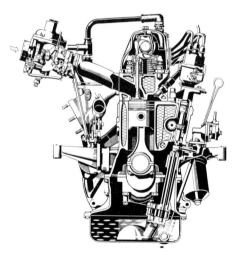

Cross section of M115 engine, 1968

Specifications

	220
Engine type	4 cyl overhead camshaft (M 115)
Bore and stroke	87.0 x 92.4mm (3.43 x 3.64 in)
Displacement	2197 cc (134 cu in)
Power output	105 hp (DIN) (116 hp SAE) @ 5200 rpm
Compression ratio	9:1
Torque	17.5 mkg @ 3600 rpm (19.7 mkg @ 3000 rpm 142.5 ft/lb)
Carburetion	2 dual downdraft carburetors Solex 36/40 PDSI (U.S.: 2 Stromberg carburetors 175 CDT)
Engine speed at 100 km/hr	3300 rpm
Gear ratios	I. 3.90:1 II. 2.30:1 III. 1.41:1 IV. 1.00:1
Rear axle ratio	3.92 (4.08 for U.S.)
Chassis	unit frame and body
Suspension	independent front and rear, with coil springs, diagonal pivot swing axle, anti-sway bars
Brakes and area	disc, power assist standard, 273/279mm (10.75/10.99 in)
Wheelbase	2750mm (108.3 in)
Track, front/rear	1440/1434mm (56.7/56.5 in)
Length	4680mm (184.3 in)
Width	1770mm (69.7 in)
Height	1440mm (56.7 in)
Ground clearance	175mm (6.9 in)
Tires	6.95 x 14 or 175 x 14
Turning circle	11.7 meters (38.4 ft)
Steering type and ratio	recirculating ball (4.6 turns); servo assisted (4.0 turns)
Weight	1314 kg (2890 lbs)
Maximum speed	161 km/hr (100 mph)
Acceleration	14 sec 0-100 km/hr
Fuel consumption	12 liters, super/100 km (19.5 mpg)
Fuel tank capacity	65 liters (17.2 gallons)

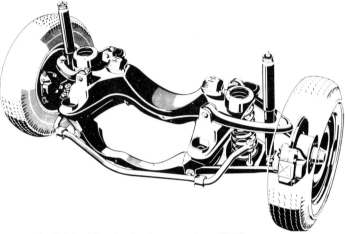

Individual front wheel suspension, 1967

Diagonal swing axle, 1967

The 220D sedan, 1968, U.S. version

Prices and Production

The 220D four-door sedan sold in 1968 for . . . . .DM 12,500
    in 1970 for. . . . . .DM 13,690
    in 1972 for. . . . . .DM 14,930
    in 1973 for. . . . . .DM 15,485
Power steering . . . . .DM   515
Automatic transmission . . . . .DM 1,440
The 220D long limousine sold in 1969 for . . . . .DM 18,315
    the price rose yearly until 1975 it was. . . . . .DM 26,075
The 220D sedan sold in the U.S. in January 1968 for
    (East coast) . . . .$ 4,494
    (West coast) . . . .$ 4,580
    in September 1971 (East coast) . . . .$ 5,900
    in September 1972 (East coast) . . . .$ 6,345
    in March 1973 (East coast) . . . .$ 6,662
        with automatic transmission . . . .$ 7,100
Power steering (1970) . . . .$ 198
Power steering (1973) . . . .$ 251
Automatic transmission (1970) . . . .$ 392

Production of the 220D model [115 D22] (from July 1967/
January 1968 until December 1976)

was in 1967	364	units
1968	50,630	units
1969	59,628	units
1970	63,314	units
1971	64,297	units
1972	73,729	units
1973	54,321	units
1974	27,510	units
1975	21,226	units
1976	5,254	units
total	420,273	units

Model 220D (1967-1976)

D = Diesel

The 220D was the fourth of the New Generation cars to share the same body style with the 200-220-200D models. It, too, was introduced to replace the smaller sedan in the United States market.

All of the outward specifications were identical with the gasoline version of this model. It was the luxury edition of the economical and reliable diesel-powerd automobile which actually went back to 1936 when a diesel passenger car was first built by Mercedes-Benz.

The four-speed manual transmission was standard, either column or floor mounted. Automatic transmission was an optional extra, as were power brakes and power steering.

The 2.2-liter diesel engine had Bosch four-plunger fuel injection and a five main bearing crankshaft. With the usual 21:1 compression ratio and maximum torque of 96 ft/lbs. at 2,400 revolutions per minute, the engine developed 65 SAE horsepower at 4,200 revolutions per minute and gave the car a maximum and cruising speed of over 80 miles per hour. (This diesel engine met the U.S. government standards for emission of hydrocarbons, carbon monoxide, and oxide of nitrogens through 1974, and the CO limit for 1975.)

Symbolic of the popularity of the diesel automobile, on May 9, 1968, the two millionth passenger car to come off the assembly lines at the Sindelfingen plant since 1946 was a 220D model — cream-colored and flower-covered.

A long wheelbase model sedan became available in December 1968. It had seats for eight persons and was similar to the 230 long limousine. The wheelbase was 3,400 mm (133.86 in) weight was 1,540 kg (3,388 lbs). Maximum speed was 130 km/hr (81 mph) and fuel consumption 11 liters per 100 km. With the optional automatic transmission, these figures were 125 km/hr and 12 liters/100 km (18 miles per gallon).

Specifications

	220D
Engine type	4 cyl diesel, overhead camshaft (OM 615)
Bore and stroke	87.0 x 92.4mm (3.43 x 3.64 in)
Displacement	2197 cc (134 cu in)
Power output	60 hp (DIN) (65 hp SAE) @ 4200 rpm
Compression ratio	21:1
Torque	12.8 mkg @ 2400 rpm (92.6 ft/lb)
Fuel injection	Bosch four plunger pump
Engine speed at 100 km/hr	3375 rpm
Gear ratios	I. 3.90:1 (15.37) II. 2.30:1 (9.01) III. 1.41:1 (5.52) IV. 1.00:1 (3.92)
Rear axle ratio	3.92 (for U.S. 4.08)
Chassis	unit frame and body
Suspension	independent front and rear, with coil springs, diagonal-pivot swing axle, anti-sway bars
Brakes and area	disc, power assist standard, 273/279mm (10.75/10.99 in)
Wheelbase	2750mm (108.3 in)
Track, front/rear	1440/1434mm (56.7/56.5 in)
Length	4680mm (184.3 in)
Width	1770mm (69.7 in)
Height	1440mm (56.7 in)
Ground clearance	175mm (6.9 in)
Tires	6.95 x 14 or 175 x 14
Turning circle	11.7 meters (38.4 ft)
Steering type and ratio	recirculating ball, (4.6 turns); servo assisted 22.7:1 (4.0 turns)
Weight	1363 kg (2997 lbs)
Maximum speed	135 km/hr (84 mph)
Acceleration	28.1 sec 0-100 km/hr
Fuel consumption	8.5 liters/100 km (27.75 mpg)
Fuel tank capacity	65 liters (17.2 gallons)

Front view of the 220D sedan, 1975

The OM 615 engine of the 220D, 1973

The 230 sedan, 1967

Model 230/6 (1973-1976)

The 230/6 model made its appearance in late 1973 when the fuel crisis became a matter of serious concern to motorists and manufacturers in Europe. Utilizing the same body style as that of the other ten cars in the medium price range, the small six-cylinder engine was placed into it to create a lower priced as well as lower fuel consumption car than the regular 2.8-liter models.

A five-speed transmission was available on request in this model as on the 250, 280, and the three coupe styles. A fifth gear was designed as a high speed gear or overdrive. It lowered the engine speed and reduced fuel consumption, engine noise, and wear. The automatic torque converter four-speed transmission, as used on the 2.8-liter models, could also be fitted.

The 230/6 model was superior in performance to the four-cylinder model which it closely resembled. The car offered the flexibility of a six-cylinder engine and even greater fuel economy than the four-cylinder model at a considerably lower price than the regular sixes.

Production figures included in the previously described 230 sedan [114 V23] until November 1976

Model 230 (1967-1976)

The 230 model, in the center of the medium price range of the New Generation cars, had the same body style as that of the 200, 220, and the 250 sedans. It replaced the former 230 model, first built in 1965.

The interior dimensions were the same as those of the other models which shared the body style, the rear center arm rest, larger door pockets, increased visibility (11 percent more glass area), arm rests on all doors, and roof-mounted assist handles, but it had the grip handles attached to the arm rest of the right front door, while the 250 model had them on all three doors (except the driver's).

The engine of the 230 model was the same as before, except for redesigned cams which improved the torque at lower engine speeds and molybdenum coated piston rings (1, 2 and 3) for longer wear and reduced oil consumption. The new gear box and newly designed clutch, now with new diaphragm spring clutch having fewer moving parts (that is, one diaphram spring instead of nine pressure springs), were fitted to all of the models which had the same chassis and body as the 230 sedan. The new hydro-pneumatic leveling device, automatic transmission, and power steering were optional items.

A long-wheelbase sedan to seat eight passengers became available in October 1968. It was also made with the 220D engine two months later. The wheelbase was 3,400 mm (133.86 in) and the total weight was 1,515 kg (3,344 lbs). The maximum speed was 170 km/hr (106 mph) and fuel consumption 16 liters per 100 kilometers. With automatic transmission these figures were 165 km/hr and 17 liters/100 km.

Prices

The 230/6 four-door sedan sold in 1973 for . . . . .DM 16,765
    in 1974 for. . . . . .DM 17,485
    in 1975 for . . . . .DM 19,270
The 230/6 long four-door sedan sold in 1973 for. . . . . .DM 23,145
    in 1974 for. . . . . .DM 24,200
    in 1975 for. . . . . .DM 26,685
    Power steering . . . . .DM   515
    Automatic transmission . . . . .DM 1,440

Specifications

	230	230/6
Engine type	6 cyl overhead camshaft (M 180)	
Bore and stroke	81.7 x 72.8mm (3.23 x 2.87 in)	
Displacement	2292 cc (139.9 cu in)	
Power output	120 hp (DIN) @ 5400 rpm (135 hp SAE @ 5600 rpm)	
Compression ratio	9:1	
Torque	18.2 mkg @ 3600 rpm; 20 mkg @ 3800 rpm (144.7 ft/lb)	
Carburetion	2 dual downdraft carburetors Zenith 35/40 INAT	
Engine speed at 100 km/hr	3180 rpm	
Gear ratios	I. 3.90:1	
	II. 2.30:1	
	III. 1.41:1	
	IV. 1.00:1	
Rear axle ratio	3.92 (4.08 for U.S.)	
Chassis	unit frame and body	
Suspension	independent front and rear, with coil springs, diagonal-pivot swing axle, anti-sway bars	
Brakes and area	disc, power assist standard, 273/279mm (10.95/10.99 in)	
Wheelbase	2750mm (108.3 in)	2750mm (108.3 in)
Track, front/rear	1444/1440mm (56.9/56.7 in)	1448/1440mm (57.0/56.7 in)
Length	4680mm (184.3 in)	4680mm (184.3 in)
Width	1770mm (69.7 in)	1770mm (69.7 in)
Height	1440mm (56.7 in)	1440mm (56.7 in)
Ground clearance	175mm (6.9 in)	175mm (6.9 in)
Tires	6.95 x 14 or 175 x 14	175 SR 14
Turning circle	11.7 meters (38.4 ft)	11 meters (36.1 ft)
Steering type and ratio	recirculating ball (4.6 turns); servo assisted (4.0 turns)	recirculating ball (3.0 turns), servo assisted
Weight	1323 kg (2911 lbs)	1365 kg (3003 lbs)
Maximum speed	165 km/hr (102 mph)	175 km/hr (109 mph)
Acceleration	14 sec 0-100 km/hr	13.5 sec 0-100 km/hr
Fuel consumption	11.2 liters, super/100 km (21 mpg)	11.2 liters/100 km (21.5 mpg)
Fuel tank capacity	65 liters (17.2 gallons)	65 liters (17.2 gallons)

Prices and Production

The 230 four-door sedan sold in 1968 for . . . . .DM 13,150
   in 1970 for. . . . . .DM 14,620
   in 1972 for. . . . . .DM 16,100
   in 1973 for. . . . . .DM 16,765
   Power steering . . . . .DM 515
   Automatic transmission . . . . .DM 1,440
The 230 long limousine sold in 1968 for . . . . .DM 18,980
   the price rose gradually every year and in 1975 was . .DM 26,685
The 230 four-door sedan sold in the United States
   in January 1968 for (East coast). . . . .$ 4,544
      (West coast) . . . .$ 4,631
   in December 1968 (East coast). . . . .$ 4,764
   Power steering (1970) . . . .$ 198
   Automatic transmission . . . .$ 392

Production of the 230 model [114 V23] (from September 1967/ January 1968 until November 1976)

was in		
1967	252 units
1968	22,064 units
1969	23,835 units
1970	25,252 units
1971	30,520 units
1972	35,270 units
1973	31,378 units
1974	25,314 units
1975	22,992 units
1976	4,906 units
total	221,783 units

The 250 sedan, 1967

Prices and Production

The 250 four-door sedan sold in 1967 for . . . . .DM 14,630
    in 1970 for. . . . . .DM 16,185
    in 1972 for. . . . . .DM 17,875
    Power steering . . . . .DM   515
    Automatic transmission . . . . .DM 1,440
The 250 four-door sedan sold in the United States
    in January 1968 for (East coast). . . . .$ 5,060
        (West coast) . . . .$ 5,150
    in October 1969 (East coast) . . . .$ 5,208
    in October 1970 (including automatic transmission)
        (East coast) . . . .$ 6,208
    in September 1971 (including automatic transmission)
        (East coast) . . . .$ 7,205
    Power steering (1970) . . . .$ 198

Production of the 250 model [114 V25] (from July/December 1967 until May 1972)

	was in 1967	2,215 units
	1968	20,475 units
	1969	18,692 units
	1970	17,329 units
	1971	15,180 units
	1972	4,412 units
	total	78,303 units

Model 250 (1967-1972)

The 250 model represented the top of the medium price range in the passenger car production line of the New Generation cars. It was distinguished by several styling refinements over the others which shared the body with this model. As the 230 model, it was fitted with a wider-spaced grill design — the box type instead of the pierced type which the 200 and 220 models had. The 250 also had a double bumper on the front and a chrome door strip.

As the best of the Medium Range, the interior was fancier than the poorer relations, the 200 and 230 models. The left side stalk on the steering column activated the headlight dimming, the windshield wipers, and the directional signals. The center console had the shift lever for the new four-speed automatic transmission, a much improved unit over the earlier one. It started always in first gear, giving an easy gliding-like move when starting off. In fact, the entire operation was considerably smoother than before and seemed a definite technological advancement.

The six-cylinder engine for the 250 was newly developed. It produced 146 SAE horsepower at 5,600 revolutions per minute. Suspension was the same as the other, less expensive models, which shared the same body style. The optional hydro-pneumatic leveler controlled the rear suspension unit, leveling the car when loaded. It had the advantage of constant leveling because the system was operative when the engine was running and maintained a constant bumper height.

The conclusion reached by the testing editors of a prestigious automotive magazine was that the car was Substantial, Safe, Spacious, and 'Spensive.

Specifications

	250
Engine type	6 cyl overhead camshaft (M 114)
Bore and stroke	81.7 x 78.8mm (3.23 x 3.1 in)
Displacement	2496 cc (152.4 cu in)
Power output	130 hp (DIN) @ 5000 rpm (146 hp SAE @ 5600 rpm)
Compression ratio	9:1
Torque	20 mkg @ 3600 rpm (22.2 mkg @ 3800 rpm 161 ft/lb)
Carburetion	2 dual downdraft carburetors Zenith 35/40 INAT
Engine speed at 100 km/hr	3180 rpm
Gear ratios	I. 3.90:1 II. 2.30:1 III. 1.41:1 IV. 1.00:1
Rear axle ratio	3.92 (4.08 for U.S.)
Chassis	unit frame and body
Suspension	independent front and rear, with coil springs, diagonal-pivot swing axle, anti-sway bars
Brakes and area	disc, power assist standard, 273/279mm (10.8/11.0 in)
Wheelbase	2750mm (108.3 in)
Track, front/rear	1444/1440mm (56.9/56.7 in)
Length	4680mm (184.3 in)
Width	1770mm (69.7 in)
Height	1440mm (56.7 in)
Ground clearance	175mm (6.9 in)
Tires	6.95 H 14 or 175 x 14
Turning circle	11.7 meters (38.4 ft)
Steering type and ratio	recirculating ball (4.6 turns); servo assisted (4.0 turns)
Weight	1370 kg (3014 lbs)
Maximum speed	180 km/hr (112 mph)
Acceleration	13 sec 0-100 km/hr
Fuel consumption	12.5 liters, super/100 km (18.75 mpg)
Fuel tank capacity	65 liters (17.2 gallons)

The 250 sedan, 1968, U.S. version

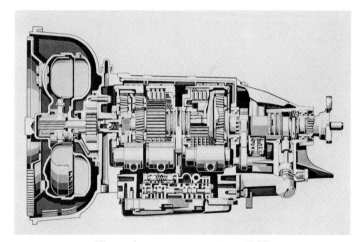

The automatic transmission, 1967

The 280S sedan, 1968

Prices and Production

The 280S four-door sedan sold in 1968 for . . . . .DM 17,000
        in 1970 for . . . . .DM 18,815
        in 1971 for . . . . .DM 19,760
        Power steering . . . . .DM   515
        Automatic transmission . . . . .DM 1,440
The 280S four-door sedan sold in the United States
        in January 1968 for (East coast). . . . .$ 5,897
        (West coast) . . . .$ 6,011
        in October 1969 (East coast) . . . .$ 6,273
        in October 1970 (including automatic transmission)
        (East coast) . . . .$ 7,019
        in March 1971 (including automatic transmission)
        (East coast) . . . .$ 7,370
        Power steering (1970) . . . .$ 198

Production of the 280S model [108 V28] (from November 1967/
January 1968 until September 1972)

was in	1967	762 units
	1968	20,110 units
	1969	25,249 units
	1970	24,882 units
	1971	16,234 units
	1972	6,429 units
	total	93,666 units

Model 280S (1967-1972)

S = Super

The 280S model was the lowest priced car in the higher priced range of the New Generation automobiles. The body style was that of the new 280SE and the 300SE models, as well as that of the older 250S first introduced in 1965, which remained in production.

The body was longer than that of the smaller-engined 250 model cars, but the wheelbase remained at 108.3 inches. Track was slightly larger and these sedans were somewhat wider, allowing more inside room for the passengers. A distinctive difference was the arrangement of the headlights. Two vertical lights made up the cluster which in the other models consisted of one headlight and amber indicator and parking lights.

The interior was more luxuriously appointed in these types than in the less expensive models. There was a definite feel of staid elegance in the dashboard layout, greater comfort in seats, and all-around conception in this model.

The engine had the dual downdraft carburetor, air oil cooler, and a new cylinder arrangement for increased cooling, and developed 140 (DIN) horsepower at 5,200 (or 157 SAE at 5,400) revolutions per minute. The seven-bearing crankshaft made for quieter and more flexible operation of this newly designed powerplant.

With this more flexible and more powerful unit, the new M130 engine, the 1,460-kilogram sedan reached a respectable maximum speed of 115 miles per hour.

The 280S was a comfortable, fast touring car in the best Mercedes tradition and it found many willing purchasers, as sales indicated. The more expensive model, the SE with identical fuel consumption but slightly superior performance, sold nearly as well over the years. This would suggest that the fuel-injection car was becoming ever more popular over the carburetor version.

Specifications

	280S
Engine type	6 cyl overhead camshaft (M 130)
Bore and stroke	86.5 x 78.8mm (3.41 x 3.10 in)
Displacement	2778 cc (169.5 cu in)
Power output	140 hp (DIN) @ 5200 rpm (157 hp SAE @ 5400 rpm)
Compression ratio	9:1
Torque	23 mkg @ 3600 rpm (25.1 mkg @ 3800 rpm 181.6 ft/lb)
Carburetion	2 dual downdraft carburetors Zenith 35/40 INAT
Engine speed at 100 km/hr	3140 rpm
Gear ratios	I. 3.90:1 II. 2.30:1 III. 1.41:1 IV. 1.00:1
Rear axle ratio	3.92 (4.08 for U.S.)
Chassis	unit frame and body
Suspension	independent front and rear, with coil springs, single joint swing axle, anti-sway bars
Brakes and area	disc, power assist standard, 273/279mm (10.8/11.0 in)
Wheelbase	2750mm (108.3 in)
Track, front/rear	1444/1440mm (56.9/56.7 in)
Length	4900mm (192.9 in)
Width	1810mm (71.3 in)
Height	1440mm (56.7 in)
Ground clearance	175mm (6.9 in)
Tires	7.35 H 14
Turning circle	12.5 meters (41 ft)
Steering type and ratio	recirculating ball (4.0 turns); servo assisted (3.0 turns)
Weight	1460 kg (3212 lbs)
Maximum speed	185 km/hr (115 mph); automatic: 180 km/hr (112 mph)
Acceleration	12.5 sec 0-100 km/hr
Fuel consumption	12.5 liters/100 km (18.75 mpg)
Fuel tank capacity	82 liters (21.7 gallons)

The 280S sedan, 1968, U.S. version

The 280S sedan, 1969

The 280SE sedan, 1968

Production

Production of the 280SE model [108 E28] (from November 1967/
January 1968 until September 1972)

was in	1967	365 units
	1968	18,685 units
	1969	25,081 units
	1970	25,627 units
	1971	14,871 units
	1972	6,422 units
	total	91,051 units

Production of the 280SEL model [108 E28] (from January 1968
until April 1971)

was in	1968	1,688 units
	1969	2,610 units
	1970	3,674 units
	1971	278 units
	total	8,250 units

Production of the 280SE coupe and convertible model [111 E28]
(from November 1967/February 1968 until May 1971)

was in	1968	55 units
	1969	1,950 units
	1970	2,501 units
	1971	613 units
	1972	68 units
	total	5,187 units

Model 280SE/SEL (1967-1972)

S = Super, E (Einspritzung) = fuel injection

The 280SE model was available as a sedan and the more luxurious coupe and convertible. The sedan body was the same as that of the 280S New Generation model, but the coupe and convertible had the same body style as the earlier 250SE which they replaced, and which were discontinued. There were no distinguishing marks between the 280S and SE sedans, except, of course, for the engine. The interior was no more elegant than that of the carburetor-engined car but the overall weight of the SE was 50 pounds more.

The fuel injected six-cylinder engine had a six-plunger pump for increased engine performance with improved economy and was not affected by altitude or by temperature. It also provided an efficient smog control system. Otherwise the 2.8-liter engines were alike. The seven main bearing crankshaft made for less vibration and longer bearing life and the greater separation between cylinders ensured better cooling. The new viscose cooling fan was also more efficient and the redesigned cams and molybdenum covered rings were all appreciable improvements. The 280SE engine developed 160 (DIN) horsepower at 5,500 (or 180 SAE at 5,750) revolutions per minute.

The 280SEL sedan went into production in January 1968. It had a longer wheelbase, by 3.9 inches, than the regular sedan, but otherwise was the same car in practically every respect.

The 280SE coupe, 1968

Prices

The 280SE four-door sedan sold in 1968 for........DM	18,600
in 1970 for............................DM	20,535
in 1971 for............................DM	21,590
The 280SEL four-door sedan sold in 1968 for.......DM	25,100
The 280SE coupe sold in 1968 for ....DM	26,510
in 1970 for............................DM	29,140
in 1971 for............................DM	30,680
The 280SE convertible sold in 1968 for...........DM	28,510
in 1970 for............................DM	31,140
in 1971 for............................DM	32,680
Power steering ....DM	515
Automatic transmission ....DM	1,440

The 280SE four-door sedan sold in the United States

in January 1968 for (East coast)..............$	6,222
(West coast)............................$	6,336
in October 1969 (East coast).................$	6,561
in September 1968 (East coast)...............$	6,310
in October 1970 (including automatic transmission)	
(East coast) ....$	7,297
in September 1971 (including automatic transmission)	
(East coast) ....$	9,546

The 280SEL sedan sold in January 1968 for

(East coast) ....$	6,622
(West coast)............................$	6,712
in September 1968 (East coast)...............$	6,722
in October 1969 (East coast).................$	6,992
in October 1970 (including automatic transmission)	
(East coast) ....$	8,088
in September 1971 (including automatic transmission)	
(East coast) ....$	10,925

The 280SE coupe sold in January 1968 for (East coast) ..$	9,174
(West coast)............................$	9,262
in September 1968 (East coast)...............$	9,424
in October 1969 (East coast).................$	11,112
in January 1970 (East coast).................$	11,612

The 280SE convertible sold in January 1968 for

(East coast) ....$	9,967
(West coast)............................$	10,054
in September 1968 (East coast)...............$	10,217
in October 1969 (East coast).................$	11,924
in January 1970 (East coast).................$	12,444
Power steering (1970) (standard on SEL model).....$	198
Automatic transmission ....$	392

Specifications

	280SE /280SEL / 280SE (coupe and convertible)
Engine type	6 cyl overhead camshaft (M 130)
Bore and stroke	86.5 x 78.8mm (3.41 x 3.10 in)
Displacement	2778 cc (169.5 cu in)
Power output	160 hp (DIN) @ 5500 rpm (180 hp SAE @ 5750 rpm)
Compression ratio	9.5:1
Torque	24.5 mkg @ 4250 rpm (26.7 mkg @ 4500 rpm 193.2 ft/lb)
Fuel injection	Bosch six plunger pump
Engine speed at 100 km/hr	3140 rpm
Gear ratios	I. 3.98:1 II. 2.39:1 III. 1.46:1 IV. 1.00:1
Rear axle ratio	3.92 (4.08 for U.S.)
Chassis	unit frame and body
Suspension	independent front and rear, with coil springs, single joint swing axle, anti-sway bars
Brakes and area	disc, power assisted, standard, 273/279mm (10.8/11.0 in)
Wheelbase	2750mm (108.3 in) SEL: 2850mm (112.2 in)
Track, front/rear	1482/1490mm (58.4/58.7 in)
Length	4900mm (192.9 in) SEL: 5000mm (196.9 in)
Width	1810mm (71.3 in) coupe and conv: 72.6 in
Height	1440mm (56.7 in) coupe: 55.9 in; conv: 56.5 in
Ground clearance	175mm (6.9 in)
Tires	7.35 H 14 or 185 H 14
Turning circle	12.5 meters (41 ft) SEL: (42 ft)
Steering type and ratio	recirculating ball (4.0 turns); servo assisted (3.0 turns)
Weight	1486 kg (3270 lbs) SEL: 3305 lbs coupe: 3330 lbs conv: 3495 lbs
Maximum speed	190 km/hr (118 mph); automatic: 185 km/hr (115 mph)
Acceleration	10.5 sec 0-100 km/hr
Fuel consumption	12.5 liters, super/100 km (18.75 mpg)
Fuel tank capacity	82 liters (21.7 gallons)

The 300SEL sedan, 1967

Prices and Production

The 300SEL four-door sedan sold in 1968 for........DM 29,760
The 300SEL sedan sold in the United States
    in January 1968 for (East coast)..............$ 9,400
       (West coast)..........................$ 9,489
    in September 1968 (East coast)..............$ 9,525
    in October 1969 (East coast)................$ 10,823
    in January 1970 (East coast)................$ 11,327

Production of the 300SEL model [109 E28] (from December 1967/
February 1968 until January 1970)

was in	1967	37 units
	1968	1,325 units
	1969	1,137 units
	1970	20 units
	total	2,519 units

Model 300SEL (1967-1970)

SE L (Lang) = long wheelbase chassis

The 300SEL sedan was the top of the line of New Generation cars for 1968. It retained the body of the former 300SE, first built in 1965, but now came equipped with the fuel injection engine of 2,778 cubic centimeter displacement and 180 SAE horsepower. The only outward difference between this and the 280 line was a more generous use of chrome around the window areas. Inwardly, the furnishings were of the finest as befitting this most elegant limousine of the New Generation class. Only the great 600 automobiles were more luxuriously built.

Such optional extras as automatic transmission, power steering, and air suspension system were standard on the 300SEL sedan. The body dimensions and chassis specifications were practically the same as those for the 300SEL 6.3 model, and the price of the car surely indicated that it was a superb automobile.

But the production life of this model was a rather short one. Sales for the first two years were quite respectable, but the superb 6.3 model, costing nearly $4,000 more, actually outsold this one by more than twice in 1969, thus accelerating its demise.

And the new V–8 engines were ready to take over from the six-cylinder units, in the top range of models.

The 300SEL sedan, 1967

Specifications

300SEL	
Engine type	6 cyl overhead camshaft (M 189)
Bore and stroke	86.5 x 78.8mm (3.41 x 3.10 in)
Displacement	2778 cc (169.5 cu in)
Power output	160 hp (DIN) @ 5500 rpm (180 hp SAE @ 5750 rpm)
Compression ratio	9.5:1
Torque	24.5 mkg @ 4250 rpm (26.7 mkg @ 4500 rpm 193.2 ft/lb)
Fuel injection	Bosch six plunger pump
Engine speed at 100 km/hr	3140 rpm
Gear ratios	I. 3.98:1
	II. 2.46:1
	III. 1.58:1
	IV. 1.00:1
Rear axle ratio	4.08
Chassis	unit frame and body
Suspension	independent front and rear, air springs, self-leveling and air suspension, single joint swing axle
Brakes and area	disc, servo assisted, 273/279mm (10.8/11.0 in)
Wheelbase	2850mm (112.2 in)
Track, front/rear	1482/1490mm (58.4/58.7 in)
Length	5000mm (196.9 in)
Width	1810mm (71.3 in)
Height	1415mm (55.7 in)
Ground clearance	175mm (6.9 in)
Tires	7.35 H 14 or 185 H 14
Turning circle	12.2 meters (40 ft)
Steering type and ratio	recirculating ball, servo assisted (3.0 turns)
Weight	1620 kg (3564 lbs)
Maximum speed	190 km/hr (118 mph)
Acceleration	11.5 sec 0-100 km/hr
Fuel consumption	12.2 liters/100 km (19 mpg)
Fuel tank capacity	82 liters (21.7 gallons)

The 300SEL sedan, 1968

The interior of the 300SEL sedan, 1967

The 250C coupe; just like this writer owned for eleven years

Production

Production of the 250C coupe model [114 V25] (from October 1968 until May 1972)

was in	1968	3 units
	1969	2,949 units
	1970	2,627 units
	1971	2,348 units
	1972	897 units
	total	8,824 units

Production of the 250CE model [114 E25] (from October 1968 until May 1972)

was in	1968	3 units
	1969	5,840 units
	1970	8,002 units
	1971	5,898 units
	1972	2,044 units
	total	21,787 units

Production of the 250C model (2,778 cc engine) [114 V28] (from July 1969 until June 1976)

was in	1969	1,213 units
	1970	2,425 units
	1971	3,621 units
	1972	2,839 units
	1973	649 units
	1974	490 units
	1975	442 units
	1976	89 units
	total	11,768 units

Model 250C/CE (1968-1976)

C = Coupe, E (Einspritzung) = fuel injection

The 250C and 250CE coupe models were introduced toward the end of 1968 as the last of the New Generation cars. The chassis, wheelbase and track, were the same as those of the 250 sedan, but the roof was nearly two inches lower and the passenger compartment was shorter. There were no pillars between the front and rear side windows and the chrome strips on the roof made the car look considerable more sportier than the staid model.

Powered either by the carburetor engine of 130 DIN (146 SAE) horsepower or the electronically controlled fuel injection engine of 150 DIN (170 SAE) horsepower, for the United States the 280 engine was fitted. This developed 157 SAE horsepower and the car had the final drive of 3.92:1 instead of the 4.08 for the former cars. The four-speed manual transmission was optional. Caliper-type disc brakes ensured safe stopping and radial tires provided superb road-holding. The base price of the 250C sporty coupe model, however, at first did not include such extras as air conditioning, automatic transmission, and power steering. (Other countries, as Great Britain, also got the 280 engine.)

Prices

The 250C coupe sold in 1969 for . . . . .DM	16,820
in 1970 for. . . . . .DM	18,430
in 1971 for. . . . . .DM	19,370
The 250CE coupe sold in 1969 for . . . . .DM	17,710
in 1970 for. . . . . .DM	19,370
in 1971 . . . . .DM	20,370
Power steering . . . . .DM	515
Automatic transmission . . . . .DM	1,440
The 250C (2.8-liter engine) sold in the United States	
in January 1970 for (East coast). . . . .$	6,625
(West coast) . . . .$	6,761
in October 1970 (including automatic transmission)	
(East coast) . . . .$	7,348
in September 1971 (including automatic transmission)	
(East coast) . . . .$	8,059
Power steering (1970) . . . .$	198

Specifications

	250C / 250CE (coupe)
Engine type	6 cyl overhead camshaft (M 114) (for U.S. M 130)
Bore and stroke	81.7 x 78.8mm (3.23 x 3.10 in) for U.S.: 86.5 x 78.8mm (3.41 x 3.10 in)
Displacement	2496 cc (152.4 cu in) for U.S.: 2778 cc (169.5 cu in)
Power output	C: 130 hp (DIN) @ 5400 rpm (146 hp SAE @ 5600 rpm) CE: 150 hp (DIN) @ 5500 rpm (170 hp SAE @ 5500 rpm) for U.S.: 157 hp SAE @ 5400
Compression ratio	9:1 (later: 8.7:1)
Torque	C: 20.3 mkg @ 3600 rpm (22.3 mkg @ 3800 rpm 161.3 ft/lb) CE: 21.5 mkg @ 4500 rpm (23.5 mkg @ 4650 rpm 170 ft/lb) for U.S.: 25.1 mkg @ 3800 rpm 181.6 ft/lb
Carburetion or Fuel injection	2 dual downdraft carburetors Zenith 35/40 INAT CE: Bosch electronic
Engine speed at 100 km/hr	3180 rpm
Gear ratios	I. 3.90:1 (optional) I. 3.96:1 II. 2.30:1 II. 2.34:1 III. 1.41:1 III. 1.43:1 IV. 1.00:1 IV. 1.00:1 V. 0.87:1
Rear axle ratio	3.92 (later: 3.69; for 5-speed 3.92)
Chassis	unit frame and body
Suspension	independent front and rear, with coil springs, diagonal-pivot swing axle, anti-sway bars
Brakes and area	disc, power assisted, 273/279mm (10.8/11.0 in)
Wheelbase	2750mm (108.3 in)
Track, front/rear	1444/1440mm (56.9/56.7 in)
Length	4680mm (184.3 in)
Width	1770mm (69.7 in)
Height	1395mm (54.9 in)
Ground clearance	175mm (6.9 in)
Tires	6.95 H 14 or 175 H 14
Turning circle	11.7 meters (38.4 ft)
Steering type and ratio	recirculating ball,(4.0 turns), servo assisted
Weight	1395 kg (3069 lbs)
Maximum speed	180 km/hr (112 mph)
Acceleration	13 sec 0-100 km/hr
Fuel consumption	12.5 liters/100 km (18.75 mpg)
Fuel tank capacity	65 liters (17.2 gallons)

The 250CE coupe, 1972

The 250C coupe, 1973

The 280SE convertible, 1969

Prices and Production

The 280SE 3.5 coupe sold in 1970 for. . . . . .DM 32,025
    in 1971 for. . . . . .DM 33,690
The 280SE 3.5 convertible sold for an additional about DM   2,000
The 280SE 3.5 coupe sold in the United States
    in January 1970 for (East coast). . . . .$ 13,430
      (West coast) . . . .$ 13,574
    in March 1971 (East coast) . . . .$ 13,766
The 280SE 3.5 convertible sold in the United States
    in January 1970 for (East coast). . . . .$ 14,155
      (West coast) . . . .$ 14,297
    in March 1971 (East coast) . . . .$ 14,509

Production of the 280SE 3.5 [111 E35/1] (from August/November 1969 until July 1971)

	was in 1969	176 units
	1970	3,300 units
	1971	1,026 units
	total	4,502 units

Model 280SE 3.5 (1969-1971)

S = Super, E (Einspritzung) = fuel injection

The 280SE 3.5 luxury coupe and convertible were introduced at the Frankfurt Auto Show in 1969. The basic body style actually dated back to the 1961 220SE model, and it was only slightly altered. The radiator was 70 millimeters lower and 100 millimeters wider and the bumpers had rubber inserts. The engine, however, was the most advanced one produced, with transistorized ignition, three-phase generator, and Bosch electronic fuel injection. Such accessories as stereo radio, air conditioning, automatic transmission, and electric windows were standard. Upholstery was of real leather and the elegant wood trim was especially selected.

The new V-8 engine, displacing 3,499 cubic centimeters (213.5 cubic inches), and developing 200 horsepower (230 SAE) was brand-new and did not share any components with the earlier and larger 6.3-liter unit. With the cast-iron block and aluminum head, it weighed only 55 pounds more (505 pounds) than the six-cylinder powerplant and gave the cars an acceleration rate of 9.5 seconds to 100 kilometers per hour and maximum speed of 125 miles per hour.

These luxurious models were the last of the long line of convertibles and coupes which were to become so very desirable and brought premium prices many years later.

The 280SE coupe, 1969

Specifications

	280SE 3.5 (coupe and convertible)
Engine type	V-8 cyl overhead camshafts, one for each bank (M 116)
Bore and stroke	92 x 65.8mm (3.62 x 2.59 in)
Displacement	3499 cc (213.5 cu in)
Power output	200 hp (DIN) @ 5800 rpm (230 hp SAE @ 6050 rpm)
Compression ratio	9.5:1
Torque	29.2 mkg @ 4000 rpm (32 mkg @ 4200 rpm 231.5 ft/lb)
Fuel injection	Bosch electronic
Engine speed at 100 km/hr	2945 rpm
Gear ratios	I. 3.98:1 (14.69) II. 2.39:1 (8.82) III. 1.46:1 (5.38) IV. 1.00:1 (3.69)
Rear axle ratio	3.69
Chassis	unit frame and body
Suspension	independent front and rear, with coil springs, single joint swing axle
Brakes and area	disc, servo assist, two circuit hydraulic, 273/279mm (10.8/11.0 in)
Wheelbase	2750mm (108.3 in)
Track, front/rear	1482/1485mm (58.4/58.6 in)
Length	4880mm (192 in)
Width	1845mm (72.6 in)
Height	1395mm (54.9 in)
Ground clearance	152mm (6 in)
Tires	7.35 H 14 or 185 H 14
Turning circle	12 meters (39.4 ft)
Steering type and ratio	recirculating ball (3.2 turns), servo assisted
Weight	convertible: 1574 kg (3463 lbs); coupe: 1655 kg (3641 lbs)
Maximum speed	205 km/hr (127 mph)
Acceleration	9.5 sec 0-100 km/hr
Fuel consumption	13 liters, super/100 km (18 mpg)
Fuel tank capacity	82 liters (21.7 gallons)

The timeless convertible, the 280SE 3.5 of 1971

The first of a long line, the 220SE of 1961

The 300SEL 3.5 sedan, 1973

Model 300SEL 3.5 (1969-1972)

SE L (Lang) = long wheelbase chassis

The 300SEL 3.5 sedan was the other car introduced at the 1969 Frankfurt Auto Show to have the new V-8 engine of 3.5-liter displacement installed. The body style was identical to the earlier 300SEL sedan which had the 6-cylinder-in-line engine of 2.8 liters and 180 SAE (160 DIN) horsepower. This, in turn, had replaced the first 300SEL sedan which actually had a 300 engine, the 2,996 cubic centimeter power unit of 160, and later 170 (DIN) horsepower.

The new 3.5-liter oversquare V–8 engine had the new Bosch electronic fuel injection system, a more accurate and less expensive method than the previously used mechanical injection. It developed a considerable 200 DIN (230 SAE) horsepower and with a torque of 231.5 ft/lb gave the 300SEL sedan a maximum speed of 205 kilometers (127 miles) per hour. It was designed for the future and would appear within only two years in enlarged form.

The new 300SEL 3.5 was again the top of the line, a most luxuriously appointed automobile, more advanced than the coming 280SE 3.5 sedan in chassis design, and, with the longer wheelbase, a somewhat better riding automobile. It had the air suspension system of the 6.3 model sedan and shared some other technological improvements of that model.

(This 300SEL 3.5 was the only one of the 3.5 models — the 280 SE 3.5 and the 280SEL 3.5 were the other two — which was sold in the U.S. Over the years 1,039 such units were sold here.)

Prices and Production

The 300SEL 3.5 four-door sedan sold in 1970 for . . . . .DM 31,025
in 1971 for. . . . . .DM 32,635
The 300SEL 3.5 four-door sedan sold in the United States
in January 1970 for (East coast). . . . .$ 12,572
(West coast) . . . .$ 12,718
in March 1971 (East coast) . . . .$ 12,886
in September 1971 (East coast) . . . .$ 14,121
in December 1971 (East coast). . . . .$ 13,768

Production of the 300SEL 3.5 model [109 E35/1] (from August/November 1969 until September 1972)

was in	1969	158 units
	1970	4,903 units
	1971	3,225 units
	1972	1,297 units
	total	9,483 units

Specifications

	300SEL 3.5
Engine type	V-8 cyl overhead camshafts, one for each bank (M 116)
Bore and stroke	92 x 65.8mm (3.62 x 2.59 in)
Displacement	3499 cc (213.5 cu in)
Power output	200 hp (DIN) @ 5800 rpm (230 hp SAE @ 6050 rpm)
Compression ratio	9.5:1
Torque	29.2 mkg @ 4000 rpm (32 mkg @ 4200 rpm 231.5 ft/lb)
Fuel injection	Bosch electronic
Engine speed at 100 km/hr	2945 rpm
Gear ratios	I. 3.98:1 (14.69)
	II. 2.39:1 (8.82)
	III. 1.46:1 (5.38)
	IV. 1.00:1 (3.69)
Rear axle ratio	3.69
Chassis	unit frame and body
Suspension	independent front and rear, air springs, self leveling and air suspension, single joint swing axle
Brakes and area	front vented disc, rear solid, servo assisted, 273/279mm (10.8/11.0 in)
Wheelbase	2850mm (112.2 in)
Track, front/rear	1482/1490mm (58.4/58.7 in)
Length	5000mm (196.9 in)
Width	1810mm (71.3 in)
Height	1415mm (55.7 in)
Ground clearance	175mm (6.9 in)
Tires	7.35 H 14 or 185 H 14
Turning circle	12.2 meters (40 ft)
Steering type and ratio	recirculating ball (3.0 turns), servo assisted
Weight	1673 kg (3680 lbs)
Maximum speed	205 km/hr (127 mph)
Acceleration	9.5 sec 0-100 km/hr
Fuel consumption	13 liters, super/100 km (18 mpg)
Fuel tank capacity	82 liters (21.7 gallons)

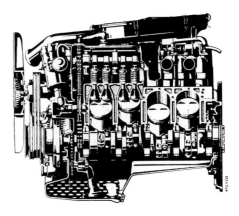

Longitudinal section of the M 116 engine, 1969

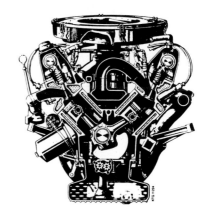

Cross section of the M 116 engine, 1969

The 250 sedan, 1974

Prices and Production

The 250 four-door sedan sold in 1970 for . . . . .DM 16,185
    in 1972 for. . . . . .DM 17,875
    in 1973 for. . . . . .DM 18,760
The 250 four-door sedan sold in the United States
    in January 1970 for (East coast). . . . .$ 5,539
    (West coast) . . . .$ 5,674
    in October 1970 (including automatic transmission)
    (East coast) . . . .$ 6,208
    in September 1971 (including automatic transmission)
    (East coast) . . . .$ 7,205
    Power steering (1970) . . . .$ 198

Production of the 250 model [114 V28] (from March/July 1970 until July 1976)

was in	1970	3,248 units
	1971	7,382 units
	1972	8,266 units
	1973	6,570 units
	1974	4,516 units
	1975	3,580 units
	1976	499 units
	total	34,061 units

Model 250 (1970-1976)

The 250 sedan, first produced March and placed into regular production in July 1970, was another model where the designation no longer indicated the displacement of the engine, for it had the 2,778 cubic centimeter engine. The true 250 was still being made (begun in July and put into production in December 1967, it was phased out in May 1972). After the appearance of the 2.8-liter 250 coupe the previous year, the 2.8-liter sedan was probably a natural 250 model to follow.

Sharing the body style of the larger 280SEL sedan, the 250 was shorter, had a smaller fuel tank, smaller sized tires, weighed 178 pounds less, but had the same specifications in other respects. In actual performance it was slightly superior to the larger sedan.

This 250 model, equipped with a 2.8-liter engine, proved that the once rigidly adhered-to model designations were now definitely discarded. A year before the 250C was — for the United States market — furnished with the 280 engine, and at the time (1970) the 280SE 3.5 and the 300 SEL 3.5 were introduced, it was believed that it was merely an exception. But now, when this new V-8 engine of 3.5 liter displacement seemed unquestionably designed for enlargement to at least 4.5 liters, it appeared certain that style designations could not be relied upon to indicate the engine's displacement in the car. Of course, the 600 limousine had actually a 6.3-liter engine, but a 630 would probably have not sounded as well. (A 600 sedan was built in 1924-1929, which had a 6.24-liter engine!) And then, earlier (in 1976), the 300SEL had a 2.8-liter engine, but it was not a 300SEL 2.8.

Specifications

	250
Engine type	6 cyl overhead camshaft (M130)
Bore and stroke	86.5 x 78.8mm (3.41 x 3.10 in)
Displacement	2778 cc (169.5 cu in)
Power output	140 hp (DIN) @ 5200 rpm (157 hp SAE @ 5400 rpm)
Compression ratio	9:1
Torque	23 mkg @ 3600 rpm (25.1 mkg @ 3800 rpm 181.6 ft/lb)
Carburetion	2 dual downdraft carburetors Zenith 35/40 INAT
Engine speed at 100 km/hr	3140 rpm
Gear ratio	I. 3.90:1 II. 2.30:1 III. 1.41:1 IV. 1.00:1
Rear axle ratio	3.92
Chassis	unit frame and body
Suspension	independent front and rear, with coil springs, diagonal-pivot swing axle, anti-sway bars
Brakes and area	disc, power assist, two circuit hydraulic, 273/279mm (10.8/11.0 in)
Wheelbase	2750mm (108.3 in)
Track, front/rear	1444/1440mm (56.9/56.7 in)
Length	4680mm (184.3 in)
Width	1770mm (69.7 in)
Height	1440mm (56.7 in)
Ground clearance	175mm (6.9 in)
Tires	6.95 H 14
Turning circle	11.7 meters (38.4 ft)
Steering type and ratio	recirculating ball (4.0 turns), servo assisted
Weight	1445 kg (3179 lbs)
Maximum speed	190 km/hr (118 mph)
Acceleration	12 sec 0-100 km/hr
Fuel consumption	12.5 liters, super/100 km (18.75 mpg)
Fuel tank capacity	65 liters (17.2 gallons)

The 250 sedan, 1971, U.S. version

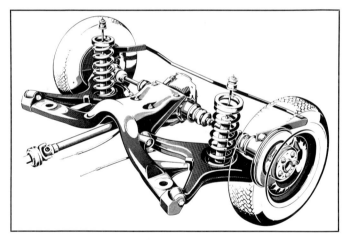

The suspension system of the 250 sedan, 1970

The 280SEL 3.5 sedan, 1971

Model 280SEL 3.5 (1970-1972)

SE L (Lang) = long wheelbase chassis

The 280SEL 3.5 sedan introduced at the Auto Show in Amsterdam, was produced for only three years. First pre-production was begun in June 1970 with only three units being built that year. Regular production did not get underway until the following March. After placing that 3.5-liter V-8 engine into the luxury coupe and convertible of the 280SE line, it seemed only natural to equip the sedan in the same manner. However, the 300SEL sedan, a more elegant model, was already in production and selling in fair numbers, even when the less expensive 280SEL was available. (The 300SEL 3.5 sold nearly 9,500 units in four years, while the 280SEL 3.5 sold less than 1,000 units in two years.)

Prices and Production

The 280SEL 3.5 four-door sedan sold in 1971 for . . . . .DM 31,420

Production of the 280SEL 3.5 model [108 E35] (from June 1970/ March 1971 until August 1972)

	was in	1970	3 units
		1971	565 units
		1972	383 units
		total	951 units

Prices and Production

The 280SE 3.5 four-door sedan sold in 1971 for . . . . . .DM 24,920

Production of the 280SE 3.5 model [108 E35] (from July 1970/ March 1971 until September 1972)

	was in	1970	3 units
		1971	7,450 units
		1972	3,856 units
		total	11,309 units

Model 280SE 3.5 (1970-1972)

S = Super, E (Einspritzung) = fuel injection

The 280SE 3.5 sedan, first produced in July 1970, but really not in regular series production until March of the following year, was a more powerful edition of the prevailing sedan model. The new V-type eight-cylinder engine had been first installed into the higher priced luxury coupe and convertible models and the longer wheelbase sedans of the 280SEL and 300SEL designation. It seemed natural to make that better performance car also available in the regular sedan style.

Still, the 280SE 3.5 sedan had a relatively short production run with slightly over 11,000 units in two years. It was then replaced by the more correctly named model and with the newer styled body and other notable improvements gained over the years.

Specifications

	280SEL 3.5	280SE 3.5
Engine type	V-8 cyl overhead camshafts, one for each bank (M 116)	V-8 cyl overhead camshafts (M 116)
Bore and stroke	92 x 65.8mm (3.62 x 2.59 in)	92 x 65.8mm (3.62 x 2.59 in)
Displacement	3499 cc (213.5 cu in)	3499 cc (213.5 cu in)
Power output	200 hp (DIN) @ 5800 rpm (230 hp SAE @ 6050 rpm)	200 hp (DIN) @ 5800 rpm (230 hp SAE @ 6050 rpm)
Compression ratio	9.5:1	9.5:1
Torque	29.2 mkg @ 4000 rpm (32 mkg @ 4200 rpm 231.5 ft/lb)	29.2 mkg @ 4000 rpm (32 mkg @ 4200 rpm 231.5 ft/lb)
Fuel injection	Bosch electronic	Bosch electronic
Engine speed at 100 km/hr	2945 rpm	2945 rpm
Gear ratios	I. 3.98:1 II. 2.39:1 III. 1.46:1 IV. 1.00:1	I. 3.98:1 II. 2.39:1 III. 1.46:1 IV. 1.00:1
Rear axle ratio	3.69	3.69
Chassis	unit frame and body	unit frame and body
Suspension	independent front and rear, with coil springs, single joint swing axle, anti-sway bars	independent front and rear, with coil springs, single joint swing axle, anti-sway bars
Brakes and area	front vented disc, rear solid, servo assisted, two circuit hydraulic, 273/279mm (10.8/11.0 in)	disc, front vented, rear solid, servo assisted, two circuit hydraulic, 273/279mm (10.8/11.0 in)
Wheelbase	2850mm (112.2 in)	2750mm (108.3 in)
Track, front/rear	1482/1490mm (58.4/58.7 in)	1482/1490mm (58.4/58.7 in)
Length	5000mm (196.9 in)	4900mm (192.9 in)
Width	1810mm (71.3 in)	1810mm (71.3 in)
Height	1440mm (56.7 in)	1440mm (56.7 in)
Ground clearance	175mm (6.9 in)	175mm (6.9 in)
Tires	7.35 H 14 or 185 H 14	7.35 H 14 or 185 H 14
Turning circle	12.2 meters (40 ft)	11.7 meters (38.4 ft)
Steering type and ratio	recirculating ball (4.0 turns), servo assisted	recirculating ball (4.0 turns), servo assisted
Weight	1762 kg (3876 lbs)	1737 kg (3821 lbs)
Maximum speed	200 km/hr (124 mph)	200 km/hr (124 mph)
Acceleration	10 sec 0-100 km/hr	10 sec 0-100 km/hr
Fuel consumption	13 liters, super/100 km (18 mpg)	13 liters, super/100 km (18 mpg)
Fuel tank capacity	82 liters, (21.7 gallons)	82 liters (21.7 gallons)

The 350SL roadster, 1971

Prices and Production

The 350SL model sold in 1971 for . . . . .DM 29,970
    in 1972 for . . . . .DM 31,415
    in 1973 for . . . . .DM 32,915
    in 1974 for . . . . .DM 34,400
    in 1975 for . . . . .DM 37,920
    in 1977 for . . . . .DM 39,360
In the United States the 350SL sold
    in September 1971 (East coast) for $11,059
    in December 1971 (East coast). $10,540

Production of the 350SL model [107 E35] (from November 1970/
April 1971 until March 1980)

was in	1970	3 units
	1971	4,802 units
	1972	4,778 units
	1973	1,647 units
	1974	574 units
	1975	390 units
	1976	540 units
	1977	650 units
	1978	743 units
	1979	934 units
	1980	243 units
	total	15,304 units

Model 350SL (1970-1980)

S = Sports, L (Leicht) = light

The 350SL model was introduced early in 1971, although the preproduction actually got started in November of the previous year. The impressive two-seater sports car was to replace the 280SL, which had actually started with the 230SL version in 1963. The body and chassis of this all-new car was considerably heavier (300 lbs.) and longer (3.3 in.) than that of the earlier sportscars, but still showed a slight resemblance to them. The front and rear axles were similar to those of the 200-250 models, with independent wheel suspension with double wishbones and anti-drive control at the front, diagonal swing axle at the rear. The steel coil springs had rubber helping springs, anti-roll bars, and double-acting hydraulic telescopic shock absorbers. Brakes were ventilated disc at front and solid on the rear, hydraulic dual circuit with vacuum boost. A fluid-coupling four-speed automatic transmission was available as an optional item. Some of the many new safety features of the 350SL were the four-spoke safety steering wheel, the fuel tank repositioned, collision-safe over the rear axle, the safety door handles, and a new type safety belt.

The engine was the 3.5-liter V-8 type with slight modifications from those of the other 3.5 models. The gear shift lever was placed on the floor and the regular four-speed transmission or automatic was available. Maximum speed was 210 km/hr and acceleration was 8.8 seconds to 100 kilometers per hour, with the standard transmission car.

The car came as an open roadster with removable hard top pagoda style roof.

The 350SL 4.5 was marketed in the U.S. It was the same car with few exceptions, but had the larger 4.5-liter engine installed. Rated at the same horsepower as the European version (3.5) the larger engine used 10 percent more fuel, but regular instead of super gasoline. Emission controls were met until 1974 with the 4.5 — the principal reason for the change to a larger displacement engine for the U.S.

Specifications

	350SL
Engine type	V-8 overhead camshafts (M 116)
Bore and stroke	92 x 65.8mm (3.62 x 2.59 in)
Displacement	3499 cc (213.5 cu in)
Power output	200 hp (DIN) @ 5800 rpm (230 hp SAE @ 6050 rpm); 1977: 195 hp (DIN) @ 5500 rpm
Compression ratio	9.5:1 1979: 9:1
Torque	29.2 mkg @ 4000 rpm (32 mkg @ 4200 rpm 231.5 ft/lb)
Fuel injection	Bosch electronic; 1979: mechanical, with air flow sensor
Engine speed at 100 km/hr	2945 rpm automatic: 3085 rpm

Gear ratios		automatic		after July, 1972	
I.	3.98:1	I.	3.96:1	I.	2.31:1
II.	2.39:1	II.	2.34:1	II.	1.46:1
III.	1.46:1	III.	1.43:1	III.	1.00:1
IV.	1.00:1	IV.	1.00:1		

Rear axle ratio	3.46
Chassis	unit frame and body
Suspension	independent front and rear, double wishbones, diagonal-pivot swing axle
Brakes and area	disc, front vented, rear solid, 278/279mm (10.9/11.0 in)
Wheelbase	2460mm (96.9 in)
Track, front/rear	1452/1440mm (57.2/56.7 in)
Length	4380mm (172.4 in) 1979: 4390mm (172.8 in)
Width	1790mm (70.5 in)
Height	1300mm (51.2 in)
Ground clearance	140mm (5.5 in)
Tires	205/70 VR 14
Turning circle	10.34 meters (33.9 ft)
Steering type and ratio	recirculating ball (3.0 turns); servo assisted 15.6:1
Weight	1585 kg (3487 lbs) 1979: 1540 kg (3388 lbs)
Maximum speed	210 km/hr (130 mph); automatic: 205 km/hr (127 mph); 1977: 205 km/hr; automatic: 200 km/hr
Accleration	8.8 sec 0-100 km/hr; automatic: 9.0 sec 0-100 km/hr; 1979: 9.5 sec 0-100 km/hr; automatic: 10.1 sec
Fuel consumption	13 liters, super/100 km (18 mpg); 1979: at 120 km/hr, 13.8 liters; automatic: 14.5 liters
Fuel tank capacity	90 liters (23 gallons)

The 350SL hard top, 1972

The 350SLC coupe, just like the writer owned for many years

Prices and Production

The 350SLC model sold in 1971 for . . . . .DM 33,690
    in 1972 for. . . . . .DM 35,635
    in 1973 for. . . . . .DM 37,300
    in 1974 for. . . . . .DM 38,980
    in 1975 for. . . . . .DM 42,970
    in 1977 for. . . . . .DM 44,910

Production of the 350SLC model [107 E35] (from June 1971/
February 1972 until March 1980)

was in	1971	6 units
	1972	5,562 units
	1973	3,750 units
	1974	864 units
	1975	589 units
	1976	671 units
	1977	822 units
	1978	807 units
	1979	775 units
	1980	79 units
	total	13,925 units

Model 350SLC (1971-1980)

S = Sports, L = Light, C = Coupe

The 350SLC model was first shown to the public at the Brussels Auto Show in 1971. It was a slightly longer edition of the SL model. The wheelbase as well as overall length was 360 millimeter (about 14 inches) longer and the car weighed 50 kilograms more. The coupe had, of course, rear passenger seats and larger trunk space than the 350SL model, but it looked just like it except for the short space of louvered rear side window area.

This newly designed luxury coupe took the place of the (111 factory designation) line of coupes and convertibles first produced as 220SE in September 1960 and followed by the steadily increased power of the 250SE and 280SE models.

It was over six inches shorter and three inches lower than the older body style car.

The 350SLC was an automobile with the sporty character of the SL model, giving superior performance, exclusive comfort, and elegant styling to the discriminating owner. Fitted with the four-speed manual or automatic transmission, the SLC had the same performance as the SL model.

For the United States, the 195 horsepower (DIN) 4.5-liter engine was installed and only the three-speed automatic transmission was available. Many items were standard equipment, such as air conditioning, automatic transmission, power brakes, power steering, central locking system, stereo radio, leather upholstery, and Michelin XVR tires, among others.

Specifications

	350SLC
Engine type	V-8 cyl overhead camshafts (M 116)
Bore and stroke	92 x 65.8mm (3.62 x 2.59 in)
Displacement	3499 cc (213.5 cu in)
Power output	200 hp (DIN) @ 5800 rpm (230 hp SAE @ 6050 rpm); 1977: 195 hp (DIN) @ 5500 rpm
Compression ratio	9.5:1 1979: 9:1
Torque	29.2 mkg @ 4000 rpm (32 mkg @ 4200 rpm 231.5 ft/lb)
Fuel injection	Bosch electronic; 1979: mechanical with air flow sensor
Engine speed at 100 km/hr	2945 rpm automatic: 3085 rpm
Gear ratios	I. 3.98:1 automatic I. 3.96:1 after July, 1972 I. 2.31:1 II. 2.39:1 II. 2.34:1 II. 1.46:1 III. 1.46:1 III. 1.43:1 III. 1.00:1 IV. 1.00:1 IV. 1.00:1
Rear axle ratio	3.64
Chassis	unit frame and body
Suspension	independent front and rear, double wishbones, diagonal swing axle
Brakes and area	disc, front vented, rear solid, 278/279mm (10.9/11.0 in)
Wheelbase	2820mm (111.0 in)
Track, front/rear	1452/1440mm (57.2/56.7 in)
Length	4740mm (186.6 in) 1979: 4750mm (187 in)
Width	1790mm (70.5 in)
Height	1300mm (51.2 in)
Ground clearance	140mm (5.5 in)
Tires	205/70 VR
Turning circle	10.34 meters (33.9 ft)
Steering type and ratio	recirculating ball (3.0 turns); servo assisted 15.6:1
Weight	1635 kg (3597 lbs) 1979: 1590 kg (3498 lbs)
Maximum speed	210 km/hr (130 mph); automatic: 205 km/hr (127 mph); 1977: 205 km/hr; automatic: 200 km/hr (124 mph)
Acceleration	8.8 sec 0-100 km/hr; automatic: 9.0 sec 0-100 km/hr; 1979: 9.5 sec; automatic: 10.1 sec
Fuel consumption	13 liters, super/100 km (18 mpg); 1979: at 120 km/hr, 13.8 liters; automatic: 14.5 liters
Fuel tank capacity	90 liters (23 gallons)

The 350SLC on the test track, 1977

The 280 sedan, 1974, U.S. version

Prices and Production

The 280 four-door sedan sold in 1972 for . . . . .DM 18,980
   in 1973 for. . . . . .DM 19,925
   in 1974 for. . . . . .DM 21,700
   in 1975 for. . . . . .DM 23,610
   Power steering . . . . .DM   515
   Automatic transmission .DM 1,440
In the United States the 280 sedan sold in 1972 for
(including automatic transmission)
     (East coast) . . . .$ 8,875
     (West coast) . . . .$ 8,978
   in November 1973 (East coast) . . . .$ 10,950
   in September 1974 (East coast) . . . .$ 12,325
   in October 1975 (East coast) . . . .$ 13,813

Production of the 280 model [114 V28] (from October 1971/May 1972 until September 1976)

was in 1971	2	units
1972	9,828	units
1973	13,718	units
1974	11,755	units
1975	6,535	units
1976	2,699	units
total	44,537	units

Model 280 (1971-1976)

The 280 sedan, fitted with the newly developed six-cylinder engine with two overhead camshafts, was introduced in early 1972. The design of an altered shape of combustion chamber and different positioning of valves and double camshafts made for more complete burning of fuel and less emission of noxious exhaust gases (15 percent less hydrocarbon and 10 percent less carbon monoxide) and was an answer to the ever-increasing stringent emission controls.

Although this newly designed twin-cam engine, particularly the detuned version for the United States market, was a considerably lower emission unit than the former six-cylinder engine it replaced. For the world market this new engine developed appreciably more power than the old one.

Equipped with the dual downdraft Solex carburetor, the M110 engine developed 160 DIN horsepower at 5,500 revolutions per minute and 23 mkg torque at 4,000. The new sedan came equipped with the all-synchromesh four-speed transmission with steering column or center floor gear shift, but had the manual five-speed transmission or the automatic unit as an optional item. It was a larger version of the 250 sedan.

The 280 sedan, 1973

Specifications

	280
Engine type	6 cyl double overhead camshafts (M 110)
Bore and stroke	86 x 78.8mm (3.41 x 3.10 in)
Displacement	2746 cc (168 cu in)
Power output	160 hp (DIN) @ 5500 rpm (180 hp SAE) later, U.S.: 120 hp SAE @ 4800 rpm
Compression ratio	9:1 (U.S.: 8:1)
Torque	23 mkg @ 4000 rpm (166.4 ft/lb)
Carburetion	dual downdraft carburetor Solex 4 A 1
Engine speed at 100 km/hr	3140 rpm
Gear ratios	I. 3.90:1 II. 2.30:1 III. 1.41:1 IV. 1.00:1
Rear axle ratio	3.69
Chassis	unit frame and body
Suspension	independent front and rear, with coil springs, diagonal-pivot swing axle, anti-sway bars
Brakes and area	disc, power assisted, two circuit hydraulic, 273/279mm (10.8/11.0 in)
Wheelbase	2750mm (108.3 in)
Track, front/rear	1444/1440mm (56.9/56.7 in)
Length	4680mm (184.3 in)
Width	1770mm (69.7 in)
Height	1440mm (56.7 in)
Ground clearance	175mm (6.9 in)
Tires	185 HR 14
Turning circle	11.7 meters (38.4 ft)
Steering type and ratio	recirculating ball (4.0 turns), servo assisted
Weight	1455 kg (3200 lbs)
Maximum speed	190 km/hr (118 mph)
Acceleration	13 sec 0-100 km/hr (18.75 mpg)
Fuel consumption	12.5 liters, super/100 km (later, U.S.: no lead fuel)
Fuel tank capacity	65 liters (17.2 gallons)

Cross section of the M 110 engine, 1972

The 280 sedan, 1973

The 280E sedan, 1974

Model 280E (1971-1976)

E (Einspritzung) = fuel injection

The 280E sedan introduced in early 1971, but not produced in any quantity until the following year, had the new double overhead camshaft six-cylinder engine, but with electronic fuel enjection. This version of the M110 engine developed 185 DIN horsepower at 6,000 revolutions per minute and 24.3 mkg torque at 4,500 revolutions. Performance was slightly better than that of the carburetor model, with maximum speed of 200 kilometers (124 miles) against the 190 of the 280 sedan, but fuel consumption was rated equal.

Inside furnishing was exactly the same and so was the exterior body style except for the designation E on the trunk lid after the 280.

Prices and Production

The 280E four-door sedan sold in 1972 for	.DM	20,535
in 1973 for.	.DM	21,535
in 1974 for.	.DM	22,500
in 1975 for.	.DM	25,465
Power steering	.DM	515
Automatic transmission	.DM	1,440

Production of the 280E model [114 E28] (from January 1971/April 1972 until September 1976)

was in	1971	18 units
	1972	8,371 units
	1973	8,214 units
	1974	3,612 units
	1975	2,277 units
	1976	344 units
	total	22,836 units

Model 280CE (1971-1976)

C = Coupe, E (Einspritzung) = fuel injection

The 280CE coupe was introduced at about the same time to the general public as the carburetor version of the car, but pre-production had actually begun in April of 1971. At that time, however, only two prototypes were made and production did not get underway until 1972 when over five thousand units of this double overhead camshaft engined model were built. The electronic fuel injected version developed 185 DIN horsepower at 6,000 revolutions per minute and a torque of 24.3 mkg at 4,500 revolutions per minute, giving the coupe a considerably livelier performance than the carburetor engined model.

Prices and Production

The 280CE sold in 1972 for	.DM	22,980
in 1973 for.	.DM	24,090
in 1974 for.	.DM	26,240
in 1975 for.	.DM	28,405
Power steering	.DM	515
Automatic transmission	.DM	1,440

Production of the 280CE coupe [114 E28] (from April 1971/May 1972 until July 1976)

was in	1971	2 units
	1972	5,389 units
	1973	3,724 units
	1974	1,429 units
	1975	844 units
	1976	130 units
	total	11,518 units

The 280CE coupe, 1974

Specifications

	280E	280CE (coupe)
Engine type	6 cyl double overhead camshafts (M 110)	6 cyl double overhead camshafts (M 110)
Bore and stroke	86 x 78.8mm (3.41 x 3.10 in)	86 x 78.8mm (3.41 x 3.10 in)
Displacement	2746 cc (168 cu in)	2746 cc (168 cu in)
Power output	185 hp (DIN) @ 6000 rpm (205 hp SAE)	185 hp (DIN) @ 6000 rpm (205 hp SAE)
Compression ratio	9:1	9:1
Torque	24.3 mkg @ 4500 rpm (175.8 ft/lb)	24.3 mkg @ 4500 rpm (175.8 ft/lb)
Fuel injection	Bosch electronic	Bosch electronic
Engine speed at 100 km/hr	3140 rpm	3140 rpm
Gear ratios	I. 3.90:1 II. 2.30:1 III. 1.41:1 IV. 1.00:1	I. 3.90:1 optional I. 3.96:1 II. 2.30:1 II. 2.34:1 III. 1.41:1 III. 1.43:1 IV. 1.00:1 IV. 1.00:1 V. 0.87:1
Rear axle ratio	3.69	3.69 (for 5-speed 3.82)
Chassis	unit frame and body	unit frame and body
Suspension	independent front and rear, with coil springs, diagonal-pivot swing axle, anti-sway bars	independent front and rear, with coil springs, diagonal-pivot swing axle, anti-sway bars
Brakes and area	disc, power assisted, 273/279mm (10.8/11.0 in)	disc, power assisted, 273/279mm (10.8/11.0 in)
Wheelbase	2750mm (108.3 in)	2750mm (108.3 in)
Track, front/rear	1444/1440mm (56.9/56.7 in)	1444/1440mm (56.9/56.7 in)
Length	4680mm (184.3 in)	4680mm (184.5 in)
Width	1770mm (69.7 in)	1770mm (69.7 in)
Height	1440mm (56.7 in)	1395mm (54.9 in)
Ground clearance	175mm (6.9 in)	175mm (6.9 in)
Tires	185 HR 14	185 HR 14
Turning circle	11.7 meters (38.4 ft)	11.7 meters (38.4 ft)
Steering type and ratio	recirculating ball (4.0 turns), servo assisted	recirculating ball (4.0 turns), servo assisted
Weight	1455 kg (3200 lbs)	1455 kg (3200 lbs)
Maximum speed	200 km/hr (124 mph)	200 km/hr (124 mph)
Acceleration	12 sec 0-100 km/hr	12 sec 0-100 km/hr
Fuel consumption	12.5 liters, super/100 km (18.75 mpg)	12.5 liters, super/100km (18.75 mpg)
Fuel tank capacity	65 liters (17.2 gallons)	65 liters (17.2 gallons)

The 280C coupe, 1974

Prices and Production

The 280C coupe sold in 1972 for . . . . .DM 21,425
in 1973 for. . . . . .DM 22,480
in 1974 for. . . . . .DM 24,500
in 1975 for. . . . . .DM 26,555
Power steering . . . . .DM   515
Automatic transmission . . . . .DM 1,440
In the United States the 280C coupe sold
in September 1972 for (East coast). . . . .$ 9,518
(West coast) . . . .$ 9,618
in November 1973 (East coast) . . . .$ 11,630
in September 1974 (East coast) . . . .$ 13,063
in October 1975 (East coast) . . . .$ 14,639

Production of the 280C coupe [114 V28] (from December 1971/
June 1972 until August 1976)

	was in		
	1971	1	unit
	1972	2,124	units
	1973	4,196	units
	1974	3,734	units
	1975	2,133	units
	1976	963	units
	total	13,151	units

Model 280C (1971-1976)

C = Coupe

The 280C coupe appeared on the scene in early 1972. It had been originated in the late period of the previous year, along with the sedan line, and one car was actually produced in December 1971. The new double overhead camshaft six-cylinder engine, equipped with the Solex dual compound downdraft carburetor, was fitted into the coupe body of the 250C model. Specifications, except for the new engine installation, were the same as those of the previous model, which remained in production, but minor alterations, such as simpler bumpers, and improved side mirror, were made.

The new regulation bumpers on the United States models were quite controversial, according to some designers. The huge, bulky rubber ends forming around the sides, front and back, were considered very ugly indeed by many experts, or design-conscious critics. It was urgently hoped that they were merely a temporary solution to the problem of compliance to stricter federal regulations, which were not always stated in precise terms and often changed quite rapidly. (Yet, on one of our visits to Germany, we found two owners of Mercedes cars who wanted to get them for their models.)

The 280C was a heavier coupe than the previous one and with the newer double overhead camshaft six-cylinder engine was a superior performing car than the older version, that is in the European trim. The U.S. version was not superior, for the engine was tuned down to develop only 120 horsepower instead of the 160 elsewhere. The same process was applied to the torque — higher in Europe, but lower in this country — which made the new coupe a rather less briskly performing, but still a pleasant car, to drive.

During the last three years of production the 280C outsold the 250C with the 2.8-liter engine by a wide margin (6,830 to 1,021), which only proved the decision a correct one.

Specifications

	280C (coupe)
Engine type	6 cyl double overhead camshafts (M 110)
Bore and stroke	86 x 78.8mm (3.41 x 3.10 in)
Displacement	2746 cc (168 cu in)
Power output	160 hp (DIN) @ 5500 rpm (180 hp SAE) later, U.S.: 120 hp SAE @ 4800 rpm; 1975 California: 123 hp SAE @ 5000 rpm
Compression ratio	9:1 (U.S.: 8:1)
Torque	23 mkg @ 4000 rom (166.4 ft/lb) later, U.S.: 15.5 mkg @ 2800 rpm (120 ft/lb); 1975: 143 ft/lb @ 2800 rpm California: 143 ft/lb @ 3600 rpm
Carburetion	dual downdraft carburetors Solex 4 A 1
Engine speed at 100 km/hr	3140 rpm
Gear ratios	I. 3.90:1 optional I. 3.96:1 II. 2.30:1 II. 2.34:1 III. 1.41:1 III. 1.43:1 IV. 1.00:1 IV. 1.00:1 V. 0.87:1
Rear axle ratio	3.69 (for 5-speed 3.92)
Chassis	unit frame and body
Suspension	independent front and rear, with coil springs, diagonal-pivot swing axle, anti-sway bars
Brakes and area	disc, power assisted, 273/279mm (10.8/11.0 in)
Wheelbase	2750mm (108.3 in)
Track, front/rear	1444/1440mm (56.9/56.7 in)
Length	4680mm (184.5 in)
Width	1770mm (69.7 in)
Height	1395mm (54.9 in)
Ground clearance	175mm (6.9 in)
Tires	185 HR 14
Turning circle	11.7 meters (38.4 ft)
Steering type and ratio	recirculating ball (4.0 turns), servo assisted
Weight	1455 kg (3200 lbs)
Maximum speed	190 km/hr (118 mph)
Acceleration	13 sec 0-100 km/hr
Fuel consumption	12.5 liters, super/100 km (18.75 mpg) (U.S.: no lead fuel)
Fuel tank capacity	65 liters (17.2 gallons)

The 280C coupe, 1974

The 280C coupe, 1974, U.S. version

The 280SE 4.5 sedan, 1971, U.S. version

Prices and Production

In the United Stated the 280SE 4.5 sedan sold
in September 1972 for (East coast)..............$ 10,283
  (West coast) ....$ 10,393

Production of the 280SE 4.5 model [108 E45] (from April/May
1971 until November 1972)

	was in 1971	5,782 units
	1972	7,745 units
	total	13,527 units

Prices and Production

In the United States the 280SEL 4.5 sedan sold
in September 1972 for (East coast)..............$ 10,875
  (West coast) ....$ 10,985

Production of the 280SEL 4.5 model [108 E45] (from May 1971
until November 1972)

	was in 1971	1,871 units
	1972	6,302 units
	total	8,173 units

Model 280SE 4.5 (1971-1972)

S = Super, E (Einspritzung) = fuel injection

The 280SE 4.5 sedan made its first appearance in early 1971, just a few months after the new 4.5-liter V-8 engine had made its debut. In fact, that model was available to the purchaser at about the same time the 3.5-liter engined sedan was produced, and gave the buyer another option in power for his car. It was, however, not the choice of as many buyers as was the 3.5-liter engined sedan the first year of production when nearly 6,000 units were sold, but the following year it outsold the smaller-engined version by a margin of two to one.

Inside and out, the two sedans were alike, with the more powerful one having, of course, better performance. Acceleration was slightly faster and the maximum speed was five miles better, but fuel consumption was 1.5 liters more for the 4.5- than for the 3.5-liter engined sedan.

The 280SE 4.5 sedan fitted into the policy of offering the customer the widest possible range in passenger automobiles. The U.S. customers were nearly the only ones who were offered this and the following two 4.5-liter engined cars, while others were able to buy and wisely preferred the 3.5-liter versions, not hampered by restrictive emission controls. (A total of 23,488 cars of the 280SE 4.5, the 280SEL 4.5, and the 300SEL 4.5 were sold in the U.S.)

Model 280SEL 4.5 (1971-1972)

SE L (Lang) = long wheelbase chassis

The 280SEL 4.5 sedan was produced at about the same time (in 1971) the regular length sedan was available. Again, this longer wheelbase car was identical to the other model, and the extra ten centimeters gave the rear-seat passengers additional space to stretch their legs. On longer journeys this was especially appreciated.

This 4.5-liter engined long sedan outsold the 3.5-liter version by about three to one during the first year of its availability and the following year this more powerful version was the choice of over 6,000 customers while only about 500 bought the less powerful car. Apparently the extra fuel consumption was of no serious concern to the buyers of the 4.5-liter long sedan.

Specifications

	280SE 4.5	280SEL 4.5
Engine type	V-8 cyl overhead camshafts (M 117)	V-8 cyl overhead camshafts (M 117)
Bore and stroke	92 x 85mm (3.62 x 3.35 in)	92 x 85mm (3.62 x 3.35 in)
Displacement	4520 cc (275.8 cu in)	4520 cc (275.8 cu in)
Power output	225 hp (DIN) @ 5000 rpm (250 hp SAE) U.S.: 230 hp SAE @ 5000 rpm	225 hp (DIN) @ 5000 rpm (250 hp SAE) U.S.: 230 hp SAE @ 5000 rpm
Compression ratio	8.8:1 U.S.: 8:1	8.8:1 U.S.: 8:1
Torque	38.5 mkg @ 3000 rpm (278.5 ft/lb)	38.5 mkg @ 3000 rpm (278.5 ft/lb)
Fuel injection	Bosch electronic	Bosch electronic
Engine speed at 100 km/hr	2865 rpm U.S.: 2740 rpm	2865 rpm U.S.: 2740 rpm
Gear ratios	I. 3.98:1 U.S. automatic I. 2.31:1 II. 2.39:1 II. 1.46:1 III. 1.46:1 III. 1.00:1 IV. 1.00:1	I. 3.98:1 U.S. automatic I. 2.31:1 II. 2.39:1 II. 1.46:1 III. 1.46:1 III. 1.00:1 IV. 1.00:1
Rear axle ratio	3.69 U.S.: 3.23	3.69 U.S.: 3.23
Chassis	unit frame and body	unit frame and body
Suspension	independent front and rear, with coil springs, single joint swing axle, anti-sway bars	independent front and rear, with coil springs, single joint swing axle, anti-sway bars
Brakes and area	disc, front and rear vented, servo assisted, two circuit hydraulic, 273/279mm (10.8/11.0 in)	disc, front and rear vented, servo assisted, two circuit hydraulic, 273/279mm (10.8/11.0 in)
Wheelbase	2750mm (108.3 in)	2850mm (112.2 in)
Track, front/rear	1482/1490mm (58.4/58.7 in)	1482/1490mm (58.4/58.7 in)
Length	4900mm (192.9 in)	5000mm (196.9 in)
Width	1810mm (71.3 in)	1810mm (71.3 in)
Height	1440mm (56.7 in)	1440mm (56.7 in)
Ground clearance	175mm (6.9 in)	175mm (6.9 in)
Tires	735 H 14 or 185 H 14	735 H 14 or 185 H 14
Turning circle	11.7 meters (38.4 ft)	12.2 meters (40 ft)
Steering type and ratio	recirculating ball (4.0 turns), servo assisted	recirculating ball (4.0 turns), servo assisted
Weight	1737 kg (3821 lbs)	1737 kg (3821 lbs)
Maximum speed	205 km/hr (127 mph) U.S.: 190 km/hr (118 mph)	205 km/hr (127 mph) U.S.: 190 km/hr (118 mph)
Acceleration	9.5 sec 0-100 km/hr U.S.: 12 sec 0-100 km/hr	9.5 sec 0-100 km/hr U.S.: 12 sec 0-100 km/hr
Fuel consumption	14.5 liters, super/100 km (16 mpg)	14.5 liters, super/100 km (16 mpg)
Fuel tank capacity	82 liters (21.7 gallons)	82 liters (21.7 gallons)

113

The 300SEL 4.5 sedan, 1973, U.S. version

Prices and Production

In the United States the 300SEL 4.5 sedan sold
in September 1972 for (East coast)............$ 14,130
(West coast) ....$ 14,240

Production of the 300SEL 4.5 model [109 E45] (from May 1971
until October 1972)

was in	1971	656 units
	1972	1,897 units
	total	2,553 units

The interior of the 300SEL 4.5, 1971

Model 300SEL 4.5 (1971-1972)

SE L (Lang) = long wheelbase chassis

The 300SEL 4.5 model sedan was produced at the same time the 280SE/SEL models, first in May 1971. It was natural that the larger and more powerful V-8 engine would be placed into the more luxurious of the longer wheelbase sedans, so as to allow this rather formal model to remain the very best of the top line. The sedan was greatly preferred as an official and generally chauffeur-driven automobile, whenever the prestigious 600 limousine was not desired.

This luxury sedan proved to be a superb fast touring car, offering the greatest comfort possible, and with its elegant interior appointment keeping up the best Mercedes tradition of superior automobiles. While the actual performance data compared with the 280SEL 4.5 model was identical, the owner of the 300SEL 4.5 sedan experienced the feeling of driving a car with truly unsurpassed roadability, the very best available model in every respect.

The 300SEL 4.5 sedan never achieved the popularity of the 280SEL 4.5 model, of course, but sales for the first year were over 600 units, while in 1972 nearly 2,000 such cars were sold. Total sales of the 300SEL 4.5 were 2,553 units and of the 280SEL 4.5 were 8,173 units during the two years of their production life.

The rather appreciative difference in price over the slightly lesser 280SEL 4.5 model contributed undoubtedly to the smaller sales of this car, yet enough buyers supported the stated Daimler-Benz policy of supplying the widest possible selection of car models to the broadest range of prospective purchasers.

Specifications

	300SEL 4.5
Engine type	V-8 cyl overhead camshafts (M 117)
Bore and stroke	92 x 85mm (3.62 x 3.35 in)
Displacement	4520 cc (275.8 cu in)
Power output	225 hp (DIN) @ 5000 rpm (250 hp SAE) U.S.: 230 hp SAE @ 5000 rpm
Compression ratio	8.8:1 U.S.: 8:1
Torque	38.5 mkg @ 3000 rpm (278.5 ft/lb)
Fuel injection	Bosch electronic
Engine speed at 100 km/hr	2865 rpm U.S.: 2740 rpm
Gear ratios	I. 3.98:1 U.S. automatic I. 2.31:1 II. 2.39:1 II. 1.46:1 III. 1.46:1 III. 1.00:1 IV. 1.00:1
Rear axle ratio	3.69 U.S.: 3.23
Chassis	unit frame and body
Suspension	independent front and rear, with coil springs, single joint swing axle, anti-sway bars
Brakes and area	disc, front vented, rear solid, servo assisted, two circuit hydraulic, 273/279mm (10.8/11.0 in)
Wheelbase	2850mm (112.2 in)
Track, front/rear	1482/1490mm (58.4/58.7 in)
Length	5000mm (196.9 in)
Width	1800mm (71.3 in)
Height	1440mm (56.7 in)
Ground clearance	175mm (6.9 in)
Tires	735 H 14 or 185 H 14
Turning circle	12.2 meters (40 ft)
Steering type and ratio	recirculating ball (4.0 turns), servo assisted
Weight	1854 kg (4079 lbs)
Maximum speed	205 km/hr (127 mph) U.S.: 190 km/hr (118 mph)
Acceleration	9.5 sec 0-100 km/hr U.S.: 12 sec 0-100 km/hr
Fuel consumption	14.5 liters, super/100 km (16 mpg)
Fuel tank capacity	82 liters (21.7 gallons)

The instrument panel of the 300SEL 4.5, 1971

The M 117 engine for the 300SEL 4.5, 1971

The 450SL roadster, 1975, U.S. version

# Model 450SL (1971-1980)
S = Sports, L (Leicht) = light

The 450SL model was shown to the public at the Geneva Auto Show in 1973 but had been produced for the United States market earlier, in 1971. It was a more powerful car than the 3.5-liter version and retained all of the fine attributes of this new model sports car.

The U.S. version of the 450SL (outwardly identifiable by the different headlight arrangement only), had a lowered compression ratio to 8:1 and milder camshafts. The car was equipped with heavier bumpers and was fitted with the new three-speed automatic transmission only. Rear axle ratio was changed to 3.07 and the maximum speed was 124 miles per hour. The 4.5-liter engine actually developed less horsepower than the original 3.5-liter unit, but that was the price to pay for the more stringent emission controls prevailing here. The car weighed 148 pounds more than the European version and had, of course, not the performance of that more powerful and lighter car.

The difference in horsepower output by the same basic engine would become even more pronounced in the coming years, and there was certainly no similarity in the same models when driving a European version over there and then driving that model in this country.

Prices and Production

The 450SL model sold in 1973 for . . . . .DM 36,630
    in 1974 for. . . . . .DM 38,300
    in 1975 for. . . . . .DM 42,215
    in 1977 for . . . . .DM 43,856
In the United States the 450SL coupe/roadster sold
    in September 1972 (East coast) for $11,688
    (West coast). $11,800
    in March 1973 (East coast) $12,733
    in November 1973 (East coast). $15,450
    in September 1974 (with automatic transmission)
    (East coast). $17,056
    in October 1975 (with automatic transmission)
    (East coast). $19,357
    in March 1977 (East coast) $21,943
    in February 1979 (East coast) $30,729

Production of the 450SL model [107 E45] (from March/July 1971 until November 1980)

was in	1971	2,131 units
	1972	7,473 units
	1973	8,654 units
	1974	6,093 units
	1975	6,011 units
	1976	6,625 units
	1977	8,110 units
	1978	7,434 units
	1979	8,184 units
	1980	5,583 units
	total	66,298 units

The 450SL roadster, 1977, U.S. version

Specifications

	450SL
Engine type	V-8 cyl overhead camshaft (M 117)
Bore and stroke	92 x 85mm (3.62 x 3.35 in)
Displacement	4520 cc (275.8 cu in)
Power output	225 hp (DIN) @ 5000 rpm (250 hp SAE); U.S.: 230 hp SAE @ 5000 rpm (200 hp DIN); later, 190 hp SAE @ 4750 rpm; 1975 California: 180 hp SAE; 1977: 217 hp (DIN); 1979: 218 hp (DIN) U.S. 1977: 180 hp (SAE) @ 4750 rpm; 1980: 160 hp (SAE) @ 4200 rpm
Compression ratio	8.8:1 U.S.: 8:1
Torque	38.5 mkg @ 3000 rpm (278.5 ft/lb); U.S.: 33.0 mkg @ 3000 rpm (238.8 ft/lb); 1975 California: 232 ft/lb U.S. 1977: 32.25 mkg @ 3000 rpm (220 ft/lb); 1980: 31.9 mkg @ 2500 rpm (230 ft/lb)
Fuel injection	Bosch electronic
Engine speed at 100 km/hr	2865 rpm U.S.: 2700 rpm
Gear ratios	I. 3.98:1 U.S. automatic I. 2.31:1 II. 2.39:1 II. 1.46:1 III. 1.46:1 III. 1.00:1 IV. 1.00:1
Rear axle ratio	3.07 U.S. 1979: 3.06; 1980: 2.65
Chassis	unit frame and body
Suspension	independent front and rear, double wishbones, diagonal-pivot swing axle
Brakes and area	disc, front vented, rear solid, 278/279mm (10.9/11.0 in)
Wheelbase	2460mm (96.9 in) 1979: 2455mm (96.6 in)
Track, front/rear	1452/1440mm (57.2/56.7 in)
Length	4380mm (172.4 in) U.S.: 182.3 in (4630mm)
Width	1790mm (70.5 in)
Height	1300mm (51.2 in)
Ground clearance	140mm (5.5 in)
Tires	205/70 VR 14
Turning circle	10.2 meters (33.5 ft); later 10.34 meters (33.9 feet); U.S.: 10.48 meters (34.4 ft)
Steering type and ratio	recirculating ball (3.0 turns); servo assisted 15.9:1
Weight	1585 kg (3487 lbs); U.S.: 1718 kg (3780 lbs); 1977: 1730 kg (3815 lbs); 1979: 1695 kg (3740 lbs); 1980: 1700 kg (3750 lbs)
Maximum speed	215 km/hr (133.5 mph); 1977: 210 km/hr; U.S.: 200 km/hr (124 mph)
Acceleration	8.5 sec 0-100 km/hr; 1979: 9.3 sec 0-100 km/hr; U.S.: 11 sec 0-100 km/hr
Fuel consumption	14.5 liters, super/100 km (16 mpg) (U.S.: no lead fuel); 1979: at 120 km/hr, 15.8 liters (15 mpg)
Fuel tank capacity	90 liters (23.8 gallons)

The 450SL roadster, 1974

The 450SLC coupe, 1973

Prices and Production

The 450SLC model sold in 1973 for . . . . .DM 41,015
in 1974 for . . . . .DM 42,860
in 1975 for . . . . .DM 47,265
In 1977 for . . . . .DM 49,406
In the United States the 450SLC coupe sold
in September 1972 (East coast) for $15,094
(West coast). $15,194
in March 1973 (East coast). $16,498
in November 1973 (East coast) $19,450
in September 1974 (with automatic transmission)
(East coast). $21,307
in October 1975 (with automatic transmission)
(East coast). $23,976
in March 1977 (East coast). $27,090
in February 1979 (East coast). $36,519

Production of the 450SLC coupe model [107 E45] (from February/
July 1972 until October 1980)

was in	1972	700 units
	1973	5,594 units
	1974	2,961 units
	1975	2,993 units
	1976	3,802 units
	1977	4,569 units
	1978	4,382 units
	1979	4,510 units
	1980	2,228 units
	total	31,739 units

Model 450SLC (1972-1980)

S = Sports, L = Light, C = Coupe

The 450SLC model was also shown at the Geneva Show in 1973. Here again, the European version of that coupe was quite differently powered than that for sale in the United States. The restrictions placed on emission and safety added weight and lessened performance because of less horsepower developed. The 4.5-liter engine actually developed 225 DIN horsepower, while the U.S. version developed 230 SAE horsepower. Considering that the German (DIN) designation means the net horsepower available and the SAE (American) horsepower is the gross measurement, one can readily see that the heavier car with less power suffered greatly in comparison.

Outwardly there was no difference in the 350SLC or the 450SLC cars. Unlike the SL model, the coupe never was designated as the 350 4.5.

The 450SL and 450SLC on the test track, 1976

Specifications

	450SLC
Engine type	V-8 cyl overhead camshafts (M 117)
Bore and stroke	92 x 85mm (3.62 x 3.35 in)
Displacement	4520 cc (275.8 cu in)
Power output	225 hp (DIN) @ 5000 rpm (250 hp SAE); 1977: 217 hp (DIN); 1979: 218 hp (DIN) U.S.: 230 hp SAE @ 5000 rpm U.S. 1977: 180 hp SAE @ 4750 rpm; 1980: 160 hp SAE @ 4200 rpm later, 190 hp SAE @ 4750 rpm; 1975 California: 180 hp SAE
Compression ratio	8.8:1 U.S. 8:1
Torque	38.5 mkg @ 3000 rpm (278.5 ft/lb); U.S. 1977: 32.25 mkg @ 3000 rpm (220 ft/lb); 1980: 31.9 mkg @ 2500 rpm (230 ft/lb) U.S.: 33.0 mkg @ 3000 rpm (238.8 ft/lb); 1975 California: 232 ft/lb
Fuel injection	Bosch electronic
Engine speed at 100 km/hr	2865 rpm U.S.: 2700 rpm
Gear ratios	I. 3.98:1 U.S. automatic I. 2.31:1 II. 2.39:1 II. 1.46:1 III. 1.46:1 III. 1.00:1 IV. 1.00:1
Rear axle ratio	3.07 U.S. 1979: 3.06; 1980: 2.65
Chassis	unit frame and body
Suspension	independent front and rear, double wishbones, diagonal-pivot swing axle
Brakes and area	disc, front vented, rear solid, 278/279mm (10.9/11.0 in)
Wheelbase	2815mm (110.8 in)
Track, front/rear	1452/1440mm (57.2/56.7 in)
Length	4740mm (186.6 in); 1979: 4750mm (187 in) U.S.: 196.4 in (4990mm)
Width	1790mm (70.5 in)
Height	1330mm (51.2 in)
Ground clearance	140mm (5.5 in)
Tires	205/70 VR 14
Turning circle	11.2 meters (36.7 ft); later 11.55 meters (36.9 feet); U.S.: 11.68 meters (38.3 feet)
Steering type and ratio	recirculating ball (3.0 turns); servo assisted 15.9:1
Weight	1635 kg (3597 lbs) U.S.: 1735 kg (3817 lbs); 1977: 1750 kg (3860 lbs); 1979: 1720 kg (3795 lbs); 1980: 1700 kg (3750 lbs)
Maximum speed	215 km/hr (133.5 mph); 1979: 210 km/hr U.S.: 200 km/hr (124 mph)
Acceleration	8.5 sec 0-100 km/hr U.S.: 11 sec 0-100 km/hr
Fuel consumption	14.5 liters, super/100 km (16 mpg) (U.S. no lead fuel); 1979: at 120 km/hr, 15.8 liters (15 mpg)
Fuel tank capacity	90 liters (23.8 gallons)

The 450SLC coupe, 1977, U.S. version

The 280S sedan, 1972

Prices and Production

The 280S four-door sedan sold in 1972 for . . . . .DM 23,810
  in 1973 for . . . . .DM 25,030
  in 1974 for . . . . .DM 26,165
  in 1975 for . . . . .DM 28,050
  in 1977 for . . . . .DM 30,158
In the United States the 280S sedan sold
  in September 1974 (fully equipped) for
  (East coast) $14,548
  (West coast) $14,698
  in October 1975 (East coast) $16,545

Production of the 280S model [116 V28] from August/September
1972 until July 1980)

was in	1972	3,787 units
	1973	15,340 units
	1974	20,808 units
	1975	21,996 units
	1976	18,031 units
	1977	17,080 units
	1978	15,307 units
	1979	9,208 units
	1980	1,291 units
	total	122,848 units

Model 280S (1972-1980)

S = Super

The 280S model, one of the newly designed cars of the S-class, was first shown at the Paris Automobile Salon in 1972. It was the least expensive representative of the almost completely restyled new line of the large six- and eight-cylinder models which shared the same basic chassis and body.

The car appeared slightly wider, lower, and longer than the previous ones. The radiator shell was longer and wider and the front light section was integrated into a wide unit curving around to the side. The rear light cluster was also redesigned in the manner of the sports models, with the dirt-repelling feature. Many new safety features had been incorporated into the design.

The modified chassis had the new suspension system of the SL and SLC models which had proved superior to the former design.

The double overhead camshaft six-cylinder engine developed 160 DIN horsepower, but for the United States a detuned version of 120 SAE horsepower was supplied, with lowered compression ratio, for improved emission. It had a torque converter four-speed automatic transmission. That car also weighed 350 pounds more than the European model, and had consequently less performance. Still, the maximum speed was 170 kilometers (105 miles) per hour.

The 280S sedan, 1974

Specifications

	280S
Engine type	6 cyl double overhead camshafts (M110)
Bore and stroke	86 x 78.8mm (3.41 x 3.10 in)
Displacement	2746 cc (168 cu in)
Power output	160 hp (DIN) @ 5500 rpm (180 hp SAE); 1977: 156 hp (DIN) U. S.: 120 hp SAE @ 4800 rpm; 1975 California: 123 hp SAE @ 5000 rpm
Compression ratio	9:1 U.S. 8:1
Torque	23 mkg @ 4000 rpm (166.4 ft/lb) U.S.: 15.5 mkg @ 2800 rpm (112.1 ft/lb) 1975: 143 ft/lb @ 2800 rpm; California: 143 @ 3600 rpm
Carburetion	dual downdraft carburetor Solex 4 A 1
Engine speed at 100 km/hr	3140 rpm by 1976: 3355 rpm
Gear ratios	I. 3.98:1 (14.69) 1976: I. 3.90:1 automatic (optional): I. 3.98:1 II. 2.39:1 (8.82) II. 2.30:1 II. 2.39:1 III. 1.46:1 (5.39) III. 1.41:1 III. 1.46:1 IV. 1.00:1 (3.69) IV. 1.00:1 IV. 1.00:1
Rear axle ratio	3.69
Chassis	unit frame and body
Suspension	independent front and rear, double wishbones, diagonal-pivot swing axle
Brakes and area	disc, front vented, rear solid, 278/279mm (10.9/11.0)
Wheelbase	2865mm (112.8 in)
Track, front/rear	1525/1505mm (60.0/59.3 in)
Length	4960mm (195.3 in)
Width	1865mm (73.4 in)
Height	1425mm (56.1 in)
Ground clearance	150mm (5.9 in)
Tires	185 HR 14
Turning circle	11.4 meters (37.4 ft)
Steering type and ratio	recirculating ball (2.7 turns); servo assisted 15.6:1
Weight	1610 kg (3542 lbs) U.S.: 3890 lbs
Maximum speed	190 km/hr (118 mph) U.S.: 170 km/hr (105.5 mph); 185 km/hr (115 mph)
Acceleration	13.5 sec 0-100 km/hr; (U.S.: no lead fuel)
Fuel consumption	12.5 liters/100 km (18.75 mpg) (U.S.: no lead fuel)
Fuel tank capacity	96 liters (25.4 gallons)

Front view of the 280S sedan, 1975, U.S. version

121

The 280SE sedan, 1972

Prices and Production

The 280SE four-door sedan sold in 1972 for . . . . .DM 25,530
    in 1973 for . . . . .DM 26,810
    in 1974 for . . . . .DM 28,020
    in 1975 for . . . . .DM 30,900
    in 1977 for . . . . .DM 32,289
In the United States the 280SE sedan sold
    in March 1977 (East coast) for $19,411
    in February 1979 (East coast). $26,177

Production of the 280SE model [116 E28] (from August/
September 1972 until July 1980)

was in	1972	3,737 units
	1973	18,266 units
	1974	18,634 units
	1975	17,376 units
	1976	17,968 units
	1977	26,903 units
	1978	23,571 units
	1979	22,568 units
	1980	1,572 units
	total	150,595 units

Model 280SE (1972-1980)

S = Super, E (Einspritzung) = fuel injection

The 280SE model, also introduced at the Paris Salon in 1972, was the fuel-injected version of the six-cylinder sedan of the newly designed S-class of passenger cars. It had the same dimensions as the carburetor model and shared the body and chassis with the more powerful eight-cylinder cars.

The new model weighed 124 kilograms (273 pounds) more than the former 280SE model which it replaced, but with the double overhead camshaft engine of 185 DIN horsepower, against the 160 formerly, the performance was actually superior to the older model.

For the United States market in 1977 the car got a detuned engine of 142 SAE horsepower (137 in California) and consequently much lower torque. Horsepower and torque were also lowered in the European version. But the performance of this fine, fast six-cylinder touring sedan was still quite good, and in subsequent years the sedan was actually made lighter by 50 kilograms.

The 280SE sedan, 1978

Specifications

	280SE
Engine type	6 cyl double overhead camshafts (M 110)
Bore and stroke	86 x 78.8mm (3.41 x 3.10 in)
Displacement	2746 cc (168 cu in)
Power output	185 hp (DIN) @ 6000 rpm (205 hp SAE); 1977: 177 hp (DIN) U.S. 1977: 142 hp SAE @ 5750 rpm; 1980: 140 hp SAE @ 5500 rpm; California: 137 hp @ 5750 rpm
Compression ratio	9:1 U.S. 1977: 8:1
Torque	24.5 mkg @ 4500 rpm (175.8 ft/lb); U.S. 1977: 21.4 mkg @ 4600 rpm (149 ft/lb); California: 20.5 mkg @ 4600 rpm (142 ft/lb)
Fuel injection	Bosch electronic
Engine speed at 100 km/hr	3140 rpm; by 1976 (automatic optional): 3375 rpm
Gear ratios	I. 3.98:1 (14.69) 1976: I. 3.90:1 I. 3.98:1 automatic (optional) II. 2.39:1 (8.82) II. 2.30:1 II. 2.31:1 III. 1.46:1 (5.39) III. 1.41:1 III. 1.46:1 IV. 1.00:1 (3.69) IV. 1.00:1 IV. 1.00:1
Rear axle ratio	3.69 U.S. 1978: 3.58
Chassis	unit frame and body
Suspension	independent front and rear, double wishbones, diagonal-pivot swing axle
Brakes and area	disc, front vented, rear solid, 278/279mm (10.9/11.0 in)
Wheelbase	2865mm (112.8 in)
Track, front/rear	1525/1505mm (60.0/59.3 in) U.S. 1977 front: 1521mm (59.9 in)
Length	4960mm (195.3 in) U.S. 1977: 5220mm (205.5 in)
Width	1865mm (73.4 in) 1976: 1870mm (73.6 in)
Height	1425mm (56.1 in)
Ground clearance	150mm (5.9 in)
Tires	185 HR 14
Turning circle	11.4 meters (37.4 ft) U.S. 1979: 11.59 meters (38 ft)
Steering type and ratio	recirculating ball (2.7 turns); servo assisted 15.6:1 U.S. 1978: 3.2 turns
Weight	1610 kg (3542 lbs); U.S. 1977: 1770 kg (3905 lbs); 1978: 1615 kg (3560 lbs); 1979: 1730 kg (3820 lbs); 1980: 1720 kg (3795 lbs)
Maximum speed	200 km/hr (124 mph) automatic: 195 km/hr (121 mph)
Acceleration	12.5 sec 0-100 km/hr
Fuel consumption	12.5 liters/100 km (18.75 mpg)
Fuel tank capacity	96 liters (25.4 gallons)

The 280SE sedan, 1978, U.S. version

The 350SE sedan, 1972

Prices and Production

The 350SE four-door sedan sold in 1972 for . . . . .DM 28,860
  in 1973 for . . . . .DM 30,260
  in 1974 for . . . . .DM 31,615
  in 1975 for . . . . .DM 34,860
  in 1977 for . . . . .DM 36,430

Production of the 350SE model [116 E35] (from March/August 1972 until September 1980)

was in	1972	4,353 units
	1973	14,340 units
	1974	7,266 units
	1975	5,447 units
	1976	4,734 units
	1977	5,723 units
	1978	4,964 units
	1979	4,099 units
	1980	214 units
	total	51,140 units

The 350SEL four-door sedan sold in 1973 for . . . . . . .DM 34,865
  in 1974 for . . . . .DM 36,415
  in 1975 for . . . . .DM 40,160
  in 1977 for . . . . .DM 38,550

Production of the 350SEL model [116 E35] (from September/November 1973 until June 1980)

was in	1973	58 units
	1974	529 units
	1975	552 units
	1976	718 units
	1977	807 units
	1978	911 units
	1979	653 units
	1980	38 units
	total	4,266 units

Model 350SE (1972-1980)

S = Super, E (Einspritzung) = fuel injection

The 350SE was the third of the newly designed cars of the S-class which made their debut at the Paris Auto Show in 1972. It was the eight-cylinder edition of this new body style automobile. With the 3.5-liter displacement engine of 200 DIN horsepower and a weight of 1,675 kilograms (3,685 pounds), the car achieved a maximum speed of 205 kilometers (127 miles) per hour and accelerated to 100 kilometers in 11.5 seconds, a fine performance figure. (Torque was rated at 32 mkg or 321 ft/lb. at 4,200 rpm.)

That these newly styled and improved cars were well accepted by the automobile-buying public is indicated by the production figures. For 1972 it was about 4,000 units (of each of the three new models) and for the first full year of manufacture it reached nearly 15,000 units.

Model 350SEL (1973-1980)

SE L (Lang) = long wheelbase chassis

The 350SEL was the other of the two new models shown first to the public at the Geneva Auto Show in 1974. It was, if anything, a more luxurious version of the other longer wheelbase sedan exhibited at the Salon. With the 3.5-liter eight-cylinder engine, identical to that of the 350SE model, developing 200 (DIN) horsepower, it had a slightly better maximum speed (205 kilometers per hour) than that of the six-cylinder 280SEL model.

With other models of the S-class, the new 350SEL sedan shared all of the newest safety and technical features of this top line of cars.

The 350SEL sedan, 1974

Specifications

	350SE	350SEL
Engine type	V-8 cyl overhead camshafts (M 116)	V-8 cyl overhead camshafts (M 116)
Bore and stroke	92 x 65.8mm (3.62 x 2.59 in)	92 x 65.8mm (3.62 x 2.59 in)
Displacement	3499 cc (213.5 cu in)	3499 cc (213.5 cu in)
Power output	200 hp (DIN) @ 5800 rpm (230 hp SAE @ 6050 rpm);1977: 195 hp (DIN)	200 hp (DIN) @ 5800 rpm (230 hp SAE @ 6050 rpm); 1977: 195 hp (DIN)
Compression ratio	9.5:1	9.5:1
Torque	29.2 mkg @ 4000 rpm (32 mkg @ 4200 rpm 231.5 ft/lb)	29.2 mkg @ 4000 rpm (32 mkg @ 4200 rpm 231.5 ft/lb)
Fuel injection	Bosch electronic	Bosch electronic
Engine speed at 100 km/hr	2945 rpm; by 1976 (automatic optional): 3295 rpm	2945 rpm; by 1976 (automatic optional): 3295 rpm
Gear ratios	I. 3.90:1 1976: I. 3.96:1 I. 2.31:1 automatic (optional) II. 2.30:1 II. 2.34:1 II. 1.46:1 III. 1.41:1 III. 1.43:1 III. 1.00:1 IV. 1.00:1 IV. 1.00:1	I. 3.90:1 1976: I. 2.31:1 automatic II. 2.30:1 II. 1.46:1 III. 1.41:1 III. 1.00:1 IV. 1.00:1
Rear axle ratio	3.46	3.46
Chassis	unit frame and body	unit frame and body
Suspension	independent front and rear, double wishbones, diagonal-pivot swing axle	independent front and rear, double wishbones, diagonal-pivot swing axle, anti-sway bars
Brakes and area	disc, front vented, rear solid, 278/279mm (10.9/11.0 in)	disc, power assisted, two circuit hydraulic, 278/279mm (10.9/11.0 in)
Wheelbase	2865mm (112.8 in)	2965mm (116.7 in)
Track, front/rear	1525/1505mm (60.0/59.3 in)	1525/1505mm (60/59.3 in)
Length	4960mm (195.3 in)	5060mm (199.2 in)
Width	1865mm (73.4 in)	1865mm (73.4 in)
Height	1425mm (56.1 in)	1430mm (56.3 in)
Ground clearance	150mm (5.9 in)	147mm (5.8 in)
Tires	205/70 HR 14	205/70 HR 14
Turning circle	11.4 meters (37.4 ft)	11.9 meters (39 ft)
Steering type and ratio	recirculating ball (2.7 turns); servo assisted 15.6:1	recirculating ball (3.0 turns), servo assisted
Weight	1675 kg (3685 lbs)	1700 kg (3740 lbs)
Maximum speed	205 km/hr (127 mph); 1977: 200 km/hr (124 mph)	205 km/hr (127 mph); 200 km/hr (124 mph)
Acceleration	11.5 sec 0-100 km/hr	11.5 sec 0-100 km/hr
Fuel consumption	13 liters/100 km (18 mpg)	13 liters/100 km (18 mpg)
Fuel tank capacity	96 liters (25.4 gallons)	96 liters (25.4 gallons)

The 230/4 sedan, 1973

Prices and Production

The 230/4 four-door sedan sold in 1973 for . . . . .DM 15,210
    in 1974 for. . . . . .DM 15,875
    in 1975 for. . . . . .DM 17,505
    Power steering . . . . .DM   515
    Automatic transmission . . . . .DM 1,440
In the United States the 230 sedan sold
    in November 1973 for (with automatic transmission)
        (East coast) . . . .$ 8,420
        (West coast) . . . .$ 8,530
    in September 1974 (East coast) . . . .$ 9,357
    in October 1975 (East coast) . . . .$ 10,497

Production of the 230/4 model [115 V23] (from January/August
1973 until December 1976)

	was in	1972	7 units
		1973	9,568 units
		1974	30,013 units
		1975	35,073 units
		1976	13,104 units
		total	87,765 units

Model 230/4 (1972-1976)

The 230/4 model was one of the two new passenger car models first introduced at the Frankfurt Auto Show in 1973. It replaced the 220 sedan which had been manufactured since 1967. The new four-cylinder engine with a stroke of 83.6 milimeters and bore of 93.75 millimeters developed 110 horsepower and gave the sedan a maximum speed of 170 kilometers (106 miles) per hour against the 161 of the former. Acceleration was the same. However, the new engine used less effort to accomplish this.

The new body had a wider radiator grille and was slightly lower in front and was similar to those of the current S-class models. With these eleven larger models the four-cylinder car shared the suspension and other, modern advanced design and safety features. A total of 24 different models of passenger cars were offered that year.

The 230 model, as it was designated for the United States market, was the lowest priced gasoline-engined Mercedes sedan, and was a good, dependable, and economical car. The roadability of this four-cylinder sedan was excellent, although it did not, of course, have the performance of the top line, the eight-cylinder models.

The 230/4 sedan, 1973

Specifications

	230/4
Engine type	4 cyl overhead camshaft (M 115)
Bore and stroke	93.75 x 83.6mm (3.69 x 3.29 in)
Displacement	2277 cc (140.8 cu in)
Power output	110 hp (DIN) @ 4800 rpm; (U.S.: 95 hp SAE @ 4800 rpm) 1975: 93 hp SAE @ 4800 rpm 1975 California: 85 hp SAE @ 4500 rpm
Compression ratio	9:1 U.S. 8:1
Torque	19 mkg @ 2500 rpm (137.5 ft/lb); U.S.: 17.7 mkg @ 2500 rpm 128 ft/lb 1975: 125 ft/lb, California: 122 ft/lb
Carburetion	Crossdraft carburetor Stromberg 175 CDT
Engine speed at 100 km/hr	3180 rpm
Gear ratios	I. 3.90:1 II. 2.30:1 III. 1.41:1 IV. 1.00:1
Rear axle ratio	3.69 U.S. 3.92
Chassis	unit frame and body
Suspension	independent front and rear, double wishbones, diagonal-pivot swing axle, anti-sway bars
Brakes and area	disc, hydraulic dual circuit, 273/279mm (10.8/11.0 in)
Wheelbase	2750mm (108.3 in)
Track, front/rear	1448/1.440mm (57.0/56.7 in)
Length	4680mm (184.3 in) U.S.: 195.5 in
Width	1770mm (69.7 in)
Height	1440mm (56.7 in)
Ground clearance	175mm (6.9 in)
Tires	175 SR 14
Turning circle	11 meters (36.1 ft)
Steering type and ratio	recirculating ball (3.0 turns), servo assisted
Weight	1350 kg (2970 lbs) U.S.: 1470 kg (3234 lbs)
Maximum speed	170 km/hr (106 mph)
Acceleration	13.7 sec 0-100 km/hr
Fuel consumption	11.4 liters, super/100 km (20.5 mpg) (U.S.: no lead fuel)
Fuel tank capacity	65 liters (17.2 gallons)

Front view of the 230/4 sedan, 1973

Rear view of the 230/4 sedan, 1973

The 240D sedan, 1974, U.S. version

Prices and Production

The 240D four-door sedan sold in 1973 for . . . . .DM 15,985
    in 1974 for. . . . . .DM 16,710
    in 1975 for. . . . . .DM 18,425
    Power steering . . . . .DM   515
    Automatic transmission . . . . .DM 1,440
The 240D long-wheelbase limousine sold in 1973 for . . .DM 22,590
    but the price increased gradually until it reached
        in 1975 . . . . .DM 26,075
In the United States the 240D sedan sold
    in November 1973 for (East coast) . . . .$ 8,140
        (West coast) . . . .$ 8,250
    and with automatic transmission (East coast) . . . . . .$ 8,715
        (West coast) . . . .$ 8,825
    in September 1974 (East coast) . . . .$ 8,862
        and with automatic transmission . . . .$ 9,479
    in October 1975 (East coast) . . . .$ 9,930
        and with automatic transmission . . . .$ 10,621

Production of the 240D model [115 D24] (from February/August
1973 until December 1976)

was in	1973	16,512 units
	1974	60,928 units
	1975	38,019 units
	1976	15,860 units
	total	131,319 units

Model 240D (1973-1976)

D = Diesel

The 240D sedan was one of two new models first shown to the public at the Frankfurt Auto Show in 1973. It was an addition to the fast-selling diesel-engined passenger cars of the 200D and 220D models. With a larger displacement, the four-cylinder engine developed 65 horsepower (against the 55 and 60 of the other two models). It shared with the new 230.4 engine other advancements in engine design.

In the customary tradition, the body style of these two cars was exactly alike. All of the new features of the gasoline-engined model were available to those who preferred the fantastic economy of the diesel-engined car. With the cylinder dimensions of the 240D, engineers believed that they had achieved the ultimate in passenger car development, for the 600 cubic centimeter displacement seemed the very ideal size.

The 240D engine ran slower than the others (at 3,180 revolutions against 3,375 at 100 kilometers per hour) and maximum speed was increased to 138 kilometers per hour against the 130 and 135 of the smaller engined cars.

In August 1973 the long chassis diesel limousine had the 240D engine installed instead of the former 220D. All of the specifications of the earlier model applied to this one except for the maximum speed (now 135 km/hr; automatic: 130 km/hr.) and the fuel consumption (now 11.5 liters; automatic: 12.5 liters per 100 kilometers). The overall weight had also increased slightly (by 15 kg) to 1,555 kg (3,421 lbs.).

The 240D sedan, 1975, U.S. version

Specifications

	240D
Engine type	4 cyl diesel overhead camshaft (OM 616)
Bore and stroke	91 x 92.4mm (3.58 x 3.64 in)
Displacement	2376 cc (146.7 cu in)
Power output	65 hp (DIN) @ 4200 rpm (62 hp SAE @ 4000 rpm)
Compression ratio	21:1
Torque	14 mkg @ 2400 rpm (13.4 mkg 97 ft/lb @ 2400 rpm)
Fuel injection	Bosch four plunger pump
Engine speed at 100 km/hr	3180 rpm
Gear ratios	I. 3.90:1 II. 2.30:1 III. 1.41:1 IV. 1.00:1
Rear axle ratio	3.69
Chassis	unit frame and body
Suspension	independent front and rear, double wishbones, diagonal-pivot swing axle, anti-sway bars
Brakes and area	disc, hydraulic dual circuit, 273/279mm (10.8/11.0 in)
Wheelbase	2750mm (108.3 in)
Track, front/rear	1448/1440mm (57.0/56.7 in)
Length	4680mm (184.3 in) U.S.: 195.5 in
Width	1770mm (69.7 in)
Height	1440mm (56.7 in)
Ground clearance	175mm (6.9 in)
Tires	175 SR 14
Turning circle	11 meters (36.1 ft)
Steering type and ratio	recirculating ball (3.0 turns), servo assisted
Weight	1390 kg (3058 lbs) U.S.: 1457 kg (3205 lbs)
Maximum speed	138 km/hr (85.7 mph)
Acceleration	24.6 sec 0-100 km/hr
Fuel consumption	9.5 liters/100 km (24.75 mpg)
Fuel tank capacity	65 liters (17.2 gallons) 1976: 80 liters (20.6 gallons)

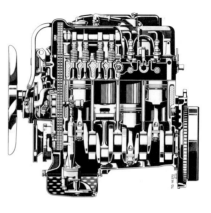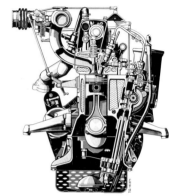

Longitudinal and cross section of the OM 616 engine, 1973

Installation of the diesel engine, 1973

129

The 280SEL sedan, 1974

Prices and Production

The 280SEL four-door sedan sold in 1974 for . . . . .DM 30,680
   in 1975 for . . . . .DM 33,340
   in 1977 for . . . . .DM 34,854

Production of the 280SEL model [116 E 28] (from October 1973/
April 1974 until May 1980)

was in		
1973	1	unit
1974	535	units
1975	716	units
1976	1,042	units
1977	1,295	units
1978	1,622	units
1979	1,551	units
1980	270	units
total	7,032	units

Model 280SEL (1973-1980)

SE L (Lang) = long wheelbase chassis

The 280SEL was first shown at the Geneva Salon in early 1974. In the true tradition of the company, it was a stretched version of the 280SE model sedan. The wheelbase was, as before on these long models, ten centimeters longer than that of the regular sedan, all of which benefitted the passengers in the rear seat. With the same engine of 2.8 liters displacement and 185 horsepower (DIN), the performance was equal to that of the shorter car. Maximum speed was calculated at 200 kilometers (124 miles) per hour.

The 280SEL model was one of 24 different passenger car models offered that year by Mercedes–Benz and fulfilled the specific needs of a wide range of preference by the motorists.

The 280SEL was meant to be a car for the executive, to travel in style, for it was a most comfortable long distance touring sedan. With the extra space for the passengers in the rear seats, easier entry and exit, the greater leg room, this sedan filled a certain need in the passenger car program of the company.

The 280SEL sedan, 1974

Specifications

	280SEL
Engine type	6 cyl double overhead camshafts (M 110)
Bore and stroke	86 x 78.8mm (3.41 x 3.10 in)
Displacement	2746 cc (168 cu in)
Power output	185 hp (DIN) @ 6000 rpm (205 hp SAE); 1977: 177 hp (DIN)
Compression ratio	9:1
Torque	24.3 mkg @ 4500 rpm (175.8 ft/lb)
Fuel injection	Bosch electronic
Engine speed at 100 km/hr	3140 rpm; 3375 rpm
Gear ratios	I. 3.90:1 1976: I. 3.98:1 automatic (optional) II. 2.30:1 II. 2.39:1 III. 1.41:1 III. 1.46:1 IV. 1.00:1 IV. 1.00:1
Rear axle ratio	3.69
Chassis	unit frame and body
Suspension	independent front and rear, double wishbones, diagonal-pivot swing axle, anti-sway bars
Brakes and area	disc, power assisted, two circuit hydraulic, 278/279mm (10.9/11.0 in)
Wheelbase	2965mm (116.7 in)
Track, front/rear	1525/1505mm (60/59.3 in)
Length	5060mm (199.2 in)
Width	1865mm (73.4 in)
Height	1430mm (56.3 in)
Ground clearance	147mm (5.8 in)
Tires	185 HR 14
Turning circle	11.9 meters (39 ft)
Steering type and ratio	recirculating ball (3.0 turns), servo assisted
Weight	1645 kg (3619 lbs)
Maximum speed	200 km/hr (124 mph); 195 km/hr (121 mph)
Acceleration	12 sec 0-100 km/hr
Fuel consumption	12.5 liters/100 km (18.75 mpg)
Fuel tank capacity	96 liters (25.4 gallons)

The 280SE sedan, 1974

The 280SE sedan, 1974

Front view of the 450SE sedan, 1974

Prices and Production

The 450SE four-door sedan sold in 1973 for . . . . .DM 33,970
   in 1974 for . . . . .DM 35,500
   in 1975 for . . . . .DM 39,150
   in 1977 for . . . . .DM 40,925
The 450SE four-door sedan sold in the United States
   in March 1973 (fully equipped) for
     (East coast) $13,396
     (West coast) $13,491
   in November 1973 (East coast) $15,820
   in September 1974 (East coast) $17,713
   in October 1975 (East coast) $19,989

Production of the 450SE model [116 E45] (from August/December
1972 until April 1980)

was in	1972	52 units
	1973	13,400 units
	1974	7,579 units
	1975	4,672 units
	1976	5,188 units
	1977	4,223 units
	1978	3,570 units
	1979	2,746 units
	1980	174 units
	total	41,604 units

# Model 450SE (1972-1980)
S = Super, E (Einspritzung) = fuel injection

The 450SE sedan was introduced to the public at the Geneva Salon in March 1973. Along with the 450SEL, 450SLC, these cars represented the top of the S-class and included all of the newest technological and safety features developed by the engineers. These incorporated design features of the C111 experimental car, such as the front axle geometry and design first tested on that amazing vehicle, and increased lateral and roll-over protection, distinct crumble zones and other safety features first tested with the experimental safety vehicles ESF 5, 13 and 22.

The 450SE was quickly recognized as one of the finest cars ever produced by Daimler-Benz and the group of forty-five European automotive journalists voted it the Car of the Year. The basic criteria were overall engineering concept with special regard to safety, aesthetic impression, styling and design, and price in relation to value offered.

While the 450SE had the 225 horsepower (DIN) engine and three- or four-speed torque converter, the U.S. version had a detuned unit which developed 190 SAE horsepower and had the three-speed automatic transmission only. Still, *Road & Track* considered the car the Best Sedan in the World.

In Europe the car was also judged Car of the Year by the automotive journalists representing six leading publications: Auto Visie of Holland, Stern of Germany, Daily Telegraph Magazine of Britain, L'Equipe of France, Quattroruote of Italy and ViBilägare of Sweden.

The 450SE sedan, 1974, U.S. version

Specifications

	450SE
Engine type	V-8 cyl overhead camshafts (M 117)
Bore and stroke	92 x 85mm (3.62 x 3.35 in)
Displacement	4520 cc (275.8 cu in)
Power output	225 hp (DIN) @ 5000 rpm; U.S.: 190 hp SAE @ 4750 rpm; 1977: 217 hp (DIN) 1975 California: 180 hp SAE
Compression ratio	8.8:1 U.S.: 8:1
Torque	38.5 mkg @ 3000 rpm (278.5 ft/lb) U.S.: 33.0 mkg @ 3000 rpm (238.8 ft/lb); 1975 California: 232 ft/lb
Fuel injection	Bosch electronic
Engine speed at 100 km/hr	2865 rpm U.S.: 2700 rpm
Gear ratios	I. 3.98:1 U.S. automatic I. 2.31:1 II. 2.39:1 II. 1.46:1 III. 1.46:1 III. 1.00:1 IV. 1.00:1
Rear axle ratio	3.07
Chassis	unit frame and body
Suspension	independent front and rear, double wishbones, diagonal-pivot swing axle
Brakes and area	disc, front vented, rear solid, 278/279mm (10.9/11.0 in)
Wheelbase	2860mm (112.6 in)
Track, front/rear	1525/1505mm (60.0/59.3 in)
Length	4960mm (195.3 in) U.S.: 205.5 in
Width	1870mm (73.6 in)
Height	1425mm (56.1 in)
Ground clearance	150mm (5.9 in)
Tires	205/70 VR 14
Turning circle	11.4 meters (37.4 ft)
Steering type and ratio	recirculating ball (2.7 turns); servo assisted 15.6:1
Weight	1740 kg (3828 lbs) U.S.: 4070 lbs
Maximum speed	210 km/hr (130 mph) U.S.: 205 km/hr (127 mph)
Acceleration	9.3 sec 0-100 km/hr U.S.: 10.8 sec 0-100 km/hr
Fuel consumption	14.5 liters/100 km (16 mpg) (U.S.: no lead fuel)
Fuel tank capacity	96 liters (25.4 gallons)

The 450SEL sedan, 1973

Prices and Production

The 450SEL four-door sedan sold in 1973 for . . . . .DM 38,575
    in 1974 for . . . . .DM 40,300
    in 1975 for . . . . .DM 44,450
    in 1977 for . . . . .DM 45,798
The 450SEL four-door sedan sold in the United States
    in March 1973 (fully equipped) for
      (East coast) $14,605
      (West coast) $14,698
    in November 1973 (East coast) $17,400
    in September 1974 (East coast) $19,106
    in October 1975 (East coast) $21,709
    in March 1977 (East coast) $24,506
    in February 1979 (East coast) $32,858

Production of the 450SEL model [116 E45] (from December 1972 until June 1980)

was in	1972	24 units
	1973	6,930 units
	1974	8,350 units
	1975	6,167 units
	1976	9,650 units
	1977	10,042 units
	1978	8,508 units
	1979	8,217 units
	1980	1,690 units
	total	59,578 units

Model 450SEL (1972-1980)

SE L (Lang) = long wheelbase chassis

The 450SEL sedan, also first shown at the Geneva Auto Show in 1973, was basically the same car as the regular length 450SE. With a fifteen-centimeter longer wheelbase, only the rear passenger benefited from that change. The interior was nearly the same as that of the SE model, with headrest, safety belts, electrically operated windows, center locking system, and such safety features as standard equipment. Velour carpeting and leather upholstery were some of the finer appointments over the 450E model.

The rear diagonal swing axle had been further developed for the 450 models because of the high torque and fitted with an anti-squat device, eliminating entirely rear end dipping when aggressively accelerating from a standstill. The hydraulic dual circuit brake with vacuum booster and disc brakes on all four wheels was, of course, standard on these models as on the other S-class cars.

In the United States, the 450SEL had the same detuned engine as the regular sedan and shared all other alterations with it to comply with the more stringent emission controls and regulations on safety.

The 450SEL sedan, 1979, U.S. version

Specifications

	450SEL
Engine type	V-8 cyl overhead camshafts (M 117)
Bore and stroke	92 x 85mm (3.62 x 3.35 in)
Displacement	4520 cc (275.8 cu in)
Power output	225 hp (DIN) @ 5000 rpm; 1977: 217 hp (DIN) U.S.: 190 hp SAE @ 4750 rpm; 1975 California: 180 hp SAE; 1977: 180 hp SAE @ 4750 rpm; 1980: 160 hp SAE @ 4200 rpm
Compression ratio	8.8:1 U.S. 8:1
Torque	38.5 mkg @ 3000 rpm (278.5 ft/lb); U.S.: 33.0 mkg @ 3000 rpm (240 ft/lb); 1975 California: 232 ft/lb U.S. 1977: 32.25 mkg @ 3000 rpm (220 ft/lb); 1979: 31.9 mkg @ 2500 rpm (230 ft/lb)
Fuel injection	Bosch electronic
Engine speed at 100 km/hr	2865 rpm U.S.: 2700 rpm
Gear ratios	I. 3.98:1 U.S. automatic I. 2.31:1 II. 2.39:1 II. 1.46:1 III. 1.46:1 III. 1.00:1 IV. 1.00:1
Rear axle ratio	3.07; U.S. 1979: 3.06; 1980: 2.65
Chassis	unit frame and body
Suspension	independent front and rear, double wishbones, diagonal-pivot swing axle
Brakes and area	disc, front vented, rear solid, 278/279mm (10.9/11.0 in)
Wheelbase	2965mm (116.7 in)
Track, front/rear	1525/1505mm (60.0/59.3 in); U.S. 1977 front: 1521mm (59.9 in)
Length	5060mm (199.2 in) U.S.: 209.4 in (5320mm)
Width	1870mm (73.6 in)
Height	1430mm (56.3 in)
Ground clearance	150mm (5.9 in)
Tires	205/70 VR 14
Turning circle	11.8 meters (38.4 ft) U.S.: 11.9 meters (39 ft)
Steering type and ratio	recirculating ball (2.7 turns); servo assisted 15.6:1
Weight	1740 kg (3828 lbs) U.S.: 4100 lbs (1864 kg); 1977: 4080 lbs (1850 kg); 1980: 3975 lbs (1800 kg)
Maximum speed	210 km/hr (130 mph) U.S.: 205 km/hr (127 mph)
Acceleration	9.3 sec 0-100 km/hr U.S.: 10.8 sec 0-100 km/hr
Fuel consumption	14.5 liters/100 km (16 mpg) (U.S.: no lead fuel)
Fuel tank capacity	96 liters (25.4 gallons)

The 240D 3.0 sedan, 1974

Model 240D 3.0/300D
(1974-1976)

D = Diesel

The 240D 3.0 made its appearance in July 1974. It was a radical and startling solution to the problem of increasing the available horsepower in a diesel-engined car and still maintain its size. Designated as the 300D in the United States, it was a luxury sedan (as was the 280) and was priced only slightly under that of the 280 sedan ($11,782 against $12,325), fully equipped with radio, air conditioning, power steering, power brakes, et al.

The five-cylinder diesel engine was basically the same as the four-cylinder unit of the 240D, except that another cylinder had been added. All dimensions and essential construction features were alike, but the Bosch injection pump was entirely redesigned. A centrifugal governor operated the metering rack and regulated the power output. The starting of the cold engine was decidedly easier than on previous diesel models, taking but a short time for the glow plug to heat up. Cylinder crank head and housing, head gasket, and the six main bearing crankshaft and oil pan were also new. Developing 80 DIN horsepower (U.S.: 77 SAE) and 17.5 mkg (U.S.: 115 ft/lb.) of torque, it gave the amazingly economical sedan a maximum speed of 92 miles (148 kilometers) per hour with the 3.46:1 rear axle ratio. The 240D, with the 3.69:1 rear axle ratio, had a maximum speed of 85.7 miles (138 kilometers) per hour.

Prices and Production

The 240D 3.0 four-door sedan sold in 1974 for . . . . . . .DM 18,815
   in 1975 for . . . . .DM 19,915
In the United States the 300D sedan sold
   in September 1974 for (fully equipped)
     (East coast) . . . .$ 11,782
     (West coast) . . . .$ 11,921
   in October 1975 (East coast) . . . .$ 13,582

Production of the 240D 3.0 four-door sedan [115 D30] (from May 1974 until November 1976)

was in	1974	7,650 units
	1975	34,420 units
	1976	11,620 units
	total	53,690 units

The diesel sedan, just like this writer owned for several years.

Specifications

	240D 3.0 / (300D)
Engine type	5 cyl diesel, overhead camshaft (OM 617)
Bore and stroke	91 x 92.4mm (3.58 x 3.64 in)
Displacement	2971 cc (183.4 cu in)
Power output	80 hp (DIN) @ 4000 rpm (77 hp SAE @ 4000 rpm)
Compression ratio	21:1
Torque	17.5 mkg @ 2400 rpm (16 mkg @ 2400 rpm 115.7 ft/lb)
Fuel injection	Bosch injector pump
Engine speed at 100 km/hr	2980 rpm
Gear ratios	I. 3.98:1 (13.77) II. 2.39:1 (8.27) III. 1.46:1 (5.05) IV. 1.00:1 (3.46)
Rear axle ratio	3.46
Chassis	unit frame and body
Suspension	independent front and rear, double wishbones, diagonal-pivot swing axle
Brakes and area	disc, front vented, rear solid, 273/279mm (10.8/11.0 in)
Wheelbase	2750mm (108.3 in)
Track, front/rear	1448/1440mm (57.0/56.7 in)
Length	4680mm (184.3 in) U.S.: 195.5 in
Width	1770mm (69.7 in)
Height	1440mm (56.7 in)
Ground clearance	175mm (6.9 in)
Tires	175 SR 14
Turning circle	11 meters (36.1 ft)
Steering type and ratio	recirculating ball (3.0 turns), servo assisted
Weight	1430 kg (3146 lbs) U.S.: 3450 lbs
Maximum speed	148 km/hr (92 mph) U.S.: 89 mph (143 km/hr)
Acceleration	20.6 sec 0-100 km/hr
Fuel consumption	10.8 liters/100 km (21.5 mpg)
Fuel tank capacity	65 liters (17.2 gallons); 1976: 80 liters (20.6 gallons)

Cutaway of the OM 617 diesel engine

Five-cylinder arrangement of the OM 617 engine

The 450SEL 6.9 sedan, 1975

Prices and Production

The 450SEL 6.9 four-door sedan sold in 1975 for . . . . .DM 70,000
in 1977 for . . . . .DM 73,093
In the United States the 450SEL 6.9 four-door sedan sold
in February (East coast) for $50,190
(West coast). $50,417

Production of the 450SEL 6.9 four-door sedan [116 E69] (from
February/September 1975 until May 1980)

was in	1975	474 units
	1976	1,475 units
	1977	1,798 units
	1978	1,665 units
	1979	1,839 units
	1980	129 units
	total	7,380 units

Sales in this country were		
in 1977		462 units
1978		457 units
1979		576 units
1980		317 units
1981		4 units
total		1,816 units

Model 450SEL 6.9 (1975-1980)

SE L (Lang) = long wheelbase chassis

The 450SEL 6.9 model was first publicly shown in 1974. It was a fast, powerful luxury sedan in the manner of the 300SEL 6.3 of 1968-1972. The sedan utilized the same body and chassis of the larger S-class, but had a hydro-pneumatic suspension system with four spring units carrying the weight of the vehicle. A constant self-leveling device kept the car at an even level under all road or load conditions, giving it a superb roadability. All of the technological improvements of the time were incorporated in the construction, making it truly an excellent automobile in every respect.

The 6.9-liter V-8 engine was an enlarged version of the tested powerplant used so successfully in the former 6.3 model and currently in the large 600 models. Many improvements had been accomplished since the time it was first introduced in the 6.3 sedan. With greater torque (405 ft/lb. against 369) and an increase in actual DIN horsepower to 286 from 250 formerly, the new 450SEL 6.9 car had a maximum speed of 140 miles (225 kilometers) per hour, although the new car weighed about 400 pounds more than the 6.3 model. The final drive had been reduced to 2.65:1 (against 2.85:1) which gave it a slightly greater maximum speed (about 3 mph), but reduced the acceleration somewhat.

In the words of *Road & Track* magazine, it was "the fastest, best sedan in the world."

The 450SEL 6.9 sedan, 1976, U.S. version

Specifications

	450SEL 6.9	
Engine type	V-8 cyl overhead camshafts (M 100)	
Bore and stroke	107 x 95mm (4.21 x 3.74 in)	
Displacement	6834 cc (417 cu in)	
Power output	286 hp (DIN) @ 4250 rpm	U.S.: 250 hp SAE @ 4000 rpm
Compression ratio	8.8:1	U.S.: 8.0:1
Torque	56 mkg @ 3000 rpm (405 ft/lb)	U.S.: 51.6 mkg @ 2500 rpm (360 ft/lb)
Fuel injection	Bosch electronic (K-Jetronic)	
Engine speed at 100 km/hr	2595 rpm	
Gear ratios	automatic I. 2.31:1 II. 1.46:1 III. 1.00:1	
Rear axle ratio	2.65	
Chassis	unit frame and body	
Suspension	independent front and rear, double wishbones, diagonal-pivot swing axle, hydropneumatic, self-leveling, torsion bar stabilizers	
Brakes and area	disc, vented front, solid rear, 278/279mm (10.9/11.0 in)	
Wheelbase	2960mm (116.5 in)	
Track, front/rear	1525/1505mm (60.0/59.3 in)	U.S.: 1521/1505mm (59.9/59.3 in)
Length	5060mm (199.2 in)	U.S.: 5335mm (210.0 in)
Width	1410mm (40mm with level adjustment) (57.1 in)	U.S.: 1425mm (56.1 in)
Height	1410mm (40mm with level adjustment) (57.1 in)	
Ground clearance	150mm (5.9 in)	
Tires	215/70 VR 14	
Turning circle	11.8 meters (38.7 ft)	U.S.: 12.18 meters (40 ft)
Steering type and ratio	recirculating ball (2.7 turns); servo assisted 15.6:1	
Weight	1935 kg (4257 lbs) U.S.: 1990 kg (4390 lbs); 1979: 2010 kg (4435 lbs)	
Maximum speed	225 km/hr (140 mph)	
Acceleration	7.4 sec 0-100 km/hr	
Fuel consumption	16 liters, super/100 km (14.75 mpg)	
Fuel tank capacity	96 liters (25.4 gallons)	

The instrument panel of the 6.9, 1976

The M 100 engine of the 450SEL 6.9, 1976

The 280SL roadster, 1974

Model 280SL (1974–1985)

S = Sports, L (Leicht) = light

The 280SL was introduced in late 1974 as a less powerful (and consequently more economical) version of the larger engined sports cars. It shared the body and all appointments with the 350SL and 450SL fast touring models.

The engine specifications were exactly those of the other 280 cars, using the identical twin overhead camshaft six-cylinder powerplant of 185 horsepower. The 280SL weighed 45 kilograms (99 pounds) less than the 350SL and 85 kilograms (187 pounds) less than the 450SL. This still gave the smallest of the three sports cars a respectable acceleration of 9.5 seconds for the 0-100 km/hr. against the 8.8 for the 350SL and 8.5 for the 450SL. Maximum speed of the 280SL was 205 kilometers per hour (127 miles). Fuel consumption was 12.5 liters per 100 kilometers.

The 280SL model was available with the regular four-speed or five-speed transmission and the fully automatic transmission, while the other two larger-engined models had the automatic transmission and only the three-speed automatic transmission. (The 350SL had a four-speed transmission until July 1972.)

Model 280SLC (1974-1981)

S = Sports, L = Light, C = Coupe

The 280SLC was brought out at the same time as the 280SL, in late 1974. As in the sports car line, this smaller engined version of the SLC model was the most economical of the three sizes available. In all appointments as well as body style and specifications, it was identical to the 350SLC and the 450SLC models.

Performance was, of course, not as brisk as that of the other two larger engined versions of the luxury coupe line, but to customers concerned with the fuel shortage and ever-increasing prices, it seemed the right answer. Weight differentials and performance figures were the same as those cited on the SL models. (The 280SLC weighed 1,550 kilograms (3,410 pound), and still attained the same maximum speed as the SL model.)

As the 280SL, this coupe also came equipped with the four- or five-speed transmission or the fully automatic transmission, while the other larger engined SLCs had only the three-speed manual and the automatic three-speed transmission.

Prices and Production

The 280SL model sold in 1974 for	DM	32,445
in 1975 for	DM	34,335
in 1977 for	DM	35,619
in 1980 for	DM	44,522

Production of the 280SL model [107 E28] (from May/August 1974 until August 1985)

was in	1974	297 units
	1975	1,020 units
	1976	1,099 units
	1977	1,347 units
	1978	1,536 units
	1979	2,155 units
	1980	2,429 units
	1981	2,628 units
	1982	3,165 units
	1983	3,393 units
	1984	3,529 units
	1985	2,838 units
	total	25,436 units

The 280SLC model sold in 1974 for	DM	37,200
in 1975 for	DM	39,385
in 1977 for	DM	41,196
in 1980 for	DM	49,155

Production of the 280SLC coupe [107 E28] (from May/August 1974 until September 1981)

was in	1974	300 units
	1975	1,312 units
	1976	1,508 units
	1977	1,624 units
	1978	1,553 units
	1979	1,741 units
	1980	1,510 units
	1981	1,118 units
	total	10,666 units

Specifications

	280SL	280SLC
Engine type	6 cyl double overhead camshafts (M 110)	
Bore and stroke	86 x 78.8mm (3.41 x 3.10 in)	
Displacement	2746 cc (168 cu in)	
Power output	185 hp (DIN) @ 6000 rpm; 1977: 177 hp (DIN); 1979: 185 hp (DIN) @ 5800 rpm	
Compression ratio	9:1	
Torque	24.3 mkg @ 4500 rpm (175.8 ft/lb)	
Fuel injection	Bosch electronic; 1979: mechanical, with air flow sensor	
Engine speed at 100 km/hr	3140 rpm; automatic: 3380 rpm	
Rear axle ratio	3.69 (for 5-speed 3.92)	
Chassis	unit frame and body	
Suspension	independent front and rear, double wishbones, diagonal-pivot swing axle	
Brakes and area	disc, front vented, rear solid, 278/279mm (10.9/11.0 in)	
Wheelbase	2460mm (96.9 in)	2820mm (111.0 in)
Track, front/rear	1452/1440mm (57.2/56.7 in)	
Length	4390mm (172.8 in)	4750mm (187 in)
Width	1790mm (70.5 in)	
Height	1300mm (51.2 in)	1330mm (52.4 in)
Ground clearance	140mm (5.5 in)	
Tires	185 HR 14	
Turning circle	10.34 meters (33.9 ft)	11.55 meters (36.9 ft)
Steering type and ratio	recirculating ball (3.0 turns); servo assisted 15.6:1	
Weight	1500 kg (3300 lbs)	1550 kg (3410 lbs)
Maximum speed	205 km/hr (127 mph); automatic: 200 km/hr (124 mph); 1977: 200 km/hr; automatic: 195 km/hr (121 mph)	
Acceleration	9.5 sec 0-100 km/hr; 1979: 10.1 sec; automatic: 11.0 sec	10.1 sec 0-100 km/hr; automatic: 11.0 sec
Fuel consumption	12.5 liters, super/100 km (18.75 mph); 1979: at 120 km/hr, 11.8 liters; automatic: 12.6 liters	
Fuel tank capacity	90 liters (23.8 gallons)	

Gear ratios

		or	1976:	automatic:	1979:	automatic:
I.	3.98:1 (14.69)	I. 3.96:1	I. 3.90:1	I. 3.98:1	I. 3.98:1	I. 3.98:1
II.	2.39:1 (8.82)	II. 2.34:1	II. 2.30:1	II. 2.39:1	II. 2.29:1	II. 2.39:1
III.	1.46:1 (5.39)	III. 1.43:1	III. 1.41:1	III. 1.46:1	III. 1.45:1	III. 1.46:1
IV.	1.00:1 (3.69)	IV. 1.00:1	IV. 1.00:1	IV. 1.00:1	IV. 1.00:1	IV. 1.00:1
		V. 0.88:1				

The 200 sedan, 1979

Prices and Production

The 200 four-door sedan sold in 1976 for . . . . .DM 18,381
   in 1979 for. . . . . .DM 20,260
   in 1980 (M102) for. . . . . .DM 22,554
   In 1982 for. . . . . .DM 25,815

Production of the 200 model [123 V20] (from July 1975/February 1976 until August 1980)

was in	1975	5 units
	1976	26,374 units
	1977	39,112 units
	1978	35,884 units
	1979	34,190 units
	1980	23,207 units
	total	158,772 units

Production of the 200 (M102) model [123 V20] (from October 1979/August 1980 until November 1985)

was in	1979	37 units
	1980	17,606 units
	1981	54,780 units
	1982	60,670 units
	1983	44,419 units
	1984	29,652 units
	1985	10,151 units
	total	217,315 units

Model 200 (1975–1985)

The 200 Sedan — W123 — was first introduced at the Geneva Auto Show in March 1976. It was the least powerful of the entire line of nine middle range sedans with the new body style, and was quite similar to the other existing models. The 200 through 250 models had round headlights, but otherwise the bodies were alike.

The new cars incorporated many new engineering features and high technical standards of the more expensive models. Some details will be mentioned in the descriptive text of subsequent models which shared these W123 body styles.

Because of the unusually high demands for the cars, production of the older W115 style 200 model, begun in 1967, was maintained and over 13,000 units were actually sold that first year when the new model was also available to the purchaser of a 200 sedan. However, production of the new 123 style was about twice that number during 1976.

In June 1980 an entirely new M102 four-cylinder carburetor engine was introduced. This new design had achieved improved fuel consumption, increased power output and smoother operation than the previous engine, the well proven M115.

Outwardly the car was the same as before, with no changes in the W123 chassis or body. Substantial changes were made, however, in the power unit and other mechanical parts. The 16% increase in power output, from 94 DIN horsepower to 109 horsepower for the new 1,997 cubic centimeter engine, allowed a longer rear axle ratio and with the 25% lighter new mechanical four-speed transmission a saving of from 9 to 13% of gasoline was accomplished.

The urban fuel consumption was rated at 13.3 liters with the manual transmission and 13.0 liters for the automatic for 100 kilometers, while the 120 kilometers per hour speed gave 10.7 and 10.9 liters, respectively, or an average of 21.5 miles per gallon, compared with the 18.3 average for the former 1,987 cc four-cylinder engine.

Production of the 200 sedan with the M102 engine began in March 1980 — although 37 units were built for exhaustive testing in October 1979 — and manufacture of the old engined models ceased in August of that year.

Specifications

	200	
Engine type	4 cyl overhead camshaft (M115)	4 cyl overhead camshaft (M102)
Bore and stroke	87 x 83.6 mm (3.43 x 3.29 in)	89 x 80.25 mm (3.50 x 3.16 in)
Displacement	1987 cc (121.27 cu in); 1979: 1988 cc	1997 cc (121.72 cu in)
Power output	94 hp (DIN) @ 4800 rpm (105 hp SAE)	109 hp (DIN) @ 5200 rpm
Compression ratio	9.0:1	9.0:1
Torque	16.1 mkg @ 3000 rpm (116.5 ft/lb)	17.3 mkg @ 3000 rpm (125.2 ft/lb)
Carburetion	Stromberg crossdraft 175 CD	Stromberg sidedraft 175 CDT
Maximum engine speed	6000 rpm	
Engine speed at 100 km/hr	3395 rpm; automatic: 3470 rpm	
Gear ratios	I. 3.90:1 I. 3.98:1 (automatic)	I. 3.91:1
	II. 2.30:1 II. 2.39:1	II. 2.52:1 (1982: 2.32:1)
	III. 1.41:1 III. 1.46:1	III. 1.42:1
	IV. 1.00:1 IV. 1.00:1	IV. 1.00:1
Rear axle ratio	3.92	
Chassis	unit frame and body	
Suspension	independent front and rear, with coil springs; diagonal swing axle, coil springs, anti-roll bar. Optional level control; standard in 1979	
Brakes and area	dual circuit discs, power assisted, front brake pad wear indicator, 278/279 mm (10.9/11.0 in)	
Wheelbase	2795 mm (110.0 in)	
Track, front/rear	1488/1446 mm (58.6/56.9 in)	
Length	4725 mm (186.0 in)	
Width	1786 mm (70.3 in)	
Height	1438 mm (56.5 in)	
Tires	175 SR 14	
Turning circle	11.25 meters (36.9 feet); 1979: 11.29 meters (37 feet)	
Steering type and ratio	recirculating ball (4.0 turns), servo assisted	
Weight	1340 kg (2948 lbs)	
Maximum speed	160 km/hr (99 mph); automatic: 155 km/hr (96 mph)	168 km/hr (104 mph); automatic: 163 km/hr (101 mph)
Acceleration	15.2 sec 0-100 km/hr; automatic: 16.3 sec	14.4 sec 0-100 km/hr; automatic: 15.4 sec 0-100 km/hr
Fuel consumption	11.1 liters/100 km (21.3 mpg) 1979: at 120 km/hr: 12.5 liters; automatic: 13.2 liters	at 120 km/hr: 10.7 liters/100 km; automatic: 10.9 liters
Fuel tank capacity	65 liters (17.2 gallons)	

The 200D sedan, 1976

Model 200D (1975–1985)

D = Diesel

The 200D model was, as usual, exactly as the gasoline-engined version and only different in the engine installation. The diesel power unit had been only slightly altered from that widely proven OM615 engine in the previous 200D line. Specifications were practically the same, but the engine speed at 100 kilometers per hour was now 3,395 revolutions per hour instead of 3,375. The maximum speed remained the same despite a 25-kilogram increase in total weight. Acceleration of the new style sedan was 31.0 seconds, just 1 second slower than before. Fuel consumption, always extremely miserly, was 8.3 liters for 100 kilometers, up 0.2 from the previous 29 miles per gallon.

All of the diesel engines had the oil filters placed so that it could be changed from above, saving time and effort. And the new type cylinder head gaskets required no maintenance.

The older model was still produced during the first year of availability of the 123 body style, but production was only slightly over 21,000 units against the nearly 39,000 built of the newer model.

Despite its relatively low power and consequently unexciting performance, this model was one of the most desired cars built by Daimler-Benz. The smallest of the diesel models had always found a huge number of enthusiastic buyers over the years, and with this latest body style, it was not different.

The fact that production was nearly twice as large as that of its gasoline-engined counterpart indicated its immense popularity. The fantastic economy of operation — and especially its miserly fuel consumption at this time when supplies were critical and rapidly becoming more expensive — this diesel model made great sense to the thousands of satisfied owners.

Over the five-year period from 1976 to 1980 a total of over 250,000 cars were manufactured, more than of any other diesel model made by Daimler-Benz.

Prices and Production

The 200D four-door sedan sold in 1976 for . . . . .DM 18,870
    in 1979 for. . . . . .DM 21,347
    in 1982 for. . . . . .DM 26,369

Production of the 200D model [123 D20] (from July 1975/February 1976 until April 1985)

was in	1975	5 units
	1976	36,894 units
	1977	56,378 units
	1978	49,359 units
	1979	52,834 units
	1980	56,435 units
	1981	51,152 units
	1982	44,633 units
	1983	20,444 units
	1984	9,308 units
	1985	696 units
	total	378,138 units

Specifications   200D

Engine type	4 cyl diesel, overhead camshaft (OM 615)
Bore and stroke	87 x 83.6mm (3.43 x 3.29 in)
Displacement	1988 cc (121.27 cu in)
Power output	55 hp (DIN) @ 4200 rpm; 1979: 60 hp (DIN) @ 4400 rpm
Compression ratio	21:1
Torque	11.5 mkg @ 2400 rpm (83.2 ft/lb)
Fuel injection	Bosch four plunger pump
Maximum engine speed	5300 rpm
Engine speed at 100 km/hr	3395 rpm automatic: 3470 rpm
Gear ratios	I. 3.90:1 automatic: I. 3.98:1 II. 2.30:1 II. 2.39:1 III. 1.41:1 III. 1.46:1 IV. 1.00:1 IV. 1.00:1
Rear axle ratio	3.92
Chassis	unit frame and body
Suspension	independent front and rear, with coil springs; diagonal swing axle, coil springs, anti-roll bar. Optional level control; standard in 1979
Brakes and area	dual circuit discs, power assisted, front brake pad wear indicator, 278/279mm (10.9/11.0 in)
Wheelbase	2795mm (110.0 in)
Track, front/rear	1488/1466mm (58.6/56.9 in)
Length	4725mm (186.0 in)
Width	1786mm (70.3 in)
Height	1438mm (56.6 in)
Ground clearance	
Tires	175 SR 14
Turning circle	11.25 meters (36.9 ft); 1979: 11.29 meters (37 ft)
Steering type and ratio	recirculating ball (4.0 turns); servo assisted
Weight	1375 kg (3025 lbs)
Maximum speed	130 km/hr (81 mph); automatic: 125 km/hr (78 mph) 1979: 135 km/hr (84 mph) automatic: 130 km/hr (81 mph)
Acceleration	31 sec 0-100 km/hr; automatic: 33.2 sec; 1979: 27.4 sec; automatic: 29.4 sec
Fuel consumption	8.3 liters/100 km (28 mpg); 1979: at 120 km/hr 10.2 liters, automatic: 11.7 liters
Fuel tank capacity	65 liters (17.2 gallons)

The 220D sedan, 1976

Prices and Production

The 220D four-door sedan sold in 1976 for . . . . .DM 19,588
   in 1977 for. . . . . .DM 20,346

Production of the 220D model [123 D22] (from July 1975/February 1976 until March 1979)

was in	1975	4 units
	1976	16,733 units
	1977	19,323 units
	1978	19,230 units
	1979	1,446 units
	total	56,736 units

Model 220D (1975-1979)

D = Diesel

The 220D model was undistinguishable outwardly from the smaller-engined diesel sedan. This intermediate model, between the 200D and 240D, had actually been the best selling of all the diesel-powered automobiles, with over 420,000 units being sold of the W115 body style (the 200D sold nearly 340,000 and the 240D over 131,000).

But sales of this new model with the W123 body — and perhaps the increasing popularity of the five-cylinder diesel-engined 3-liter sedan — did never even challenge the other available models and the 220D was discontinued early in 1979.

The 2,197-cubic centimeter diesel engine developed only five more horsepower than the 2-liter unit, and the curb weight of both models was within five kilograms of each other. Acceleration figures for the 220D were 28.1 seconds for the 0-100 kilometers per hour, about 3 seconds faster, and the top speed was 5 kilometers faster. Fuel consumption of this larger engined diesel was 9 liters against the 8.3 liters per 100 kilometers for the 200D. The critical power-to-weight ratio for the 200D was 25 kilograms per horsepower but that of the 220D was 23 kilograms.

Offered to satisfy the buyer of a most economic sedan, yet also giving him a slightly more powerful car than the 2-liter model, this 220D had lost popularity over the past years. Ever since the introduction of the 123 line of body styles, only about half as many of the smaller size were built, and it was only because the sales department believed that it should offer the largest possible choice of model sizes to its prospective customers that this 220D was kept in production. Its demise was clearly indicated long before manufacture of the model was stopped. Still, a production run of 56,736 units during the lifetime of this 220D was not too insignificant.

Specifications

	220D
Engine type	4 cyl diesel, overhead camshaft (OM 615)
Bore and stroke	87.0 x 92.4mm (3.43 x 3.64 in)
Displacement	2197 cc (134 cu in)
Power output	60 hp (DIN) @ 4200 rpm
Compression ratio	21:1
Torque	12.8 mkg @ 2400 rpm (92.6 ft/lb)
Fuel injection	Bosch four plunger pump
Engine speed at 100 km/hr	3395 rpm automatic: 3470 rpm
Gear ratios	I. 3.90:1 automatic: I. 3.98:1 II. 2.30:1 II. 2.39:1 III. 1.41:1 III. 1.46:1 IV. 1.00:1 IV. 1.00:1
Rear axle ratio	3.92
Chassis	unit frame and body
Suspension	independent front and rear, with coil springs; diagonal swing axle, coil springs, anti-roll bar. Optional level control; standard in 1979
Brakes and area	dual circuit discs, power assisted, front brake pad wear indicator, 278/279mm (10.9/11.0 in)
Wheelbase	2795mm (110.0 in)
Track, front/rear	1488/1466mm (58.6/56.9 in)
Length	4725mm (186.0 in)
Width	1786mm (70.3 in)
Height	1438mm (56.6 in)
Ground clearance	
Tires	175 SR 14
Turning circle	11.25 meters (36.9 ft)
Steering type and ratio	recirculating ball (4.0 turns); servo assisted
Weight	1380 kg (3036 lbs)
Maximum speed	135 km/hr (84 mph); automatic: 130 km/hr (81 mph)
Acceleration	28.1 sec 0-100 km/hr; automatic: 29.1 sec
Fuel consumption	9.0 liters/100 km (26 mpg)
Fuel tank capacity	65 liters (17.2 gallons)

Injection part of OM 615 engine

The 230 sedan, 1976

Prices and Production

The 230 four-door sedan sold in 1976 for . . . . .DM 19,203
    in 1979 for. . . . . .DM 21,336
    in 1980 (M102) for. . . . . .DM 25,221

Production of the 230 model [123 V23] (from July 1975/February 1976 until September 1981)

was in	1975	9 units
	1976	32,060 units
	1977	49,426 units
	1978	42,270 units
	1979	47,739 units
	1980	23,549 units
	1981	1,132 units
	total	196,185 units

Production of the 230E (M102) model [123 E23] (from October 1979/ July 1980 until November 1985)

was in	1979	37 units
	1980	24,997 units
	1981	62,125 units
	1982	60,777 units
	1983	50,931 units
	1984	38,298 units
	1985	8,717 units
	total	245,882 units

Model 230 (1975-1981)

The 230 model, the middle range of the smaller sedans, was also first shown at the Geneva Auto Show in 1976. It shared the body style with the 200 and 250 models, and as in those cars, it was outwardly recognizable by the round headlights.

Some of the features of these new bodies were that the entire roof frame and the front, center and rear pillars had a profile of a closed cross section for greater roll-over resistance. Lateral strength had also been improved over the old body style.

The front axle required no maintenance. The fuel tank, holding 65 liters (17.2 gallons), was positioned above the rear axle and the spare wheel was laid down horizontally to absorb tail end impact energy.

For the U.S. market and in the 1977 model year, this 230 sedan had gained 100 kilograms in weight (1450 kg or 3195 lbs) and 123 millimeters (to 109.0 in) in length over the European version. It was sold for another year and then dropped.

Again, production of the previous 230 model remained with over 13,000 cars built, but of the new style, more than 32,000 were produced that first year.

Model 230E (1979 – 1985)

E (Einspritzung) = fuel injection

The 230E sedan, introduced in June 1980, also had a brand new M102 four-cylinder fuel injected engine. Similar to the 2-liter unit, this mechanical fuel injection type displayed 2,299 cubic centimeters and developed 136 DIN horsepower at 5,100 revolutions per minute.

Fuel economy was considerably improved, and developing greater power, lower revolutions were sufficient for the same performance with consequently less stress on engine and driver than previously with the carburetor model. Urban cycle fuel consumption was rated at 13.6 liters for 100 kilometers with manual transmission (14.7 for the M115) and 13.5 with automatic transmission. At 120 kilometers per hour, fuel consumption was 10.4 and 11.0 liters, respectively, which gave an average of 22 miles per gallon (12.5 and 12.8 liters for the M115).

Over 25,000 units were built the first year, including the 37 cars for testing constructed the previous year, and it seemed that the regular 230 sedan would soon be phased out. For 1981 a greatly curtailed official manufacturing schedule was listed.

Specifications

	230		230E
Engine type	4 cyl overhead camshaft (M115)		4 cyl overhead camshaft (M102)
Bore and stroke	93.75 x 83.6 mm (3.69 x 3.29 in)		95.5 x 80.25 mm (3.74 x 3.16 in)
Displacement	2307 cc (140.8 cu in)		2299 cc (140.12 cu in)
Power output	109 hp (DIN) @ 4800 rpm; U.S. 1977: 86 hp SAE @ 4600 rpm		136 hp (DIN) @ 5100 rpm
Compression ratio	9.0:1	U.S. 1977: 8:1	9.0:1
Torque	18.9 mkg @ 3000 rpm (136.7 ft/lb) U.S. 1977: 16.8 mkg @ 3000 rpm (116 ft/lb)		20.9 mkg @ 3500 rpm (151.2 ft/lb)
Carburetion	Stromberg crossdraft 175 CD		Bosch mechanical (fuel injection)
Maximum engine speed	6000 rpm		6000 rpm
Engine speed at 100 km/hr	3195 rpm	automatic: 3275 rpm	
Gear ratios	I. 3.90:1 II. 2.30:1 III. 1.41:1 IV. 1.00:1	I. 3.98:1 (automatic) II. 2.39:1 III. 1.46:1 IV. 1.00:1	I. 3.91:1 II. 2.32:1 III. 1.42:1 IV. 1.00:1
Rear axle ratio	3.69		3.58
Chassis	unit frame and body		
Suspension	independent front and rear, with coil springs; diagonal swing axle, coil springs, anti-roll bar. Optional level control; standard in 1979		
Brakes and area	dual circuit discs, power assisted, front brake pad wear indicator, 278/279 mm (10.9/11.0 in)		
Wheelbase	2795 mm (110.0 in)		
Track, front/rear	1488/1446 mm (58.6/56.9 in)		
Length	4725 mm (186.0 in)	U.S. 1977: 4848 mm (190.9 in)	
Width	1786 mm (70.3 in)		
Height	1438 mm (56.5 in)		
Tires	175 SR 14		175 HR 14
Turning circle	11.25 meters (36.9 feet); 1979: 11.29 meters (37 feet) U.S. 1977: 11.29 meters (37 feet)		11.29 meters (37 feet)
Steering type and ratio	recirculating ball (4.0 turns), servo assisted; U.S. 1977: 2.7 turns		recirculating ball
Weight	1350 kg (2970 lbs)	U.S. 1977: 1450 kg (3195 lbs)	1360 kg (2992 lbs)
Maximum speed	170 km/hr (106 mph); automatic: 165 km/hr (103 mph)		180 km/hr (112 mph); automatic: 175 km/hr (109 mph)
Acceleration	13.7 sec 0-100 km/hr; automatic: 13.9 sec 0-100 km/hr		11.5 sec 0-100 km/hr; automatic: 12.3 sec 0-100 km/hr
Fuel consumption	11.7 liters/100 km (20.6 mpg) 1979: at 120 km/hr: 12.5 liters; automatic: 12.8 liters		at 120 km/hr: 10.4 liters/100 km; automatic: 11 liters
Fuel tank capacity	65 liters (17.2 gallons); U.S. 1977: 80 liters (21.1 gallons)		

The 240D sedan, 1976

Prices and Production

The 240D four-door sedan sold in 1976 for . . . . .DM 20,146
in 1979 for. . . . . .DM 22,825
in 1982 for. . . . . .DM 28,109
The 240D sedan sold in the United States
in February 1979 for (East Coast). $15,068
with automatic transmission. $16,313
in November 1980 (East Coast) $19,312
with automatic transmission. $20,558
in October 1981 (East Coast). $20,989
in September 1982 (East Coast) $22,470
with automatic transmission. $23,800

Production of the 240D model [123 D24] (from July 1975/February 1976 until November 1985)

	was in 1975	7 units
	1976	21,247 units
	1977	40,382 units
	1978	42,816 units
	1979	62,678 units
	1980	69,908 units
	1981	73,162 units
	1982	74,627 units
	1983	44,718 units
	1984	23,338 units
	1985	1,897 units
	total	454,780 units

Model 240D (1975–1985)

D = Diesel

The 240D, the third diesel sedan with the same new body style of the other middle class models, also went into full production in January 1976. The older style was still built to ease the demand for these most economical cars.

The wheelbase of all of the W123 bodies was 45 millimeters longer than on the previous models and the front axle track 40 millimeters wider to give improved comfort and better roadhandling.

The bumpers had rubber guards and side strips with rubber inlets to protect the body from negligent and careless opening of doors. Windshield wipers were parallel running instead of the former butterfly style and were black to prevent reflections. Seat belts had been repositioned for improved comfort and safety. The heating and ventilating system was simplified and made more efficient and the easy-to-read panel with round instruments had a heavily inclined glass plate which eliminated glare and was easier to keep clean. A key-operated starter was available by 1977.

Acceleration figures for the 0 to 100 kilometers per hour were 24.6 seconds with the manual, and 27.4 seconds with the automatic transmission. In 1980 the figures were 22 seconds and 24.7, respectively. However, for that year the power output in the cars in the United States was raised to 67 SAE horsepower, but the weight of the sedan had increased to 1,415 kilograms (3,120 pounds).

The Environmental Protection Agency rating for the 240D for 1979 was 30 miles per gallon for city driving and 34 miles per gallon for the highway cycle. In 1980 this was changed to 28 mpg for city and 34 for highway, or a combined average rating of 30 miles per gallon of fuel. With the automatic transmission the figures were 26 and 29, or 27 combined. The 1981 figures were 29 and 33 for manual and 27 and 31 for the automatic.

The longer wheelbase (LW) model also became available in 1979 in the new body style. The rear suspension of that long limousine had a leveling control devise as standard equipment.

Specifications

	240D	240D (LW)
Engine type	4 cyl diesel, overhead camshaft (OM 616)	*In 1979 the 240D model became also available with a longer wheelbase as an eight-passenger limousine.*
Bore and stroke	91 x 92.4mm (3.58 x 3.64 in) 1979: 90.9 x 92.4mm	
Displacement	2402 cc (146.7 cu in) 1979: 2399 cc (146.4 cu in)	*The basic specifications were as those of the regular model, but with the following exceptions:*
Power output	65 hp (DIN) @ 4200 rpm; 1977: 64 hp 1979: 72 hp (DIN) @ 4400 rpm U.S. 1977: 62 hp SAE @ 4000 rpm U.S. 1980: 67 hp (SAE) @ 4000 rpm	
Compression ratio	21:1	
Torque	14 mkg @ 2400 rpm (101.3 ft/lb) U.S. 1977: 13.4 mkg @ 2400 rpm (97 ft/lb) 1982: 13.5 mkg (97 lb/ft)	
Fuel injection	Bosch four plunger pump	
Maximum engine speed	5400 rpm; 1979: 5300 rpm; U.S. 1977: 4350 rpm U.S. 1980: 4000 rpm	
Engine speed at 100 km/hr	3195 rpm; automatic: 3275 rpm 1980: 4000rpm, 1982: 4600 rpm	
Gear ratios	I. 3.90:1 automatic: I. 3.98:1 1980: I. 3.91:1 II. 2.30:1 II. 2.39:1 II. 2.32:1 III. 1.41:1 III. 1.46:1 III. 1.42:1 IV. 1.00:1 IV. 1.00:1	
Rear axle ratio	3.69	
Chassis	unit frame and body	
Suspension	independent front and rear, with coil springs; diagonal swing axle, coil springs, anti-roll bar. Optional level control; standard in 1979	
Brakes and area	dual circuit discs, power assisted, front brake pad wear indicator, 278/279 mm (10.9/11.0 in)	
Wheelbase	2795mm (110.0 in)	3425mm (134.8 in)
Track, front/rear	1488/1466mm (58.6/56.9 in)	1477/1430mm (58.1/56.3 in)
Length	4725mm (186.0 in) U.S. 1977: 4848mm (190.9 in)	5355mm (210.8 in)
Width	1786mm (70.3 in)	
Height	1438mm (56.6 in)	1480mm (58.3 in)
Ground clearance		
Rear suspension		level control standard
Tires	175 SR 14	
Turning circle	11.25 meters (36.9 ft) 1979: 11.29 meters (37 ft) U.S. 1977: 11.29 meters (37 ft)	13.35 meters (43.8 ft)
Steering type and ratio	recirculating ball (4.0 turns); servo assisted U.S. 1977: 2.7 turns; U.S. 1980: 3.2 turns	
Weight	1385 kg (3047 lbs) U.S. 1977: 1455 kg (3210 lbs) U.S. 1980: 1415 kg (3120 lbs)	1565 kg (3443 lbs)

The 240D sedan, 1981, U.S. version

Regular and long wheelbase 240D sedans

	240D	240D (LW)
Maximum speed	138 km/hr (86 mph) automatic: 133 km/hr (83 mph) 1979: 143 km/hr (89 mph) automatic: 138 km/hr (86 mph)	
Acceleration	24.6 sec 0-100 km/hr; automatic: 27.4 sec 1979: 22.0 sec; automatic: 24.7 sec	0-100 km/hr: 24.6 sec automatic: 27.2 sec
Fuel consumption	9.5 liters/100 km (24.75 mpg); 1979: at 120 km/hr: 10.9 liters; automatic: 11.4 liters	at 120 km/hr: 11.1 liters automatic: 12.2 liters
Fuel tank capacity	65 liters (17.2 gallons) U.S. 1977: 80 liters (21.1 gallons) U.S. 1980: 65 liters (17.2 gallons)	

The 250 sedan, 1976

The M 123 2.5-liter engine

Prices and Production

The 250 four-door sedan sold in 1976 for . . . . .DM 21,767
   in 1979 for. . . . . .DM 24,662

Production of the 250 model [123 V25] (from July 1975/April 1976 until December 1985)

was in	1975	5 units
	1976	14,915 units
	1977	25,183 units
	1978	23,306 units
	1979	21,758 units
	1980	17,447 units
	1981	8,029 units
	1982	5,392 units
	1983	3,246 units
	1984	2,232 units
	1985	1,311 units
	total	122,864 units

Model 250 (1975–1985)

The 250 model was the third of the newly introduced cars at the Geneva Auto Show in 1976, having the identical 123 style body as the 200 and 230 models with the round headlights.

It replaced the 250 model, in production since 1967 and built until 1972, when the designated 250 sedan, built from 1970 until 1976, actually had a 2.8-liter engine. The six-cylinder 230.6 model (1973-1976) was perhaps closer to the true 250, with the 2.3-liter engine of 120 horsepower, and it was really considered a replacement for that model.

But the engine for this W123 model style was a newly designed 2.5-liter six-cylinder unit developing 129 (DIN) horsepower at 5,500 revolutions per minute. It was a high performance engine built for economical operation. The four-bearing crankshaft had nine counterweights for improved balance, while the 2.3-liter engine had only three. Overhead camshaft with single roller chain drive, hydraulic chain tensioner and a Solex four-barrel carburetor were other features of the new power unit.

As in all of these new models, the oil change for the engine was simplified by the use of a sucking-out method, thus eliminating the need for a hoist, and making for quicker service.

This new 250 sedan, the smallest of the six-cylinder line of cars, was a lively performer and promised to be a good choice in the wide range of 30 models then offered to the public by Daimler-Benz. Still, the smaller four-cylinder 230 model outsold it by about two to one over the next five years and the 250 sedan sold as well as the larger six-cylinder 280 and 280E models combined.

Specifications

	250			250 (LW)

The 250 sedan, 1976

	250			250 (LW)
Engine type	6 cyl overhead camshaft (M123)			
Bore and stroke	86 x 72.45 mm (3.38 x 2.85 in)			
Displacement	2525 cc (154.1 cu in)			
Power output	129 hp (DIN) @ 5500 rpm; 1979: 140 hp (DIN) @ 5500 rpm			
Compression ratio	8.7:1; 1979: 9:1			
Torque	20 mkg @ 3500 rpm (144.7 ft/lb)			
Carburetion	Solex dual-compound downdraft 4A1			
Maximum engine speed	6000 rpm			
Engine speed at 100 km/hr	3195 rpm	automatic: 3275 rpm		
Gear ratios	I. 3.90:1 II. 2.30:1 III. 1.41:1 IV. 1.00:1	I. 3.98:1 (automatic) II. 2.39:1 III. 1.46:1 IV. 1.00:1	I. 3.98:1 (1979: manual transmission) II. 2.29:1 III. 1.45:1 IV. 1.00:1	
Rear axle ratio	3.92			
Chassis	unit frame and body			
Suspension	independent front and rear, with coil springs; diagonal swing axle, coil springs, anti-roll bar. Optional level control; standard in 1979			
Brakes and area	dual circuit discs, power assisted, front brake pad wear indicator, 278/279 mm (10.9/11.0 in)			
Wheelbase	2795 mm (110.0 in)			3425mm (134.8 in)
Track, front/rear	1488/1446 mm (58.6/56.9 in)			1477/1430mm (58.1/56.3 in)
Length	4725 mm (186.0 in)			5355mm (210.8 in)
Width	1786 mm (70.3 in)			
Height	1438 mm (56.6 in)			1480mm (58.3 in)
Tires	175 SR 14			
Turning circle	11.25 meters (36.9 feet); 1979: 11.29 meters (37 feet)			13.35 meters (43.8 feet)
Steering type and ratio	recirculating ball (4.0 turns), servo assisted			
Weight	1360 kg (2992 lbs); 1979: 1375 kg (3025 lbs)			1540 kg (3388 lbs)
Maximum speed	180 km/hr (112 mph); automatic: 175 km/hr (109 mph)			
Acceleration	11.5 sec 0-100 km/hr; automatic: 12.4 sec			0-100 km/hr: 12.4 sec.; automatic: 13.3 sec
Fuel consumption	11.8 liters/100 km (20.5 mpg); 1979: at 120 km/hr: 12.1 liters; automatic: 12.9 liters			at 120 km/hr: 11.9 liters; automatic: 13.1 liters
Fuel tank capacity	65 liters (17.2 gallons)			

In 1979 the 250 model became also available with a longer wheelbase as an eight-passenger limousine, but with the following exceptions:

The 280 sedan, 1975

The 280 sedan, 1975

Prices and Production

The 280 four-door sedan sold in 1976 for . . . . .DM 24,997
   in 1979 for. . . . . .DM 27,899

Production of the 280 model [123 V28] (from July/December 1975 until July 1981)

was in	1975	957 units
	1976	12,821 units
	1977	7,530 units
	1978	4,103 units
	1979	3,139 units
	1980	3,477 units
	1981	1,179 units
	total	33,206 units

Model 280 (1975-1981)

The 280 model, also first shown at the Geneva Auto Show in 1976, was distinguishable from the smaller engined cars by the halogen headlights. Otherwise, the W123 body style was the same.

The reflector surface of the main headlights was increased by 13%, standard with halogen lamps, signifying a definite safety contribution to the 280 and 280E models. Fog lights were also standard equipment and these had a 40% larger reflector surface on these models.

Interior appointments also incorporated many new safety features, such as recessed and easier to read instruments, improved padding of roof frame, relocated mounting seat belts, newly arranged combination switches stalk mounted on left of steering column, and redesigned heating and cooling systems, among others.

The front seats had better lateral support at hip height and had seat height control adjustments as standard equipment. It also extended the seat adjustment to the rear by 86 millimeters, a feature especially appreciated by long-legged drivers and normal body size who did not need the height adjustment.

The new exhaust system on all 123 models used an improved corrosion resistant material which extended its service life. The cars also had a hydraulic two-circuit braking system with vacuum brake booster and, of course, disc brakes on all four wheels, as all previous models. A brake pad wear indicator, up to then only used on the S-class cars, was included in all models. The foot-operated parking brake needed 30% less pressure to achieve the same effect as before.

The 280 was powered by the double overhead camshaft six-cylinder engine of 2,746 cubic centimeter displacement and developed 156 DIN horsepower.

Specifications

	280
Engine type	6 cyl double overhead camshafts (M110)
Bore and stroke	86 x 78.8 mm (3.39 x 3.10 in)
Displacement	2746 cc (167.6 cu in)
Power output	156 hp (DIN) @ 5500 rpm
Compression ratio	8.7:1
Torque	22.7 mkg @ 4000 rpm (164.2 ft/lb)
Carburetion	Solex dual-compound downdraft 4A1
Maximum engine speed	6500 rpm
Engine speed at 100 km/hr	3065 rpm automatic: 3155 rpm
Gear ratios	I. 3.90:1 I. 3.98:1 (automatic) I. 3.98:1 (1979: manual transmission)
	II. 2.30:1 II. 2.39:1 II. 2.29:1
	III. 1.41:1 III. 1.46:1 III. 1.45:1
	IV. 1.00:1 IV. 1.00:1 IV. 1.00:1
Rear axle ratio	3.54
Chassis	unit frame and body
Suspension	independent front and rear, with coil springs; diagonal swing axle, coil springs, anti-roll bar. Optional level control; standard in 1979
Brakes and area	dual circuit discs, power assisted, front brake pad wear indicator, 278/279 mm (10.9/11.0 in)
Wheelbase	2795 mm (110.0 in)
Track, front/rear	1488/1446 mm (58.6/56.9 in)
Length	4725 mm (186.0 in)
Width	1786 mm (70.3 in)
Height	1438 mm (56.6 in)
Tires	175 SR 14; 1979: 195/70 HR 14
Turning circle	11.25 meters (36.9 feet); 1979: 11.29 meters (37 feet)
Steering type and ratio	recirculating ball (4.0 turns), servo assisted
Weight	1455 kg (3201 lbs)
Maximum speed	190 km/hr (118 mph) automatic: 185 km/hr (115 mph)
Acceleration	10.6 sec 0-100 km/hr; automatic: 11.3 sec
Fuel consumption	12.5 liters/100 km (18.75 mph); 1979: at 120 km/hr: 12.7 liters; automatic: 13.5 liters
Fuel tank capacity	65 liters (17.2 gallons); 1979: 80 liters (21.1 gallons)

The 280 sedan, 1976

The 280E sedan, 1976

Instrument panel of the 280E, 1976

Prices and Production

The 280E four-door sedan sold in 1976 for . . . . .DM 26,895
 in 1979 for. . . . . .DM 30,016
The 280E sedan sold in the United States
 (with automatic transmission)
 in February 1979 for (East Coast). $22,318
 in November 1980 (East Coast) $26,848

Production of the 280E model [123 E28] (from July/December 1975 until December 1985)

was in	1975	607 units
	1976	17,638 units
	1977	17,651 units
	1978	14,904 units
	1979	18,383 units
	1980	17,703 units
	1981	12,723 units
	1982	10,757 units
	1983	8,545 units
	1984	5,946 units
	1985	1,518 units
	total	126,375 units

Model 280E (1975–1985)

E (Einspritzung) = fuel injection)

The 280E model, resembling in every detail the 280, was also first introduced at the Geneva Auto Show in 1976. It was, of course, the fuel-injection engine (E for Einspritzung) which made it different from the 280 model.

Fuel injection was by means of a mechanically controlled unit (Bosch K-Jetronic) with air volume control instead of the electronic system used previously. This improved type had been employed to a certain extent in the S-class models and had been introduced first in the 6.9-liter engine of the 450 SEL.

The optional sunroof on the 123 bodied models, where available, had an automatically operating wind deflector which popped up when the sunroof was opened. It was a most desirable feature.

The earlier 280E sedan (of the 114 body style) was gradually phased out. Only 344 units were built during the first year of production of this new model style when nearly 18,000 units of the 123 bodied 280E sedan were built.

As the least expensive six-cylinder model in the United States, this 280E was offered fully equipped. Many optional and extra cost items were, as was customary in this country, included in the price. The car had the four-wheel power disc brakes, variable assisted power steering, quartz clock, central locking system, fog lights, tinted windshield, heated rear window, electric window lifts, cruise control, arm rests front and rear, and radio as standard equipment.

Because of stringent emission controls and safety devices, the 280E was quite different from the regular European version. The engine developed only 137 SAE horsepower, instead of the 177 DIN, and the weight of the sedan was 1,600 kilograms (or 3,530 pounds), instead of 1,460 kilograms (or 3,212 pounds) for the other version. In 1977 a total of 4,166 units were imported into the U.S., outselling the more expensive and larger 280SE model by a small margin. Sales dropped the following years, and by 1980, 8,551 units had been brought to this country, against the 8,080 for the 280SE model sedan.

Specifications

	280E
Engine type	6 cyl double overhead camshafts (M110)
Bore and stroke	86 x 78.8 mm (3.39 x 3.10 in)
Displacement	2746 cc (167.6 cu in)
Power output	177 hp (DIN) @ 6000 rpm; 1979: 185 hp (DIN) @ 5800 rpm; U.S. 1977: 142 hp SAE @ 5750 rpm; 1980: 140 hp SAE @ 5500 rpm California: 137 hp SAE @ 5750 rpm
Compression ratio	8.7:1 1979: 9:1 U.S. 1977: 8:1
Torque	23.8 mkg @ 4500 rpm (172 ft/lb); U.S. 1977: 21.4 mkg @ 4600 rpm (149 ft/lb); 1980: 20.1 mkg California: 20.5 mkg @ 4600 rpm (142 ft/lb)
Fuel injection	Bosch mechanical with air metering device
Maximum engine speed	6500 rpm; US 1980: 6650 rpm
Engine speed at 100 km/hr	3065 rpm
Gear ratios	I. 3.90:1 I. 3.98:1 (automatic) I. 3.98:1 (1979: manual transmission) II. 2.30:1 II. 2.39:1 II. 2.29:1 III. 1.41:1 III. 1.46:1 III. 1.45:1 IV. 1.00:1 IV. 1.00:1 IV. 1.00:1
Rear axle ratio	3.54; 1982: 3.58 U.S. 1980: 3.58
Chassis	unit frame and body
Suspension	independent front and rear, with coil springs; diagonal swing axle, coil springs, anti-roll bar. Optional level control; standard in 1979
Brakes and area	dual circuit discs, power assisted, front brake pad wear indicator, 278/279 mm (10.9/11.0 in)
Wheelbase	2795 mm (110.0 in)
Track, front/rear	1488/1446 mm (58.6/56.9 in)
Length	4725 mm (186.0 in); U.S. 1977: 4848 mm (190.9 in)
Width	1786 mm (70.3 in)
Height	1438 mm (56.6 in)
Tires	175 SR 14; 1979: 195/70 HR 14
Turning circle	11.25 meters (36.9 feet); 1979: 11.29 meters (37 feet)
Steering type and ratio	recirculating ball (4.0 turns), servo assisted U.S. 1977: 2.7 turns
Weight	1460 kg (3212 lbs) U.S. 1977: 1600 kg (3530 lbs); 1980: 1570 kg
Maximum speed	200 km/hr (124 mph); automatic: 195 km/hr (121 mph)
Acceleration	9.9 sec 0-100 km/hr; automatic: 10.8 sec
Fuel consumption	12.5 liters/100 km (18.75 mpg); 1979: at 120 km/hr: 12.1 liters; automatic: 13 liters
Fuel tank capacity	65 liters (17.2 gallons); 1979: 80 liters (21.1 gallons)

The 280E sedan, 1977, U.S. version

Model 300D (1975–1985)

D = Diesel

The 300D sedan, 1976

Prices and Production

The 300D four-door sedan sold in 1976 for . . . . .DM 22,311
   in 1979 for. . . . . .DM 24,897
   in 1982 for. . . . . .DM 30,465
The 300D sedan sold in the United States
(with automatic transmission)
   in February 1979 for (East Coast). $20,911
   in November 1980 (East Coast) $25,640
   in October 1981 (East Coast). $28,483
   in September 1982 (East Coast) $30,530

Production of the 300D model [123 D30] (from July 1975/February 1976 until November 1985)

was in	1975	9 units
	1976	28,996 units
	1977	48,605 units
	1978	49,908 units
	1979	52,296 units
	1980	50,197 units
	1981	38,858 units
	1982	30,720 units
	1983	18,773 units
	1984	10,920 units
	1985	2,717 units
	total	331,999 units

Production of the 300D (turbo) model [123 D30A] (from July/September 1981 until August 1985)

was in	1981	4,505 units
	1982	20,178 units
	1983	20,005 units
	1984	19,673 units
	1985	10,900 units
	total	75,261 units

The 300D, the five-cylinder diesel-engined sedan, shared with the other eight models the same body style introduced at the Geneva Auto Show in 1976.

Over 53,000 of these sedans had been produced since their introduction in 1974 as the 240D 3.0 models, attesting to the enormous popularity of this larger diesel engine with buyers who valued the economy of a diesel.

The W123 body had, as the others mentioned earlier, the synchronized four-speed transmission with floor shift or, as an optional extra, the automatic four-speed with torque converter. It had an improved, more rigid clutch bell housing and transmission case, which reduced the bending vibration and made for smoother running.

The front had individual wheel suspension by means of double control arms, two coil springs with additional rubber springs, hydraulic telescopic shock absorbers and anti-roll bar. The rear had a diagonal pivot swing axle, two coil springs with additional rubber springs, hydraulic shock absorbers and anti-roll bar. Level control was an optional extra item.

The fuel injection pump for this diesel was entirely redesigned. A centrifugal governor operated the metering rack and regulated the power output. Cylinder crankhead and housing, head gasket, and the six main bearing crankshaft and oil pan were also new.

Automatic transmission was standard on this 300D model. Acceleration was 19.9 seconds for the 0 to 100 kilometers per hour, and with the rear axle ratio of 3.46 to 1, maximum speed was 89 miles per hour in the United States version, but 92 miles per hour for the European model.

The Environmental Protection Agency rating for 1979 and 1980 was 23 miles per gallon for city and 28 miles per gallon for the highway cycle, for an average of 25 miles per gallon fuel consumption. For 1981 the rating was 24 and 28 miles per gallon.

The 300D LW (long wheelbase) model was also available with the new body style.

The 300D outsold the 240D in the United States for the five-year period from 1979 to 1980 with 39,075 units against 38,777; but for the last two years the four-cylinder diesel had topped it.

For the 1982 model year the OM617A turbo-charged diesel engine replaced the regularly aspirated version. With the significant increase in power (45%), fuel economy was actually improved.

Specifications

	300D	300D (LW)	300D (turbo)
Engine type	5 cyl diesel, overhead camshaft (OM 617)	*In 1979 the 300D model became also available with a longer wheelbase as an eight-passenger limousine.* *The basic specifications were as those of the regular model, but with the following exceptions:*	5 cyl diesel, overhead camshaft, with turbo-charger (OM 617A)
Bore and stroke	91 x 92.4mm (3.58 x 3.64 in) 1979: 90.9 x 92.4mm		91 x 92.4mm (3.58 x 3.64 in)
Displacement	3055 cc (183.4 cu in) U.S. 1979: 2998 cc (183.0 cu in)		2998 cc (182.9 cu in)
Power output	80 hp (DIN) @ 4000 rpm 1979: 88 hp (DIN) @ 4400 rpm U.S. 1977: 77 hp (SAE) @ 4000 rpm U.S. 1980: 83 hp (SAE) @ 4200 rpm		125 hp (DIN) @4350 rpm U.S.: 120 hp (SAE) 1984: 123 hp; Cal. 1985: 118 hp
Compression ratio	21:1		21.5:1
Torque	17.5 mkg @ 2400 rpm (126.6 ft/lb) U.S. 1977: 15.9 mkg @ 2400 rpm (115 ft/lb) U.S. 1980: 16.7 mkg @ 2400 rpm (120 ft/lb)		25.5 mkg @ 2400 rpm U.S.: 23.6 mkg (170 ft/lb) 1984: 184 ft/lb; Cal. 1985: 177 ft/lb
Fuel injection	Bosch five plunger pump		Bosch five plunger pump w/injection timer
Maximum engine speed	5100 rpm; 1979: 5300 rpm U.S. 1977: 4350 rpm; U.S. 1980: 4200 rpm		5100 rpm; U.S.: 4350 rpm; 1982: 4500 rpm; 1983: 4640 rpm 1984: 5000 rpm; 1985: 5200 rpm
Engine speed at 100 km/hr			
Gear ratios	I. 3.90:1 automatic I. 3.98:1 II. 2.30:1 II. 2.39:1 III. 1.41:1 III. 1.46:1 IV. 1.00:1 IV. 1.00:1		I. 3.90:1 II. 2.30:1 III. 1.41:1 IV. 1.00:1
Rear axle ratio	3.46		3.07; U.S. 1985: 2.88
Chassis	unit frame and body		
Suspension	independent front and rear, with coil springs; diagonal swing axle, coil springs, anti-roll bar. Optional level control; standard in 1979		
Brakes and area	dual circuit discs, power assisted, front brake pad wear indicator (278/279mm (10.9/11.0 in)		
Wheelbase	2795mm (110.0 in)	3425mm (134.8 in)	
Track, front/rear	1488/1466mm (58.6/56.9 in)	1477/1430mm (58.1/56.3 in)	
Length	4725mm (186.0 in) U.S. 1977: 4848mm (190.9 in)	5355mm (210.8 in)	
Width	1786mm (70.3 in)		
Height	1438mm (56.6 in)	1480mm (58.3 in)	
Ground clearance			
Rear suspension		level control standard	
Tires	175 SR 14		1982: 195/70 SR-14
Turning circle	11.25 meters (36.9 ft) 1979: 11.29 meters (37 ft) U.S. 1977: 11.29 meters (37 ft)	13.35 meters (43.8 ft)	
Steering type and ratio	recirculating ball (4.0 turns), servo assisted U.S. 1977: 2.7 turns; U.S. 1980: 3.2 turns		
Weight	1445 kg (3179 lbs) U.S. 1977: 1595 kg (3515 lbs) U.S. 1978: 1600 kg (3530 lbs) U.S. 1980: 1555 kg (3430 lbs)	1615 kg (3553 lbs)	1982: 1625 kg (3585 lbs)
Maximum speed	148 km/hr (92 mph) automatic: 143 km/hr (89 mph) 1979: 155 km/hr automatic: 150 km/hr (93 mph)		
Acceleration	19.9 sec 0-100 km/hr automatic: 20.8 sec; 1979: 17.8 sec automatic: 19.2 sec	19.4 sec 0-100 km/hr automatic: 20.8 sec	
Fuel consumption	10.8 liters/100 km (21.5 mpg) 1979: at 120 km/hr 11.5 liters automatic: 12.4 liters	at 120 km/hr: 12.4 liters automatic: 12.0 liters	
Fuel tank capacity	65 liters (17.2 gallons) U.S. 1977: 80 liters (21.1 gallons)		

The 300D sedan, 1976

*The 280TE station wagon, 1977
similar to the 240TD*

Prices and Production

The 240TD station wagon sold in 1977 for . . . . .DM 25,052
in 1980 for . . . . .DM 28,159

Production of the 240TD station wagon [123 D24] (from February/May
1978 until January 1986)

was in	1978	3,003 units
	1979	6,387 units
	1980	5,820 units
	1981	5,078 units
	1982	5,881 units
	1983	5,134 units
	1984	4,491 units
	1985	3,103 units
	1986	6 units
	total	38,903 units

Model 240TD (1978–1986)

T (Touristik und Transport) = station wagon, D = Diesel

The 240TD, as the entire range of T models — the five different engined station wagons but with identical bodies — were first shown at the Frankfurt Auto Show in 1977. Regular production was scheduled to begin in the Bremen factory in April 1978, but actually started a month earlier than planned.

The T stood for Tourism and Transport, and the figures in that designation indicated the engine type.

Two diesel-engined and three gasoline-engined models were built, affording a great variety and satisfying nearly every conceivable preference.

It was the first time that Daimler-Benz manufactured a station wagon, although such type vehicles had been made available over the years, beginning with the 180/180D, by body building specialists, such as Christian Miesen of Bonn and Binz & Co. of Lorch, and the Belgiam IMA assembly plant.

The station wagons were based on the 123 sedan line of passenger cars and shared many components used in those vehicles. The roof line had been harmoniously integrated into the body shape, retaining the character of the sedan, but at the same time dramatically increasing the usable space. Other description details will be mentioned in connection with the following models.

The 240TD was powered by a 2.4-liter four-cylinder engine of 65 (DIN) horsepower. The 1,485-kilogram (3,267-pound) station wagon had a maximum speed of 138 kilometers per hour with manual transmission and 133 km/hr (83 miles per hour) with the automatic. Fuel consumption was rated at 9.5 liters per 100 kilometers (24.75 miles per gallon).

This diesel-powered model proved the best selling station wagon, except for the five-cylinder diesel sold also in the United States. The reliability and economy of the diesel engine proved irresistible to many buyers.

Specifications

	240TD
Engine type	4 cyl diesel, overhead camshaft (OM 616)
Bore and stroke	91 x 92.4mm (3.58 x 3.64 in) 1979: 90.9 x 92.4mm
Displacement	2404 cc (146.7 cu in) 1979: 2399 cc (146.4 cu in)
Power output	65 hp (DIN) @ 4200 rpm 1979: 72 hp @ 4400 rpm
Compression ratio	21:1
Torque	14 mkg @ 2400 rpm (101.3 ft/lb) 1979: 13.9 mkg @ 2400 rpm
Fuel injection	Bosch four plunger pump
Maximum engine speed	5300 rpm

Gear ratios		automatic:		1980:	
I.	3.90:1	I.	3.98:1	I.	3.91:1
II.	2.30:1	II.	2.39:1	II.	2.32:1
III.	1.41:1	III.	1.46:1	III.	1.42:1
IV.	1.00:1	IV.	1.00:1		

Rear axle ratio	3.69
Chassis	unit frame and body
Suspension	independent front and rear, coil springs; diagonal swing axle, coil springs, torsion bar stabilizer, standard level control
Brakes and area	dual circuit discs, front brake pad wear indicator, 278/279mm (10.9/11.0 in)
Wheelbase	2795mm (110.0 in)
Track, front/rear	1488/1453mm (58.6/57.2 in)
Length	4725mm (186.0 in)
Width	1786mm (70.3 in)
Height	1425mm (56.1 in) 1979: 1470mm (57.9 in)
Tires	195 SR 14
Turning circle	11.29 meters (37 ft)
Steering type and ratio	recirculating ball (3.2 turns), power assisted
Weight	1485 kg (3267 lbs) 1979: 1505 kg (3311 lbs)
Maximum speed	138 km/hr (86 mph) automatic: 133 km/hr (83 mph) 1979: 143 km/hr; automatic: 138 km/hr
Acceleration	24.6 sec 0-100 km/hr automatic: 27.4 sec 1979: 23.2 sec; automatic: 26.1 sec
Fuel consumption	9.5 liters/100 km (24.75 mpg) 1979: at 120 km/hr — 11.0 liters; automatic: 11.6
Fuel tank capacity	70 liters (18.5 gallons)

Rear lid open of 280TE, 1977

Front view of 280TE, 1977

161

The 300TD station wagon, 1978, U.S. version

Prices and Production

The 300TD station wagon sold in 1977 for . . . . .DM 27,317
    in 1980 for . . . . .DM 30,736
The 300TD station wagon sold in the United States
    (with automatic transmission)
    in February 1979 for (East Coast) $23,900
    in November 1980 (East Coast) $31,373

Production of the 300TD station wagon [123 D30] (from September 1977/May 1978 until January 1986)

was in	1977	1 unit
	1978	3,144 units
	1979	11,180 units
	1980	7,523 units
	1981	3,308 units
	1982	3,712 units
	1983	3,149 units
	1984	2,823 units
	1985	2,030 units
	1986	4 units
	total	36,874 units

Model 300TD (1977–1986)

T (Touristik und Transport) = station wagon, D = Diesel

The 300TD was the other of diesel-engined and another of the same bodied station wagons introduced at the Frankfurt Auto Show in 1977.

It was the only model destined for sale in the United States market and would have the identical mechanical specifications as the 300D sedans.

The interior was the very same as that of the sedan, with the instrument panel, console and gear shift exactly alike. A sunroof was available, but only the manual operated kind was offered because of lack of space for the electrical mechanism.

The wide opening rear door of the vehicle gave easy access to the normal loading area of 1.23 meters long and 1.48 meters wide. With the rear seat-back folded down, this could be extended to 1.78 meters, giving a volume of 525 or 879 liters (45.9 cubic feet). And by removing the rear seat, the floor length could be increased to 2.03 meters, or with the passenger seat folded down another 2.86 meters could be gained. There appeared to be almost no limit to the various loading possibilities available to suit practically every purpose. The load-carrying capacity was increased to 700 kilograms (1,540 pounds). An automatic self-leveling device on the rear axle was standard on these station wagons.

The 300TD was powered by the 3,005 cubic centimeter diesel engine of 80 (DIN) horsepower. The 1,545 kilogram (3,090 pound) vehicle had a maximum speed of 148 kilometers (92 miles) per hour with manual transmission and 143 km/hr (89 mph) with the automatic. Fuel consumption was rated at 10.8 liters per 100 kilometers (21.5 miles per gallon).

The 300TD became available first in the United States in March 1979. Specifications were consequently different from the regular version, with the 77SAE horsepower engine and a curb weight of 1,715 kilograms (3,780 pounds). The Environmental Protection Agency fuel consumption rate was 23 miles per gallon for city driving and 28 miles per gallon for the highway cycle, the same as for the 300D sedan, for an average of 25 miles per gallon.

Specifications

300TD

Engine type	5 cyl diesel, overhead camshaft (OM 617)	Wheelbase	2795mm (110.0 in)
		Track, front/rear	1488/1453mm (58.6/57.2 in)
Bore and stroke	91 x 92.4mm (3.58 x 3.65 in)	Length	4725mm (186.0 in)
	1979: 90.9 x 92.4mm		U.S.: 4848mm (190.9 in)
Displacement	3005 cc (183.4 cu in)	Width	1786mm (70.3 in)
	1979: 2998 cc (183 cu in)	Height	1425mm (56.1); 1979: 1470mm (57.9 in)
Power output	80 hp (DIN) @ 4000 rpm		
	1979: 88 hp @ 4400 rpm; U.S.: 77 hp	Tires	195 SR 14
	SAE @ 4000 rpm	Turning circle	11.29 meters (37 ft)
	U.S. 1980: 83 hp (SAE) @ 4200 rpm	Steering type and ratio	recirculating ball (3.2 turns), power assisted
Compression ratio	21:1		
Torque	17.5 mkg @ 2400 rpm (126.6 ft/lb)	Weight	1545 kg (3399 lbs); 1979: 1565 kg
	1979: 17.5 mkg @ 2400 rpm		(3443 lbs); U.S.: 1715 kg (3773 lbs)
	U.S.: 15.9 mkg (115 ft/lb); U.S. 1980:		U.S. 1980: 1635 kg (3597 lbs)
	16.7 mkg @ 2400 rpm (120 ft/lb)	Maximum speed	148 km/hr (92 mph)
Fuel injection	Bosch five plunger pump		automatic: 143 km/hr (89 mph)
Maximum engine speed	5300 rpm; U.S.: 4350 rpm		1979: 155 km/hr; automatic: 150 km/hr
	U.S. 1980: 4200 rpm	Acceleration	19.9 sec 0–100 km/hr; automatic: 20.8 sec
Gear ratios	I. 3.90:1 automatic: I. 3.98:1		1979: 18.9 sec; automatic: 20.4 sec
	II. 2.30:1 II. 2.39:1		
	III. 1.41:1 III. 1.46:1	Fuel consumption	10.8 liters/100 km (21.5 mpg)
	IV. 1.00:1 IV. 1.00:1		1979: at 120 km/hr: 11.3 liters;
			automatic: 13.0
Rear axle ratio	3.46	Fuel tank capacity	70 liters (18.5 gallons)
Chassis	unit frame and body		
Suspension	independent front and rear, coil springs; diagonal swing axle, coil springs, torsion bar stabilizer, standard level control		
Brakes and area	dual circuit discs, front brake pad wear indicator, 278/279mm (10.9/11.0 in)		

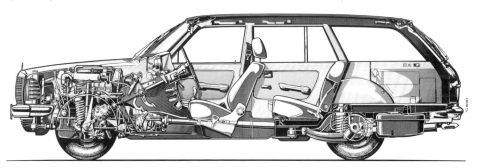

Schematic drawing of station wagon

The 230T station wagon, 1979

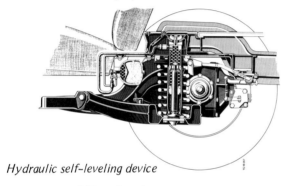

Hydraulic self-leveling device

Prices and Production

The 230T station wagon sold in 1977 for . . . . .DM 23,976
    in 1979 for. . . . . .DM 25,704

Production of the 230T station wagon [123 V23] (from February/
May 1978 until April 1980)

was in	1978	1,793 units
	1979	3,829 units
	1980	1,262 units
	total	6,884 units

The 230TE station wagon sold in 1980 for . . . . .DM 28,781

Production of the 280TE station wagon [123 E23] (from October 1979/
April 1980 until January 1986)

was in	1979	2 units
	1980	3,750 units
	1981	5,655 units
	1982	7,158 units
	1983	9,731 units
	1984	9,617 units
	1985	6,340 units
	1986	31 units
	total	42,284 units

Model 230T (1978-1980)

T (Touristik und Transport) = station wagon

The 230T was the same bodied station wagon as the others shown first at the Frankfurt Auto Show in 1977. It had the smallest gasoline engine of the three vehicles so powered.

The entire range of station wagons had available a large assortment of special equipment which was especially developed for these vehicles, which were meant also for leisure driving, as well as for light commercial purposes. Special rails were built into the roof, able to take roof racks with aerodynamically styled luggage containers, or ski and ski boot cases, and protect them from possible inclement weather and potential thieves. In addition, various racks were offered for the convenient carrying of boats, surfboards, bicycles, and such recreation equipment.

The 230T was powered by the regular 2,307 cubic centimeter four-cylinder engine of 109 (DIN) horsepower, giving the 1,450 kilogram (3,190 lb) station wagon a top speed of about 170 kilometers per hour with manual or 165 km/hr (102 mph) with the automatic transmission. Fuel consumption was rated at 11.7 liters per 100 kilometers (20 miles per gallon).

Model 230TE (1979-1986)

T = station wagon, E = fuel injection

The 230TE model station wagon with the newly designed M102 fuel-injection engine appeared in early 1980 when the regular carburetor engined model was phased out in April of that year.

These 2,299 cubic centimeter four-cylinder engines with better fuel consumption and greater smoothness of operation developed 136 DIN horsepower, actually 25% more power than the carburetor units they replaced.

The 230TE had a maximum speed of 180 kilometers per hour, and acceleration of 0-100 kilometers per hour was 12.2 seconds with manual and 13.1 seconds with the automatic transmission. Fuel consumption was rated at 14.2 liters with manual and 13.8 liters with automatic transmission for the urban cycle, and for the 120 kilometers per hour speed, the figures were 10.6 and 11.5, respectively.

Specifications

	230T	230TE
Engine type	4 cyl overhead camshaft (M115)	4 cyl overhead camshaft (M102)
Bore and stroke	93.75 x 83.6 (3.69 x 3.29 in)	95.5 x 80.25 mm (3.74 x 3.16 in)
Displacement	2307 cc (140.8 cu in)	2299 cc (140.12 cu in)
Power output	109 hp (DIN) @ 4800 rpm	136 hp (DIN) @ 5100 rpm
Compression ratio	9.0:1	9.0:1
Torque	18.9 mkg @ 3000 rpm (136.7 ft/lb) 1979: 18.9 mkg @ 3000 rpm	20.9 mkg @ 3500 rpm (151.2 ft/lb)
Carburetion	Stromberg crossdraft 175 CD	Bosch mechanical (fuel injection)
Maximum engine speed	6000 rpm	6000 rpm
Gear ratios	I. 3.90:1 I. 3.98:1 (automatic) II. 2.30:1 II. 2.39:1 III. 1.41:1 III. 1.46:1 IV. 1.00:1 IV. 1.00:1	I. 3.91:1 II. 2.32:1 III. 1.42:1 IV. 1.00:1
Rear axle ratio	3.69	
Chassis	unit frame and body	
Suspension	independent front and rear, with coil springs; diagonal swing axle, coil springs, torsion bar stabilizer, standard level control	
Brakes and area	dual circuit discs, front brake pad wear indicator, 278/279 mm (10.9/11.0 in)	
Wheelbase	2795 mm (110.0 in)	
Track, front/rear	1488/1453 mm (58.6/57.2 in)	
Length	4725 mm (186.0 in)	
Width	1786 mm (70.3 in)	
Height	1425 mm (56.1 in) 1979: 1470 mm (57.9 in)	1470 mm (57.9 in)
Tires	195 SR 14	195/70 HR 14
Turning circle	11.29 meters (37 feet)	
Steering type and ratio	recirculating ball (3.2 turns), power assisted	
Weight	1450 kg (3190 lbs) 1979: 1470kg (3234 lbs)	1455 kg (3205 lbs)
Maximum speed	170 km/hr (106 mph); automatic: 165 km/hr (103 mph)	168 km/hr (105 mph); automatic: 163 km/hr (102 mph)
Acceleration	13.7 sec 0-100 km/hr; automatic 13.9 sec 1979: 14.4 sec 0-100 km/hr; automatic: 14.8 sec	11.5 sec 0-100 km/hr; automatic: 12.3 sec 0-100 km/hr
Fuel consumption	11.7 liters/100 km (20.6 mph) 1979: at 120 km/hr: 12.5 liters; automatic 12.8	at 120 km/hr: 10.7 liters/100 km; automatic: 11.4 liters 70 liters (18.5 gallons)
Fuel tank capacity	70 liters (18.5 gallons)	

Model **250T** (1977-1982)

Rear view of the 280TE, 1977

Prices and Production

The 250T station wagon in 1977 sold for .... DM 26,751
    in 1980 for .... DM 30,600

Production of the 250T station wagon [123 V25] (from September 1977/May 1978 until August 1982)

was in	1977	1 unit
	1978	1,382 units
	1979	2,946 units
	1980	2,761 units
	1981	402 units
	1982	213 units
	total	7,704 units

The 280TE station wagon sold in 1977 for .... DM 32,056
    in 1980 for .... DM 35,798

Production of the 280TE station wagon [123 E28] (from September 1977/May1978 until January 1986)

was in	1977	3 units
	1978	1,260 units
	1979	4,059 units
	1980	3,614 units
	1981	1,956 units
	1982	2,545 units
	1983	2,716 units
	1984	2,293 units
	1985	1,329 units
	1986	14 units
	total	19,789 units

T (Touristik und Transport) = station wagon

The 250T was the fourth of the five station wagons shown first at the Frankfurt Auto Show in 1977. This medium powered vehicle actually proved to be the slowest selling model of the whole range of these utility vehicles.

The entire line of the station wagons shared the same body style and features of this utilitarian wagon. The interior design was a fine example of the most ingenious use of space. Built to carry five adult persons in comfort, with either all or some of the seats folded down, it offered an immense variety of space to carry a vast diversity of objects.

When raising the tailgate, the hinges and shock absorber units were discreetly tucked into the roof, allowing an absolutely smooth inner roof surface so that bulky packages would not snag on outjutting hinges.

The 250T was powered by the 2,525 cubic centimeter six-cylinder engine of 129 (DIN) horsepower. This 1,460 kilogram (3,212 pound) heavy station wagon had a maximum speed of about 180 kilometers per hour with standard transmission and 175 km/hr (109 mph) with automatic transmission. Fuel consumption was rated at 11.8 liters per 100 kilometers (20 miles per gallon).

Model **280TE** (1977–1986)

T = station wagon, E = fuel injection

The 280TE was the last and fastest of the five differently powered station wagons, introduced publicly at the Frankfurt Auto Show in 1977.

The interior outfitting compared in practically every detail to the sedans, including carpeting for the entire loading area.

The specifications for this line of vehicles was the same as those of the sedans — wheelbase, length and width. The fuel tank had a capacity of 70 liters (18.2 gallons). The regular manual four-speed Mercedes–Benz transmission was standard equipment, with the automatic transmission as an optional choice.

The 280TE had the 2,746 cubic centimeter six-cylinder fuel injection engine of 177 (DIN) horsepower to give it a maximum speed of 200 kilometers per hour with the manual and 195 km/hr (121 mph) with the automatic transmission. Fuel consumption was rated at 12.5 liters per 100 kilometers (18.75 miles per gallon).

Specifications

	250T				280 TE	
Engine type	6 cyl overhead camshaft (M123)				6 cyl double overhead camshafts (M110)	
Bore and stroke	86 x 72.45 mm (3.38 x 2.85 in)				86 x 78.8 mm (3.39 x 3.10 in)	
Displacement	2525 cc (154.1 cu in)				2746 cc (167.6 cu in)	
Power output	129 hp (DIN) @ 5500 rpm 1979: 140 hp (DIN) @ 5500 rpm				177 hp (DIN) @ 6000 rpm 1979: 185 hp (DIN) @ 5800 rpm	
Compression ratio	8.7:1	1979: 9:1			8.7:1	1979: 9.0:1
Torque	20 mkg @ 3500 rpm (144.7 ft/lb) 1979: 20 mkg @ 3500 rpm				23.8 mkg @ 4500 rpm (172.2 ft/lb) 1979: 24.4 mkg	
Carburetion	Solex dual-compound downdraft 4A1				Bosch mechanical with air metering device (fuel injection)	
Maximum engine speed	6000 rpm				6500 rpm	
Gear ratios	I. 3.90:1 II. 2.30:1 III. 1.41:1 IV. 1.00:1	I. 3.98:1 (automatic) II. 2.39:1 III. 1.46:1 IV. 1.00:1	I. 3.98:1 (1979: manual transmission) II. 2.29:1 III. 1.45:1 IV. 1.00:1		I. 3.90:1 II. 2.30:1 III. 1.41:1 IV. 1.00.1	
Rear axle ratio	3.69				3.58	
Chassis	unit frame and body					
Suspension	independent front and rear, with coil springs; diagonal swing axle, coil springs, torsion bar stabilizer, standard level control					
Brakes and area	dual circuit discs, front brake pad wear indicator, 278/279 mm (10.9/11.0 in)					
Wheelbase	2795 mm (110.0 in)					
Track, front/rear	1488/1453 mm (58.6/57.2 in)					
Length	4725 mm (186.0 in)					
Width	1786 mm (70.3 in)					
Height	1425 mm (56.1 in) 1979: 1470 mm (57.9 in)					
Tires	195 SR 14					
Turning circle	11.29 meters (37 feet)					
Steering type and ratio	recirculating ball (3.2 turns), power assisted					
Weight	1460 kg (3212 lbs) 1979: 1495 kg (3289 lbs)				1525 kg (3355 lbs) 1979: 1545 kg (2542 lbs)	
Maximum speed	180 km/hr (112 mph); automatic: 175 km/hr (109 mph) 1979: 185 km/hr; automatic: 180 km/hr				200 km/hr (124 mph); automatic: 195 km/hr (121 mph)	
Acceleration	11.5 sec 0-100 km/hr; automatic: 12.4 sec 1979: 11.9 sec; automatic: 12.9 sec				9.9 sec 0-100 km/hr; automatic: 10.8 sec 1979: 10.2 sec; automatic: 11.2 sec	
Fuel consumption	11.8 liters/100 km (20.5 mpg)		1979: at 120 km/hr: 12.1 liters automatic: 12.9 liters		12.5 liters/100 km (18.75 mpg) 1979: at 120 km/hr: 12.2 liters automatic: 13.4 liters	
Fuel tank capacity	70 liters (18.5 gallons)					

The 450SLC 5.0 coupe, 1977

Front view of the 450SLC 5.0 coupe, 1977

Prices and Production

The 450SLC 5.0 coupe sold in 1977 for . . . . .DM 58,841

Production of the 450SLC 5.0/500SLC coupe [107 E50] (from September 1977/May 1978 until September 1981)

was in	1977	9 units
	1978	524 units
	1979	937 units
	1980	816 units
	1981	483 units
	total	2,769 units

Model 450SLC 5.0 (1977-1981)

S = Sports, L = Light, C = Coupe

The 450SLC 5.0 coupe was first shown to the general public at the Frankfurt Auto Show in September 1977. It was equipped with a new light-alloy V-8 gasoline fuel injection engine of 240 (DIN) horsepower.

Mainly urged by the desire to improve fuel consumption efficiency, this new engine was based on the existing V-8 units. The improved power output reduced the noise level and gave the car the finest performance of any model built then.

In addition to the lighter engine (by 43 kilograms or 94.6 pounds), the wheels, hood and trunk lid were also of light alloy, thus achieving a weight reduction of over 100 kg (220 lbs), or 7% over the former 450SLC. By the installation of front and rear spoilers, wind resistance was reduced by 9%. The car had a maximum speed of 225 kilometers (140 miles) per hour. Fuel consumption was rated at only 14.5 liters per 100 kilometers (16 miles per gallon).

The 450SLC 5.0 was a rather limited production model and never reached the sales figures of the 6.9 model, except for the 1980 year of manufacture. It seemed that it rather afforded a glimpse of future models with lighter engines and lighter bodies and greater fuel economy.

This new coupe was a car for driving enthusiasts, offering high performance and great driving comfort. It was quite suitable for sporting events and the use in rallies by private entries was apparently not disapproved of by the factory.

In fact, eventually some factory-prepared cars — 450SLC 5.0 and 280E models — participated in several selected rally events over the years, but the cars were never able to win the coveted world's rally championships. Although occasionally they won the first several places in a rally, their weight and power were not suited to all twelve of the international events rallies, which counted toward the championship.

Specifications

Rear view of the 450SLC 5.0 coupe, 1977

	450SLC 5.0	
Engine type	V-8 cyl overhead camshafts (M117)	
Bore and stroke	97 x 85 mm (3.82 x 3.35 in)	1979: 96.5 x 85 mm (3.80 x 3.35 in)
Displacement	4990 cc (304.5 cu in)	1979: 4973 cc (303.5 cu in)
Power output	240 hp (DIN) @ 5000 rpm	
Compression ratio	8.8:1	
Torque	41 mkg @ 3200 rpm (296.6 lb/ft)	
Fuel injection	Bosch mechanical with air flow sensor	
Maximum engine speed	5800 rpm	
Gear ratios	I. 2.31:1 (automatic, standard) II. 1.46:1 III. 1.00:1	
Rear axle ratio	2.72	
Chassis	unit frame and body	
Suspension	independent front and rear, with coil springs, anti-roll bar; diagonal swing axle, coil springs, anti-roll bar, level control	
Brakes and area	dual circuit discs, power assisted, brake pad wear indicator, 278/279 mm (10.9/11.0 in)	
Wheelbase	2815 mm (110.8 in)	
Track, front/rear	1452/1440 mm (57.2/56.7 in)	
Length	4750 mm (187 in)	
Width	1790 mm (70.5 in)	
Height	1330 mm (52.3 in)	
Tires	205/70 VR 14	
Turning circle	11.55 meters (37.9 feet)	
Steering type and ratio	recirculating ball (3.0 turns), servo assisted	
Weight	1515 kg (3333 lbs)	
Maximum speed	225 km/hr (140 mph)	
Acceleration	8.5 sec 0-100 km/hr	
Fuel consumption	14.5 liters/100 km (16 mpg) 1979: at 120 km/hr: 13.3 liters/100 km	
Fuel tank capacity	90 liters (23.8 gallons)	

Instrument panel of the 450SLC 5.0 coupe, 1977

The 300SD sedan, 1978, U.S. version

The 300SD sedan, 1979, U.S. version

Prices and Production

The 300SD sedan sold in the United States
(with automatic transmission)
in February 1979 for (East Coast) $26,265

Production of the 300SD model [116D 30A] (from February 1977/
May 1978 until September 1980)

was in	1977	51 units
	1978	5,970 units
	1979	13,194 units
	1980	9,419 units
	total	28,634 units

Model 300SD (1977-1980)

S = turbo charged, D = Diesel

The 300SD sedan, the first turbo-charged diesel-engined passenger car, was introduced at the Frankfurt Auto Show in September 1977. However, at that time it was intended for the United States market only, beginning in the spring of 1978.

The body style was that of the S-class cars, the larger displacement gasoline models (die Oberklasse), with a 2,865 millimeter (112.8 inch) wheelbase and overall length of 5,220 millimeters (205.5 inches). The turbo-charged five-cylinder diesel engine of 2,998 cubic centimeters, with the Garrett turbo charger unit, developed 115 (DIN) horsepower, an increase of 44% of power over the naturally aspirated 300D 80 horsepower unit. Torque was increased by 37%, and fuel economy was actually improved by 9%.

Turbo-charging was, of course, a long tradition with Daimler-Benz, having begun in the 1940s with airplane engines, then large industrial units and finally truck engines.

The new engine had been widely tested, and installed in somewhat modified trim — to develop 200 horsepower — in the experimental coupe C 111, it established on the track at Nardo absolute long distance world records at continuous speeds of more than 250 kilometers (156 miles) per hour.

In 1979 the 300SD was the best selling diesel sedan in the United States, leading the second place 240D (11,066 units sold) with sales of 11,067 cars. In fact, that year, diesels sold constituted 67.4% of total of all cars sold in this country by Mercedes-Benz. (In 1980 diesels were 73% of all cars sold.) The Environmental Protection Agency rating was 24 for city and 29 for highway, with an average of 26 miles per gallon fuel consumption, — the best of the entire diesel line, and beating by 1 mile per gallon the five-cylinder regularly aspirated diesel models. This becomes an even greater feat when considering that the 300D sedan weighed (in the U.S.) 1,600 kilograms (3,530 pounds) and the 300SD 1,745 kilograms (3,850 pounds).

Specifications

	300SD
Engine type	5 cyl diesel, overhead camshaft, with turbo-charger (OM 617A)
Bore and stroke	90.9 x 92.4mm (3.58 x 3.64 in)
Displacement	2998 cc (182.9 cu in)
Power output	115 hp (DIN) @ 4200 (110 SAE hp); U.S. 1980: 120 hp (SAE) @ 4350 rpm
Compression ratio	21.5:1
Torque	23.2 mkg @ 2400 rpm (168 ft/lb); U.S. 1980: 23.6 mkg @ 2400 rpm (170 ft/lb)
Maximum engine speed	4350 rpm
Fuel injection	Bosch five plunger pump with injection timer
Engine speed at 100 km/hr	2580 rpm
Gear ratios	automatic, standard: I. 3.98:1 II. 2.39:1 III. 1.46:1 IV. 1.00:1
Rear axle ratio	3.07
Chassis	unit frame and body
Suspension	independent front and rear, coil springs, anti-roll bar; diagonal swing axle, coil springs, anti-roll bar, standard level control
Brakes and area	dual circuit discs, power assisted, brake pad wear indicator, 278/279mm (10.9/11.0 in)
Wheelbase	2865mm (112.8 in)
Track, front/rear	1521/1505mm (59.9/59.3 in)
Length	5220mm (205.5 in)
Width	1870mm (73.6 in)
Height	1425mm (56.1 in)
Tires	185 HR 14
Turning circle	11.59 meters (38 feet)
Steering type and ratio	recirculating ball (2.7 turns); servo assisted
Weight	1765 kg (3883 lbs); U.S.: 1745 kg (3839 lbs); 1980: 1715 kg (3773 lbs)
Maximum speed	165 km/hr (103 mph)
Acceleration	12.7 sec 0-100 km/hr
Fuel consumption	10.6 liters/100 km (22 mph)
Fuel tank capacity	82 liters (21.7 gallons)

The OM 617A engine for the 300SD, 1979

The short-lived insignia for the turbo-diesel

171

The 280CE coupe, 1978, U.S. version

Prices and Production

The 280CE coupe sold in 1977 for . . . . .DM 31,834
    in 1980 for. . . . . .DM 36,566
The 280CE coupe sold in the United States
  (with automatic transmission)
  in February 1979 for (East Coast). $24,951
  in November 1980 (East Coast) $30,314

Production of the 280CE coupe [123 E28] (from October 1976/April 1977 until August 1985)

was in 1976	2 units
1977	6,413 units
1978	6,958 units
1979	5,091 units
1980	4,013 units
1981	2,774 units
1982	2,509 units
1983	2,237 units
1984	1,476 units
1985	665 units
total	32,138 units

Model 280CE (1976–1985)

C = Coupe, E (Einspritzung) = fuel injection

The 280CE coupe was first shown at the Geneva Auto Show in March 1977. This new body style was based on the W123 sedan body, introduced just a year before at the same exhibition.

The wheelbase of the coupe was actually 2,710 millimeters (106.7 inches), or 85 millimeters (3.3 inches), shorter than that of the sedans, but the resemblance to the new style was unmistakable. It was to replace the C114 line of coupes originally introduced in late 1968 as the 250C and four years later as the 280C coupe. Now the coupes were available as the 230C, 280C, and 280CE.

The 280CE had the double overhead camshaft six-cylinder engine of 2,746 cubic centimeters (168 cubic inches), the very same as the 280SE sedan, and it was the most spirited performer of the trio. In overall appearance and in the rather elegant distinct interior appointments, all of the coupes were alike.

The 185 DIN horsepower fuel injected engine gave the coupe a good acceleration, from 0 to 100 kilometers per hour in 9.9 seconds with the manual transmission and 10.8 seconds with the automatic. Maximum speed was an even 200 kilometers (124 miles) per hour, and 195 kilometers with the manual transmission, the same figures as the sedan which actually weighed 10 kilograms more than the 1,450 kilograms given for the coupe.

For the United States market, the engine for the 280CE developed 142 SAE horsepower (California: 137 hp), and the coupe weighed 1,590 kilograms (3,510 lbs) when it was first introduced for the 1978 model year. For 1980 these specifications had changed to a weight of 1,560 kilograms (3,440 pounds), and the engine developed 140 SAE horsepower at 5,500 revolutions per minute. Torque was 145 feet/pounds, or 20.1 mkg at 4,500 revolutions.

Specifications

	280CE		
Engine type	6 cyl double overhead camshafts (M110)		
Bore and stroke	86 x 78.8 mm (3.39 x 3.10 in)		
Displacement	2746 cc (167.6 cu in)		
Power output	177 hp (DIN) @ 6000 rpm	1979: 185 hp (DIN) @ 5800 rpm	
	U.S. 142 hp SAE @ 5750 rpm	1980: 140 hp @ 5500 rpm	
	California: 137 hp SAE @ 2750 rpm		
Compression ratio	8.7:1	1979: 9:1 U.S.: 8:1	
Torque	23.8 mkg @ 4500 rpm (172.2 ft/lb)		
	U.S.: 21.4 mkg @ 4600 rpm (149 ft/lb; California: 142 ft/lb)		
Fuel injection	Bosch mechanical with air metering device		
Maximum engine speed	6500 rpm	U.S. 1980: 6650 rpm	
Engine speed at 100 km/hr	3065 rpm	automatic: 3155 rpm	
Gear ratios	I. 3.90:1	I. 3.98:1 (automatic)	I. 3.98:1 (1979: manual transmission)
	II. 2.30:1	II. 2.39:1	II. 2.29:1
	III. 1.41:1	III. 1.46:1	III. 1.45:1
	IV. 1.00:1	IV. 1.00:1	IV. 1.00:1
Rear axle ratio	3.58	U.S. 3.54	1978: 3.58
Chassis	unit frame and body		
Suspension	independent front and rear, with coil springs; diagonal swing axle, coil springs, anti-lift control, stabilizer bar		
Brakes and area	dual circuit discs, power assisted, 278/279 mm (10.9/11.0 in)		
Wheelbase	2710 mm (106.7 in)		
Track, front/rear	1488/1446 mm (58.6/56.9 in)		
Length	4640 mm (182.6 in)	U.S.: 4763 mm (187.5 in)	
Width	1786 mm (70.3 in)		
Height	1395 mm (54.9 in)		
Tires	175 SR 14	1979: 195/70 HR 14	U.S. 195/70 HR 14
Turning circle	11 meters (36.1 feet)		
Steering type and ratio	recirculating ball (3.2 turns), servo assisted		
Weight	1450 kg (3190 lbs)	U.S.: 1590 kg (3510 lbs)	1980: 1570 kg
			1981: 1565 kg
Maximum speed	200 km/hr (124 mph); automatic: 195 km/hr (121 mph)		
Acceleration	9.9 sec 0-100 km/hr; automatic: 10.8 sec		
Fuel consumption	12.5 liters/100 km (18.75 mpg); 1979: at 120 km/hr: 11.8 liters; automatic: 13.2 liters		
Fuel tank capacity	80 liters (21.1 gallons)		

The 280CE coupe, 1979, U.S. version

Model 280C (1976-1980)

C = Coupe

The 280C coupe was another variation of that introduced at the Geneva Auto Show in 1977. The new body style of the 123, with a graceful arc of the roofline and pillarless design, gave the cars a rakish shape.

The front suspension linked the zero offset front axle with a sway bar to provide unusual tracking and superb roadability on any surface. The rear suspension, fully independent, incorporated a patented design with parallel constant velocity couplings and another sway bar. Power-assisted disc brakes were standard equipment, as were radial tires.

The 2,746 cubic centimeter six-cylinder engine had a Solex dual downdraft carburetor and developed 156 (DIN) horsepower at 5,500 revolutions per minute in that form. The 280C weighed 1,445 kilograms (3,179 pounds) and maximum speed was 190 kilograms (118 miles) per hour with the manual transmission.

Prices and Production

The 280C coupe sold in 1977 for . . . . .DM 29,847

Production of the 280C coupe [123 V28] (from November 1976/ April 1977 until March 1980)

was in	1976	2 units
	1977	1,577 units
	1978	1,243 units
	1979	757 units
	1980	125 units
	total	3,704 units

The 230C coupe sold in 1977 for . . . . .DM 25,063

Production of the 230C coupe [123 V23] (from November 1976/ June 1977 until June 1980)

was in	1976	1 unit
	1977	3,484 units
	1978	7,049 units
	1979	6,538 units
	1980	1,603 units
	total	18,675 units

The 230CE coupe sold in 1980 for . . . . .DM 30,837

Production of the 230CE coupe [123 E23] (from February/April 1980 until August 1985)

was in	1980	4,818 units
	1981	7,192 units
	1982	6,734 units
	1983	6,038 units
	1984	4,052 units
	1985	1,024 units
	total	29,858 units

Model 230C (1976-1980)

C = Coupe

The 230C was the third version of the coupe first shown at the Geneva Auto Show in 1977. In outward appearance it was just as the other two models.

The interior was as sumptious as the more powerful cars, except that it had the 2,307 cubic centimeter four-cylinder engine of 109 horsepower (DIN) installed. The curb weight of the coupe was 1,375 kilograms (3,025 lbs), giving it a power-to-weight ratio of 12.6. The others had a ratio of 9.3 and 8.2, respectively. Still, the acceleration of the 230C was 13.7 seconds for the 0-100 kilometers per hour, and maximum speed was 170 kilometers (106 miles) per hour. Of course, it was the most economical of the elegant coupes, using only 12.1 liters of gasoline for 100 kilometers (over 19 miles per gallon), driving at 120 kilometers per hour.

Model 230CE (1980−1985)

C = Coupe

The 230CE coupe with the same body style but with the newly designed M102 four-cylinder engine went into production in April 1980. The 230C model was phased out in June.

It was in keeping with the policy of replacing the older 2-liter and 2.3-liter gasoline engines in sedans and station wagons as well. The 230CE had improved acceleration times and top speed was bettered by 10 km/hr. Fuel consumption was also greatly improved.

The 230CE coupe, 1980

Specifications

	280C			230C		230CE
Engine type	6 cyl double overhead camshafts (M110)			4 cyl overhead camshaft (M115)		4 cyl overhead camshaft (M102)
Bore and stroke	86 x 78.8 mm (3.39 x 3.10 in)			93.75 x 83.6 mm (3.69 x 3.29 in)		95.5 x 80.25 mm (3.74 x 3.16 in)
Displacement	2746 cc (167.6 cu in)			2307 cc (140.8 cu in)		2299 cc (140.12 cu in)
Power output	156 hp (DIN)@ 5500 rpm			109 hp (DIN) @ 4800 rpm		136 hp (DIN) @ 5100 rpm
Compression ratio	8.7:1			9.0:1		9.0:1
Torque	22.7 mkg @ 4000 rpm (164.2 ft/lb)			18.9 mkg @ 3000 rpm (136.7 ft/lb)		20.9 mkg @ 3500 rpm (151.2 ft/lb)
Carburetion	Solex dual compound downdraft 4A1			Stromberg crossdraft 175 CD		Bosch mechanical (fuel injection)
Maximum engine speed	6500 rpm			6000 rpm		6000 rpm
Engine speed at 100 km/hr	3065 rpm	automatic: 3155 rpm		3195 rpm	automatic: 3275 rpm	
Gear ratios		automatic	1979: manual transmission			
	I. 3.90:1	I. 3.98:1	I. 3.98:1			I. 3.91:1
	II. 2.30:1	II. 2.39:1	II. 2.29:1			II. 2.32:1
	III. 1.41:1	III. 1.46:1	III. 1.45:1			III. 1.42:1
	IV. 1.00:1	IV. 1.00:1	IV. 1.00:1			IV. 1.00:1
Rear axle ratio	3.54					
Chassis	unit frame and body					
Suspension	independent front and rear, with coil springs; diagonal swing axle, coil springs, anti–lift control, stabilizer bar					
Brakes and area	dual circuit discs, power assisted, 278/279 mm (10.9/11.0 in)					
Wheelbase	2710 mm (106.7 in)					
Track, front/rear	1488/1446 mm (58.6/56.9 in)					
Length	4640 mm (182.6 in)					
Width	1786 mm (70.3 in)					
Height	1395 mm (54.9 in)					
Tires	175 SR 14; 1979: 195/70 HR 14					
Turning circle	11 meters (36.1 feet)					
Steering type and ratio	recirculating ball (3.2 turns), servo assisted					
Weight	1445 kg (3179 lbs)			1375 kg (3025 lbs)		1390 kg (3060 lbs)
Maximum speed	190 km/hr (118 mph); automatic: 185 km/hr (115 mph)			170 km/hr (106 mph) automatic: 165 km/hr (103 mph)		180 km/hr (112 mph) automatic: 175 km/hr (109 mph)
Acceleration	10.6 sec 0-100 km/hr; automatic: 11.3 sec			13.7 sec 0-100 km/hr automatic: 13.9 sec 0-100 km/hr		11.5 sec 0-100 km/hr automatic: 12.3 sec 0-100 km/hr
Fuel consumption	12.5 liters/100 km (18.75 mpg) 1979: at 120 km/hr: 12.8 liters; automatic: 14.0 liters			11.7 liters/100 km (20.6 mpg) 1979: at 120 km/hr: 12.1 liters automatic: 13.7 liters		at 120 km/hr: 10.4 liters/100 km automatic: 11.9 liters
Fuel tank capacity	80 liters (21.1 gallons)					65 liters (17.2 gallons)

The 300CD coupe, 1981 U.S. version, just like this writer owned for over 10 years

Instrument panel of the 300CD, 1980

Prices and Production

The 300CD coupe sold in the United States
(with automatic transmission)
in February 1979 for (East Coast) $23,619
in November 1980 (East Coast) $29,231
in October 1981 (East Coast) $31,541
in September 1982 (East Coast) $33,750

Production of the 300CD coupe [123 D30] (from May/September 1977 until August 1981)

was in	1977	1,078 units
	1978	2,485 units
	1979	1,834 units
	1980	1,770 units
	1981	335 units
	total	7,502 units

Production of the 300CD (turbo) coupe [123 D30A] (from July/September 1981 until August 1985)

was in	1981	777 units
	1982	1,985 units
	1983	2,031 units
	1984	1,923 units
	1985	1,291 units
	total	8,007 units

Model 300CD (1977–1985)

C = Coupe, D = Diesel

The 300CD became available by August 1977 when 98 units were produced, although a single unit had been built in May of that year. (Another one was manufactured in July.) It shared the body style with the other three coupes introduced at the Geneva Auto Show in March 1977.

This diesel coupe, using the 3-liter five-cylinder OM617 engine of 77 SAE horsepower, was as luxuriously appointed as any of the high-line automobiles of previous years, and was fitted with the latest and most advanced technological concepts. The climate control and radio were positioned in the center console and the instruments were logically arranged, all graced generously with real burled walnut trim. Cruise control, centrally locking system, and such items were standard equipment on this model sold in the United States. In fact, the diesel-engined coupe was built expressly for sales in the North American market.

The 1,585 kilogram (3,495 pound) coupe, weighing 20 pounds less than the sedan, had a maximum speed of about 150 kilometers (93 miles) per hour and, of course, the outstanding economy of that five-cylinder diesel engine. The rated Environmental Protection Agency mileage was 23 for the city and 28 for highway, giving the 300CD a combined rating of 25 miles per gallon for 1979.

This luxury diesel-engined coupe was quite similar to the gasoline-engined 280CE coupe, also sold in the United States. The performance of the diesel was naturally considerably less spirited, but it compared favorably with that of the 300D sedan. Apparently production of the 300CD was clearly justified by sales in the United States over a four-year period compared with the CE coupe.

As all five-cylinder diesel models in this country, the coupe also had the turbo-charged engine for 1982. The EPA mileage rating was 27 miles per gallon for city and 33 for highway driving. This welcome change was reflected in the production figures, which showed an increase of nearly 100% in 1982 over the previous year.

Specifications

	300CD	(turbo)
Engine type	5 cyl diesel, overhead camshaft (OM 617)	5 cyl diesel, overhead camshaft, with turbo-charger (OM 617A)
Bore and stroke	91 x 92.4mm (3.58 x 3.64 in)	91 x 92.4mm (3.58 x 3.64 in)
Displacement	3005 cc (183.4 cu in); 1979: 2998 cc (183 cu in)	2998 cc (182.9 cu in)
Power output	80 hp (DIN) @ 4000 rpm; 1979: 88 hp (DIN) @ 4400 rpm; U.S. 1977: 77 hp (SAE) @ 4000 rpm; 1980: 83 hp (SAE) @ 4200 rpm	125 hp (DIN) @4350 rpm U.S.: 120 hp (SAE) 1984: 123 hp; Cal. 1985: 118 hp
Compression ratio	21:1	21.5:1
Torque	17.5 mkg @ 2400 rpm (126.6 ft/lb); 1979: 17.5 mkg @ 2400 rpm; U.S. 1977: 15.9 mkg (110.0 ft/lb); U.S. 1980: 16.7 mkg @ 2400 rpm (120 ft/lb)	25.5 mkg @ 2400 rpm U.S.: 23.6 mkg (170 ft/lb) 1984: 184 ft/lb; Cal. 1985: 177 ft/lb
Fuel injection	Bosch five plunger pump	Bosch five plunger pump w/injection timer
Maximum engine speed	5300 rpm; U.S. 1980: 4200 rpm	5100 rpm; U.S.: 4350 rpm; 1982: 4500 rpm; 1983: 4640 rpm 1984: 5000 rpm; 1985: 5200 rpm
Engine speed at 100 km/hr	2995 rpm; automatic: 3090 rpm	
Gear ratios	I. 3.90:1 automatic: I. 3.98:1 II. 2.30:1 II. 2.39:1 III. 1.41:1 III. 1.46:1 IV. 1.00:1 IV. 1.00:1	I. 3.90:1 II. 2.30:1 III. 1.41:1 IV. 1.00:1
Rear axle ratio	3.46	3.07; U.S. 1985: 2.88
Chassis	unit frame and body	
Suspension	independent front and rear, with coil springs; diagonal swing axle, coil springs, anti-lift control, stabilizer bar	
Brakes and area	dual circuit discs, power assisted, 278/279mm (10.9/11.0 in)	
Wheelbase	2710mm (106.7 in)	
Track, front/rear	1488/1446mm (58.6/56.9 in)	
Length	4640mm (182.6 in); U.S.: 4763mm (187.5 in)	
Width	1786mm (70.3 in)	
Height	1395mm (54.9 in)	
Tires	175 SR 14; 1979: 195/70 HR 14; U.S.: 195/70 HR 14	
Turning circle	11 meters (36.1 ft)	
Steering type and ratio	recirculating ball (3.2 turns), servo assisted	
Weight	1445 kg (3179 lbs); U.S.: 1585 kg (3487 lbs); U.S.: 1978: 1575 kg (3465 lbs); U.S. 1980: 1545 kg (3399 lbs)	U.S. 1981: 1550 kg (3420 lbs) 1625 kg (3583 lbs)
Maximum speed	148 km/hr (92 mph); automatic: 143 km/hr (89 mph); 1979: 155 km/hr; automatic: 150 km/hr (93 mph)	
Acceleration	19.9 sec 0-100 km/hr; automatic: 20.8 sec; 1979: 17.8 sec; automatic: 19.2 sec	
Fuel consumption	10.8 liters/100 km (21.5 mpg); 1979: at 120 km/hr: 11.5 liters; automatic: 12.4 liters	
Fuel tank capacity	80 liters (21.1 gallons)	

The 280S sedan, 1979

The 280S sedan, 1979

Prices and Production

The 280S four-door sedan sold in 1981 for. . . . . .DM 40,511

Production of the 280S model [126 V28] (from April/December 1979 until November 1985)

was in	1979	408 units
	1980	6,348 units
	1981	7,212 units
	1982	8,761 units
	1983	8,568 units
	1984	6,203 units
	1985	5,496 units
	total	42,996 units

Model 280S (1979–1985)

S = Super

The 280S sedan of the new S-class was introduced to the public at the Frankfurt Auto Show in 1979. It was one of seven models which had the new W126 body style.

By redesigning and completely reconstructing the body, with a lower and rather wedge-shaped hood line, recessing the windshield wipers, and such refinements, this new aerodynamic design resulted in a drag coefficient improvement of 14% over the previous W116 S-class bodies. The use of lighter material in construction resulted in a considerable saving of weight also, thus greatly contributing to superior economy of operation.

Actually, work on the design of this new S-class of model had begun some seven years previously, long before the oil shortage and ever escalating fuel cost was a known factor. Yet the Daimler-Benz engineers concentrated on the creation of a vehicle which would use considerably less gasoline because of lighter body weight and vastly improved engine design.

The 280S model was the least expensive of the new luxury line (Oberklasse) of sedans, and as such would find many anxious buyers who desired the top line car even if only the least powerful one of that type, which was still the most economical one as well.

The proven six-cylinder carburetor engine was improved to give better elasticity and combustion efficiency. The 2,746 cubic centimeter engine now developed 156 (DIN) horsepower at 5,500 revolutions per minute, giving the 1,560 kilogram (3,432 pound) sedan a top speed of 200 kilometers (124 miles) per hour with the manual transmission, and 195 km/hr with the automatic. (The old 280S weighed 1,610 kilograms (3,542 pounds) and had a maximum speed of 190 kilometers (118 miles) per hour.)

Specifications

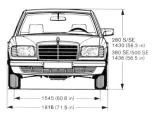

	280S
Engine type	6 cyl double overhead camshafts (M110)
Bore and stroke	86 x 78.8 mm (3.39 x 3.10 in)
Displacement	2746 cc (167.6 cu in)
Power output	156 hp (DIN) @ 5500 rpm
Compression ratio	9:1
Torque	22.6 mkg @ 4000 rpm (164 ft/lb)
Carburetion	Solex dual compound downdraft 4A1
Maximum engine speed	6500 rpm
Gear ratios	I. 3.98:1 I. 3.68:1 (automatic) II. 2.29:1 II. 2.41:1 III. 1.45:1 III. 1.44:1 IV. 1.00:1 IV. 1.00:1
Rear axle ratio	3.46
Chassis	unit frame and body
Suspension	independent front and rear, with coil springs, anti-roll bar; diagonal swing axle, coil springs, anti-roll bar, level control
Brakes and area	dual circuit discs, power assisted, brake pad wear indicator, 278/279 mm (10.9/11.0 in)
Wheelbase	2935 mm (115.5 in)
Track, front/rear	1545/1517 mm (60.8/59.7 in)
Length	4995 mm (196.6 in)
Width	1820 mm (71.6 in)
Height	1430 mm (56.3 in)
Tires	195/70 HR 14
Turning circle	11.80 meters (38.7 feet)
Steering type and ratio	recirculating ball (2.75 turns), servo assisted
Weight	1560 kg (3432 lbs)
Maximum speed	200 km/hr (124 mph); automatic: 195 km/hr (121 mph)
Acceleration	10.8 sec 0-100 km/hr; automatic: 12 sec
Fuel consumption	at 120 km/hr: 11.1 liters/100 km (21 mpg); automatic: 11.6 liters (20.6 mpg)
Fuel tank capacity	90 liters (23.8 gallons)

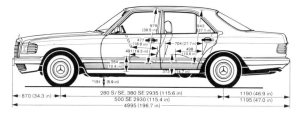

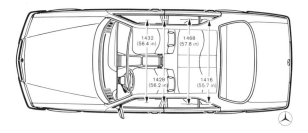

Dimensions of the S-Class cars, 1979

Drawing of the S-Class sedans, 1979

179

The 280SE sedan, 1979

Prices and Production

The 280SE four-door sedan sold in 1981 for . . . . DM 43,980

Production of the 280SE model [126 E28] (from February/December 1979 until September 1985)

was in 1979	812	units
1980	22,482	units
1981	26,654	units
1982	23,287	units
1983	25,229	units
1984	22,656	units
1985	12,835	units
total	133,955	units

The 280SEL four-door sedan sold in 1981 for . . . . DM 57,174

Production of the 280SEL model [126 E28] (from December 1979/June 1980 until September 1985)

was in 1979	1	unit
1980	887	units
1981	2,423	units
1982	3,843	units
1983	4,302	units
1984	4,598	units
1985	4,601	units
total	20,655	units

Model 280SE/SEL (1979–1985)

S = Super, E (Einspritzung) = fuel injection

SE L (Lang) = long wheelbase chassis

The 280SE and 280SEL, introduced at the Frankfurt Auto Show in 1979, were the other six-cylinder sedans which shared the new W126 bodies. As in all of the models, the bodies were actually 3.5 centimeters (1.4 inches) longer and 5 centimeters (1.97 inches) wider than the previous W116 S-class bodies. The drag coefficient was only 0.38, considerably less than that of the modern sedans then being offered by the competitive automobile manufacturers. The new body style car was, of course, easily recognized as a Mercedes. By using newly developed materials and new body structures, the weight of the body shell was reduced by about 50 kilograms (110 pounds) and yet considerably improved in resistance in crash tests.

The 280SE offered the same driving performance of the former 350SE model which it replaced. The 280SEL was, of course, the longer wheelbase (121.1-inch) version of the 116.4-inch SE car. By changing the front wheel suspension and further reducing engine and wind noise, smoother running and handling were achieved.

The fuel-injected 280 engine, using mechanical fuel injection (K-Jetronic) with air flow metering device, developed 185 (DIN) horsepower at 5,800 revolutions per minute. The 280SE weighed 1,560 kilograms (3,432 pounds), while the longer SEL weighed 1,590 kg (3,498 lbs). Maximum speed was 210 kilometers (130 miles) per hour with manual transmission and 205 km/hr with automatic transmission. The 350SE weighed 1,675 kg (3,685 lbs) and had a top speed of 205 km/hr (127 mph).

The 280SE and 280SEL models were good touring cars with the characteristic features expected of this upper class line of cars, but with their six-cylinder fuel-injection engines they were still economical to operate, using about 11.3 liters of fuel for 100 kilometers, driving at 120 kilometers per hour, thus averaging about 20.5 miles per gallon with the manual transmission. The power-to-weight ratio of these models was 11.5 and 11.7 kilograms per horsepower, while the more powerful V-8 engined 380SE and 380SEL models had a 9.96 and 10.09 kilograms ratio, respectively, with consequently better acceleration and a 10 miles per hour higher maximum speed.

Specifications

280SE/SEL

Engine type	6 cyl double overhead camshafts (M110)
Bore and stroke	86 x 78.8 mm (3.39 x 3.10 in)
Displacement	2746 cc (167.6 cu in)
Power output	185 hp (DIN) @ 5800 rpm
Compression ratio	9:1
Torque	24.4 mkg @ 4500 rpm (176.5 ft/lb)
Fuel injection	Bosch mechanical with air flow sensor
Maximum engine speed	6500 rpm

Gear ratios

I. 3.98:1		I. 3.68:1 (automatic)	
II. 2.29:1		II. 2.41:1	
III. 1.45:1		III. 1.44:1	
IV. 1.00:1		IV. 1.00:1	

Rear axle ratio	3.46
Chassis	unit frame and body
Suspension	independent front and rear, with coil springs, anti-roll bar; diagonal swing axle, coil springs, anti-roll bar, level control
Brakes and area	dual circuit discs, power assisted, brake pad wear indicator, 278/279 mm (10.9/11.0 in)
Wheelbase	2935 mm (115.5 in) SEL: 3075 mm (121 in)
Track, front/rear	1545/1517 mm (60.8/59.7 in)
Length	4995 mm (196.6 in) SEL: 5135 mm (202.1 in)
Width	1820 mm (71.6 in)
Height	1430 mm (56.3 in) SEL: 1434 mm (56.4 in)
Tires	195/70 VR 14
Turning circle	11.80 meters (38.7 feet) SEL: 12.26 meters (40.2 feet)
Steering type and ratio	recirculating ball (2.75 turns), servo assisted
Weight	1560 kg (3432 lbs) SEL: 1590 kg (3498 lbs)
Maximum speed	210 km/hr (130 mph); automatic: 205 km/hr (127 mph)
Acceleration	9.8 sec 0-100 km/hr; automatic: 11.1 sec
Fuel consumption	at 120 km/hr: 11.3 liters/100 km (20.8 mpg); automatic: 11.7 liters (20.5 mpg)
Fuel tank capacity	90 liters (23.8 gallons)

The 280SE sedan, 1979

The SE sedans of 1979

The 380SE sedan, 1979

Prices and Production

The 380SE four-door sedan sold in 1980 for .... DM 48,510

Production of the 380SE model [126 E38] (from May 1979/January 1980 until November 1985)

was in 1979	217 units	
1980	7,935 units	
1981	8,603 units	
1982	7,429 units	
1983	8,174 units	
1984	14,618 units	
1985	11,290 units	
total	58,239 units	

The 380SEL four-door sedan sold in 1980 for .... DM 50,974
The 380SEL sedan sold in the United States
(with automatic transmisstion)
in November 1980 for (East Coast) $44,298
in September 1982 (East Coast) $47,870

Production of the 380SEL model [126 E38] (from October 1979/June 1980 until September 1985)

was in 1979	1 unit	
1980	1,648 units	
1981	6,726 units	
1982	8,496 units	
1983	6,270 units	
1984	2,016 units	
1985	1,857 units	
total	27,014 units	

Model 380SE/SEL (1979–1985)

S = Super, E (Einspritzung) = fuel injection

SE L (Lang) = long wheelbase chassis

The 380SE and 380SEL, with the new S–class body style, were also first shown at the Frankfurt Auto Show in 1979. This line of cars was to replace the previous 450 line of sedans, and with the smaller displacement engines and lighter bodies, appeared to be worthy successors to the 450 line of sedans.

With the newly designed lighter V–8 engines of 218 (DIN) horsepower and favorable body weight of 1,595 kilograms (3,509 pounds), and 1,615 kilograms (3,553 lbs), respectively, they were spirited performers. Acceleration from 0 to 100 kilometers per hour was 8.9 seconds and maximum speed was 215 kilometers (133.5 miles) per hour with the automatic transmission. The 450SE sedan (1,740 kg or 3,828 lbs) had posted acceleration figures of 9.3 seconds and a top speed of 210 kilometers (130 miles) per hour. Fuel consumption was reduced by 10%, partly due to the new four–speed automatic transmission.

The 380SEL model became available in the United States for the 1981 model year. It was, however, a greatly altered car and, because of strict emission control and safety standards, appreciably different from the European version.

The engine, with a bore of 88 millimeters and stroke of 78.9 millimeters, displaced 3,839 cubic centimeters instead of the 3,818 and developed only 155 SAE horsepower at 4,750 revolutions per minute instead of 218. Torque was 196 lb/ft (27.1 mkg) at 2,750 rpm. Compression ratio was 8.3:1 instead of 9:1. The weight of the sedan had increased by 90 kilograms (110 pounds) to 1,685 kg (3,715 lbs). With the rear axle ratio of 2.47:1 (3.27:1 in Europe), the car had a maximum speed of about 115 miles per hour. The power-to-weight ratio of this model was 25.5 pounds per horsepower against the 16.28 for the European version.

Despite all of these changes, the character of the car had not changed much, and the 380SEL was still a most desirable automobile, and in the words of a most prestiguous reviewer magazine, *Road & Track,* "the best four-door sedan in the world today" (January 1981).

Specifications

	380SE/SEL		
Engine type	V-8 cyl overhead camshafts (M116)		
Bore and stroke	92 x 71.8 mm (3.62 x 2.83 in)	1981: 88 x 78.9 mm (3.46 x 3.10 in)	
Displacement	3818 cc (233 cu in)	1981: 3839 cc (234 cu in)	
Power output	218 hp (DIN) @ 5500 rpm	1981: 204 hp (DIN) @ 5250 rpm	SEL U.S. 1981: 155 hp SAE @ 4750 rpm
Compression ratio	9:1	1981: 9.4:1	SEL U.S. 1981: 8.3:1
Torque	31 mkg @ 4000 rpm (224.3 ft/lb)	1981: 32 mkg @ 3250 rpm (230.0 ft/lb)	SEL U.S. 1981: 27.1 mkg @ 2750 rpm
Fuel Injection	Bosch mechanical with air flow sensor		
Maximum engine speed	6600 rpm		SEL U.S. 1981: 5300 rpm; 1983: 5500 rpm
Gear ratios	I. 3.68:1 (automatic, standard) II. 2.41:1 III. 1.44:1 IV. 1.00:1		
Rear axle ratio	3.27		SEL U.S. 1981: 2.47
Chassis	unit frame and body		
Suspension	independent front and rear, with coil springs, anti-roll bar; diagonal swing axle, coil springs, anti-roll bar, level control, hydropneumatic, optional		
Brakes and area	dual circuit discs, power assisted, brake pad wear indicator, 278/279 mm (10.9/11.0 in)		
Wheelbase	2935 mm (115.5 in)		SEL: 3075 mm (121 in)
Track, front/rear	1545/1517 mm (60.8/59.7 in)		
Length	4995 mm (196.6 in)		SEL: 5135 mm (202.1 in); U.S.: 5285 mm (208 in)
Width	1820 mm (71.6 in)		
Height	1436 mm (56.5 in)		SEL: 1440 mm (56.7 in)
Tires	205/70 VR 14		
Turning circle	11.80 meters (38.7 feet)		SEL: 12.26 meters (40.2 feet)
Steering type and ratio	recirculating ball (2.75 turns), servo assisted		
Weight	1595 kg (3509 lbs)		SEL: 1615 kg (3553 lbs) SEL U.S.: 1685 kg (3715 lbs) SEL 1982: 1715 kg (3780 lbs)
Maximum speed	215 km/hr (134 mph)		SEL 1981: 210 km/hr
Acceleration	8.9 sec 0-100 km/hr		SEL 1981: 9.8 sec 0-100 km/hr
Fuel consumption	at 120 km/hr: 13.3 liters/100 km (17.6 mpg)		SEL 1981: 10.8 liters/100 km
Fuel tank capacity	90 liters (23.8 gallons)		

The 500SE sedan, 1979

Prices and Production

The 500SE four-door sedan sold in 1980 for . . . . DM 52,680

Production of the 500SE model [126 E50] (from September 1979/
January 1980 until October 1991

was in 1979	149 units
1980	5,312 units
1981	3,308 units
1982	3,349 units
1983	3,646 units
1984	2,790 units
1985	3,194 units
1986	2,351 units
1987	1,722 units
1988	1,895 units
1989	2,676 units
1990	2,308 units
1991	718 units
total	33,418 units

The 500SEL sedan sold in the United States in 1985 for $51,200

Production of the 500SE model [126 E50] (from September 1979/
June 1980 until October 1991)

was in 1979	2 units
1980	2,206 units
1981	5,942 units
1982	8,966 units
1983	12,095 units
1984	14,808 units
1985	17,251 units
1986	4,032 units
1987	2,163 units
1988	2,087 units
1989	1,560 units
1990	1,331 units
1991	244 units
total	72,687 units

Model 500SE/SEL (1979–1991)

S = Super, E (Einspritzung) = fuel injection

SE L (Lang) = long wheelbase chassis

The 500SE and 500SEL were the top of the line cars of the new S-class shown first at the Frankfurt Auto Show in 1979. They were the most luxurious sedans built by Daimler-Benz.

The newly bodied sedans replaced the former star performer, the 450SEL 6.9. The light allow 4,973-cubic centimeter engine, already used in the 450SLC 5.0 since its debut in 1977, developed 240 (DIN) horsepower at 4,750 revolutions per minute in the new sedans. (The SLC engine ran at 5,000 revolutions per minute.)

This engine was not only widely tested in the former luxury coupe, but also in a number of highly competitive rally events under most trying conditions. As an example, in the 1979 Bandama Rally in December 1979, four factory-prepared coupes, weighing 1,350 kilograms and their engines developing 300 horsepower, won the first four places of this 5,600-kilometer long and extremely brutal rally event.

All of these new models with the V-8 engines had the newly designed four-speed automatic transmission and showed improved fuel economy. At a speed of 90 kilometers (56 miles) per hour, the 2,175-kilogram (4,785-pound) car used 11.3 liters per 100 kilometers and at 120 kilometers (75 miles) per hour it used 13.5 liters, or 17.4 miles per gallon. Acceleration was 7.7 seconds for the 0 to 100 kilometers (0–62 miles) per hour and maximum speed for the 500SE and SEL was 225 kilometers (140 miles) per hour. For the 6.9 sedan, weighing 1,935 kilograms (4,257 pounds), the acceleration figures had been 7.4 seconds, and top speed achieved by the 500SEL was the same.

At the time of their introduction, Werner Breitschwerdt, Chief of Development at Daimler-Benz, said, "The new 500SE and 500SEL five-liter models are equal or even superior to our 450SEL 6.9 in design and equipment." His and his predecessor's (Hans Scherenberg) team of able designers and engineers had indeed achieved an exceedingly high level of comfort and performance in the new models.

Specifications

Instrument panel of the 500SE sedan, 1979

500SE/SEL

Engine type	V-8 cyl overhead camshafts (M117)
Bore and stroke	96.5 x 85 mm (3.80 x 3.35 in)
Displacement	4973 cc (303.5 cu in)
Power output	240 hp (DIN) @ 4750 rpm U.S.: 184 hp (SAE) 137 Kw @ 4500 rpm
Compression ratio	8.8:1 U.S.: 8.0:1
Torque	41 mkg @ 3200 rpm (296.6 ft/lb) U.S.: 335 Nm @ 2000 rpm (247 ft/lb)
Fuel injection	Bosch mechanical with air flow sensor
Maximum engine speed	5950 rpm
Gear ratios	I. 3.68:1 (automatic, standard) II. 2.41:1 III. 1.44:1 IV. 1.00:1
Rear axle ratio	2.82 U.S.: 2.47 1981: 2.24
Chassis	unit frame and body
Suspension	independent front and rear, with coil springs, anti-roll bar; diagonal swing axle, coil springs, anti-roll bar, level control, hydropneumatic, optional
Brakes and area	dual circuit discs, power assisted, brake pad wear indicator, 278/279 mm (10.9/11.0 in)
Wheelbase	2855 mm (112.4 in) 1981: 2930 mm SEL: 2955 mm (116.3 in); 1981: 3070 mm (120.8 in)
Track, front/rear	1545/1517 mm (60.8/59.7 in)
Length	4995 mm (196.6 in) SEL: 5135 mm (202.1 in)
Width	1820 mm (71.6 in)
Height	1436 mm (56.5 in) SEL: 1440 mm (56.7 in)
Tires	205/70 VR 14
Turning circle	11.80 meters (38.7 feet) SEL: 12.26 meters (40.2 feet)
Steering type and ratio	recirculating ball (2.75 turns), servo assisted
Weight	1620 kg (3564 lbs) U.S.: 1755 kg (3870 lbs) SEL: 1655 kg (3641 lbs)
Maximum speed	225 km/hr (140 mph)
Acceleration	7.7 sec 0–100 km/hr
Fuel consumption	at 120 km/hr: 13.5 liters/100 km (17.4 mpg) 1981: 11.4 liters/100 km
Fuel tank capacity	90 liters (23.8 gallons)

The 300TD turbo station wagon, 1980

Prices and Production

The 300TD (turbo) station wagon sold in 1980 for . . . .DM 36,521
    in 1982 for. . . . . .DM 40,940
The 300TD station wagon sold in the United States
    (with automatic transmission)
    in November 1980 for (East Coast) $31,373
    in September 1982 (East Coast) $33,850

Production of the 300TD turbo station wagon [123 D30A] (from
November 1979/October 1980 until January 1986)

was in	1979	2 units
	1980	1,852 units
	1981	6,710 units
	1982	6,302 units
	1983	4,898 units
	1984	4,739 units
	1985	3,713 units
	1986	3 units
	total	28,219 units

Model 300TD (1979–1986)

T = station wagon, D = Diesel

The 300TD turbo-charged diesel-engined station wagon was introduced at the Frankfurt Auto Show in 1979, but was not scheduled to go into production until the middle of 1980.

This newest addition to the line of five differently powered wagons would use up to 10% less fuel, gave superior performance, and had a higher load capacity than the regular five-cylinder diesel-engined vehicle.

The OM617A turbo diesel engine was the same as had been available in the United States only in the SD sedan and developed 125 (DIN) horsepower at 4,350 revolutions per minute. Maximum torque was 25.5 mkg (184.4 pounds/feet) at 2,400 revolutions per minute. In the U.S., this turbo diesel developed 120 SAE horsepower and had a torque of 23.6 mkg (170 lbs/ft).

Appointments of this station wagon, available now in other countries than the United States, were those of the more luxurious 280TE. Automatic transmission was standard, and with over 40% greater output and lower fuel consumption than the regular aspirated five-cylinder diesel, this new model was expected to be a good choice. A new, quicker starting system, available from August 1980, would reduce the starting time to some five seconds at outside temperatures of 0 degrees Centigrade (32 degrees Fahrenheit). At higher temperatures the engine could be started in an even shorter time.

For the model year 1981, the turbo charged diesel-engined station wagon was the only model station wagon sold in the United States market. It replaced the former model with the naturally aspirated OM617 five-cylinder diesel engine, but the old designation of 300TD remained. The body style and appointments were the same as previously, but the performance had, of course, greatly improved. And so had the price.

The Environmental Protection Agency rated for 1981 the 300TD at 26 miles per gallon for the city cycle and 30 miles per gallon for highway travel, or an average fuel consumption of 28 miles per gallon.

Specifications

300TD (turbo)

Engine type	5 cyl diesel, overhead camshaft, with turbo-charger (OM 617A)
Bore and stroke	91 x 92.4mm (3.58 x 3.64 in)
Displacement	2998 cc (182.9 cu in)
Power output	125 hp (DIN) @4350 rpm U.S.: 120 hp (SAE) 1984: 123 hp; Cal. 1985: 118 hp
Compression ratio	21.5:1
Torque	25.5 mkg @ 2400 rpm U.S.: 23.6 mkg (170 ft/lb) 1984: 184 ft/lb; Cal. 1985: 177 ft/lb
Fuel injection	Bosch five plunger pump w/injection timer
Maximum engine speed	5100 rpm; U.S.: 4350 rpm; 1982: 4500 rpm; 1983: 4640 rpm 1984: 5000 rpm; 1985: 5200 rpm
Gear ratios	I. 3.90:1 II. 2.30:1 III. 1.41:1 IV. 1.00:1
Rear axle ratio	3.07; U.S. 1985: 2.88
Chassis	unit frame and body
Suspension	independent front and rear, coil springs; diagonal swing axle, coil springs, torsion bar stabilizer, standard level control
Brakes and area	dual circuit discs, front brake pad wear indicator, 278/279mm (10.9/11.0 in)

Wheelbase	2795mm (110.0 in)
Track, front/rear	1488/1453mm (58.6/57.2 in)
Length	4725mm (186.0 in) U.S.: 4848mm (190.9 in)
Width	1786mm (70.3 in)
Height	1470mm (57.9 in)
Tires	195/70 SR 14
Turning circle	11.29 meters (37 ft)
Steering type and ratio	recirculating ball (3.2 turns), power assisted
Weight	1610 kg (3542 lbs) U.S.: 1695 kg (3729 lbs), 1715 kg (3780 lbs)
Maximum speed	automatic: 165 km/hr (103 mph)
Acceleration	automatic: 15 sec 0–100 km/hr
Fuel consumption	at 120 km/hr: 11.1 liters
Fuel tank capacity	70 liters (18.5 gallons)

The 300TD turbo station wagon, 1981, U.S. version

The 200T station wagon, 1980

The M 102 engine for the 200T, 1980

The 200T, 1980

Prices and Production

The 200T station wagon sold in 1980 for . . . . .DM 26,114

Production of the 200T station wagon [123 V20] (from May/November 1980 until January 1986)

was in	1980	648 units
	1981	3,142 units
	1982	3,809 units
	1983	4,742 units
	1984	4,092 units
	1985	2,422 units
	1986	5 units
	total	18,860 units

Model 200T (1980–1986)

T (Touristik und Transport) = station wagon

The 200T station wagon model was built when the newly designed, greatly advanced four-cylinder gasoline engine was created in early 1980. The 200 sedan was the only other model then available with this smoother, fuel-saving, and more powerful M102 engine.

The 200T was like the other station wagons in body style and appointments, and it represented just another addition to the already wide range of those popular utility vehicles first shown in 1977 and enthusiastically received by the public. For buyers who wanted a gasoline-engined version with the greatest economy possible, this new model proved most satisfactory.

Fuel saving was the ultimate concern at that time and this least powerful of station wagon models was in keeping with the times of serious fuel shortages and steadily advancing costs.

Real production began in September, but one unit was produced in May, a month after the manufacture of the 230T model had ceased, with another one following in June, none in July, and two in August. These early units were, of course, used mainly for testing purposes, and sales began with the fall production. By December, 349 units of the 200T were built.

The 1,997-cubic centimeter displacement engine developed 109 DIN horsepower at 5,200 revolutions per minute, had a 9:1 compression ratio, and torque of 17.3 mkg at 3,000 rpm. The acceleration of the 1,455-kilogram heavy 200T wagon was 14.4 seconds for the 0 to 100 kilometers per hour speed with the manual, and 15.4 seconds with the automatic transmission. The maximum speed was 168 kilometers per hour with the manual and 163 kilometers per hour with the automatic transmission.

Fuel consumption was rated at 14.2 liters per 100 kilometers of driving the urban cycle with the manual, and 13.8 liters with the automatic transmission. At a speed of 120 kilometers per hour, consumption was 10.6 liters with manual, and 11.5 liters with the automatic tranmission.

Specifications

	200T
Engine type	4 cyl overhead camshaft (M102)
Bore and stroke	89 x 80.25 (3.50 x 3.16 in)
Displacement	1997 cc (121.72 cu in)
Power output	109 hp (DIN) @ 5200 rpm
Compression ratio	9.0:1
Torque	17.3 mkg @ 3000 rpm (125.2 ft/lb)
Carburetion	Stromberg sidedraft 175 CDT
Maximum engine speed	6000 rpm
Gear ratios	I. 3.91:1 I. 3.98:1 (automatic) II. 2.32:1 II. 2.39:1 III. 1.42:1 III. 1.46:1 IV. 1.00:1 IV. 1.00:1
Rear axle ratio	3.69
Chassis	unit frame and body
Suspension	independent front and rear, with coil springs; diagonal pivot axle; coil springs, anti-roll bar
Brakes and area	dual circuit discs, front brake pad wear indicator, 278/279 mm (10.9/11.0 in)
Wheelbase	2795 mm (110.0 in)
Track, front/rear	1488/1446 mm (58.6/56.9 in)
Length	4725 mm (186.0 in)
Width	1786 mm (70.3 in)
Height	1438 mm (56.6 in)
Tires	195/70 SR 14
Turning circle	11.29 meters (37 feet)
Steering type and ratio	recirculating ball (3.2 turns), power assisted
Weight	1455 kg (3204 lbs)
Maximum speed	168 km/hr (104 mph); automatic: 163 km/hr (101 mph)
Acceleration	15.3 sec 0-100 km/hr; automatic: 16.4 sec 0-100 km/hr
Fuel consumption	at 120 km/hr: 10.2 liters/100 km; automatic: 11.0 liters
Fuel tank capacity	70 liters (18.5 gallons)

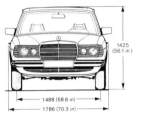

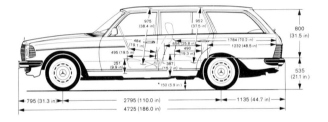
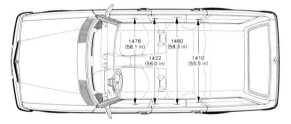

Dimensions for the T-models

The 380SL roadster, 1981, U.S. version

Prices and Production

The 380SL roadster sold in 1980 for . . . . DM 54,014
The 380SL roadster sold in the United States
  (with automatic transmission)
  in November 1980 for (East Coast) $38,993
  in September 1982 (East Coast) $43,030

Production of the 380SL model [107 E38] (from February/May 1980 until August 1985)

was in	1980	3,347 units
	1981	9,470 units
	1982	9,926 units
	1983	11,198 units
	1984	11,115 units
	1985	8,144 units
total		53,200 units

Model 380SL (1980–1985)

S = Sports, L = Light, C = Coupe

The 380SL model was first publicly shown in March 1980 at the 50th Geneva Auto Show, the traditional exhibition for the introduction of Mercedes sports models. This sporty roadster was one of the three open cars still being manufactured — the others were the 280SL and 500SL — and considering that since 1971 more than 85,000 of the 107 type roadsters had been produced, it was a sound decision to continue the model with a practically unchanged body.

Since the introduction of the latest S-class sedans, all of these 3.8-liter eight-cylinder models were equipped with the economical new generation light-alloy engines of 3,818 cubic centimeter displacement, producing 218 DIN horsepower.

The 1,540 kilogram (3,396 pounds) heavy 380SL had a maximum speed of 215 kilometers per hour and acceleration of 9.0 seconds for the 0 to 100 kilometers per hour speed. The figures for the older 450SL of 1,585 kilograms, which it replaced, had been 8.5 seconds and also 215 km/hr (133.5 mph) top speed, thus this smaller displacement and lighter engined model was practically the identically performing car.

For the United States market, the 380SL was, like the sedan, altered to conform with the government regulations. The 3,839 cubic centimeter engine had a longer stroke for better emission controls, but aside from the slightly differing size, was constructed of the same weight-saving materials. It developed 155 SAE horsepower, had a compression ratio of only 8.3:1, and a torque of 27.1 mkg (196 lbs/ft). The car weighed 1,635 kilograms (3,605 lbs), and maximum speed was about 120 miles per hour.

Despite the alterations, the 380SL was still a superbly performing car, and a fine replacement for the 450 SL (with the considerably larger engine) of which over 57,000 units (including the 350SLs) had been sold in this country over the past ten years. Even during 1980, when the 380SL was first introduced for the 1981 model year, a total of 1,624 cars had already been imported.

Specifications

	380SL		
Engine type	V-8 cyl overhead camshafts (M116)		
Bore and stroke	92 x 71.8 mm (3.62 x 2.83 in)	1981: 88 x 78.9 mm	U.S.: 88 x 78.9 mm (3.46 x 3.11 in)
Displacement	3818 cc (233 cu in)	1981: 3839 cc	U.S.: 3839 cc (234.3 cu in)
Power output	218 hp (DIN) @ 5500 rpm	1981: 204 hp (DIN) @ 5250 rpm	U.S.: 155 hp SAE @ 4750 rpm
Compression ratio	9:1	1981: 9.4:1	U.S.: 8.3:1
Torque	31 mkg @ 4000 rpm (224.3 ft/lb)		U.S.: 27.1 mkg @ 2750 rpm (196 ft/lb)
Fuel injection	Bosch mechanical with air flow sensor		
Maximum engine speed	6600 rpm		U.S.: 5300 rpm; 1983: 5500 rpm
Gear ratios	I. 3.68:1 (automatic, standard) II. 2.41:1 III. 1.44:1 IV. 1.00:1		
Rear axle ratio	3.27		U.S.: 2.47
Chassis	unit frame and body		
Suspension	independent front and rear, coil springs, anti-roll bar; diagonal swing axle, coil springs, anti-roll bar, level control, hydropneumatic, optional		
Brakes and area	dual circuit discs, power assisted, brake pad wear indicator, 278/279 mm (10.9/11.0 in)		
Wheelbase	2455 mm (96.7 in)		
Track, front/rear	1452/1440 mm (57.2/56.7 in)		
Length	4390 mm (172.8 in)		U.S.: 4630 mm (182.3 in)
Width	1790 mm (70.5 in)		
Height	1300 mm (51.2 in)		
Tires	205/70 VR 14		U.S.: 205/70 HR 14
Turning circle	10.74 meters (35.2 ft)		U.S.: 10.48 meters (34.4 ft)
Steering type and ratio	recirculating ball (3.0 turns), servo assisted		
Weight	1540 kg (3392 lbs)		U.S.: 1635 kg (3605 lbs); 1983: 1650 kg
Maximum speed	215 km/hr (134 mph)		
Acceleration	9 sec 0–100 km/hr	1981: 9.8 sec 0–100 km/hr	
Fuel consumption	at 120 km/hr: 13.6 liters/100 km (17.3 mpg); 1981: 11.3 liters		
Fuel tank capacity	90 liters (23.8 gallons)		U.S.: 85 liters (22.4 gallons)

The 380SLC coupe, 1980

Prices and Production

The 380SLC coupe sold in 1980 for . . . . .DM 57,743
The 380SLC coupe sold in the United States
(with automatic transmission)
in November 1980 for (East Coast). $46,638

Production of the 380SLC model [107 E38] (from February/May 1980 until September 1981)

was in	1980	1,737 units
	1981	2,052 units
	total	3,789 units

Model 380SLC (1980-1981)

S = Sports, L = Light, C = Coupe

The 380SLC coupe, the companion model to the roadster, was also first shown at the Geneva Auto Show in 1980. Here, too, it was pointed out that these style coupes, with the different engine sizes, were steady sellers with over 54,000 units sold since their inception in 1972, when this 107SLC body type was first produced.

The bodies of the new cars remained as before, but had a front spoiler added, and only the power units were new. Engine specifications were as in the SL models, the usual practice in this line of cars.

These eight-cylinder models had the new four-speed torque converter automatic transmission as standard equipment, while in the six-cylinder 280SL/SLC line it was an optional extra cost item. This new transmission was considered quite suitable for sporty driving as well as for a more fuel-conscious driving style. New brake calipers were fitted with larger brake pads and rear anti-squat suspension linkage was provided.

The fuel consumption of the 380SL/SLC was rated at 18.8 liters per 100 kilometers in urban driving and at 120 kilometers per hour at 13.6 liters for highway driving, again identical with both models.

In the United States the 380SLC was, of course, the true counterpart to the SL. The engine was the very same as in the 380SEL sedan, and practically all essential specifications were identical in all these 380 models. Performance figures of the SLC were also the same as those for the SL, although the weight was 10 kilograms (22 pounds) less for the coupe than for the roadster.

Fuel consumption rated by the Environmental Protection Agency for 1981 was 17 miles per gallon for the city driving cycle and 24 miles per gallon for highway driving, for a combination average rating of 20 miles per gallon.

Over the nine-year period, a total of 13,890 units of the SLC 450 model had been brought to this country (against about 57,000 of the SLs) and in 1980 already 380 cars had been imported by the distributor.

Specifications

	380SLC	
Engine type	V-8 cyl overhead camshafts (M116)	
Bore and stroke	92 x 71.8 mm (3.62 x 2.83 in)	U.S.: 88 x 78.9 mm (3.46 x 3.11 in)
Displacement	3818 cc (233 cu in)	U.S.: 3839 cc (234.3 cu in)
Power output	218 hp (DIN) @ 5500 rpm	U.S.: 155 hp SAE @ 4750 rpm
Compression ratio	9:1	U.S.: 8.3:1
Torque	31 mkg @ 4000 rpm (224.3 ft/lb)	U.S.: 27.1 mkg @ 2750 rpm (196 ft/lb)
Fuel injection	Bosch mechanical with air flow sensor	
Maximum engine speed	6600 rpm	U.S.: 5300 rpm
Gear ratios	I. 3.68:1 (automatic, standard) II. 2.41:1 III. 1.44:1 IV. 1.00:1	
Rear axle ratio	3.27	U.S.: 2.47
Chassis	unit frame and body	
Suspension	independent front and rear, coil springs, anti-roll bar; diagonal swing axle, coil springs, anti-roll bar, level control, hydropneumatic optional	
Brakes and area	dual circuit discs, power assisted, brake pad wear indicator, 278/279 mm (10.9/11.0 in)	
Wheelbase	2820 mm (111 in)	
Track, front/rear	1452/1440 mm (57.2/56.7 in)	
Length	4750 mm (187.0 in)	U.S.: 4990 mm (196.4 in)
Width	1790 mm (70.5 in)	
Height	1330 mm (52.4 in)	
Tires	205/70 VR 14	U.S.: 205/70 RH 14
Turning circle	11.55 meters (37.9 ft)	
Steering type and ratio	recirculating ball (3.0 turns), servo assisted	
Weight	1560 kg (3435 lbs)	U.S.: 1625 kg (3585 lbs)
Maximum speed	215 km/hr (134 mph)	
Acceleration	9 sec 0-100 km/hr	
Fuel consumption	at 120 km/hr: 13.6 liters/100 km (17.3 mpg)	
Fuel tank capacity	90 liters (23.8 gallons)	U.S.: 85 liters (22.4 gallons)

The M 116 engine for the 380SLC, 1980

193

The 500SL roadster, 1980

Prices and Production

The 500SL roadster sold in 1980 for .... DM 61,924

Production of the 500SL model [107 E50] (from April 1980 until August 1989)

was in	1980	501 units
	1981	899 units
	1982	1,297 units
	1983	1,563 units
	1984	1,793 units
	1985	2,719 units
	1986	1,192 units
	1987	768 units
	1988	739 units
	1989	341 units
	total	11,822 units

	1992	2,682 units
SL500	1993	6,090 units
	1994	6,172 units

The 500SLC coupe sold in 1980 for .... DM 67,122

Production of the 500SLC coupe [107 E50] (from February/May 1980 until September 1981)

was in	1980	816 units
	1981	483 units
	total	1,299 units

Model 500SL/SLC (1980-   )

S = Sports, L (Leicht) = light

S = Sports, L = Light, C = Coupe

The 500SL and 500SLC were nearly identical to the 380SL/SLC sports models introduced also in March at the Geneva Auto Show, except, of course, for the power.

The body style was similar to the old 107 style except that the cars had the rear spoiler, formerly only used on the 450SLC 5.0 model. The front spoiler, also made of dark grey foamed plastic, was a feature of both eight-cylinder SL and SLC models. This innovation definitely improved the handling characteristics at higher speeds because of the great reduction in air resistance. All models also had the light-allow hoods for weight saving.

The running gear was nearly identical with the former models, although some details had been improved, such as the double wishbone axle with coil springs and anti-roll bar in front and the diagonal swing axle with them in the rear, and as the larger brake pads, increasing their serviceable life by about 30%. As an option, the anti-lock braking system was available on all SL and SLC models, which prevented wheel lock-up when braking, particularly under certain road conditions when the car had a tendency to skid. These models also had the anti-squat device on the swing axle which kept the rear end from sagging during fast acceleration.

Acceleration was considerably better than that of the 380 line, taking but 7.8 seconds for the 0 to 100 kilometer per hour speed, with a maximum speed for the 500SL/SLC of 225 kilometers per hour.

Since the cars had a 240 horsepower engine, just as the almost legendary 300SL had almost 30 years ago, comparison with that sports car might be of interest. The 1,330 kilogram 300SL coupe accelerated in 8.7 seconds, the roadster in 8.1 seconds, from 0 to 100 kilometers per hour. (The weight of the 500SL was 1,540 kilograms and that of the 500SLC, strangely, only 1,515 kilograms. However, the 500SL and SLC were quite comfortable sporty cars compared with the real sports characteristics of the 300SL models.) The 500SL and SLC cars were truly splendid performers.

Specifications

500SL/SLC

Engine type	V-8 cyl overhead camshafts (M117)	
Bore and stroke	96.5 x 85.0 mm (3.80 x 3.35 in)	
Displacement	4973 cc (303.5 cu in)	
Power output	240 hp (DIN) @ 5000 rpm	1981: 231 hp (DIN) @ 4750 rpm
Compression ratio	8.8:1	1981: 9.2:1
Torque	41 mkg @ 3200 rpm (296.6 ft/lb)	
Fuel injection	Bosch mechanical with air flow sensor	
Maximum engine speed	5950 rpm	
Gear ratios	I. 3.68:1 (automatic, standard)	
	II. 2.41:1	
	III. 1.44:1	
	IV. 1.00:1	
Rear axle ratio	2.72	1981: 2.24
Chassis	unit frame and body	
Suspension	independent front and rear, coil springs, anti-roll bar; diagonal swing axle, coil springs, anti-roll bar	
Brakes and area	dual circuit discs, power assisted, brake pad wear indicator, 278/279 mm (10.9/11.0 in)	
Wheelbase	2455 mm (96.7 in)	SLC: 2820 mm (111.0 in)
Track, front/rear	1452/1440 mm (57.2/56.7 in)	
Length	4390 mm (172.8 in)	SLC: 4750 mm (187.0 in)
Width	1790 mm (70.5 in)	
Height	1300 mm (51.2 in)	SLC: 1330 mm (52.4 in)
Tires	205/70 VR 14	
Turning circle	10.74 meters (35.2 ft)	SLC: 11.55 meters (37.9 ft)
Steering type and ratio	recirculating ball (3.0 turns), servo assisted	
Weight	1540 kg (3392 lbs)	SLC: 1515 kg (3336 lbs)
Maximum speed	225 km/hr (140 mph)	
Acceleration	7.8 sec 0-100 km/hr	1981: 8.1 sec 0-100 km/hr
Fuel consumption	at 120 km/hr: 13.3 liters/100 km (17.6 mpg)	1981: 11.5 liters
Fuel tank capacity	90 liters (23.8 gallons)	

The 500SLC coupe, 1980

The 300SD sedan, 1981, U.S. version

Prices and Production

The 300SD four-door sedan in 1981 sold for . . . . . . .DM 37,815
The 300SD sedan sold in the United States
  (with automatic transmission)
  in November 1980 for (East Coast). $34,185
  in September 1982 (East Coast) $37,970

Production of the 300SD model [126 D30A] (from September 1979/
October 1980 until August 1985)

was in 1979	3	units
1980	4,857	units
1981	16,595	units
1982	18,122	units
1983	20,291	units
1984	12,546	units
1985	6,311	units
total	78,725	units

Production of the 300SDL [126 D30A] (from February 1985/February
1986 until September 1987)

was in 1985	47	units
1986	8,274	units
1987	5,509	units
total	13,830	units

The 300SDL (turbo) sedan sold in the United States in
  1987 (East Coast) for $47,000

Model 300SD (1979-1987) SDL (1985-1987)

S = turbo-charged, D = Diesel

The 300SD sedan with the W126 body of the S-class was introduced to the public at the Frankurt Auto Show in 1979. It was one of the four models which shared that upper class body style. The gasoline-engined 280SE/SEL, 380SE/SEL, and 500SE/SEL sedans were the other luxury models.

These lighter cars (by as much as 176 pounds) were indeed "engineered for the future — to meet the demands of today," although development work had begun seven years before when the economic factor was not a dominating concern, but emission and safety received the main emphasis. The lower and smoother hood line gave the W126 bodies a drag coefficient of only .36, an improvement of 14% over the older body style.

Square halogen sealed beam headlights replaced the previous round style. Windshield wipers were recessed. The hood and rear deck lid were of aluminum. Bumpers were redesigned, stronger yet lighter. Climate control was electronically controlled instead of vacuum operated.

The 300SD was available in Europe soon after introduction and production of over 500 units in September, climbing to over 1,500 by November, indicated good sales. In the United States the new 300SD model was first sold in the 1981 model year. That car weighed then 1,705 kilograms (3,760 pounds), fully equipped, and had undergone some changes to comply with government regulations. Alloy wheels were standard, but leather upholstery was an optional extra item.

The Environmental Protection Agency rated the 300SD at 26 miles per gallon for the city cycle of driving and 30 miles per gallon for highway cruising. (The 240D manual got 29/33 mpg, automatic 27/31 mpg.) With the 20.3 gallon fuel tank, the turbo-charged five-cylinder diesel had a driving range of 609 miles, the longest distance of all models then sold in this country. Anticipating an extraordinary demand for this model (quite correctly when using 20/20 hindsight), the distributor brought 2,443 units into this country in 1980 already, just to be prepared for this eventuality.

The 300SDL six-cylinder turbo diesel sedan became available in the United States in 1986.

Specifications

	300SD	300SDL
Engine type	5 cyl diesel, overhead camshaft, with turbo-charger (OM 617A)	6 cyl diesel, overhead camshaft, with turbo-charger (OM 603A)
Bore and stroke	91 x 92.4mm (3.58 x 3.64 in)	87.0 x 84.0 mm (3.43 x 3.31 in)
Displacement	2998 cc (182.9 cu in)	2996 cc (182.8 cu in)
Power output	125 hp (DIN) @4350 rpm U.S.: 120 hp (SAE) 1984: 123 hp; Cal. 1985: 118 hp 1987: All U.S.: 143 hp	148 hp (SAE) 110 Kw @ 4600 rpm; Calif: 143 hp (107 Kw) 1987: All U.S.: 195 ft/lb
Compression ratio	21.5:1	22:1
Torque	25.5 mkg @ 2400 rpm U.S.: 23.6 mkg (170 ft/lb) 1984: 184 ft/lb; Cal. 1985: 177 ft/lb	201 lb/ft $ 2400 rpm; Calif: 195 lb/ft
Maximum engine speed		
Fuel injection	Bosch five plunger pump w/injection timer	
Engine speed at 100 km/hr	5100 rpm; U.S.: 4350 rpm; 1982: 4500 rpm; 1983: 4640 rpm 1984: 5000 rpm; 1985: 5200 rpm	5150 rpm
Gear ratios	I. 3.90:1 II. 2.30:1 III. 1.41:1 IV. 1.00:1	
Rear axle ratio	3.07; U.S. 1985: 2.88	2.88
Chassis	unit frame and body	
Suspension	independent front and rear, coil springs; diagonal swing axle, coil springs, anti-roll bar, level control standard	
Brakes and area	dual circuit discs, power assisted, brake pad wear indicator, 278/279mm (10.9/11.0 in)	
Wheelbase	2935mm (115.6 in)	3075 mm (121.1 in)
Track, front/rear	1545/1517mm (60.8/59.7 in)	1555/1527 mm (61.1/60.1 in)
Length	4995mm (196.6 in); U.S.: 5145mm (202.6 in)	5285 mm (208.1 in)
Width	1820mm (71.6 in)	1820 mm (71.6 in)
Height	1430mm (56.3 in)	1441 mm (56.7 in)
Tires	195/70 RS 14	205/65 R 15 93 H
Turning circle	11.80 meters (38.7 ft)	12.4 meters (40.6 ft)
Steering type and ratio	recirculating ball (2.7 turns); servo assisted	(3 turns)
Weight	1705 kg (3751 lbs) 1982: 1715 kg (3780 lbs)	1740 kg (3835 lbs)
Maximum speed	165 km/hr (103 mph) automatic	119 mph (191 km/hr) automatic
Acceleration	15 sec 0-100 km/hr	
Fuel consumption	11.1 liters at 120 km/hr	
Fuel tank capacity	77 liters (20.3 gallons)	90 liters (23.8 gallons)

Model 380SEC (1980–1985)

S = Super, E (Einspritzung) = fuel injection, C = Coupe

The 380SEC coupe was first shown at the Frankfurt Auto Show in 1981. Developed from the W126 sedan of the S-class of cars introduced two years before, the lines of this coupe showed clearly their heritage. However, the front end had the lower, sportier looking profile of the 380SLC which it replaced.

Air resistance of 0.34 cw of the newer model was actually 14% less than that of the former coupe and 6% less than that of the sedan. Wheelbase was 80 millimeters shorter and the body 30 millimeters lower, but the older 380SLC had been 30 millimeters shorter and 64 millimeters lower, and weighed 25 kilograms less. The new model was indeed a larger car and a coupe with sufficient room for the rear seat passengers.

Rear seats were separate, styled like single seats, and the wide doors made for easier passenger entry. Safety belts were offered by an electrically activated device to the driver and front seat after entering the vehicle to encourage greater use of this safety feature.

The V-8 light alloy gasoline engine was modified to save energy and obtain the highest possible torque at lower engine speeds. The stroke/bore ratio was close to that of the 5-liter unit. Bore was reduced and stroke increased for more compact combustion and less heat losses, and displacement was slightly changed from the previous unit. Compression ratio was also changed and 94% of total torque was available already at 2,000 revolutions per minute. Actually, these dimensions were those of the 3.8-liter engines already used in the U.S. cars two years before. Even the compression ratio and rear axle ratio were the same.

The U.S. version of the 380SEC model was, of course, again a somewhat different car. The 3.8-liter engine was the same as that used in these 380 line cars before, developing 155 horsepower at 4,750 rpm and 196 lb/ft torque at 2,750 rpm. Compression ratio was still 8.3:1. The rear axle ratio was, as on all of these cars, again 2.47:1.

The 380SEC weighed 1,705 kg (3,760 lbs), nearly 100 kilograms more than the European model. It had, consequently, slightly less maximum speed, but was still an excellently performing automobile. And in these days of fuel shortages and higher prices, the average EPA mileage figures of 17 miles per gallon for the city cycle and 22 mpg for highway driving were of definite importance to the buyer of even such a luxury car as this.

There is little doubt that this truly most luxurious 380SEC coupe would be rated, as was the sedan, the best coupe in the world.

Prices and Production

The 380SEC coupe sold in 1981 for . . . . .DM 69,495
The 380SEC model sold in the United States
    (with automatic transmission)
    in October 1981 for (East Coast) $49,827
    in September 1982 (East Coast) $53,570

Production of the 380SEC coupe [126 E38] (from September 1980/October 1981 until September 1985)

was in	1980	3 units
	1981	945 units
	1982	4,393 units
	1983	3,829 units
	1984	1,310 units
	1985	787 units
	total	11,267 units

The 380SEC coupe, 1981

Specifications

380SEC

Engine type	V-8 cyl overhead camshafts (M116)	
Bore and stroke	88 x 78.9 mm (3.46 x 3.10 in)	
Displacement	3839 cc (234.3 cu in)	
Power output	204 hp (DIN) @ 5250 rpm	U.S.: 155 hp SAE @ 4750 rpm
Compression ratio	9.4:1	U.S.: 8.3:1
Torque	315 Nm @ 3250 rpm (31 mkg, 224.3 ft/lb)	U.S.: 196 lb/ft (27.5 mkg)
Fuel injection	Bosch mechanical with air flow sensor	
Maximum engine speed	5950 rpm	U.S.: 5300 rpm; 1983: 5500 rpm
Gear ratios	I. 3.68:1 (automatic, standard) II. 2.41:1 III. 1.44:1 IV. 1.00:1	
Rear axle ratio	2.47	
Chassis	unit frame and body	
Suspension	double control arm axle, coil springs, anti-roll bar; diagonal swing axle, coil springs, anti-roll bar	
Brakes and area	dual circuit discs, power assisted, brake pad wear indicator, 278/279 mm (10.9/11.0 in)	
Wheelbase	2850 mm (112.2 in)	
Track, front/rear	1545/1517 mm (60.8/59.7 in)	
Length	4910 mm (193.3 in)	U.S.: 5060 mm (199.2 in)
Width	1828 mm (72.0 in)	
Height	1406 mm (55.4 in)	
Tires	205/70 VR 14	
Turning circle	11.53 meters (35.14 feet)	U.S.: 11.62 meters (38.12 feet)
Steering type and ratio	recirculating ball (2.89 turns), servo assisted	
Weight	1585 kg (3487 lbs)	U.S.: 1705 kg (3760 lbs)
Maximum speed	210 km/hr (131 mph)	
Acceleration	9.8 sec 0-100 km/hr	
Fuel consumption	at 120 km/hr: 10.8 liters (21.5 mpg)	
Fuel tank capacity	90 liters (23.8 gallons)	

The 380SEC coupe, 1982, U.S. version

Model 500SEC (1980–1991)

S = Super, E (Einspritzung) = fuel injection, C = Coupe

The 500SEC coupe was also introduced to the public at the 1981 Frankfurt Auto Show. It was the identical body style to the 380SEC model, and as in that case, also replaced the former SLC, a body style which had been in production for ten years.

The absolutely best materials went into this top-line coupe, which included all of the safety demands of the S-line sedans, the generously comfortable arrangement of controls and utilization of available space. Longer by 160 mm, wider by 38 mm, and higher by 76 mm, the SEC body also had a 30 mm longer wheelbase than the SLC coupe. The engine hood, trunk lid, and bulk head between tank and trunk were made of light alloy to achieve a curb weight of 1,610 kg, just 25 kg (55 lbs) more than the 3.8-liter coupe.

Besides the luxurious features mentioned for the 380SEC, a choice of eight velour or leather color combinations with matching trim was made available to the buyer. Burl walnut finish of the wood used in the instrument range, center console, and door trim was used (reminiscent of my own 300S coupe of 1957).

The V-8 light alloy fuel-injection gasoline engine was somewhat modified to save energy and to obtain the highest possible torque at low engine speeds. The four-speed converter automatic transmission, first introduced in the S-class sedans, was used. In the 500SEC model, driving off proceeded in second gear when "D" was engaged, but a pedal kickdown resulted in first gear. A new position, "B," used in both coupes, utilized better the engine braking effect, and was especially designed for downhill mountain driving.

The rear axle ratios were changed to obtain lower engine speeds at the same previous vehicle speeds, 18% in the 500SEC and 24% in the 380SEC models. Another new feature was the floating caliper disc brakes in front, reducing the heating-up of brake fluid, thus practically eliminating vapor lock and consequently increasing safety. The ABS (anti-lock breaking system) feature was available as an optional extra.

The fuel mileage figures, according to the German DIN method, showed that the new 500SEC needed 5.5 liters less in the city cycle and 1.8 liters less at 120 km/hr highway driving than did the 500SLC. But acceleration took 8.1 seconds against 7.8 seconds of the former coupe, for the 0-100 km/hr while the maximum speed remained the same for both models at 225 kilometers per hour (140 mph).

Prices and Production

The 500SEC coupe sold in 1981 for . . . . DM 73,902

In the United States for 500SEC coupe sold in 1984

for . . . . (East Coast) $56,800

for . . . . (West Coast) $57,100

Production of the 500SE coupe [126 E50] (from July 1980/ October 1981 until September 1991)

was in 1980	1 unit
1981	726 units
1982	4,059 units
1983	6,058 units
1984	6,664 units
1985	5,865 units
1986	2,020 units
1987	1,107 units
1988	1,056 units
1989	1,062 units
1990	1,067 units
1991	499 units
total	30,184 units

The 500SEC coupe, 1981

Specifications

	500SEC	
Engine type	V-8 cyl overhead camshafts (M117)	
Bore and stroke	96.5 x 85.0 mm (3.80 x 3.35 in)	
Displacement	4973 cc (303.5 cu in)	
Power output	231 hp (DIN) @ 4750 rpm 1989: 252 hp (DIN) 185 Kw @ 5200 rpm	U.S.: 184 hp (SAE) 137 Kw @ 4500 rpm
Compression ratio	9.2:1 1989: 10.0:1	U.S.: 8.0:1
Torque	405 Nm @ 3000 rpm (41 mkg, 296.6 ft/lb) 1989: 390 Nm @ 3750 rpm	U.S.: 335 Nm @ 2000 rpm (247 ft/lb)
Fuel injection	Bosch mechanical with air flow sensor	
Maximum engine speed	5950 rpm	U.S.: 5500 rpm
Gear ratios	I. 3.68:1 (automatic, standard)	
	II. 2.41:1	
	III. 1.44:1	
	IV. 1.00:1	
Rear axle ratio	2.24	U.S.: 2.47
Chassis	unit frame and body	
Suspension	double control arm axle, coil springs, anti-roll bar; diagonal swing axle, coil springs, anti-roll bar	
Brakes and area	dual circuit discs, power assisted, brake pad wear indicator, 278/279 mm (10.9/11.0 in)	
Wheelbase	2850 mm (112.2 in)	
Track, front/rear	1545/1517 mm (60.8/59.7 in)	
Length	4910 mm (193.3 in)	
Width	1828 mm (72.0 in)	
Height	1406 mm (55.4 in)	
Tires	205/70 VR 14	
Turning circle	11.53 meters (35.14 feet)	
Steering type and ratio	recirculating ball (2.89 turns), servo assisted	
Weight	1610 kg (3542 lbs)	U.S.: 1755 kg (3870 lbs)
Maximum speed	225 km/hr (140 mph)	
Acceleration	8.1 sec 0-100 km/hr	
Fuel consumption	at 120 km/hr: 11.4 liters/100 km (20.5 mpg)	
Fuel tank capacity	90 liters (23.8 gallons)	

The elegant interior of the 500SEC, 1981

The 190 sedan, 1982

Prices and Production

The 190 four-door sedan sold in 1982 for . . . . DM 25,538

Production of the 190 four-door sedan [201 V20] (from February/
October 1982 until January 1991)

was in	1982	1,635 units
	1983	25,746 units
	1984	15,415 units
	1985	15,790 units
	1986	14,402 units
	1987	13,474 units
	1988	14,183 units
	1989	14,116 units
	1990	3,796 units
until Jan. 1991		4 units
	total	118,561 units

The 190E four-door sedan sold in 1982 for . . . . DM 27,742

Production of the 190E four-door sedan [201 E20] (from February/
October 1982 until January 1991)

was in	1982	2,987 units
	1983	73,284 units
	1984	80,149 units
	1985	77,752 units
	1986	69,875 units
	1987	64,558 units
	1988	64,050 units
	1989	75,463 units
	1990	51,430 units
	1991	39,900 units
	1992	29,361 units
	1993	9,371 units
	total	205,525 units

Model 190/190E (1982–1991)

E (Einspritzung) = fuel injection

The 190 and 190E models made their debut in early December 1982 near Seville, Spain, where they were shown to representatives of the press. These cars had undergone extensive and exhaustive testing for a long time before their initial production period. This chronicler had seen examples of them already being driven in the factory grounds at Untertuerkheim some three years previously. This new line of cars had the smaller W201 body style, a scaled-down version of the S-class W126 style, and looked as if they were merely a smaller edition of those popular Mercedes models. From the front, the cars looked more like these larger types than the medium range of the current models with the W123 body style.

The sloping front end and integrated headlights resulted in an improved coefficient of aerodynamic drag, and the 190 cars with 0.33 actually bested the 0.36 of the W126 models. Strips of molding placed along the roof conducted rainwater from the windshield, washed by a single arm, double-blade wiper, and away from the side windows.

Despite its smaller size, the interior space was nearly as roomy as that of the larger models. Front leg room was almost identical and headroom and kneeroom in the rear seats was only 0.3 and 0.4 inches less than that in the 240D model. The placement of the driving controls and switches was similar to that of the larger sedans. The seats were all newly designed, combining safety with comfort.

New systems to maintain a high standard of ride, handling, and controllability had been developed. The multi-link rear suspension was a totally new design. Five independent links allowed for a relatively light system which ensured ride comfort and excellent roadhandling. The suspension was new and incorporated anti-squat and anti-dive controls. Gas-filled shock absorber struts with wishbones supported the front wheels. Coil springs were separate from the shocks, unlike the MacPherson strut system. Floating caliper front disc brakes were used, as first found on the 380SEC models, resulting in better front end geometry because of their greater compactness. Disc brakes were also used in the rear, and the entire system was vacuum boosted.

Manual transmission was standard, but a five-speed manual unit with overdrive or an automatic transmission was available as an optional item.

Specifications

	190	190E
Engine type	4 cyl overhead camshaft (M102)	
Bore and stroke	89 x 80.25 mm (3.50 x 3.16 in)	
Displacement	1997 cc (121.72 cu in)	
Power output	90 hp (DIN) @ 5000 rpm 1988: 102 hp (DIN) 75 Kw @ 5500 rpm	122 hp (DIN) @ 5100 rpm 1989: 105 hp (DIN) 77 Kw @ 5700 rpm
Compression ratio	9.0:1	9.1:1 1989: 9.0:1 1989: 118 hp (DIN) @ 5200 rpm
Torque	165 Nm @ 2500 rpm	178 Nm @ 3500 rpm 1989: 158 Nm @ 3500 rpm 1989: 172 Nm @ 3500 rpm
Carburetion/ Fuel Injection	175 CDT cross-draught carburetor	mechanically/electronically controlled fuel injection
Maximum engine speed	6000 rpm	
Gear ratios	I. 3.91:1 (4 speed) I. 3.91:1 (5 speed) 4.25:1 (automatic) II. 2.32:1 II. 2.32:1 2.41:1 III. 1.42:1 III. 1.42:1 1.49:1 IV. 1.00:1 IV. 1.00:1 1.00:1 V. 0.78:1	
Rear axle ratio	3.23	1989: 3.46 (5-speed); 3.23 (automatic)
Chassis	unit frame and body	
Suspension	shock absorber strut with anti-dive control, coil springs, anti-roll bar; multi-link independent rear, anti-dive, anti-squat control, coils, anti-roll bar	
Brakes and area	hydraulic dual circuit, discs; anti-locking system optional	
Wheelbase	2665 mm (104.9 in)	
Track, front/rear	1428/1415 mm (56.2/55.7 in)	
Length	4420 mm (174.0 in)	
Width	1678 mm (66.0 in)	
Height	1383 mm (54.4 in)	
Tires	175/70 R 14 82T 1985: 15 in wheels	175/70 R 14 82H 1985: 15 in wheels
Turning circle	10.60 meters (32.3 feet)	
Steering type and ratio	recirculating ball (5 turns); servo-assisted optional	
Weight	1080 kg (2376 lbs)	1100 kg (2420 lbs)
Maximum speed	175 km/hr (109 mph); 167 (5th); 1988: 183 km/hr [Max speed] automatic 170 km/hr (106 mph)	195 km/hr (120 mph); 187 (5th); automatic 190 km/hr (118 mph)
Acceleration	13.2 sec 0-100 km/hr; automatic 13.8 sec 0-100 km/hr	10.5 sec 0-100 km/hr; automatic 11 sec 0-100 km/hr
Fuel consumption	at 120 km/hr: 8.4 liters/100 km; automatic 8.9 liters	at 120 km/hr: 8.3 liters/100 km; automatic 8.7 liters
Fuel tank capacity	55 liters (14.5 gallons)	

The 190E 2.3 sedan, 1984, U.S. version

Prices and Production

The 190E 2.3 sedan sold in 1983 for (East Coast) $23,430
in 1985 for (West Coast) $23,730

Production of the 190E 2.3 sedan [201 E23] (from March/September 1983)

was in	1983	3,945 units
	1984	20,743 units
	1985	23,123 units
	1986	25,449 units
	1987	29,726 units
	1988	20,471 units
	1989	10,696 units
	1990	14,260 units
	1991	16,341 units
	1992	15,863 units
	1993	5,993 units
	total	65,153 units

The 190E 2.3 sedan, 1985, U.S. version

Model 190E 2.3 (1983–1993)

E (Einspritzung) = fuel injection

The 190E 2.3 was created solely for the North American market. It first became available in 1983. The single overhead camshaft M102 four-cylinder gasoline engine had a larger bore (95.5 millimeters against 89 millimeters) than that of the European version and displaced 2,299 cubic centimeters (140 cubic inches) instead of the 1,997 cubic centimeters of that 190E 2-liter unit. The added designation 2.3 stood, of course, for the 2.3-liter displacement.

The larger displacement engine developing 113 SAE horsepower at 5,000 revolutions per minute, against the 122 DIN horsepower of the smaller one, was necessitated because of the stringent emission controls prevailing in this country. Torque was about the same in both versions, 180 Nm (133 pounds/feet) at 3,500 rpm of the American against 178 Nm for the European.

The engine was slanted 15 degrees for a lower hood line. The block was of cast iron and the head of aluminum alloy with hemispherical combustion chambers and cross-flow ports. The forged crankshaft had five main bearings and eight counterweights and vibration damper, ensuring smooth running for this relatively large four-cylinder engine. The smooth and precise five-speed manual transmission was the first one designed by factory engineers. A completely new four-speed automatic was also available. Idle creep was reduced by starting in second gear in the automatic transmission.

The excellent, computer-designed rear suspension "incorporated race car precision but maintained great comfort," according to the designers. This new five-link rear suspension was indeed a tremendous improvement over the previous designs.

The 190E 2.3 was heavier, 1,219 kilograms against 1,100, and the acceleration figures were 11.2 seconds against 10.5 seconds for the 0 to 100 kilometers run. Maximum speed was also less for our version, 114 miles per hour, against the 120 miles per hour for the European 190E. But there was really not too much difference in the overall performance of these two similar cars. This "near equal performance" goal was of course the aim of the factory engineers when solving that problem of severe modifications made necessary by the demands of the countries to which the cars are being exported.

Specifications

	190E 2.3
Engine type	4 cyl overhead camshaft (M102)
Bore and stroke	3.76 x 3.16 in (95.5 x 80.25 mm)
Displacement	140.3 cu in (2299 cc)
Power output	113 hp (SAE) 84 Kw @ 5000 rpm 1985: 120 hp 1987: U.S.: 130 hp (SAE) 97 Kw @ 5100 rpm
Compression ratio	8.0:1 1987: U.S. 9.0:1 1988: U.S.: 132 hp (SAE) 97 Kw @ 5100 rpm
Torque	133 ft/lb (181 Nm) @ 3500 rpm 1985: 136 ft/lb (184 Nm) 1987: U.S.: 146 ft/lb (198 Nm)
Fuel injection	KE Bosch Jetronic 1989: U.S.: 198 ft/lb
Maximum engine speed	5700 rpm 1985: 6200 rpm

The M 102 engine of the 190E 2.3, 1984

Gear ratios	I.	3.91:1	(5-speed)	I.	4.25:1	(automatic)
	II.	2.17:1		II.	2.41:1	
	III.	1.37:1		III.	1.49:1	
	IV.	1.00:1		IV.	1.00:1	
	V.	0.78:1				

Rear axle ratio	3.27; automatic: 3.23 1987: U.S.: 3.27 1989: U.S.: 3.92 (5-speed); 3.27 (automatic)
Chassis	unit frame and body
Suspension	shock absorber strut with anti-dive control, coil springs, anti-roll bar; multi-link independent rear, anti-dive, anti-squat control, coils, anti-roll bar
Brakes and area	hydraulic dual circuit, discs; 373 sq in (2411 sq mm) 262/258 mm (10.3/10.2 in)
Wheelbase	104.9 in (2665 mm)
Track, front/rear	56.2/55.7 in (1428/1415 mm)
Length	175.0 in (4445 mm)
Width	66.1 in (1678 mm)
Height	54.5 in (1383 mm)
Tires	175/70 R 14 82T 1985: 15 in wheels 1986: 185/65 R 15 87H
Turning circle	35.0 ft (10.7 meters)
Steering type and ratio	recirculating ball (3.3 turns); servo-assisted
Weight	2655 lbs (1205 kg) 1985: 2670 lbs (1210 kg) 1986: 2745 lbs (1245 kg)
Maximum speed	114 mph (184 km/hr) 1988: U.S.: 197 km/hr 1987: U.S.: 1260 kg (2780 lbs)
Acceleration	11.2 sec 0-60 mph
Fuel consumption	manual: 23 mpg city, 37 mpg highway; automatic: 23 mpg city, 31 mpg highway
Fuel tank capacity	14.5 gallons (55 liters)

The instrument panel of the 190E 2.3, 1984

The 190E 2.3-16 sedan, 1985

Prices and Production

The 190E 2.3-16 sedan sold in 1984 for DM55,158.90

The 190E 2.3-16 sedan sold in in the United States in 1986 (East Coast)
for $34,800
automatic $600

Production of the 190E 2.3-16 sedan [201 E23/2] (from September 1983/
September 1984 until June 1988)

was in 1983	5 units
1984	2,445 units
1985	8,656 units
1986	5,473 units
1987	2,374 units
1988	534 units
total	17,037 units

Production of the 190E 2.5-16 sedan [201 E25] from July 1988)

was in 1988	959 units
1989	2,645 units
1990	1,270 units
1991	566 units
1992	197 units
1993	106 units
total	4,784 units

The 190E 2.5-16 sold in 1988 for DM67,944

Production of the 190E 2.5 EV (chassis only) (from January until July
1990)

was in 1990	502 units

Model 190E 2.3-16 (1983–1988)
190E 2.5-16 (1988–1993)

E (Einspritzung) = fuel injection

The 190E 2.3-16 model, the high performance version of the small Mercedes line, was first publicly exhibited at the Frankfurt Auto Show in September 1983, but its well-deserved reputation for a fantastically fast car had already preceded it.

In August at the Nardo, Italy, track the 190 2.3-16 had set three world records; the fastest average speed of 154.06 miles (247.939 kilometers) per hour was for 50,000 kilometers. And twelve international class endurance records were also established there—from 1,000 kilometers at 153.54 miles per hour to the 24 hours at 153.30 miles (246.713 km) per hour.

Those cars were only slightly modified from the regularly available stock version. The windshield wipers, headlight wipers, and outside rearview mirrors were removed, and headlight and grille shields were fitted. The rear axle ratio was changed to 2.65:1. Tires were Pirelli P7s. Otherwise, the cars were standard. The engine of the 2.3-16 model, developed by Cosworth engineers, had the light alloy cylinder head with twin overhead camshafts and four valves per cylinder, electronically controlled ignition and idling, mechanically and electronically controlled (Bosch LE Jetronic) fuel injection, air-bathed injection valves, single poly V-belt, hydraulically damped engine bearings, and an oil cooler. (It developed 72 more horsepower and 41 lbs/ft more torque than the regular single overhead camshaft 190 engine.)

This M102 2.3-liter (2,299 cc) engine developed 185 DIN (136 kw) horsepower at 6,000 rpm. Torque was 174 lbs/ft at 4,500 rpm. Acceleration was about 8 seconds from 0 to 100 kilometers (62 miles) per hour, and maximum speed with the standard 3.07 rear axle was 230 kilometers (144 miles) per hour. The flexible engine allowed the car to be driven in fifth gear also at 50 kilometers (31 miles) per hour.

The slight increase in engine size did not give the car a greatly improved performance. The power output increased by 10 hp and the torque remained the same, but it was in keeping with the current trend of improving the existing lines.

For competition purposes in Germany an "Evolution" version of 502 units was produced in March 1989. The slightly altered short-stroke engine developed in competition trim 315-320 horsepower and improved torque characteristics. It sold to selected competitors for DM 87,204.

Specifications

	190E 2.3-16		109E 2.5-16	
				Evolution model:
Engine type	4 cyl overhead camshaft (M102)			
Bore and stroke	95.5 x 80.25 mm (3.76 x 3.16 in)		95.50 x 87.20 mm (3.76 x 3.43 in)	97.30 x 82.80 mm (3.83 x 3.26 in)
Displacement	2299 cc (140.3 cu in)		2497 cc (152.3 cu in)	2463 cc (150.2 cu in)
Power output	185 hp (DIN) 136 Kw @ 6200 rpm	U.S.: 167 (SAE) hp @ 5800 rpm	195 hp (DIN) 143 Kw @ 6800 rpm; 1989: 170 hp (DIN) 125 Kw @ 5800 rpm	
Compression ratio	10.5:1	U.S.: 9.7:1		
Torque	235 Nm (167.2 ft/lb) @ 4500 rpm (23.1 mkg)	U.S.: 162 ft/lb @ 4750 rpm	235 Nm (167.2 ft/lbs) @ 5000-5500 rpm;	
Fuel injection	Bosch mechanically/electronically controlled			
Maximum engine speed	7000 rpm			
Gear ratios	I. 4.08:1 II. 2.52:1 III. 1.77:1 IV. 1.26:1 V. 1.00:1			
Rear axle ratio	3.07	U.S.: 3.27		3.27
Chassis	unit frame and body			
Suspension	shock absorber strut with anti-dive control, coil springs, anti-roll bar; multi-link independent rear, anti-dive, anti-squat control, coils, anti-roll bar, pneumatic self-leveling			
Brakes and area	hydraulic dual circuit, discs; ABS standard 373 sq in			
Wheelbase	2665 mm (104.9 in)			
Track, front/rear	1446/1429 mm (56.9/56.2 in)			
Length	4430 mm (174.4 in)			
Width	1706 mm (67.1 in)			
Height	1361 mm (53.6 in)			
Tires	205/55 VR 15			225/50 ZR 16 on 8" rims
Turning circle	10.6 meters (35.0 feet)			
Steering type and ratio	recirculating ball (3.3 turns); servo-assisted			
Weight	1260 kg (2772 lbs)	U.S.: 3030 lbs (1375 kg)		
Maximum speed	230 km/hr (143.5 mph)		220 km/hr	
Acceleration	7.5 sec 0-100 km/hr			
Fuel consumption	at 120 km/hr 7.9 liters (29.0 mpg)			
Fuel tank capacity	70 liters (18.5 gallons)			

The 190D sedan, 1985

Prices and Production

The 190D sedan sold in 1983 for DM27,310.00
    in 1985 for .... DM 28,306.20

Production of the 190D sedan [201 D20] (from August 1982/November 1983)

was in 1982	28 units	
1983	3,500 units	
1984	71,221 units	
1985	71,766 units	
1986	65,126 units	
1987	58,426 units	
1988	42,287 units	
1989	38,222 units	
1990	31,070 units	
1991	33,953 units	
1992	31,083 units	
1993	6,124 units	
total	140,452 units	

Rear view of the 190D sedan, 1985

Model 190D (1983–1993)

D = Diesel

The 190D model was first publicly shown at the Frankfurt Auto Show in September 1983, but deliveries of cars were not made until that December.

As in past instances, this economical diesel-engined model shared its outward appearance and inside appointments with the gasoline-engined 190 model, of which nearly 3,000 had already been built the previous year. There was absolutely no visible difference between these two sedans, and the proper identification could only be made by the designation on the trunk lid. Even the usual diesel noise was now so subdued that while driving, this car seemed practically as quiet as the gasoline version. Noise level of this newly designed engine had been reduced by half over the previous levels by the highly effective "encapsulation system" and the generous utilization of insulating materials all around.

Compared to the engine in the 200D models with the W123 body, a 23% weight saving of 50 kilograms (110 pounds) was achieved, and the power output was actually increased from 60 to 72 horsepower, or 20% over that 1,988 cc engine.

The completely new OM601 2-liter (actually 1,997 cc) diesel engine produced 72 DIN (53 kw) horsepower, giving the 1,110-kilogram (2,442 pounds) sedan an acceleration from 0 to 100 kilometers (62 miles) per hour of 18.1 seconds, and a maximum speed of 160 kilometers (100 miles) per hour. Despite this relatively superior performance of the diesel model, fuel consumption was rated at 7 liters for 100 kilometers of driving, or 34 miles per gallon. A manual four-speed transmission was standard, or a five-speed manual or four-speed automatic was optional.

A new feature of the engine was the bucket tappet control with hydraulic valve clearance compensation. The compact arrangement of the timing gear considerably reduced mass and drag and raised rigidity, thus also increasing the overall strength and insensitivity to overrevving of the engine. The tappets were supplied with oil through special holes drilled in the cylinder head. The usual method of driving the auxiliaries by numerous belts had been dispensed with and all were driven by a single V-belt operating in one plane. An automatic tensioner ensured maintenance-free operation and distributed the tension more evenly. It also gave it greater reliability and durability. A new fuel heating system was installed, assuring that the diesel fuel is of the correct viscosity and making jellification impossible in winter climates.

Specifications

	190D
Engine type	4 cyl diesel, overhead camshaft (MO 601)
Bore and stroke	87.0 x 84.0 mm (3.43 x 3.31 in)
Displacement	1997 cc (121.72 cu in)
Power output	72 hp (DIN) 53 Kw @ 4600 rpm 1989: 75 hp (DIN) 55 Kw @ 4600 rpm
Compression ratio	22:1
Torque	123 Nm (87.3 ft/lb) @ 2800 rpm (12.1 mkg) 1989: 126 Nm @ 2700 rpm
Fuel injection	Bosch four-plunger pump
Maximum engine speed	5150 rpm

Gear ratios						
I.	4.23:1	(4-speed)	I.	4.24:1 (automatic)	I.	4.23:1 (5-speed)
II.	2.36:1		II.	2.41:1	II.	2.36:1
III.	1.49:1		III.	1.49:1	III.	1.49:1
IV.	1.00:1		IV.	1.00:1	IV.	1.00:1
					V.	0.84:1

Rear axle ratio	3.23 1989: 3.91 (5-speed)
Chassis	unit frame and body
Suspension	shock absorber strut with anti-dive control, coil springs, anti-roll bar; multi-link independent rear, anti-dive, anti-squat control, coils, anti-roll bar
Brakes and area	hydraulic dual circuit, discs; anti-locking system optional; 373 sq in (2411 sq mm)
Wheelbase	2665 mm (104.9 in)
Track, front/rear	1428/1415 mm (56.2/55.7 in)
Length	4420 mm (174.0 in)
Width	1678 mm (66.1 in)
Height	1383 mm (54.4in)
Tires	175/70 R 14 82S 1985: 15 in wheels
Turning circle	10.60 meters (32.3 feet)
Steering type and ratio	recirculating ball (5 turns); servo-assisted
Weight	1110 kg (2442 lbs)
Maximum speed	160 km/hr (100 mph); automatic: 156 km/hr (97 mph)
Acceleration	18.1 sec 0-100 km/hr; automatic: 18.6 sec
Fuel consumption	at 120 km/hr: 6.9 liters (34 mpg); automatic: 7.3 liters; 5-speed: 6.6 liters (35.5 mpg)
Fuel tank capacity	55 liters (14.5 gallons)

The 190D 2.2 sedan, 1984, U.S. version

Prices and Production

The 190D 2.2 sedan sold in 1983 for (East Coast) $23,510
in 1985 for (West Coast) $23,810

Production of the 190D 2.2 sedan [201D 22] (from February 1983/
November 1984 until August 1985)

was in	1983	3,357 units
	1984	5,327 units
	1985	1,876 units
	total	10,560 units

Model 190D 2.2 (1983–1985)

D = Diesel

For the United States, the 190D became the 190D 2.2. Instead of the 2-liter engine, by increasing the stroke to 92.4 millimeters, the displacement was enlarged to 2.2 liters—actually 2,197 cubic centimeters—but because of the stringent emission standards imposed, the horsepower output remained at 72, the same as that of the (1,997 cc) European version of the diesel engine used. The torque here was slightly increased over that of the European version as well, from 123 Nm to 130 Nm.

As usual, the 190D 2.2 shared the body style and interior appointments with the gasoline-powerd model.

In performance, however, this diesel version was overshadowed by the more powerful (113 hp to 72 hp for the D 2.2) yet not lighter gasoline model (2,655 lbs to 2,645 lbs for the diesel), but this OM601 diesel engine, based on the newly designed 2-liter unit was considerably more powerful than any previous diesel engine of comparable size. And, of course, it was fantastically economical. Fuel consumption was rated at 35 miles per gallon for the city cycle and 44 miles per gallon for highway driving. (The 190E 2.2 was rated at 23 and 31 mpg, respectively.)

Many otherwise extra cost optional items were standard equipment on these models in the U.S. and a partial list of these mentioned no less than 30 items, among them alloy wheels, tinted glass, cruise control, electric windows, central locking, and interior wood trim. The instrumentation included, of course, the speedometer, tachometer, quartz chronometer, and outside air temperature indicator. Two transmissions were available—the five-speed manual or the four-speed automatic. The automatic transmission started in first gear. The European optional dual mode economy shift program selector was not offered, because for the larger displacement engine here it did not result in any benefits.

The 190D 2.2 was indeed a most economical diesel sedan, but sales in its first year did not anywhere approach those of the popular larger 300D model. In fact, the 5,309 units sold during 1984 were but 32% of that of the best-selling diesel model in the United States, and only 33% of the companion gasoline 190E 2.3 model.

Specifications

190D 2.2

Engine type	4 cyl diesel, overhead camshaft (OM601)
Bore and stroke	3.43 x 3.64 in (87.0 x 92.4 mm)
Displacement	134.1 cu in (2197 cc)
Power output	72 hp (SAE) 54 Kw @ 4200 rpm
Compression ratio	22.0:1
Torque	96 ft/lb (130 Nm) @ 2800 rpm
Fuel injection	Bosch four-plunger pump
Maximum engine speed	5000 rpm 1985: 5100 rpm

The OM 601 engine of the 190D 2.2, 1984

Gear ratios

I.	4.23:1	(5-speed)	I.	4.25:1	(automatic)
II.	2.25:1		II.	2.41:1	
III.	1.48:1		III.	1.49:1	
IV.	1.00:1		IV.	1.00:1	
V.	0.84:1				

Rear axle ratio	3.42
Chassis	unit frame and body
Suspension	shock absorber strut with anti-dive control, coil springs, anti-roll bar; multi-link independent rear, anti-dive, anti-squat control, coils, anti-roll bar
Brakes and area	hydraulic dual circuit, discs; 373 sq in
Wheelbase	104.9 in (2665 mm)
Track, front/rear	56.2/55.7 in (1428/1415 mm)
Length	175.0 in (4445 mm)
Width	66.1 in (1678 mm)
Height	54.4 in (1383 mm)
Tires	175/70 R14 82S 1985: 15 in wheels
Turning circle	35.0 ft (10.7 meters)
Steering type and ratio	recirculating ball (3.3 turns); servo-assisted
Weight	2645 lbs (1200 kg) 1985: 2700 lbs (1225 kg)
Maximum speed	97 mph (156 km/hr)
Acceleration	18.6 sec 0-60 mph
Fuel consumption	manual: 35 mpg city, 51 mpg highway; automatic: 35 mpg city, 44 mph highway
Fuel tank capacity	14.5 gallons (55 liters)

The 200 sedan, 1985

Prices and Production

The 200 sedan sold in 1984 for .... DM 31,635

Production of the 200 sedan [124 V20] (from March 1984 until June 1990)

was in	1984	811 units
	1985	21,688 units
	1986	26,294 units
	1987	23,731 units
	1988	25,589 units
	1989	10,213 units
	1990	2,028 units
	total	110,354 units

The 200E sedan sold in 1988 for .... DM 42,066

Production of the 200E sedan [124 E20] (from January/July 1985)

was in	1985	1,039 units
	1986	2,511 units
	1987	3,577 units
	1988	10,054 units
	1989	38,957 units
	1990	55,147 units
	1991	42,337 units
	1992	23,308 units
	total	159,749 units

Model 200 (1984-1992)
Model 200E (1985–)

The 200 model was one of seven (four gasoline and three diesel) models which shared the new W124 body style, first introduced in late 1984. It replaced the nine-year-old W123 style, of which over 2.6 million units had been sold.

The new body design was a logical continuation of the trend initiated with the W126 S-class of 1979 and the W201 style of the compact line three years later, and only on closer inspection could a difference between these last two styles be noted.

It included further improvements in aerodynamics, suggested by the shape of the high trailing edge. The easier low loading edge of the trunk was uniquely integrated with the rear lights positioned in the actual body.

The new bodies were 12 inches longer than those of the 190 line cars, but only slightly longer (0.6 inches) than those which they replaced. The width was 2 inches narrower, giving them a smaller frontal area which brought about a more favorable drag coefficient of 0.29 to 0.30. This was about 30% lower than that of the older style. Along with a considerable saving in overall weight, this gave all of the new models an appreciably better performance.

The improved front and rear suspension systems from the W201 bodies were used, that is the revised McPherson design in front and the greatly advanced multi-links system in the rear. Low profile tires 185/65 x 15 with 6-inch rims were fitted to the 200 model cars to accommodate the optional anti-lock (ABS) brake system.

The four-cylinder 2-liter M102 engine was the same since March 1980, but the weight of the new model was actually 176 pounds less. Consequently, the performance was greatly improved, with a maximum speed of 187 km/hr (116 mph) against the 168 km/hr (104 mph) of the former model, with manual transmission. Acceleration figures were also considerably better, the 0-100 km/hr being 12.6 seconds against the 14.4 seconds for the older model. And with the new five-speed transmission (with the 0.78:1 ratio and rear axle of 3.42), the fuel consumption figures showed an equally remarkable improvement. With the four-speed manual transmission, at 120 km/hr the new model used 8.5 liters of fuel, or gave 28 miles per gallon, while the older model used 10.2 liters, or gave 22 miles per gallon. (Earlier figures showed 10.7 liters.) The anti-skid braking system (ABS) was an optional extra on all models.

Specifications

	200	200E
Engine type	4 cyl overhead camshaft (M102)	
Bore and stroke	89.0 x 80.25 mm (3.50 x 3.16 in)	
Displacement	1997 cc (121.9 cu in)	
Power output	109 hp (DIN) 80 Kw @ 5200 rpm	122 hp (DIN) 90 Kw @ 5100 rpm
Compression ratio	9:1	1989: 105 hp (DIN) 77 Kw @ 5700 rpm
Torque	170 Nm (125.2 ft/lb) @ 2500 rpm (17.3 mkg)	178 Nm (131.4 ft/lb) @ 3500 rpm (18.2 mkg)
		1989: 158 Nm @ 3500 rpm
Carburetion	175 CD cross draught carburetor	Bosch KE jetronic
Maximum engine speed	6000 rpm	
Gear ratios	I. 3.92:1 (4-speed) I. 4.25:1 (automatic) I. 3.92:1 (5-speed) II. 2.17:1 II. 2.41:1 II. 2.17:1 III. 1.37:1 III. 1.49:1 III. 1.37:1 IV. 1.00:1 IV. 1.00:1 IV. 1.00:1 V. 0.78:1	
Rear axle ratio	3.42	1989: 3.46
Chassis	unit frame and body	
Suspension	shock absorber strut with anti-dive control, coil springs, anti-roll bar; multi-link independent rear, anti-dive, anti-squat control, coils, anti-roll bar	
Brakes and area	hydraulic dual circuit, discs; 373 sq in	
Wheelbase	2800 mm (110.0 in)	
Track, front/rear	1497/1488 mm (58.9/58.6 in)	
Length	4740 mm (186.6 in)	
Width	1740 mm (68.5 in)	
Height	1440 mm (56.7 in)	
Tires	185/65 R 15 87H	195/65 R 15 91H
Turning circle	11.2 meters (44 feet)	
Steering type and ratio	recirculating ball (3.3 turns); servo-assisted	
Weight	1260 kg (2772 lbs)	
Maximum speed	187 km/hr (116 mph); automatic: 182 km/hr (113 mph)	195 km/hr (121 mph)
Acceleration	12.6 sec. 0-100 km/hr; automatic: 13.1 sec	11 sec. 0-100 km/hr; automatic: 11.8 sec
Fuel consumption	at 120 km/hr: 8.5 liters (28 mpg); automatic: 9.0 liters; 5-speed: 7.7 liters (31 mpg)	
Fuel tank capacity	70 liters (18.5 gallons)	

The 230E sedan, 1985

Prices and Production

The 230E sedan sold in 1984 for .... DM 35,397

Production of the 230E sedan [124 E23] (from March 1984/January 1985)

was in 1984	1,324 units
1985	44,697 units
1986	52,040 units
1987	51,022 units
1988	56,285 units
1989	47,504 units
1990	46,738 units
1991	44,716 units
1992	30,096 units
total	169,054 units
1994	19 units

The 230E sedan, 1985

Model 230E (1984-   )

E (Einspritzung) = fuel injection

The 230E model was another one which shared the new W124 body style, first shown in late 1984. It was the smaller (four cylinders) of the gasoline-injected cars. In every respect, these seven various models resembled each other. The only visible difference was the designation on the trunk, but even that was not always there, because many Mercedes owners—especially of the smaller displacement models—removed that designation, and thus the visible means of identification.

Appointments were alike, and many refinements had been included in these middle range line of cars. For instance, the front seat belts had three height-adjustable slots at the center post for easier accommodation to the driver. An ingenous single-blade windshield wiper with a clever variable-length arm to reach into the corners was used. It cleared 86% of the entire windshield. The comfortable seats were electronically adjustable and the rear headrests could be recessed for unobstructed vision by the driver. These goodies, however, were here optional extra cost items.

The newer W124 body style was a considerably more economical car and performed better than the one it replaced, which was built from 1979 on, and had sold well over 200,000 units.

The four-cylinder 2.3-liter fuel-injection engine based on the newer M102 unit was of the same size as used in the older 230E model and the 190E 2.3 model. The mechanical electronic fuel injection system and completely electronic ignition system were entirely new. But the overall weight of the car was 2,816 lbs against the 2,992 lbs of the older one. Again, as in the other new models, the overall performance was greatly improved. Maximum speed of the new 230E was 203 km/hr (127 mph) with the manual transmission and 198 km/hr (124 mph) with the automatic transmission. Fuel economy showed an appreciable advancement. Using the manual transmission, it took 8.5 liters (28 mpg) for 100 kilometers of driving at 120 km/hr for the new model, while the older one used 10.3 liters (22 mpg).

Acceleration of 0-100 km/hr now took only 10.4 seconds with manual as well as automatic transmission, against the 11.4 for the former model with the manual and 12.3 with the automatic.

Again, the improvements of this newer model over the one it replaced were considerable—in riding comfort, economy, and overall performance.

Specifications

	230E
Engine type	4 cyl overhead camshaft (M102)
Bore and stroke	89.0 x 80.25 mm (3.50 x 3.16 in)
Displacement	2299 cc (140.3 cu in)
Power output	136 hp (DIN) 100 Kw @ 5100 rpm
Compression ratio	9.0:1
Torque	205 Nm (151.3 ft/lb) @ 3500 rpm (20.9 mkg)
Fuel injection	Bosch KE jetronic
Maximum engine speed	6000 rpm

Power output — 1989: 132 hp (DIN) 97 Kw @ 5100 rpm

Torque — 1989: 198 Nm @ 3500 rpm

Gear ratios

I.	3.92:1 (4-speed)	I.	4.25:1 (automatic)	I.	3.92:1 (5-speed)
II.	2.17:1	II.	2.41:1	II.	2.17:1
III.	1.37:1	III.	1.49:1	III.	1.37:1
IV.	1.00:1	IV.	1.00:1	IV	1.00:1
				V.	0.78:1

Rear axle ratio	3.27
Chassis	unit frame and body
Suspension	shock absorber strut with anti-dive control, coil springs, anti-roll bar; multi-link independent rear, anti-dive, anti-squat control, coils, anti-roll bar
Brakes and area	hydraulic dual circuit, discs; 373 sq in
Wheelbase	2800 mm (110.0 in)
Track, front/rear	1497/1488 mm (58.9/58.6 in)
Length	4740 mm (186.6 in)
Width	1740 mm (68.5 in)
Height	1446 mm (56.9 in)
Tires	195/65 R 15 90H
Turning circle	11.2 meters (44 feet)
Steering type and ratio	recirculating ball (3.3 turns); servo-assisted
Weight	1280 kg (2816 lbs)
Maximum speed	203 km/hr (127 mph); 198 km/hr (124 mph) automatic
Acceleration	10.4 sec 0-100 km/hr; automatic: 10.4 sec
Fuel consumption	at 120 km/hr: 8.5 liters (28 mpg); automatic: 8.7 liters; 5-speed: 7.7 liters (31 mpg)
Fuel tank capacity	70 liters (18.5 gallons)

Rear axle ratio — 1989: 3.46 (5-speed)

Front view of the 230E sedan, 1985

The 260E sedan, 1985

Model 260E (1984–1992)
Model 300E 2.6

E (Einspritzung) = fuel injection

The 260E model was the third of the gasoline-engined cars introduced in late 1984, and was the smaller displacement version of the new six-cylinder fuel-injected cars. It replaced the 250 model of 1975, actually first shown at the Geneva Auto Show in the spring of 1976. At any rate, that model had been sold for nine years.

The 260E shared the new W124 body style with the other six models and was undistinguishable from them as far as the outward appearance was concerned. The designation on the trunk lid was the only identification mark.

As in all of the new models, this 260E was considerably superior to the 250 model which it replaced. With a slightly larger displacement engine than the former, the new model was a better performer, but with the 163 horsepower which the 2,599 cc engine produced (against the 129 hp of the former 2,525 cc engine) the difference was actually tremendously noticeable.

The six-cylinder fuel-injected engine was an all new design. The mechanical/electronic injection and new completely electronic ignition, which reduced fuel consumption and lowered emission, were perhaps the main features. The lower weight—by some 42 kg (93 lbs) of the engine—of course contributed greatly to the lower fuel consumption as well.

The 260E sedan became available in late 1985 with the 4Matic system.

The 260E sedan became also available in a long-wheelbase version (3,600 mm) and overall length of 5,600 mm, with six doors.

Prices and Production

The 260E sedan sold in 1984 for .... DM 39,957

With 4Matic in 1985 .... DM 55,153

The 260E sedan sold in the United States (East Coast)
in 1987 for $33,700
automatic $34,500

Production of the 260E sedan [124 E26] (from August 1984/September 1985)

was in 1984	17 units		
1985	5,062 units		
1986	21,958 units	55 chassis; 4matic,	3 units
1987	28,827 units	4matic,	511 units
1988	26,687 units	4matic,	741 units
1989	21,070 units	4matic,	383 units
1990	21,973 units	4matic,	218 units
1991	19,099 units	4matic,	87 units
1992	9,715 units		
total	71,857 units		

The 300E 2.6 sedan sold in the United States in 1990 for $39,950

In 1990 the 260E became the 300E 2.6 in the United States. It was essentially the same 124-bodied car as before.

In 1989 (for testing) 6 units of the 250DV were built.

260EV 1989	5 units	260E VF	179 units
1990	544 units		179 units
1991	345 units		180 units
long wheelbase 1992	112 units		132 units
total	1,006 units	total	670 units

Specifications

	260E	300E 2.6
Engine type	6 cyl overhead camshaft (M103)	
Bore and stroke	89.0 x 80.25 (3.50 x 3.16 in)	
Displacement	2599 cc (158.6 cu in)	
Power output	170 hp (DIN) 125 Kw @ 5800 rpm 1987: U.S.: 158 hp (SAE) 118 Kw @ 5800 rpm 1988: 166 hp (DIN) 122 Kw	158 hp (SAE) 118 Kw @ 5800 rpm
Compression ratio	10.0:1 1987: U.S.: 9.2:1 1989: 160 hp (DIN) 118 Kw	9.2:1
Torque	230 Nm (170.1 ft/lb) @4500 rpm (23.5 mkg) 1987: U.S.: 162 ft/lb 220 Nm @ 4600 rpm	162 ft/lb (220 Nm) @ 4600 rpm
Fuel injection	Bosch KE jetronic	
Maximum engine speed	6200 rpm	
Gear ratios	I. 4.25:1 (automatic) I. 3.86:1 (5-speed) II. 2.41:1 II. 2.18:1 III. 1.49:1 III. 1.38:1 IV. 1.00:1 IV. 1.00:1 V. 0.80:1	automatic (4-speed)
Rear axle ratio	3.27 1989: 3.92 (5-speed); 3.27 (automatic) 1990: U.S.: 3.07	3.07
Chassis	unit frame and body	
Suspension	shock absorber strut with anti-dive control, coil springs, anti-roll bar; multi-link independent rear, anti-dive, anti-squat control, coils, anti-roll bar	
Brakes and area	hydraulic dual circuit, discs; 373 sq in	
Wheelbase	2800 mm (110.0 in)	
Track, front/rear	1497/1488 mm (58.9/58.6 in)	
Length	4740 mm (186.6 in)	
Width	1740 mm (68.5 in)	
Height	1446 mm (56.9 in)	
Tires	195/65 VR 15	195/65 R15 91V
Turning circle	11.2 meters (44 feet)	
Steering type and ratio	recirculating ball (3.3 turns); servo-assisted	
Weight	1330 kg (2926 lbs) 1987: U.S.: 1455 kg (3210 lbs)	1480 kg (3265 lbs)
Maximum speed	220 km/hr (137 mph); automatic: 215 km/hr (134 mph)	
Acceleration	8.5 sec 0-100 km/hr; automatic: 9.1 sec	
Fuel consumption	at 120 km/hr: 8.4 liters (28 mpg); automatic: 9.5 liters (25 mpg)	
Fuel tank capacity	70 liters (18.5 gallons)	

The 300E sedan, 1985

Prices and Production

The 300E sedan sold in 1984 for .... DM 44,004

With 4Matic in 1985 .... DM 59,326

in the United States in 1986 (East Coast) for $33,900
automatic $800

Production of the 300E sedan [124 E30] (from April 1984)

was in 1984	16 units			
1985	24,989 units			
1986	46,191 units,	4matic,	18 units	
1987	41,696 units,	4matic,	2,050 units	
1988	35,046 units,	4matic,	2,672 units	
1989	33,655 units,	4matic,	1,914 units	
1990	34,869 units,	4matic,	3,095 units	
1991	30,073 units,	4matic,	2,215 units	
1992	11,537 units,	4matic,	1,233 units	
total	110,161 units,	4matic,	494 units	
	units,	4matic,	344 units	
300E 24 1989	2,377 units			
1990	7,528 units			
1991	6,497 units			
1992	2,884 units			
total	19,286 units			

Model 300E (1984–1992)

E (Einspritzung) = fuel injection

The 300E model, also introduced in late 1984 with the other six new models using the W124 body style, was the top performer of the entire new middle-class cars. The newly designed 2,962 cc six-cylinder fuel-injection gasoline engine of 190 DIN horsepower gave the 1,340 kg (2,948 lbs) car truly fantastic performance and economy and left the 280E model, first shown in early 1976 and which it replaced, way behind in every category.

The six-cylinder engine of the 300E was 105 lbs lighter than that of the 280E and while it had but 5 hp more than the 1979 engine (13 more than the 1976 one), the weight of the new W124-bodied car was only 1,340 kg (2,948 lbs) against the 1,460 kg (3,212 lbs) of the W123-bodied 280E model.

The five-speed manual and the four-speed automatic transmissions were standard. Gear ratios were different from the former models, as were the rear axle ratios (3.07 for the 300E and 3.54 [3.58 in 1982] for the 280E). The automatic transmission had two modes of operation—sport and economic. The maximum speed of the 300E was 230 km/hr (144 mph) with the manual transmission, while the 280E had a top speed of 200 kilometers per hour (124 mph). Acceleration also showed a remarkable improvement over the model it replaced. From 0-100 km/hr it took but 7.7 seconds, against the 9.9 seconds for the 280E. With the automatic, the figures were equally startling, 8.3 seconds against 10.8, a really tremendous improvement.

The 300E sedan became available in late 1985 with the 4Matic (four-wheel drive) system.

The 300E sedan became available also with the optional 24-valve 220 horsepower (162 Kw) six-cylinder engine. The car was then equipped with ZR rated tires.

Production of the 300E 24 was (from April 1988)

was in 1988	14 units
1989	2,377 units

The 300E 24 sedan sold in 1989 for .... DM 65,664
in 1989 .... DM 61,503
with 4Matic .... DM 74,100

Specifications

	300E			
Engine type	6 cyl overhead camshaft (M103)			
Bore and stroke	89.0 x 80.25 mm (3.50 x 3.16 in)			
Displacement	2962 cc (180.8 cu in)			
Power output	190 hp (DIN) 140 Kw @ 5600 rpm	U.S.: 177 (SAE) hp @ 5700 rpm	1988: 188 hp (DIN) 138 Kw	
Compression ratio	10.0:1	U.S.: 9.2:1	1989: 180 hp (SAE) 132 Kw @ 5700 rpm	
Torque	260 Nm (191.8 ft/lb) @ 4250 rpm (26.5 mkg)	U.S.: 188 ft/lb @ 4400 rpm	1989: 255 Nm @ 4400 rpm	
Fuel injection	Bosch KE jetronic			
Maximum engine speed	6200 rpm			
Gear ratios	I. 3.68:1 (automatic) II. 2.41:1 III. 1.44:1 IV. 1.00:1	I. 3.86:1 (5-speed) II. 2.18:1 III. 1.38:1 IV. 1.00:1 V. 0.80:1	1989: U.S.: 3.69 (5-speed); 3.07 (automatic)	
Rear axle ratio	3.07		1990: 2.87	
Chassis	unit frame and body			
Suspension	shock absorber strut with anti-dive control, coil springs, anti-roll bar; multi-link independent rear, anti-dive, anti-squat control, coils, anti-roll bar			
Brakes and area	hydraulic dual circuit, discs; 373 sq in			
Wheelbase	2800 mm (110.0 in)			
Track, front/rear	1497/1488 mm (58.9/58.6 in)			
Length	4740 mm (186.6 in)			
Width	1740 mm (68.5 in)			
Height	1446 mm (56.9 in)			
Tires	195/65 VR 15			
Turning circle	11.2 meters (44 feet)			
Steering type and ratio	recirculating ball (3.3 turns); servo-assisted			
Weight	1340 kg (2948 lbs)	U.S.: 3295 lbs (1495 kg) 1987: 1460 kg (3220 lbs)		
Maximum speed	230 km/hr (144 mph); automatic: 225 km/hr (140 mph)	1989: 1480 kg (3265 lbs)		
Acceleration	7.9 sec 0-100 km/hr; automatic: 8.3 sec	1990: 1505 kg (3315 lbs) 4-Matic: 1640 kg (3615 lbs)		
Fuel consumption	at 120 km/hr: 8.3 liters (29 mpg); automatic: 9.6 liters (25 mpg)			
Fuel tank capacity	70 liters (18.5 gallons)			

The M 102 engine of the 300E, 1985

The 200D sedan, 1985

Prices and Production

The 200D sedan sold in 1984 for .... DM 32,604

Production of the 200D sedan (124D 20] (From May 1984/January 1985)

was in 1984	1,034 units
1985	28,109 units
1986	32,894 units
1987	30,887 units
1988	29,077 units
1989	20,356 units
1990	20,283 units
1991	22,782 units
1992	21,012 units
1993	14,307 units
1994	9,900 units
E220D 1994	6 units

Model 200D (1984-   )

D = Diesel

The 200D model was the most economical diesel sedan with the new W124 body, introduced in late 1984. It replaced the 200D with the W123 body style, of which nearly 400,000 units had been sold during the nine years of its production.

This, as every diesel-engined model, shared practically everything—except the engine, of course—with the gasoline-powerd version and, just as all other new models, showed tremendous improvements over the car it replaced.

All of these new diesel models were extremely quiet because of the new, much quieter running diesel engines and their unique engine encapsulation system.

The new OM601 four-cylinder overhead camshaft diesel engine of 1,997 cc developed 72 horsepower, while the former 200D model had a 55 hp (in 1979 increased to 60 hp) power unit. The weight of the new model sedan was actually 209 pounds less, weighing 2,816 lbs against the 3,025 lbs of the former W123 model. Consequently, performance was greatly improved.

The maximum speed was 20 miles faster—now 160 kilometers per hour (100 mph) against the 130 km/hr. Acceleration, never a strong point in a diesel, from 0-100 km/hr now took 18.5 seconds while the older model (in 1979) took fully 27.4 seconds to reach that speed. (The 190D had the same engine and the same maximum speed, but a slightly better acceleration and a mite better fuel economy.)

Fuel consumption, certainly the strong point in any diesel model, was 7 liters per 100 kilometers (34 mpg) against the 8.3 liters (28 mpg) of the former 200 sedan.

The four-speed manual transmission was standard with a five-speed manual or the automatic optional. As in all of the intermediate range models, the anti-lock braking system (ABS) was also available as an extra cost item.

The 200D was a fine economical and roomy sedan with better performance than ever. It promised again to be one of the best selling diesels made.

Specifications

	200D		
Engine type	4 cyl diesel, overhead camshaft (OM601)		
Bore and stroke	87.0 x 84.0 (3.43 x 3.31 in)		
Displacement	1997 cc (121.9 cu in)		
Power output	72 hp (DIN) 53 Kw @ 4600 rpm		1989: 75 hp (DIN) 55 Kw @ 4600 rpm
Compression ratio	22:1		
Torque	123 Nm (90.5 ft/lb) @ 2800 rpm (12.5 mkg)		1989: 126 Nm @ 2700 rpm
Fuel injection	Bosch four-plunger pump		
Maximum engine speed	5150 mph		

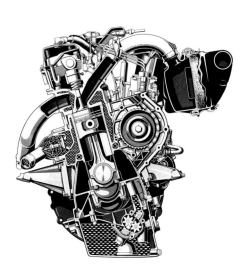

Gear ratios	I. 4.32:1 (4-speed)	I. 4.25:1 (automatic)	I. 4.23:1 (5-speed)
	II. 2.36:1	II. 2.41:1	II. 2.36:1
	III. 1.49:1	III. 1.49:1	III. 1.49:1
	IV. 1.00:1	IV. 1.00:1	IV. 1.00:1
			V. 0.84:1

Rear axle ratio	3.42; 5-speed: 3.64	1989: 3.42 (4-speed); 3.91 (5-speed)
Chassis	unit frame and body	
Suspension	shock absorber strut with anti-dive control, coil springs, anti-roll bar; multi-link independent rear, anti-dive anti-squat control, coils, anti-roll bar	
Brakes and area	hydraulic dual circuit, discs; 373 sq in	
Wheelbase	2800 mm (110.0 in)	
Track, front/rear	1497/1488 mm (58.9/58.6 in)	
Length	4740 mm (186.6 in)	
Width	1740 mm (68.5 in)	
Height	1440 mm (56.7 in)	
Tires	185/65 R 15 87T	
Turning circle	11.2 meters (44 feet)	
Steering type and ratio	recirculating ball (3.3 turns); servo-assisted	
Weight	1280 kg (2816 lbs)	
Maximum speed	160 km/hr (100 mph); automatic: 155 km/hr (96.7 mph)	
Acceleration	18.5 sec 0-100 km/hr; automatic: 20.4 sec	
Fuel consumption	at 120 km/hr: 7.0 liters (34 mpg); automatic: 7.6 liters (31 mpg)	
Fuel tank capacity	70 liters (18.5 gallons)	

Longitudinal and cross section of the OM601 engine, 1984

The 250D sedan, 1985

Prices and Production

The 250D sedan sold in 1984 for .... DM 36,138

Production of the 250D sedan (124D 25] (from November 1984/
May 1985)

was in 1984	13 units	(from January 1989) 250D turbo	
1985	18,250 units		
1986	32,417 units	1988	800 units
1987	38,674 units	1989	4,112 units
1988	33,143 units	1990	10,129 units
1989	24,749 units	1991	12,547 units
1990	24,234 units, 141 chassis	1992	12,339 units
1991	28,298 units, 160 chassis	1993	5,634 units
1992	28,673 units, 163 chassis		
1993	8,360 units, 34 chassis	E250D turbo 1992	2 units
		1993	3,181 units
E250D 1992	2 units	1994	2,264 units
1993	12,005 units, 60 chassis		
1994	18,645 units, 141 chassis		

long wheelbase 1988	305 chassis
1989	6 units, 262 chassis
1990	308 units, 274 chassis
1991	209 units, 392 chassis
1992	202 units, 300 chassis
1993	51 units, 101 chassis

E250D long 1993	44 units, 150 chassis
1994	137 units, 215 chassis

Production of the 250D (turbo) sedan (124D 25] (from March 1988)

was in 1988	800 units
1989	4,112 units

Model 250D (1984-   )

D = Diesel

The 250D with the new W124 body style, first shown in late 1984, was to replace the 240D, by a wide margin the best selling (with over 450,000 units) diesel sedan since 1976.

This new sedan shared, of course, all specifications mentioned in previous pages about the W124-bodied cars, with the other six models then introduced, but as one of the three diesel models, it had the newly developed regularly aspirated OM602 five-cylinder engine.

The cylinder size of 87.0 x 84.0 mm was believed to be the ideal size and all new diesel engines used these specifications. The 250D had five cylinders, a displacement of 2,497 cc, and developed 90 horsepower. The 240D had finally the OM616 four-cylinder engine of 2,399 cc of 72 hp. (The new OM602 engine, based on the progressive diesel engine concept for the 190 cars, developed 36.2 horsepower per liter). In addition, the new W124 bodies were also lighter by 134 lbs, thus giving the new model appreciably better performance and economy. With the engine encapsulation method, the inherent diesel engine noise was practially eliminated.

Maximum speed of the 250D was 175 kilometers per hour (109 miles) with the five-speed manual transmission, against the 138 km/hr (86 mph) with the 240D four-speed. With the automatic, the top speed was 170 km/hr (106 mph) to the former 138 km/hr (86 mph).

Acceleration was 16.2 seconds for the 0-100 km/hr against the 24.6 seconds for the 240D; a tremendous improvement indeed. The new five-speed manual and four-speed automatic transmissions were standard in the 250D. The rear axle ratios were 3.42 and 3.07, respectively.

Fuel consumption also showed a noticeable improvement. The 250D, with the five-speed transmission, used 7 liters for 100 kilometers at 120 km/hr (34 mpg) against the 8.7 liters (27.5 mpg) for the 240D.

Thus, the 250D with the five-cylinder regularly aspirated diesel engine was indeed a vastly superior performing car than the 240D which it replaced.

The 250D sedan became also available with six doors on a longer wheelbase (3,600 mm) and overall length of 5,600 mm.

In 1989 (for testing) 5 units of the 260EV were built.

A turbo-charged diesel engine became available in 1989 for the popular 250D model. The car gave a better performance all around; increased horsepower and torque, greatly improved acceleration and considerable higher maximum speed.

Specifications

	250D	250D turbo
Engine type	5 cyl diesel, overhead camshaft (OM602)	
Bore and stroke	87.0 x 84.0 mm (3.43 x 3.31 in)	
Displacement	2497 cc (152.4 cu in)	
Power output	90 hp (DIN) 66 Kw @ 4600 rpm 1989: 94 hp (DIN) 69 Kw @ 4600 rpm	125 hp (DIN) 93 Kw @ 4600 rpm
Compression ratio	22:1	
Torque	154 Nm (113.6 ft/lb) @ 2800 rpm (15.7 mkg) 1989: 158 Nm @ 2600 rpm	231 Nm (170.5 ft/lb) @ 2400 rpm
Fuel injection	Bosch four-plunger pump	
Maximum engine speed	5150 rpm	
Gear ratios	I. 4.23:1 (5-speed) I. 4.25:1 (automatic) II. 2.36:1 II. 2.41:1 III. 1.49:1 III. 1.49:1 IV. 1.00:1 IV. 1.00:1 V. 0.84:1	I. 3.86:1 (5-speed) II. 2.18:1 III. 1.38:1 IV. 1.00:1 V. 0.75:1
Rear axle ratio	3.42; automatic: 3.07 1989: 3.64 (5-speed); 3.07 (automatic)	3.46 (5-speed); 2.85 (automatic)
Chassis	unit frame and body	
Suspension	shock absorber strut with anti-dive control, coil springs, anti-roll bar; multi-link independent rear, anti-dive, anti-squat control, coils, anti-roll bar	
Brakes and area	hydraulic dual circuit, discs; 373 sq in	
Wheelbase	2800 mm (110.0 in)	
Track, front/rear	1497/1488 mm (58.9/58.6 in)	
Length	4740 mm (186.6 in)	
Width	1740 mm (68.5 in)	
Height	1446 mm (56.9 in)	
Tires	195/65 R 15 90T	
Turning circle	11.2 meters (44 feet)	
Steering type and ratio	recirculating ball (3.3 turns); servo-assisted	
Weight	1320 kg (2904 lbs)	1440 kg (3080 lbs)
Maximum speed	175 km/hr (109 mph); automatic: 170 km/hr (106 mph)	198 km/hr (124 mph); 195 km/hr (122 mph) automatic
Acceleration	16.2 sec 0-100 km/hr; automatic: 17.0 sec	12.3 sec 0-100 km/hr
Fuel consumption	at 120 km/hr: 7 liters (34 mpg); automatic: 7.7 liters (30 mpg)	7.4 liters (32 mpg); automatic: 7.9 liters (29 mpg)
Fuel tank capacity	70 liters (18.5 gallons)	

The 300D sedan, 1985

Model 300D (1984-   )

D = Diesel

The 300D sedan with the new W124 body style was the most powerful of the three diesel models introduced in late 1984. It also had the first six-cylinder passenger car diesel engine, based on the newly developed progressive engine first used in the 190 line.

The body incorporated all of the features (mentioned on previous pages) of this new intermediate range, the "Mittelklasse" of cars. The resemblance to the W201 body of the smaller range and the W126 of the S-class was carefully planned and such refinements as the multi-link rear suspension were naturally incorporated in the new body style.

The OM603 six-cylinder naturally aspirated diesel engine had the same ideal sized bore and stroke of the new design and displaced 2,966 cc. It developed 109 horsepower. The 300D of 1976 had a five-cylinder engine of 3,055, and then 2,988 cc, with 80 and 88 hp, respectively, but that W123-bodied model weighed 3,179 pounds. The new replacement weighed only 3,014 pounds and with 21 more horsepower (and 165 lbs. less weight) performance and economy were naturally greatly improved.

The 300D sedan became available in late 1985 with the 4Matic (four-wheel drive) system.

In 1986 The 300D turbo sedan became available in the United States.

Prices and Production

The 300D sedan sold in 1984 for .... DM 39,672
With 4Matic in 1985 .... DM 54,184

Production of the 300D sedan [124D 30] (from March 1984/January 1985)

was in 1984	269 units	
1985	15,035 units, 4matic,	2 units
1986	21,882 units, 4matic,	20 units
1987	19,885 units, 4matic,	540 units
1988	15,167 units, 4matic,	542 units
1989	11,393 units, 4matic,	205 units
1990	13,878 units, 4matic,	136 units
1991	15,609 units, 4matic,	40 units
1992	14,183 units	
1993	4,348 units	

E300D 1992	2 units
1993	6,886 units
1994	11,552 units

The 300D turbo sedan sold in the United States in 1986 for
(East Coast) $39,500
(West Coast) $39,900

Production of the 300D (turbo) sedan [124D 30A] (from May 1985)

was in 1985	16 units	
1986	7,254 units	
1987	3,960 units, 4matic,	2 units
1988	4,046 units, 4matic,	385 units
300DT (turbo) 1989	3,636 units 4matic,	396 units
1990	4,325 units, 4matic,	387 units
1991	5,546 units, 4matic,	393 units
1992	5,119 units, 4matic,	299 units
1993		135 units
1994		175 units

E300DT 1992	2 units
1993	1,906 units
1994	1,687 units

Specifications

	300D	300D turbo	300D 2.5 turbo
Engine type	6 cyl diesel, overhead camshaft (MO 603)	U.S.: turbo (OM 603A)	
Bore and stroke	87.0 x 84.0 mm (3.43 x 3.31 in)		
Displacement	2996 cc (182.8 cu in)		
Power output	109 hp (DIN) 80 Kw @ 4600 rpm 1989: 113 hp (DIN) 83 Kw	U.S.: 148 (SAE) hp @ 4600 rpm 1989: 147 hp (SAE) 108 Kw @ 4600 rpm	
Compression ratio	22:1	U.S. 1987: 143 hp (SAE) 107 Kw @ 4600 rpm	
Torque	185 Nm (136.8 ft/lb) @ 2800 rpm (18.9 mkg) 1989: 191 Nm	U.S.: 201 ft/lb @ 2400 rpm	
Fuel injection	Bosch four-plunger pump	1987: 195 ft/lb (265 Nm) @ 2400 rpm	1989: 273 Nm @ 2400 rpm
Maximum engine speed	5150 rpm		
Gear ratios	I. 3.86:1 (5-speed) I. 4.25:1 (automatic) II. 2.18:1 II. 2.41:1 III. 1.38:1 III. 1.49:1 IV. 1.00:1 IV. 1.00:1 V. 0.80:1	U.S.: automatic only	
Rear axle ratio	3.46; automatic: 2.88	U.S.: 2.65	
Chassis	unit frame and body		
Suspension	shock absorber strut with anti-dive control, coil springs, anti-roll bar; multi-link independent rear, anti-dive, anti-squat control, coils, anti-roll bar		
Brakes and area	hydraulic dual circuit, discs; 373 sq in		
Wheelbase	2800 mm (110.0 in)		
Track, front/rear	1497/1488 mm (58.9/58.6 in)		
Length	4740 mm (186.6 in)		
Width	1740 mm (68.5 in)		
Height	1446 mm (56.9 in)		
Tires	195/65 R 15 90H		
Turning circle	11.2 meters (44 feet)		
Steering type and ratio	recirculating ball (3.3 turns); servo-assisted		
Weight	1370 kg (3014 lbs)	U.S.: 3375 lbs (1530 kg)	
Maximum speed	190 km/hr (118 mph); automatic: 185 km/hr (115 mph)		
Acceleration	13.7 sec 0-100 km/hr; automatic: 14.1 sec		
Fuel consumption	at 120 km/hr: 7 liters (34 mpg); automatic: 7.9 liters (29 mpg)		
Fuel tank capacity	70 liters (18.5 gallons)		

The OM 603 engine of the 300D, 1985

The 190D 2.5 sedan, 1985

Prices and Production

The 190D 2.5 sedan sold in 1985 for DM33,915
The 190D 2.5 sedan sold in the United States in 1986 (East
Coast) for $23,700
    automatic $600

Production of the 190D 2.5 sedan [201D 25] (from August 1984/
June 1985)

was in 1984	46	units
1985	1,284	units
1986	29,072	units
1987	26,812	units
1989	16,855	units
1990	13,130	units
1991	14,700	units
1992	14,593	units
1993	2,001	units
total	61,279	units

The 190D 2.5 (turbo) sedan sold in the United States in 1987 for
  (East Coast) $29,800

Production of the 190D 2.5 (turbo) sedan [201D 25A] (from February
1986)

was in 1986	132	units
1987	1,349	units
1988	3,287	units
1989	3,383	units
1990	4,177	units
1991	4,572	units
1992	3,535	units
1993	480	units
total	16,147	units

Model 190D 2.5 (1984–1993)
Turbo (1986–1993)

D = Diesel

The 190D 2.5 model appeared in May 1984. It was in line with the expansion of the W201 body style and the trend toward improved performance of these smaller Mercedes gasoline-powered cars. This increase in diesel power was the natural approach, especially since the 2.5-liter five-cylinder diesel engine was used already in the W124 body style 200D sedan. This lighter weight 190D 2.5 model was, of course, a better all-around performer with a weight difference of 198 pounds (2,816 pounds for the 200D and 2,681 for the 190D 2.5).

For the North American market, this 93-horsepower OM602 diesel engine was used in the 190D cars for the 1986 model year. Torque was increased to 122 ft/lb against the 96 ft/lb before. The performance over the former 72-horsepower 190D 2.2 was appreciably improved and fitted well into the overall program of offering better performance and greater economy in the newer models. The weight difference in these cars was only 155 pounds (2,855 pounds for the 2.5 and 2,700 for the 2.2 model).

The change in rear axle ratio for the five-cylinder diesel to 3.07 in the 4-speed automatic transmission version resulted in smoother and quieter operation in all speeds and in greater economy in fuel consumption. The 5-speed manual transmission retained the 3.42 rear axle ratio, and with the 0.78 to 1 fifth gear—actually an overdrive—the maximum speed was now reached in fifth gear, rather than fourth as previously.

This diesel model was one of the quietest diesels offered, not merely for the near-noiseless engine but also because of the encapsulation system used in the design of the car.

With the sophisticated EGR system, based on that employed in the 2.2 engines, the Federal limit for NOx and the California (0.2 g/m) particulate limit was reached without the use of a trap oxidizer. CO and HE emissions are also lower and fuel economy was expected to be about 5% better.

Specifications

	190D 2.5		190D 2.5 turbo
Engine type	5 cyl diesel, overhead camshaft (OM 602)		
Bore and stroke	87.0 x 84.0 mm (3.43 x 3.31 in)		
Displacement	2497 cc (152.4 cu in)		
Power output	90 hp (DIN) 66Kw @ 4600 rpm	U.S.: 93 hp (SAE) 69Kw 1987: U.S.: 123 hp (SAE) 92 Kw @ 4600 rpm	1989: 90 hp 67 Kw @ 4600 rpm 1989: 94 hp 69 Kw
Compression ratio	22:1		
Torque	154 Nm (113.6 ft/lb) @ 2800 rpm (15.7 mkg)	U.S.: 122 ft/lb @ 2800 rpm 1987: U.S.: 168 ft/lb (228 Nm) @ 2400 rpm	1989: 117 ft/lb 158 Nm @ 2800 rpm 1989: 150 Nm @ 2600 rpm
Fuel injection	Bosch four-plunger pump		
Maximum engine speed	5150 rpm		
Gear ratios	I. 3.91:1 (manual) I. 4.25:1 (automatic) II. 2.17:1 II. 2.41:1 III. 1.37:1 III. 1.49:1 IV. 1.00:1 IV. 1.00:1 V. 0.78:1		
Rear axle ratio	3.64 manual; 3.07 automatic	U.S.: 3.42 manual, 3.07 automatic	1987: 2.65
Chassis	unit frame and body		
Suspension	shock absorber strut with anti-dive control, coil springs, anti-roll bar; multi-link independent rear, anti-dive, anti-squat control, coils, anti-roll bar		
Brakes and area	dual circuit discs, power-assisted; anti-locking system optional		
Wheelbase	2665 mm (104.9 in)		
Track, front/rear	1428/1415 mm (56.2/55.7 in)	U.S.: 56.6/55.8 in (1437/1418 mm)	
Length	4420 mm (174.0 in)	U.S.: 175.0 in (4445 mm)	
Width	1678 mm (66.1 in)		
Height	1383 mm (54.4 in)	U.S.: 54.7 in (1390 mm)	
Tires	185/65 R 15 87 S/T	U.S.: 185/65 R 15 87 T	
Turning circle	10.6 meters (32.3 feet)		
Steering type and ratio	recirculating ball (3.3 turns); servo-assisted		
Weight	1175 kg (2585 lbs)	U.S.: 2855 lbs (1295 kg)	1987: 1365 kg (3010 lbs)
Maximum speed	174 km/hr (109 mph); automatic: 170 km/hr (106 mph)	U.S.: manual: 107 mph; automatic: 104 mph	
Acceleration	15.1 sec 0-100 km/hr; automatic: 16.1 sec	U.S.: manual: 14.8 sec; automatic: 15.2 sec	
Fuel consumption	at 120 km/hr: 7.1 liters (34 mpg) automatic: 7.7 liters (31 mpg)	U.S.: manual: 32 mpg; automatic: 31 mpg (average)	
Fuel tank capacity	55 liters (14.5 gallons)		

The 200TD station wagon, 1985

Prices and Production

The 200TD station wagon sold in 1985 for .... DM 39,444
The 250TD station wagon sold in 1985 for .... DM 42,807

Production of the 250TD station wagon [124D 25] (from June/November 1985)

			turbo
was in 1985	413 units		
1986	8,158 units, chassis 334 units		
1987	6,710 units, chassis 383 units		
1988	5,534 units, chassis 423 units		
1989	4,669 units, chassis 364 units		
1990	4,173 units, chassis 415 units	488 units	
1991	5,624 units, chassis 552 units	1,275 units	
1992	6,692 units, chassis 463 units	1,697 units	
1993	1,653 units, chassis 101 units	758 units	
1994	5,452 units, chassis 215 units	279 units	

Production of the 200TD station wagon [124D 20] (from November until June 1991)

was in 1985	342 units
1986	2,354 units
1987	1,680 units
1988	1,176 units
1989	855 units
1990	603 units
1991	363 units
total	7,373 units

Model 200TD (1985–1991)

T = station wagon, D = Diesel

The 200TD model was one of six new style station wagons introduced at the September 1985 Frankfurt Auto Show. It was based on the W124 sedan body and appeared just a few months after that successor to the W123 had been made available to buyers. By the time of the showing of the added station wagon line, over 100,000 units of the new W124 sedans had already been sold.

The 200TD model had the proven four-cylinder diesel engine of 72 DIN horsepower (53 Kw) with the five-speed manual transmission. It was the most economical of the T-line of cars, using about 8 liters of fuel for 100 kilometers of average city cycle and of country driving at 120 kilometers per hour.

Model 250TD (1985-   )

T = station wagon, D = Diesel

The 250TD was the next in the diesel line of station wagons. It shared the body style and the appointments of the entire line, but had the 2,497 cc five-cylinder diesel engine of 90 DIN horsepower (66 Kw) with the five-speed manual transmission.

The new line of T models replaced those first built almost eight years before and successfully (about 200,000 units) marketed. The new models included, of course, all of the new forward-looking technology as found in the middle range (W124) and incorporated further developments of the preceeding models, thus reaching a new standard of perfection in station wagons.

Specifications

	200TD	250TD
Engine type	4 cyl diesel, overhead camshaft (OM 601)	5 cyl diesel, overhead camshaft (OM 602)
Bore and stroke	87.0 x 84.0 mm (3.43 x 3.31 in)	
Displacement	1997 cc (121.9 cu in)	2497cc (152.4 cu in)
Power output	72 hp (DIN) 53 Kw @ 4600 rpm 1989: 75 hp (DIN) 55 Kw @ 4600 rpm	90 hp (DIN) 66 Kw @ 4600 rpm 1989: 94 hp (DIN) 69 Kw @ 4600 rpm
Compression ratio	22.:1	22:1
Torque	123 Nm (90.5 ft/lb) @ 2800 rpm (12.5 mkg) 1989: 126 Nm @ 2700 rpm	154 Nm (113.6 ft/lb) @2800 rpm (15.7 mkg) 1989: 158 Nm @ 2600 rpm
Fuel injection	Bosch four-plunger pump	
Maximum engine speed	5150 rpm	

	200TD	250TD
Gear ratios	I. 4.32:1 (4-speed) I. 4.25:1 (automatic) I. 4.23:1 (5-speed) II. 2.36:1 II. 2.41:1 II. 2.36:1 III. 1.49:1 III. 1.49:1 III. 1.49:1 IV. 1.00:1 IV. 1.00:1 IV. 1.00:1 V. 0.84:1	
Rear axle ratio	3.42; 5-speed: 3.64 1989: 3.91 (manual); 3.64 (automatic)	3.42; automatic: 3.07 1989: 3.91 (manual) 323 (automatic)
Chassis	unit frame and body	
Suspension	shock absorber strut with anti-dive control, coil springs, anti-roll bar; multi-link independent rear, anti-dive, anti-squat control, coils, anti-roll bar	
Brakes and area	hydraulic dual circuit, discs (373 sq in); 262/258 mm (10.3/10.2 in)	
Wheelbase	2800 mm (110.2 in)	
Track, front/rear	1497/1488 mm (58.9/58.6 in)	
Length	4765 mm (187.6 in)	
Width	1740 mm (68.5 in)	
Height	1490 mm (58.7 in)	
Tires	195/65 R 15	
Turning circle	11.2 meters (44 feet)	
Steering type and ratio	recirculating ball (3.3 turns); servo-assisted	
Weight	1410 kg (3102 lbs)	1440 kg (3168 lbs)
Maximum speed	160 km/hr (100 mph); automatic: 155 km/hr (96.7 mph)	175 km/hr (109 mph); automatic: 170 km/hr (106 mph)
Acceleration	18.5 sec 0-100 km/hr; automatic: 20.4 sec	16.2 sec 0-100 km/hr; automatic: 17.0 sec
Fuel consumption	at 120 km/hr: 7.0 liters (34 mpg); automatic: 7.6 liters (31 mpg)	automatic: 7.7 liters (30 mpg)
Fuel tank capacity	70 liters (18.5 gallons)	

The 300TD turbo station wagon, 1985

Model 300TD (1985-   )

T = station wagon, D = Diesel

The 300TD turbo-diesel station wagon was prominently featured at the 1985 Frankfurt Auto Show. Cleverly displayed—slightly elevated with mirrors below—to show the details of the 4Matic (four-wheel drive) system, it was one of the outstanding exhibits.

The four-wheel drive system was actually a part of the Dynamics Driving Concept which consisted of three electronic-automatic systems matched to different requirements, the automatic locking differential (ASD), the acceleration skid control (ASR), and the Mercedes-Benz 4Matic.

The ASD system increased traction on road surfaces, where adhesion differed, by automatic intervention when one wheel is about to spin. The ASR system was an extension of the ABS brake system by an additional hydraulic unit, an extended electronic control unit, and the so-called electronic accelerator. This combination made the car controllable to an extent which cannot be achieved in any other way.

The 4Matic system engaged automatically and represented the ultimate in traction-improving systems. Depending on requirement, three stages would be engaged: all differentials remain unlocked; or the differential between front and rear axle is also locked; or thirdly, the differential in the rear axle is also locked. Wheel sensors measured the wheel revolving speeds and passed the results on to the electric control unit.

The three combined systems were considered to be an important step in the maximum active Safety Concept by the Daimler-Benz engineers.

The 300TD station wagon had the new 2,996 cc six-cylinder turbo charged diesel engine of 143 DIN horsepower (105 Kw), had 270 Nm torque, and weighed 1,540 kilograms. It came with the automatic transmission only.

Although shown prominently on the 300TD turbo station wagon only at the Frankfurt Auto Show in September 1985, this new 4Matic (four-wheel drive) system was also made available in three models of the 124 sedan line—the 300D, 260E, and 300E cars.

This new 300TD four-wheel drive turbo-engined station wagon model was scheduled to be sold in the North American market in the spring of 1986 in only slightly modified form from that shown and so greatly lauded for the many technical advances it incorporated.

Prices and Production

The 300TD turbo station wagon sold in the United States in 1967 for
(East Coast) $42,500
(West Coast) $42,900

The 300TD station wagon sold in 1986 for . . . . DM 54,549
with 4Matic . . . . DM 67,773

Production of the 300TD (turbo) station wagon [124D 30A] (from May 1985)

was in 1985	2 units		
1986	1,379 units,	4matic,	2 units
1987	2,386 units,	4matic,	297 units
1988	1,319 units,	4matic,	552 units
1989	957 units ,	4matic,	281 units
1990	1,301 units,	4matic,	267 units
1991	1,906 units,	4matic,	243 units
1992	2,425 units,	4matic,	286 units
1993	1,312 units,	4matic,	171 units
1994	1,087 units,	4matic,	175 units

Production of the 300TD station wagon [124D 30] (from March/September 1986)

was in 1986	688 units	
1987	3,022 units	
1988	2,700 units	
1989	2,373 units	
1990	3,175 units	
1991	4,047 units	
1992	4,733 units	
1993	1,161 units	
total	15,489 units	
E300TD	1992	2 units
	1993	1,906 units
	1994	3,672 units

Specifications

	300TD turbo		300TD
Engine type	6 cyl diesel, overhead camshaft, with turbo-charger, (OM 603A)		
Bore and stroke	87.0 x 84.0 mm (3.43 x 3.31 in)		
Displacement	2996 cc		
Power output	143 hp (DIN) 105 Kw @ 4600 rpm U.S.: 143 hp (SAE) 107 Kw @ 4600 rpm 1989: 147 hp (DIN) 108 Kw @ 4600 rpm		109 hp (DIN) 80 Kw
Compression ratio	22:1		
Torque	270 Nm (1978 ft/lb) @ 2400 rpm (27.5 mkg) U.S.: 195 ft/lb (265 Nm) @ 2400 rpm 1989: 273 Nm @ 2400 rpm		185 Nm (135.5 ft/lb) @ 2800 rpm
Fuel injection	Bosch five-plunger pump with injection timer		
Maximum engine speed	5100 rpm		5150 rpm
Gear ratios	I.　　4.25:1　(automatic) II.　　2.41:1 III.　1.49:1 IV.　1.00:1		
Rear axle ratio	2.88	U.S.: 2.65	3.07
Chassis	unit frame and body		
Suspension	shock absorber strut with anti-dive control, coil springs, anti-roll bar; multi-link independent rear, anti-dive, anti-squat control, coils, anti-roll bar		
Brakes and area	hydraulic dual circuit, discs; 262/258 mm (10.3/10.1 in)		
Wheelbase	2800 mm (110.2 in)		
Track, front/rear	1497/1488 mm (58.9/58.6 in)		
Length	4765 mm (187.6 in)		
Width	1740 mm (68.5 in)		
Height	1490 mm (58.7 in)		
Tires	195/65 R 15		
Turning circle	11.2 meters (44 feet)		
Steering type and ratio	recirculating ball (3.3 turns); servo-assisted		
Weight	1540 kg (3388 lbs)	U.S.: 1665 kg (3670 lbs)	1500 kg (3300 lbs)
Maximum speed	190 km/hr (118 mph)		
Acceleration	13.7 sec 0-100 km/hr		
Fuel consumption	at 120 km/hr: 7.9 liters (29 mpg)		
Fuel tank capacity	70 liters (18.5 gallons)		

Prices and Production

The 200T station wagon sold in 1985 for .... DM 38,076
The 230TE station wagon sold in 1985 for .... DM 42,009

Production of the 200T station wagon [124V 20] (from March 1985 until May 1990)

was in	1985	77 units
	1986	2,241 units
	1987	2,236 units
	1988	2,313 units
	1989	493 units
	1990	107 units
	total	7,467 units
E200T	1992	1,520 units
	1993	4,679 units
	1994	3,954 units

Production of the 200TE station wagon [124E 20] (from July 1988)

was in	1985	712 units
	1986	8,850 units, chassis 151 units
	1987	9,265 units, chassis 143 units
	1988	11,436 units, chassis 133 units
	1989	9,774 units, chassis 134 (105 long of total)
	1990	9,199 units chassis 106 (85 long of total)
	1991	9,196 units chassis 183 (141 long of total)
	1992	6,513 units chassis 87 (73 long of total)
	total	34,682 units 404 units

Production of the 230TE station wagon [124E 23] (from April 1985)

was in	1988	314 units
	1989	5,201 units
	1990	5,864 units
	1991	5,475 units
	1992	3,701 units
	total	20,241 units

Production of the 220T station wagon [124V 20] (from March 1985 until May 1990)

1992	2,204 units
1993	7,000 units
1994	5,751 units

Model 200T (1985–   )

T = station wagon

The 200T station wagon was the smallest gasoline-engined version shown at the 1985 Frankfurt Auto Show. It shared the body style, based on the W124 sedan line, with all other station wagons, but was the most economical gasoline model.

In these new models loading and unloading was improved, and the cargo space was increased by about 10%. A seat divider in the rear became a standard feature. The electronical closing aid ensured quiet, automatic closing of the cargo door in an easy and safe manner.

The four-cylinder carburetor engine developed 109 DIN horsepower (80 Kw) and 170 Nm torque, and the car weighed 1,390 kilograms.

Model 230TE (1985–1992)

T = station wagon, E (Einspritzung) = fuel injection

The 230TE station wagon, the middle performer of the gasoline-engine powered line, had all of the characteristics of the new T models, the harmonious styling, with back seat doors especially suited to a station wagon, and roof rails that were substantially improved over those of the previous model.

The four-cylinder fuel injection engine developed 136 DIN horsepower (100 Kw) and 205 Nm torque. The 230TE weighed 1,400 kilograms.

Model 200TE (1988–   )

T = Station wagon, E (Einspritzung) = fuel injection

The 200TE station wagon was essentially the same as the T carburetor version, except that it had the new Bosch KE jetronic fuel injected engine which developed nine more horsepower and consequently gave superior performance. It placed just between the regular 200T and the 230TE versions of the same station wagon model.

Model 220TE (1992–   )

T = station wagon, E (Einspritzung) = fuel injection

The 220TE station wagon was similar in practically everything to the others except for the engine size which developed 150 horsepower, thus providing the customer with a wide variety to choose from.

Specifications

	200T	230TE	200TE	220TE
Engine type	4 cyl overhead camshaft (M102)	6 cyl overhead camshaft (M103)	4 cyl overhead camshaft (M102)	
Bore and stroke	89.0 x 80.25 mm (3.50 x 3.16 in)	95.5 x 80.25 mm (3.75 x 3.16 in)		89.9 x 86.6 mm
Displacement	1997 cc (121.9 cu in)	2299 cc (140.3 cu in)		2199 cc
Power output	109 hp (DIN) 80 Kw @ 5200 rpm 1989: 105 hp (DIN) 77 Kw @ 5700	136 hp (DIN) 100 KW @ 5100 rpm 1989: 132 hp (DIN) 97 Kw @ 5100 rpm	118 hp (DIN) 87 Kw @ 5100 rpm	150 hp (DIN) 110 Kw @ 5500 rpm
Compression ratio	9.1:1	9.0:1		10.0:1
Torque	170 Nm (125.2 ft/lb) @ 2500 rpm (17.3 mkg)	205 Nm (151.3 ft/lb) @ 3500 rpm 1989: 198 Nm @ 3500 rpm	178 Nm @ 3500 rpm	210 Nm @ 4000 rpm
Fuel injection	175 CD cross draught carburetor	Bosch KE jetronic	Bosch KE jetronic	microprocess HFM
Maximum engine speed	6000 rpm	6000 rpm		
Gear ratios	I. 3.92:1 (4-speed) II. 2.17:1 III. 1.37:1 IV. 1.00:1	I. 4.25:1 (automatic) II. 2.41:1 III. 1.49:1 IV. 1.00:1	I. 3.92:1 (5-speed) II. 2.17:1 III. 1.37:1 IV. 1.00:1 V. 0.78:1	
Rear axle ratio	3.42 1989: 3.64	1989: 3.67 (manual); 346 (automatic)		
Chassis	unit frame and body			
Suspension	shock absorber strut with anti-dive control, coil springs, anti-roll bar; multi-link independent rear, anti-dive, anti-squat control, coils, anti-roll bar			
Brakes and area	hydraulic dual circuit, discs; 262/258 mm (10.3/10.1 in)			
Wheelbase	2800 mm (110.2 in)			
Track, front/rear	1497/1488 mm (58.9/58.6 in)			
Length	4765 mm (187.6 in)			
Width	1740 mm (68.5 in)			
Height	1490 mm (58.7 in)		Maximum speed	198 km/hr manual; 193 km/hr automatic
Tires	195/65 R 15		Acceleration	11.1 sec 0-100 km/hr manual; 11.6 sec automatic
Turning circle	11.2 meters (44 feet)			
Steering type and ratio	recirculating ball (3.3 turns); servo-assisted			
Weight	1390 kg (3058 lbs)	1400 kg (3080 lbs)		
Maximum speed	187 km/hr (116 mph); automatic: 182 km/hr (113 mph)	203 km/hr (127 mph); automatic: 198 km/hr (124 mph)	182 km/hr (114 mph) automatic: 177km/hr (110 mph)	
Acceleration	12.6 sec 0-100 km/hr; automatic: 13.1 sec	10.4 sec 0-100 km/hr; automatic: 10.4 sec	12.4 sec 0-100 km/hr automatic: 12.5 sec	
Fuel consumption	at 120 km/hr: 8.5 liters (28 mpg); automatic: 9.0 liters (30 mpg); 5-speed: 7.7 liters (31 mpg)	at 120 km/hr: 8.5 liters (28 mpg) automatic: 8.7 liters		
Fuel tank capacity	70 liters (18.5 gallons)			

The 190E 2.6 sedan, 1985

Prices and Production

The 190E 2.6 sedan sold in 1986 for .... DM 39,102

The 190E 2.6 sold in the United States in 1987
(East Coast) for $30,300
(automatic) $31,000

Production of the 190E 2.6 sedan [201E 26] (from April 1986)

	was in 1986	1,480 units
	1987	17,048 units
	1988	15,392 units
	1989	22,584 units
	1990	17,513 units
	1991	14,399 units
	1992	12,654 units
	1993	3,837 units
	total	70,987 units

Prices and Production

The 190E 1.8 sedan sold in 1992 for .... DM 37,090

Production of the 190E 1.8 sedan [201E 18] (from January 1990)

	was in 1990	4,442 units
	1991	63,173 units
	1992	47,903 units
	1993	17,837 units
	total	133,355 units

Model 190E 2.6 (1986–1993)

E (Einspritzung) = fuel injection

The 190E 2.6 model was first introduced at the Frankfurt Auto Show in September 1985. It was the sixth version (counting the American models, the eighth)) of the W201 body style sedans, and the most powerful one, except for the high performance special 2.3-liter 16-valve car.

The new M103 six-cylinder fuel injected engine displacing 2,599 cc, was also used in the W124 body style 260E model and the W126 bodied 260SE of the S-class line. The engine developed 166 DIN horsepower (122 Kw) and 200 Nm torque. The car weighed 1,210 kilograms (2,662 lbs.), reached a kilometer from a standing start in 30 seconds, and had a fuel consumption of less than 10 liters per 100 kilometers.

"The 190E 2.6 represented the logical conclusion of the concept of motorization which made the current passenger car range the most successful--and the most technically sophisticated and unique—in Daimler-Benz history," a spokesman stated.

The car had the emission control technology, standard for all six- and eight-cylinder models. It is a reconverted type—that is, originally without the closed loop three-way catalytic converter with oxygen sensor, which can be fitted as an optional extra. The car, equipped with the multi-functional electronically controlled mixture formation and ignition system, can be operated on unleaded premium or regular gasoline.

The 190E 2.6 was available with the standard five-speed manual transmission, or with the four-speed automatic with program selector an an optional extra. Suspension, tires, and brakes were in keeping with the high technical standards of the entire compact W201 range of cars.

Model 190E 1.8 (1990–1993)

E (Einspritzung) = Fuel injection

The 190E 1.8 model was made available to offer a wider range of this best selling line of 201 body style cars. With very good fuel economy and quite acceptable performance, this smallest engined model proved a favorite of buyers of the compact class of Mercedes cars.

Specifications

	190E 2.6		190E 1.8
Engine type	6 cyl overhead camshaft (M 103)		4 cyl overhead camshaft (M102)
Bore and stroke	82.9 x 80.25 mm (3.26 x 3.16 in)		89.0 x 72.2 mm (3.24 x 2.63 in)
Displacement	2599 cc (158.6 cu in)		1797 cc (109.6 cu in)
Power output	166 hp (DIN) 122 Kw @ 5800 rpm	1989: 160 hp (DIN) 118 Kw @ 5800 rpm	109 hp (DIN) 80 kw @ 5500 rpm
Compression ratio	9.2:1	U.S.: 158 hp (SAE) 118 Kw @ 5800 rpm	9.0:1
Torque	228 Nm (167.1 ft/lb) @ 4600 rpm (23.2 mkg)	1989: 220 Nm @ 4600 rpm	150 Nm @ 3700 rpm
Fuel injection	Bosch KE jetronic	U.S.: 162 ft/lb 220 Nm @ 4600 rpm	Bosch KE jetronic
Maximum engine speed	6200 rpm		6000 rpm

Gear ratios	I.	4.25:1	(automatic)	I.	3.86:1	(5-speed)	I. 3.91:1 (5-speed manual)
	II.	2.41:1		II.	2.18:1		II. 2.17:1
	III.	1.49:1		III.	1.38:1		III. 1.37:1
	IV.	1.00:1		IV.	1.00:1		IV. 1.00:1
				V.	0.80:1		V. 0.81:1

	190E 2.6		190E 1.8
Rear axle ratio	3.23	U.S.: 3.27; 2.87 automatic	3.46
Chassis	unit frame and body		
Suspension	shock absorber strut with anti-dive control, coil springs, anti-roll bar; multi-link independent rear, anti-dive, anti-squat control, coils, anti-roll bar		
Brakes and area	hydraulic dual circuit, discs; anti-locking system optional		
Wheelbase	2665 mm (104.9 in)		
Track, front/rear	1437/1418 (56.6/55.8 in)		
Length	4427 mm (174.2 in)		
Width	1678 mm (66.1 in)		
Height	1390 mm (54.7 in)		
Tires	185/65 VR 15		
Turning circle	10.7 meters (35.0 feet)		
Steering type and ratio	recirculating ball (3.3 turns); servo-assisted		
Weight	1210 kg (2662 lbs)	1285 kg (2835 lbs); 1988: 1305 kg; 1989: 1340 kg	1170 kg (2574 lbs)
Maximum speed	218 km/hr (136 mph); automatic: 213 km/hr (133 mph)		185 km/hr automatic; 180 km/hr manual (115/112 mph)
Acceleration	8.2 sec 0-62 mph		12.3 sec 0-100 km/hr; 13.0 sec automatic
Fuel consumption	at 120 km/hr:manual: 8.8 liters (27 mpg); automatic: 9.6 liters (25 mpg)		manual:8.8 liters; automatic:9.3 liters (27/26 mpg)
Fuel tank capacity	55 liters (14.5 gallons)		

The 300SE sedan, 1985

Model 260SE (1985-1992)

S = Super, E (Einspritzung) = fuel injection

The 260SE sedan was introduced to the public at the 1985 Frankfurt Auto Show. It was the smallest engined model of the W126 body style and offered that rather luxurious S-line of cars at a more reasonable price. The new six-cylinder fuel injection engine of 2,599 cc developed 166 DIN horsepower (122 Kw) in the reconverted version (RUF). The model shared all of the further aerodynamic refinements, contemporary standards of economy, and maximum active and passive safety of this further enlarged and improved range of the S-class of cars.

Prices and Production

The 260SE sedan sold in 1985 for .... DM 50,673   *0.923*
The 300SE sedan sold in 1985 for .... DM 54,891   *1.000*
The 300SEL sedan sold in 1985 for .... DM 58,596   *1.067*

$45?

Production of the 260SE sedan [126E 26] (from June/October 1985 until February 1991)

was in	1985	2,222 units
	1986	6,198 units
	1987	4,657 units
	1988	3,120 units
	1989	2,455 units
	1990	2,100 units
	1991	84 units
	total	20.836 units

Production of the 300SE sedan [126E 30] (from August/September 1985 until October 1991)

was in	1985	5,432 units
	1986	18,134 units
	1987	15,104 units
	1988	20,431 units
	1989	20,289 units
	1990	21,058 units
	1991	4,974 units
? →	1992	24,099 units
	total	105,422 units

Production of the 260SEL sedan [126E 30] (from August/September 1985 until August 1991)

was in	1985	1,379 units
	1986	4,815 units
	1987	6,886 units
	1988	8,686 units
	1989	10,985 units
	1990	6,428 units
	1991	1,777 units
? →	1992	9,412 units
	total	40,956 units

Model 300SE/SEL (1985–1991)

S = Super, E (Einspritzung) = fuel injection
SE L (Lang) = long wheelbase chassis

The 300SE and 300SEL sedans were also first shown at the 1985 Frankfurt Auto Show and represented the next in the line of five different engine sizes offered in the top S-class sedan range. The 3-liter engine developed 188 DIN horsepower (138 Kw). The reconverted engines had the injection and ignition systems already prepared for installation of the catalytic converter. The lead-sensitive parts such as catalyzer and lambda sensor could be installed subsequently at the customer's request. All of the larger engines for 1986 had been originally designed for catalytic converters, but the countries of the European Market could not agree on such changes and Mercedes cars had to be reconverted to become acceptable to all customers.

Specifications

	260SE	300SE	300SEL
Engine type	6 cyl overhead camshaft (M103)	6 cyl overhead camshaft (M103)	
Bore and stroke	82.9 x 80.25 cc	88.5 x 80.25 cc	
Displacement	2599 cc	2962 cc	
Power output	166 hp (DIN) 122 KW @ 5800 rpm 1989: 160 hp (DIN) 118 Kw @ 5800 rpm	188 hp (DIN) 138 Kw @ 5700 rpm	1989: U.S.: 177 hp (SAE) 132 Kw @ 5700 rpm [300SE]
Compression ratio	9.2:1	9.2:1	
Torque	228 Nm (167 ft/lb) @ 4600 rpm (23.2 mkg) 1989: 220 Nm @ 4600 rpm	260 Nm (191.8 ft/lb) @ 4400 rpm (26.5 mkg)	1989: U.S.: 188 ft/lb 255 Nm @ 4400 rpm
Fuel injection	Bosch KE jetronic		
Maximum engine speed	6200 rpm		
Gear ratios	I. 3.86:1 (5-speed) II. 2.18:1 III. 1.38:1 IV. 1.00:1 V. 0.80:1	I. 4.25:1 (automatic) II. 2.41:1 III. 1.49:1 IV. 1.00:1	I. 3.68:1 (automatic) II. 2.41:1 III. 1.44:1 IV. 1.00:1
Rear axle ratio	3.46		
Chassis	unit frame and body		
Suspension	independent front and rear, coil springs, anti-roll bar; diagonal swing axle, coil springs, anti-roll bar, level control, hydropneumatic optional		
Brakes and area	dual circuit, discs; power assisted, wear indicator, anti-locking system optional; 278/279 mm		
Wheelbase	2935 mm (115.5 in)		3075 mm (121 in)
Track, front/rear	1545/1517 mm (60.8/59.7 in)		
Length	5020 mm (197.6 in)		5135 mm (202.1 in)
Width	1820 mm (71.6 in)		
Height	1437 mm (56.6 in)		
Tires	195/70 VR 15		205/65 VR 15
Turning circle	11.8 meters (38.7 feet)		12.26 meters (40.2 feet)
Steering type and ratio	recirculating ball (2.75 turns); servo-assisted		
Weight	1510 kg (3322 lbs)	1990: 1695 kg	1540 kg (3388 lbs) 1690 kg (3730 lbs) 1710 kg (3770 lbs) 1990: 1715 kg
Maximum speed	205 km/hr (128 mph)	210 km/hr (131 mph)	
Acceleration	10.2 sec 0-100 km/hr	9.6 sec 0-100 km/hr	
Fuel consumption	at 120 km/hr: 9.6 liters (25 mpg)	9.7 liters (24.75 mpg)	
Fuel tank capacity	90 liters (23.8 gallons)		

The M 102 engine of the 260SE, 1985

The 420SE sedan, 1985

Prices and Production

The 420SE sedan sold in 1985 for .... DM 70,623
The 420SEL sedan sold in 1985 for .... DM 74,328
   in the United States in 1986 (East Coast) for $45,100

Production of the 420SE sedan [126E 42] (from June/September 1985 until December 1991)

was in	1985	1,689 units
	1986	4,181 units
	1987	2,704 units
	1988	2,368 units
	1989	1,528 units
	1990	1,345 units
	1991	181 units
	total	13,996 units

Production of the 420SEL sedan [126E 42] (from June/October 1985 until October 1991)

was in	1985	6,102 units
	1986	19,238 units
	1987	18,623 units
	1988	9,467 units
	1989	9,181 units
	1990	8,324 units
	1991	3,082 units
	total	74,017 units

Model 420SE/SEL (1985–1991)

S = Super, E (Einspritzung) = fuel injection
SE L (Lang) = long wheelbase chassis

The 420SE and 420SEL models were also first introduced at the Frankfurt Auto Show in 1985. They were, as middle range of the eight S-line models, powered by the new M116 lightweight 4,196 cc V-eight fuel injection gasoline engine, developing 218 DIN horsepower (180 Kw). This engine replaced the smaller 3.8-liter powerplant of the former line of sedans, made necessary because of the anticipated catalytic converter. However, it was, as in the case of all the newly developed engines, offered in the "reconverted" trim. These new engines were—again as all of the other new styles—more economical and more technically advanced than those they replaced.

These new six- and eight-cylinder engines were designed for superior running on unleaded premium fuel, but because an adequate supply of unleaded premium grade gasoline was not then available everywhere, the engines were designed to operate on leaded or unleaded premium fuel, utilizing a multi-functional mixture formation and ignition system (MF), by means of the adapter plug in the engine compartment. The appropriate ignition map is selected for the grade of fuel used. This applied to both the standard reconverted versions as well as to those equipped with catalytic converters.

All of the eight-cylinder engines were further improved using the latest electronics technology. The electronic ignition timing system took into account engine operating conditions by means of an integrated microprocessor. In place of the CIS injection system, all of these engines had the new CIS-E III mechanical-electronic gasoline injection system.

The front axle of the W126 line was unchanged from the previous design, but the diagonal swing axle had been further improved for greater ride comfort and smoother running. The rear axle housing, previously rigidly connected to the rear axle carrier, now had a flexible three-point mounting. The limited slip differential was optionally available on all 126 cars, but standard on the 560 models. The sedans were fitted with fixed caliper disc brakes at the front. The 15-inch wheels allowed larger thermally more efficient ones to be used.

For the United States, the 420SEL, in somewhat modified form from the European version, replaced the 380SEL sedan. The engine developed 201 SAE horsepower, 228 lbs/ft of torque, and the car weighed 3,850 pounds (1,745 kg), while the previous model (380SEL) had only 155 SAE horsepower, 196 lbs/ft of torque, and weighed 3,715 pounds (1,685 kg). The replacement was a better performer in acceleration and maximum speed.

Specifications

	420SE	SEL	
Engine type	V-8 cyl overhead camshaft (M116)		
Bore and stroke	92.0 x 78.9 cc (3.62 x 3.11 in)		
Displacement	4196 cc (256 cu in)		
Power output	218 hp (DIN) 160 KW @ 5200 rpm 1989: 224 hp (DIN) 165 Kw @ 5400 rpm		U.S.: 201 SAE hp 150 KW
Compression ratio	9.0:1		
Torque	330 Nm (241.8 ft/lb) @ 3750 rpm (33.6 mkg) 1989: 325 Nm @ 4000 rpm		U.S.: 228 ft/lb @ 3600 rpm
Fuel injection	Bosch KE jetronic		
Maximum engine speed	6000 rpm		
Gear ratios	I. 3.68:1 (automatic) II. 2.41:1 III. 1.44:1 IV. 1.00:1		
Rear axle ratio	2.47	1990: 3.46	
Chassis	unit frame and body		
Suspension	independent front and rear, coil springs, anti-roll bar; diagonal swing axle, coil springs, anti-roll bar, level control, hydropneumatic optional		
Brakes and area	dual discs, power assisted, anti-locking system, 278/279 mm (10.9/11.0 in)		
Wheelbase	2935 mm (115.5 in)	2935 mm (115.5 in)	
Track, front/rear	1555/1527 mm (61.2/60.1 in)		
Length	5020 mm (197.6 in)	5160 mm (203.1 in)	U.S.: 5285 mm (208.1 in)
Width	1820 mm (71.6 in)		
Height	1437 mm (56.6 in)	1441 mm (56.7 in)	
Tires	205/65 R 15		U.S.: 205/65 VR 15
Turning circle	11.8 meters (38.7 feet)	12.3 meters (40.2 feet)	
Steering type and ratio	recirculating ball (2.75 turns); servo-assisted		
Weight	1600 kg (3520 lbs)	1630 kg (3586 lbs) 1988: 1760 kg; 1990: 1695 kg	U.S.: 1745 kg (3850 lbs)
Maximum speed	215 km/hr (134 mph)		U.S.: 131 mph
Acceleration	9.0 sec 0-100 km/hr		U.S.: 9.2 sec 0-60 mph
Fuel consumption	at 120 km/hr: 11.0 liters (21.5 mpg)		U.S.: 16 mpg (average)
Fuel tank capacity	90 liters (23.8 gallons)		

The 560SEL sedan, 1985

Prices and Production

The 560SEL sedan sold in 1985 for .... DM 121,410
    in the United States in 1986 (East Coast) for $53,300

Production of the 560SEL sedan [126E 56] (from September/
October 1985)

was in	1985	2,097 units
	1986	16,559 units
	1987	13,494 units
	1988	12,832 units
	1989	12,990 units
	1990	13,728 units
	1991	3,339 units
	1992	32 units
	total	30,089 units

Production of the 560SE sedan [126E 56] (from April/June 1988
until January 1991)

was in	1988	486 units
	1989	428 units
	1990	337 units
	1991	1 unit
	total	1,252 units

Model 560SEL (1985–1992)

S = Super, E (Einspritzung) = fuel injection
SE L (Lang) = long wheelbase chassis

560SE (1988–1991)

The 560SEL model was first shown publicly at the prestigious Automobile Show at Frankfurt in September 1985. It was the new "flagship" of the new Sonderklasse, the S-class, of the Mercedes cars.

Powered by the newly designed M117 light-alloy eight-cylinder V-shaped fuel injection gasoline engine, developing 300 DIN horsepower (220 Kw) from the 5,547 cc displacement, the 560SEL sedan reached a maximum speed of 250 km/hr (156 mph) of exhilerating, luxurious driving. Acceleration was 7.2 seconds for the 0-100 km speed. The RUF reconversion (Ruckrustversion) engine had a 9.0:1 compression ratio (instead of the 10.0:1) and developed 272 DIN horsepower (200 Kw) with a maximum speed of 235 km/hr (147 mph) and acceleration of 7.4 seconds, only minutely slower performance figures.

Although first introduced in 1979, the S-class models had undergone some styling changes. Modifications of the exterior included new, integral front and rear spoilers for enhanced appearance and improved directional control. Suspension modifications were also made to provide better handling, safety, and riding comfort.

The luxurious interior included naturally all of the latest features and represented the utmost in Mercedes' outstanding quality design. For the American market, the 560SEL was slightly altered, of course, to conform to the various government regulations. Yet, performance was still superb.

The 5,547 cc (338.5 cubic inch) V-eight fuel injection engine developed 238 SAE horsepower (178 Kw) at 5,200 rpm with a 9.0:1 compression ratio. Torque was 287 lbs/ft at 3,500 rpm. The four-speed automatic transmission was standard and the rear axle ratio was 2.47, as on all eight-cylinder models. Limited slip differential and hydropneumatic level control was used. The aerodynamic alloy wheels provided were of an improved design.

Standard equipment included new flush-face halogen headlights with washers and wipers, electric sunroof with rear pop-up, removable footrests for rear passengers, electronically adjustable steering column, warning indicators for low oil, coolant and windshield washer fluid levels, warning indicators for exterior light failures, improved automatic climate control with recirculation feature, leather-covered steering wheel and gearshift lever, and as formerly, ABS and SRS systems. A new option was the Arametta upholstery, a suede-like synthetic material, but only offered in conjunction with the SEC two-place rear seating package, first offered on the 1985 models.

Specifications

	560SEL		560SE
Engine type	V-8 cyl overhead camshaft (M 117)		
Bore and stroke	96.5 x 94.8 cc (3.80 x 3.73 in)		
Displacement	5547 cc (338.5 in)		
Power output	300 hp (DIN) 220 Kw @ 5000 rpm 1989: 279 hp (DIN) 205 Kw @ 5200 rpm 1987: U.S.: 238 hp (SAE) 178 Kw @ 4800 rpm		
Compression ratio	10.0:1	U.S. 9.0:1	
Torque	455 Nm (333.5 ft/lb) @ 3750 rpm (46.3 mkg)	U.S.: 287 ft/lb @ 3500 rpm	
Fuel injection	Bosch mechanical/electronic CIS-E		
Maximum engine speed	6000 rpm		
Gear ratios	I. 3.87:1 (automatic) I. 3.68:1 (KAT) II. 2.25:1 II. 2.41:1 III. 1.44:1 III. 1.44:1 IV. 1.00:1 IV. 1.00:1		
Rear axle ratio	2.65	U.S.: 2.47	
Chassis	unit frame and body		
Suspension	independent front and rear, coil springs, anti-roll bar; diagonal swing axle, coil springs, anti-roll bar, level control, hydropneumatic optional		
Brakes and area	dual discs, power-assisted, anti-locking system, 278/279 mm (10.9/11.0 in)		
Wheelbase	3070 mm (120.9 in)		
Track, front/rear	1555/1527 mm (61.2/60.1 in)		
Length	5160 mm (203.1 in)	U.S.: 5285 mm (208.1 in)	5020 mm (197.6 in)
Width	1820 mm (71.7 in)		
Height	1441 mm (56.7 in)		1437 mm (56.6 in)
Tires	215/65 VR 15	U.S.: 205/65 VR 15 1990: 205/65 R15 94V	
Turning circle	12.3 meters (40.2 feet)		11.8 meters (38.7 ft)
Steering type and ratio	recirculating ball (3.0 turns); servo-assisted		
Weight	1810 kg (3982 lbs)	U.S.: 1870 kg (4125 lbs) 1989: 1830 kg (4035 lbs) 1990: 1860 kg (4100 lbs)	1780 kg (3916 lbs)
Maximum speed	250 km/hr (156 mph)	U.S.: 140 mph	
Acceleration	7.2 sec 0-100 km-hr	U.S.: 8.0 sec 0-60 mph	
Fuel consumption	at 120 km/hr: 12.8 liters (18 mpg)	U.S.: 15 mpg (average)	
Fuel tank capacity	90 liters (23.8 gallons)		

The 300SL coupe, 1985

Prices and Production

The 300SL roadster sold in 1985 for . . . . DM 63,441
The 420SL roadster sold in 1985 for . . . . DM 80,826

Production of the 300SL roadster [107E 30] (from May/September 1985 until August 1989)

was in	1985	1,356 units
	1986	4,331 units
	1987	3,261 units
	1988	2,746 units
	1989	2,048 units
	total	13,742 units

Production of the 420SL roadster [107E 42] (from July/November 1985 until August 1989)

was in	1985	215 units
	1986	1,003 units
	1987	479 units
	1988	325 units
	1989	126 units
	total	2,148 units

Model 300SL (1985–1989)

S = Sports, L = Light

The new 300SL model was first shown at the Frankfurt Auto Show in 1985. It was to replace the 280SL and with the newly designed engine provided again a six-cylinder SL model.

The designation was certainly correct but would cause much confusion and disturbance to owners and admirers of the esteemed 300SL gullwing coupe and roadster of thirty years before. Perhaps it should have been retired as the jersey number of a favorite irreplaceable star athlete.

The 2,962 cc light alloy engine developed 188 DIN horsepower (138 Kw) and gave the car a maximum speed of 203 km/hr (127 mph) and 0 to 100 km acceleration of 9.6 seconds. Comparison figures for the 280SL were 105 km/hr and 9.5 seconds (for the 1974, the first W107 model).

The open roadster—with coupe top—was still a popular model and good seller. In fact, at that Auto Show a considerably larger number of new roadster models were shown by other important manufacturers, attesting to the then increased popularity and demand of this style of enjoyment in driving an automobile.

Model 420SL (1985–1989)

S = Sports, L = Light

The 420SL model was also first introduced at the 1985 Frankfurt Auto Show. With the newly developed 4,196 cc V-eight engine of 218 DIN horsepower (160 Kw), it was to replace the 380SL model first marketed in 1980. Basically, the cars were the same in performance and 107 body style, but the 420SL had some refinements. The 218 horsepower engine—the same output as that of the former—gave the new model a top speed of 213 km/hr (144 mph) and a 0 to 100 kilometer acceleration time of 9 seconds, again about the same as that of the 380SL (215 km and 9 seconds, respectively).

Specifications

	300SL	420SL
Engine type	6 cyl overhead camshaft (M103)	V-8 cyl overhead camshaft (M116)
Bore and stroke	88.5 x 80.25 cc (3.50 x 3.16 in)	92.0 x 78.9 cc (3.62 x 3.11 in)
Displacement	2962 cc (180.8 cu in)	4196 cc (256.0 cu in)
Power output	188 hp (DIN) 138 Kw @ 5700 rpm	218 hp (DIN) 160 Kw @ 5200 rpm
Compression ratio	9.2:1	9.0:1
Torque	260 Nm (191.8 ft/lb) @ 4400 rpm (26.5 mkg)	330 Nm (241.8 ft/lb) @ 3750 rpm (33.6 mkg)
Fuel injection	Bosch KE jetronic	
Maximum engine speed	6200 rpm	6000 rpm

The 300SL coupe, 1985

Gear ratios	I. 3.86:1 (5-speed) I. 3.68:1 (automatic) II. 2.18:1 II. 2.41:1 III. 1.38:1 III. 1.44:1 IV. 1.00:1 IV. 1.00:1 V. 0.80:1	
Rear axle ratio	3.46	2.47
Chassis	unit frame and body	
Suspension	independent front and rear, coil springs, anti-roll bar; diagonal swing axle, coil springs, anti-roll bar, level control, hydropneumatic optional	
Brakes and area	dual discs, power-assisted, wear indicator, 278/279mm (10.9/11.0 in)	
Wheelbase	2455 mm (96.7 in)	
Track, front/rear	1462/1440 mm (57.6/56.7 in)	
Length	4580 mm (180.3 in)	
Width	1790 mm (70.5 in)	
Height	1290 mm (50.8 in)	
Tires	205/65 VR 15	
Turning circle	10.6 meters (35 feet)	
Steering type and ratio	recirculating ball (3.0 turns); servo-assisted	
Weight	1500 kg (3300 lbs)	1600 kg (3520 lbs)
Maximum speed	203 km/hr (127 mph)	213 km/hr (133 mph)
Acceleration	9.6 sec 0-100 km/hr	9.0 sec 0-100 km/hr
Fuel consumption	at 120 km/hr: 10.2 liters (23 mpg)	11.4 liters (20.5 mpg)
Fuel tank capacity	85 liters (22.5 gallons)	

The M 103 engine of the 300SL coupe, 1985

The 560SEC coupe, 1985

Model 420SEC (1985–1991)

S = Sports, E (Einspritzung) = fuel injection, C = Coupe

The 420SEC coupe was introduced at the Frankfurt Auto Show in 1985. It was one of three SEC models available, and with the smallest displacement V-eight engine, the least expensive of these luxury coupes, first shown in 1981.

This replacement for the 380SEC had the new M116 light alloy low pollution engine of 4,196 cc developing 218 DIN horsepower (160 kw) in the reconverted form, and 380 Nm torque. Its design incorporated many new technological features not found in the former power plant.

The 420SEC had a maximum speed of 218 km/hr (136 mph) and accelerated from 0 to 100 km/hr in 9.0 seconds. It took just 30 seconds to reach 1 kilometer from a standing start. As all SEC models, the 420SEC was only offered with the automatic transmission.

Prices and Production

The 420SEC coupe sold in 1985 for	....	DM 94,563
The 560SEC coupe sold in 1985 for	....	DM 133,608
in the United States in 1986 (East Coast) for	....	$58,700

Production of the 420SEC coupe [126E 42] (from August/October 1985 until October 1991)

was in	1985	273 units
	1986	896 units
	1987	714 units
	1988	593 units
	1989	534 units
	1990	451 units
	1991	219 units
	total	3,680 units
E420C	1994	384 units

Production of the 560SEC coupe [126E 56] (from June/October 1985 until October 1991)

was in	1985	989 units
	1986	4,745 units
	1987	5,476 units
	1988	5,012 units
	1989	5,299 units
	1990	5,270 units
	1991	2,138 units
	total	28,929 units

Model 560SEC (1985–1991)

S = Sports, E (Einspritzung) = fuel injection, C = Coupe

The 560SEC coupe, shown first at the 1985 Frankfurt Auto Show, was the most powerful of the three luxury coupes then built. It shared the outward appearance and inside appointments with the others, but had the newly designed M117 type 5,547 cc V-eight engine of 300 DIN horsepower (220 Kw) and 455 Nm torque. The maximum speed was 250 km/hr (156 mph), and acceleration from 0 to 100 km/hr took 7.2 seconds. The 272 DIN horsepower reconverted version reached 235 km/hr and acceleration figures were 7.4 seconds. Performance was considerably better than that of the 5-liter car.

For the North American market, the 560SEC had a 238 SAE horsepower (178 Kw) engine and 2.47 rear axle ratio. Compression ratio was 9.0 to 1. There were but minor changes in the other specifications or outward appearance of the model sold elsewhere in the world.

Specifications

	420SEC	560SEC	
Engine type	V-8 cyl overhead camshaft (M116)	V-8 cyl overhead camshaft (M117)	
Bore and stroke	92.0 x 78.9 mm	96.5 x 94.8 mm (3.80 x 3.73 in)	
Displacement	4196 cc	5547 cc (338.5 cu in)	
Power output	218 hp (DIN) 160 Kw @ 5200 rpm	300 hp (DIN) 220 Kw @ 5000 rpm	U.S.: 238 hp @ 5200 rpm
	1989: 224 hp (DIN) 165 Kw @ 5400 rpm	1989: 279 hp (DIN) 205 Kw @ 5200 rpm	
Compression ratio	9.0:1 1989: 10.0:1	10.0:1	U.S.: 9.0:1
Torque	380Nm (278.4 ft/lb) @ 3750 rpm (38.7 mkg)	455 Nm (333.5 ft/lb) @ 3750 rpm (46.3 mkg)	U.S.: 287 ft/lb @ 3500 rpm
	1989: 325 Nm @ 4000 rpm	1989: 430 Nm @ 3750 rpm	
Fuel injection	Bosch KE jetronic	Bosch mechanical/electronic CIS-E	
Maximum engine speed	6000rpm		
Gear ratios	I. 3.68:1 (automatic) II. 2.41:1 III. 1.44:1 IV. 1.00:1		
Rear axle ratio	2.47	2.65	
Chassis	unit frame and body		
Suspension	independent front and rear, coil springs, anti-roll bar; diagonal swing axle, coil springs, anti-roll bar, level control, hydropneumatic optional		
Brakes and area	dual discs, power-assisted, anti-locking system, 278/279 mm (10.9/11.0 in)		
Wheelbase	2845 mm (111.9 in)		
Track, front/rear	1555/1527 mm (61.2/60.1 mm)		

The M 117 engine of the 560SEC coupe, 1985

	420SEC	560SEC	
Length	4935 mm (194.2 in)		U.S.: 5060 mm (199.2 in)
Width	1828 mm (72.0 in)		
Height	1407 mm (55.4 in)		
Tires	205/65 VR 15	215/65 VR 15	U.S.: 205/65 VR 15
Turning circle	11.53 meters (37.7 feet)		
Steering type and ratio	recirculating ball (2.89 turns); servo-assisted		
Weight	1600 kg (3520 lbs)	1750 kg (3850 lbs)	U.S.: 1795 kg (3960 lbs)
Maximum speed	218 km/hr (136 mph)	250 km/hr (156 mph)	U.S.: 140 mph
Acceleration	9.0 sec 0-100 km/hr	7.2 sec 0-100 km/hr	U.S.: 8.0 sec 0-60 mph
Fuel consumption	at 120 km/hr: 11 liters (21.5 mpg)	12.8 liters (19 mpg)	U.S.: 15 mpg (average)
Fuel tank capacity	90 liters (23.8 gallons)		

The 560SL coupe, 1985

Prices and Production

The 560 SL sold in the United States in 1986 (East Coast)
for $48,200
Production of the 560SL roadster [107E 56] (from June/September 1985
until August 1989)

was in 1985	3,907 units
1986	13,788 units
1987	14,770 units
1988	11,531 units
1989	5,351 units
1990	502 units
total	49,347 units

The 560SL coupe, 1986, U.S. version

Model 560SL (1985–1990)

S = Sports, L = Light

The 560SL model was especially created for the North American market for the 1986 model year to replace the 380SL. The W107 body style, actually built for fourteen years, had undergone many refinements inside and out, and would perhaps soon be replaced completely by a new style.

The newly designed 5,547 cc V-eight fuel injection engine installed was rated at 227 SAE horsepower, somewhat less than the same sized power unit of the 238 horsepower 560SE and 560SEC models, because of the more restrictive exhaust system dictated by tighter underbody dimensions of the 107 chassis. Still, the new engine represented a 47% increase of power over the 155 SAE horsepower of the 380SL model. The 560SL weighed 3,780 pounds (1,715 kg), the 380SL weighed 3,605 pounds (1,635 kg).

An anti-squat/dive torque compensation feature had been added to the rear axle, along with a limited slip differential and the noise-reducing change in its mounting to the body. The front suspension geometry had been revised to have less positive wheel offset and new caster and camber settings, helping straight-ahead tracking. An air dam had also been added under the front bumper, reducing front end lift by 17%.

The new alloy wheel design and the brake light on the rear deck were the only visible changes, except for the new style S-class door handles. Inside, leather upholstery was a standard feature and the seats had more lateral support. Guides to keep the seatbelt away from the backrest adjustment wheel had also been installed. Standard equipment of the new 560SL raodster/coupe included the ABS anti-locking brake system, SRS, thermostatically heated windshield washer jets, anti-theft alarm system, leather-covered steering wheel and shift lever, warning lights for low-level fluids and exterior lamp failures, as well as an improved climate control system and the radio-cassette.

The main reason for offering the 560SL in this country was unquestionably to counteract the large number of privately imported European 500SL models. These cars had a 231 DIN horsepower engine (the 380SL had 204 horsepower) and the overall performance—even with the federally demanded (EPA) emission controls installed—was still quite superior to the 380SL models sold by the authorized dealers here. (Maximum speed for the 500SL European models was 140 mph and acceleration 0-100 took 8. 1 seconds against the 134 mph and 9.8 seconds for the 1981 version of the U.S. 380SL.) The new 560SL was expected to equal—or even exceed—the performance of the converted European 500SL model.

Specifications

	560SL
Engine type	V-8 cyl overhead camshaft (M117)
Bore and stroke	96.5 x 94.8 mm (3.80 x 3.73 in)
Displacement	5547 cc (338.5 cu in)
Power output	227 SAE hp (170 Kw) @ 4750 rpm
Compression ratio	9.0:1
Torque	279 ft/lb @ 3250 rpm (28.4 mkg)
Fuel injection	Bosch mechanical/electronic CIS-E
Maximum engine speed	6000 rpm
Gear ratios	I. 3.68:1 (automatic)
	II. 2.41:1
	III. 1.44:1
	IV. 1.00:1
Rear axle ratio	2.47
Chassis	unit frame and body
Suspension	independent front and rear, coil springs, anti-roll bar; diagonal swing axle, coil springs, anti-roll bar, level control, hydropneumatic optional
Brakes and area	dual discs, power-assisted, anti-locking system, 278/279 mm (10.9/11.0 in)
Wheelbase	2455 mm (96.7 in)
Track, front/rear	1462/1440 mm (57.6/56.7 in)
Length	4580 mm (180.3 in)
Width	1790 mm (70.5 in.)
Height	1290 mm (50.8 in)
Tires	205/65 VR 15
Turning circle	10.6 meters (35 feet)
Steering type and ratio	recirculating ball (3.0 turns); servo-assisted
Weight	1715 kg (3780 lbs) U.S.: 1680 kg (3705 lbs)
Maximum speed	137 mph
Acceleration	8 sec 0-60 mph
Fuel consumption	14 mpg city; 17 mpg highway
Fuel tank capacity	90 liters (23.8 gallons)

The instrument panel of the 560SL, 1985

The M 116 engine of the 420SEC, 1985

The 300TE station wagon, 1988 U.S. version

Prices and Production

The 300 TE 24 station wagon sold in 1989 for DM71,706
The 300 TE station wagon sold in the U.S. in 1990 for $49,650
(with 4matic) $56,250

Production of the 300TE station wagon [124E 30] (from June 1985)

was in 1985	129 units		
1986	3,780 units,	4matic	8 units
1987	5,670 units,	4matic	1,192 units
1988	7,650 units,	4matic	2,201 units
1989	7,623 units,	4matic	1,574 units
1990	6,110 units,	4matic,	2,790 units
1991	6,889 units,	4matic,	2,016 units
1992	3,928 units,	4matic,	1,262 units
total	24,550 units,	4matic,	488 units 1993
		units, 4matic,	401 units 1994

Production of the 300TE 24 station wagon [124E 30] (from June 1989)

300TE-24 1989	543 units
1990	2,285 units
1991	2,286 units
1992	1,168 units
total	6,282 units

Production of the 260TE chassis only [124E 26] (from 1986)

was in 1986	55 units
1987	151 units
1988	173 units
4matic 1989	179 units

Model 300TE (1985–)

T = Station Wagon, E (Einspritzung) = Fuel injection

The 300TE, shown at the 1985 Frankfurt Auto Show, was the largest gasoline-engined version of the line. As all six new style station wagons, this one shared body style and features with the other five models. The newer 124 W form had reduced aerodynamics by 15% and combined with the new engines appreciably showed improved fuel economy of each of these new models.

The 300TE had the fuel-injected six-cylinder gasoline engine which developed 188 horsepower (138 Kw) and had 260 Nm (191.8 ft/lbs) torque, giving the 3,234 pound station wagon a more spirited performance than that with the three-liter, 143 horse-power, diesel engine.

Maximum speed of 230 km/hr (144 mph) against the diesel-powered 190 km/hr (118 mph) and the considerably better acceleration of 7.9 seconds for the 0-100 km/hr against the 13.7 seconds required for the 300TD, made this 300TE model infinitely more desirable for the driver in a hurry and was expected to outsell the slower model.

With ever increasing punitive restrictions and regulations against the diesel engines, in Europe as well as in this country, the once fantastic advantage in fuel prices and maintenance, became gradually less and less financially beneficial.

By 1988 the 300TE station wagon was offered to the American buyer. The TD model had been replaced by the gasoline-engined version. (However, an improved diesel engine to recapture the loss was hinted at.)

The 300TE station wagon became available also with the optional 24-valve 220 horsepower (162 Kw) six-cylinder engine. It was then equipped with ZR rated tires.

Model 260TE (1986–)

T = Station wagon, E (Einspritzung) = fuel injection

The 260TE was, apparently, available only as a chassis. The production listing showed it as a 260 E VF, which I translated as Verlängertes Fahrgestell = long chassis.

Specifications

	300TE	
Engine type	6 cyl overhead camshaft (M103)	
Bore and stroke	88.5x 80.25 (3.48 x 3.16 in)	
Displacement	2962 cc (180.8 cu in)	
Power output	188 hp (DIN) 138 Kw @ 5700 rpm	U.S.: 177 hp (SAE) 132 Kw @ 5700 rpm 1989: 180 hp 132 Kw @ 5700 rpm
Compression ratio	9.2:1	
Torque	260 Nm (191.8 ft/lb) @ 4400 rpm (26.5 mkg)	U.S.: 188 ft/lb (255 Nm) @ 4400 rpm
Fuel injection	Bosch KE jetronic	
Maximum engine speed	6200 rpm	U.S.:

Gear ratios

I.	3.92:1	(4-speed)	I.	4.25:1	(automatic)	I.	3.92:1	(5-speed)	1988: I.	3.86:1	(5-speed)	I. 3.87:1 (automatic)
II.	2.17:1		II.	2.41:1		II.	2.17:1		II.	2.18:1		II. 2.25:1
III.	1.37:1		III.	1.49:1		III.	1.37:1		III.	1.38:1		III. 1.44:1
IV.	1.00:1		IV.	1:00:1		IV.	1.00:1		IV:	1:00:1		IV. 1.00:1
						V.	0.78:1					

Rear axle ratio	3.42	U.S.: 4-speed automatic 3.27 (automatic); 3.92 (5-speed)
Chassis	unit frame and body	
Suspension	schock absorber strut with anti-dive control, coil springs, anti-roll bar; multi-link independent rear, anti-dive, anti-squat control, coils, anti-roll bar	
Brakes and area	hydraulic dual circuit, discs; 262/258 mm (10.3/10.1in)	
Wheelbase	2800 mm (110.2 in)	
Track, front/rear	1497/1488 mm (58.9/58.6 in)	
Length	4765 mm (187.6 in)	U.S.: 4780 mm (188.2 in)
Width	1740 mm (68.5 in)	
Height	1490 mm (58.7 in)	
Tires	195/65 VR 15	
Turning circle	11.2 meters (44 feet)	
Steering type and ratio	recirculating ball (3.3 turns); servo-assisted	U.S.: 3.0 turns
Weight	1470 kg (3234 lbs)	U.S.: 1575 kg (3475 lbs) 1989: 1600 kg; 1990: 1615 kg
Maximum speed	230 km/hr (144 mph); automatic: 225 km/hr (140 mph)	

260TE

82.9 x 80.25 mm (3.26 x 3.16 in)

2599 cc

166 hp (DIN) 122 Kw @ 5800 rpm

Acceleration	7.9 sec 0-100 km/hr; automatic: 8.3 sec
Fuel consumption	at 120 km/hr: 8.3 liters (29 mpg); automatic: 9.6 liters (25 mpg)
Fuel tank capacity	70 liters (18.5 gallons)

The 300CE coupe, 1988, similar to all coupe models

Prices and Production

The 230CE coupe sold in 1988 for . . . . DM 54,180

Production of the 230CE coupe [C124] (from July 1986)

was in 1986	4 units	
1987	3,370 units	
1988	7,741 units	
1989	6,423 units	
1990	5,556 units	
1991	5,969 units	
1992	4,612 units	
total	22,560 units	

The 200CE coupe sold in 1990 for . . . . DM 50,255

Production of the 200CE coupe [124] (from March 1990)

was in 1990	1,166 units
1991	2,401 units
1992	2,354 units
Total	5,921 units

Production of the 200CE 4-V [124]

was in 1992	487 units
1993	2,732 units
1994	1,684 units

The 220CE coupe sold in 1992 for . . . . DM 64,296

Production of the 220CE coupe [124]

was in 1992	1,370 units
1993	4,841 units
1994	3,379 units

Production of the 220CE convertible [124]

was in 1992	1 unit
1993	1,322 units
1994	2,180 units

Model 230CE (1987–1992)

C = Coupe, E (Einspritzung) = Fuel injection

The 230CE coupe was first shown at the Geneva Auto Show in 1987. This new coupe had its own distinctively different styling, yet was unmistakenly a part of the entire new line of cars. Based on the 124 body style, it had actually only the identical front and tail lights. The wheelbase of the coupe was reduced over that of the sedan, as was the overall height, but the overall weight of the four-cylinder engined 230CE was increased by 30 kilograms because of more effective insulation and extra reinforcements. It also had considerably more comprehensive appointments. Compared to the predecessor model the 124 coupe was actually lighter by 40 kilograms, had a reduced (by 33%) drag coefficient, used 17% less fuel, and accelerated faster by 8% and had an 11% increased top speed.

Model 200CE (1990–   )

C = Coupe, E (Einspritzung) = Fuel injection

The 200CE coupe was added to the line in 1990, thus offering a wider range, and satisfying customers who preferred a coupe, yet hesitated purchasing the more powerful versions. Equipped with the new 4-valve per cylinder 2-liter engine this 200CE 4V model was available in 1992.

Model 220CE (1992–   )

C = Coupe, E (Einspritzung) = Fuel injection

The 220CE coupe was also offered in 1992, still expanding the smaller engined models of this popular body style.

And one convertible with the 2.2-liter engine was also produced that year.

Specifications

	230CE	200CE	220CE
Engine type	4 cyl overhead camshaft (M 102)		
Bore and stroke	95.5 x 80.25 mm (3.74 x 3.16 in)	89.9 x 78.7 mm (3.15 x 3.16 in)	89.9 x 86.6 mm
Displacement	2299 cc (140.3 cu in)	1998 cc	2199 cc
Power output	136 hp (DIN) 100 Kw @ 5100 rpm 1989: 132 hp (DIN) 97 Kw 220 hp (DIN) 162 Kw @ 6400 rpm	87 Kw 118 hp (DIN) @ 5200 rpm	110 Kw 150 hp (DIN) @ 5500 rpm
Compression ratio	9.0:1	9.0:1	10.0:1
Torque	205 Nm (151.3 ft/lb) @ 3500 rmp (20.9 mkg) 1989: 198 Nm 265 Nm @ 4600 rpm	172 Nm @ 3500 rpm	210 Nm @ 4000 rpm
Fuel injection	Bosch KE mech, electronic		
Maximum engine speed	6000 rpm		
Gear ratios	I. 3.91:1 (manual) I. 4.25:1 (automatic) II. 2.17:1 II. 2.41:1 III. 1.37:1 III. 1.49:1 IV. 1.00:1 IV. 1.00:1 V. 0.78:1		
Rear axle ratio	3.27 1989:3.46 manual, 3.27 automatic		3.67
Chassis	unit frame and body		
Suspension	shock absorber strut with anti-dive control, coil springs, anti-roll bar; multi-link independent rear, anti-drive, anti-squat control, coils, anti-roll bar		
Brakes and area	hydraulic dual circuit, discs; 373 sq in		
Wheelbase	2715 mm		
Track, front/rear	1501/1491 mm		
Length	4655 mm (183 in)		
Width	1740 mm (68.5 in)		
Height	1395 mm (55.5 in)		
Tires	195/65 R 15 91 H		
Turning circle	10.92. meters (43 feet)		
Steering type and ratio	recirculating ball (3.3 turns); servo-assisted		
Weight	1340 kg (2948 lbs) 1390 kg		
Maximum speed	203 km/hr (126.7 mph); automatic: 198 km/hr (123.5 mph)		
Acceleration	10.4 sec 0-100 km/hr; automatic: 10.4 sec		
Fuel consumption	at 120 km/hr: 8.7 liters (27.5 mpg); automatic: 7.7 liters		
Fuel tank capacity	70 liters (18.5 gallons)		

The 300CE-24 Convertible, 1990

Prices and Production

The 300CE coupe sold in 1989 for . . . . DM 68,115
The 300E-24 coupe sold in 1989 for . . . . DM 77,748
The 300CE coupe sold in the United States
  in 1988 for $53,880

Production of the 300CE coupe [C124] (from August 1986)

was in	1986	5 units
	1987	5,010 units
	1988	13,711 units
	1989	9,957 units
	1990	6,143 units
	1991	5,299 units
	1992	3,361 units
	total	24,760 units

Production of the 300CE 24 coupe [C124] (from March 1988)

was in	1988	14 units
	1989	3,165 units
	1990	8,927 units
	1991	8,461 units
	1992	3,896 units
	total	24,449 units

The 300CE convertible sold in 1992 for . . . . DM 99,638

The 300CE convertible sold in the United States in 1993 for . . . $76,500

Production of the 300CE convertible [124] (from August 1990/January 1992)

was in	1990	2 units
	1991	16 units
	1992	4,469 units
	1993	1,856 units
	total	6,343 units

Model 300CE (1987–1993)

C = Coupe, E (Einspritzung) = Fuel injection

The 300CE coupe, also introduced at the same time and place as the less powerful one, had the six-cylinder engine. Outwardly it was identical, except for the dual exhaust pipes, to the four-cylinder car. The ABS anti-lock brake system was standard in the 300CE model, an optional item in the other. Appointments were similar to the cars in the prestigious S-class.

The 300 CE coupe became also available with the optional 24-valve 220 horsepower (162 Kw) six-cylinder engine. The car was then equipped with ZR rated tires.

The 300CE convertible, introduced at the Geneva Auto Show in 1992, was based on the coupe. It had the same six-cylinder engine with 4 valves per cylinder and equipped with a retractable top and automatic roll bar similar to that of the SL models.

Model 320CE (1992–   )

C = Coupe, E (Einspritzung) = Fuel injection

The 320CE coupe appeared in 1992 to replace the regular six-cylinder model. Although the engine was slightly larger (3.2 liters instead of 3), the power output was actually the same as that of the 24 valve 3-liter unit, but at a lower engine speed (5500 rpm to 6400). Torque was also considerably higher (310 Nm to 265), and thus offered a livelier acceleration than the 300CE (8.3 sec 0-100 km/hr and 7.9 against the 9.0 and 8.8 sec).

Prices and Production

The 320CE coupe sold in 1992 for . . . . DM 82,821

Production of the 320CE coupe [124]

was in	1992	2,690 units
	1993	5,914 units
	1994	3,234 units

The 320CE convertible sold in 1993 for . . . . DM 102,637.50

Production of the 320CE convertible [124]

was in	1992	599 units
	1993	3,685 units
	1994	2,964 units

Specifications

	300CE	300CE 24 and Convertible	320CE
Engine type	6 cyl overhead camshaft (M103)	6 cyl double overhead camshaft (M104)	
Bore and stroke	88.5 x 80.2 mm (3.48 x 3.16 in)	89.9 x 84.0 mm (3.54 x 3.31 in)	89.9 x 84.0 mm (3.54 x 3.31 in)
Displacement	2960 cc (180.8 cu in)	3199 cc (195.1 cu in)	3199 cc (195.1 cu in)
Power output	188 hp (DIN) 138 Kw @ 5700 rpm 1989: 180 hp (DIN) 132 Kw U.S.:177 hp (SAE)	220 hp (DIN) 162 Kw @ 6400 rpm U.S.:217 hp	
Compression ratio	9.2:1 U.S.:10:1	10:1	
Torque	260 Nm (191.8 ft/lbs) @ 4400 rmp (26.5 mkg) 1989: 255 Nm U.S.:188 ft/lb (255 Nm)	265 Nm @ 4600 rpm U.S.: 229 ft/lb @ 3750 rpm	310 Nm @ 3750 rpm
Fuel injection	Bosch KE mech.electronic		
Maximum engine speed	6200 rpm	7000 rpm	6400 rpm
Gear ratios	I. 3.86:1 (manual) I. 3.89:1 (automatic) II. 2.18:1 II. 2.25:1 III. 1.38:1 III. 1.44:1 IV. 1.00:1 IV. 1.00:1 V. 0.80:1	I. 4.15:1 (manual) I. 3.87:1 (automatic) II. 2.52:1 II. 2.25:1 III. 1.69:1 III. 1.44:1 IV. 1.24:1 IV. 1.00:1 V. 1.00:1 V. 0.75:1	
Rear axle ratio	3.07 1989: 3.67 manual; 3.07 automatic U.S.:3.27	3.27 manual 3.69 automatic U.S.: 2.65	3.06 manual
Chassis	unit frame and body		
Suspension	shock absorber strut with anti-dive control, coil springs, anti-roll bar; multi-link independent rear, anti-squat control, anti-dive, coils and anti-roll bar		
Brakes and area	hydraulic dual circuit, discs; 373 sq in		
Wheelbase	2715 mm (106.8 in)		
Track, front/rear	1501/1491 mm (58.9/58.6 in)		
Length	4655 mm (183 in) U.S.:183.9 (4670 mm)		
Width	1740 mm (68.5 in)		
Height	1395 mm (55.5 in)		
Tires	195/65 VR 15 U.S.:195/65 R 15 91V	195/65 ZR 15	
Turning circle	10.92 meters (43 feet)		Convertible: 1710 kg (3762 lbs) 230/225 km/hr (140 mph)
Steering type and ratio	recirculating ball (3.3 turns); servo-assisted		
Weight	1390 kg (3058 lbs) U.S.:1590 kg (3505 lbs)	1480 kg (3256 lbs)	1490 Kg (3278 lbs)
Maximum speed	228 km/hr (142.3 mph); automatic: 223 km/hr (139 mph)	237 km/hr (148 mph); automatic 232 km/hr	235/230 km/hr (137/144 mph)
Acceleration	10.4 sec 0-100 km/hr; automatic: 10.4 sec U.S.:8.5 sec; 1990:8 sec	8 sec 0-100 km/hr; automatic: 7.8 sec 14.6 liters (16 mpg); 9.9 liters	8.3 sec 0-100 km/hr; automatic 7.9
Fuel consumption	8.3 liters (29 mpg); automatic: 10 liters	U.S.: city 17 mpg; highway 23 mpg	15.2 liters (15 mpg) 10.5 liters
Fuel tank capacity	70 liters (18.5 gallons)		

The 300SL roadster, 1989

Prices and Production

The 300SL sold for in 1989 . . . . DM 85,000
The 300SL sold in the United States in 1990 for $73,500

Production of the 300SL [R129] (from May 1988)

was in 1988	28	units
1989	1,507	units
1990	7,902	units
1991	7,833	units
1992	7,417	units
1993	2,297	units
total	26,956	units

Production of the 300SL 24 [R129] (from June 1988)

was in 1988	27	units
1989	407	units
1990	2,236	units
1991	3,115	units
1992	4,543	units
1993	1,692	units
total	11,993	units

Model 300SL (1989–1993)

S = Sports, L = Light

The newly styled SL models were first exhibited at the 59th Geneva Auto Show in March 1989. Designated as the 129 body style, they were a worthy successor to the 107, first introduced in 1971 — three units were actually built in November 1970 — as the 350SL open roadster and hard top and produced over the years with many different engine sizes and appropriate model designations. Now, the models were available with three different engines.

The 300SL had the M103 six-cylinder, single overhead camshaft 2960 cc engine of 190 hp (DIN) at 5,700 rpm. It gave a brisk performance, with 9.3 seconds for the 0-100 km/hr (62.4 mph) and a maximum speed of 228 km/hr (142 mph). The 300SL was the least powerful model in this line of cars.

The new SL models incorporated an abundance of innovative engineering features. This trend-setting technology provided excellent sporty driving with ultimate comfort, not usually found in such high performance cars. The new SL was designed to be the undisputed leader in the luxury sports car category, and was a worthy successor to the earlier 107 body style cars, which were in production for eighteen years and still most admired and immensely desirable cars.

Model 300SL 24 (1989–1993)

S = Sports, L = Light

The 300SL 24 was, of course, the same body style as the above, except with a stronger engine installed, and consequently improved performance. The M104 double overhead camshaft, four valves per cylinder 2,960 cc engine developed 231 hp (DIN) at 6,300 rpm. (228 hp SAE for the U.S. at 7,000 rpm) The compression ratio was also slightly increased over the regular 3-liter engine, 10:1 against 9.2:1, and torque was rated higher as well. Thus, the 0-100 km acceleration figures were 8.4 seconds and the top speed 240 km/hr (150 mph). Both models had different rear axle ratios and were available with either a 5-speed manual or a 4-speed automatic transmission, but the U.S. version had the 5-speed automatic.

Specifications

	300SL	300SL 24
Engine type	6 cyl single overhead camshaft (M103)	6 cyl overhead camshafts (M104)
Bore and stroke	88.5 x 80.25 mm (3.50 x 3.16 in)	88.5 x 80.25 mm (3.50 x 3.16 in)
Displacement	2960 cc (180.8 cu in)	2960 cc (180.8 cu in)
Power output	190 hp (DIN) 140 Kw @ 5700 rpm	231 hp (DIN) 170 Kw @ 6300 rpm U.S.: 228 hp (SAE) 170 Kw @ 6300 rpm
Compression ratio	9.2:1	10.0:1
Torque	260 Nm (191.9 ft/lb) @ 4500 rpm	272 Nm (200.7 ft/lb) @ 4600 rpm U.S.: 201 ft/lb 272 Nm @ 4600 rpm
Fuel injection	CIS-E5 mech. electronic	CIS-E5 mech. electronic
Maximum engine speed	6300 rpm	7000 rpm
Gear ratios	I. 3.86:1 (manual) I. 3.87:1 (automatic) II. 2.18:1 II. 2.25:1 III. 1.38:1 III. 1.44:1 IV. 1.00:1 IV. 1.00:1 V. 0.80:1	I. 4.15:1 (manual) I. 3.87:1 (automatic) II. 2.52:1 II. 2.25:1 III. 1.69:1 III. 1.44:1 IV. 1.24:1 IV. 1.00:1 V. 1.00:1
Rear axle ratio	3.92 (manual) 3.29 (automatic)	3.46 (manual) 3.69 (automatic)
Chassis	integral all-steel body	integral all-steel body
Suspension	shock absorber strut with anti-dive control, coil springs, anti-roll bar; multi-link independent rear, anti-dive, anti-squat control, coils, anti-roll bar	
Brakes and area	hydraulic, dual circuit, discs; ABS system	
Wheelbase	2515 mm (99.0 in)	
Track, front/rear	1532/1521 mm (60.3/59.9 in)	
Length	4465 mm (175.74 in)	
Width	1812 mm (71.3 in)	
Height	1286 mm (50.4 in)	
Tires	255/55 ZR 16	
Turning circle	10.75 meters (42.3 feet)	
Steering type and ratio	recirculating ball (3 turns); servo-assisted	
Weight	1650 kg (3630 lbs)	1690 kg (3718 lbs) U.S.: 1800 kg (3970 lbs)
Maximum speed	228 km/hr (142 mph)	240 km/hr (150 mph)
Acceleration	9.3 sec 0-100 km/hr	8.4 sec 0-100 km/hr
Fuel consumption	urban cycle: 15.9 liters; at 90 km/hr: 8.5 1; 120 km/hr:10.3	urban cycle: 16.2 liters; at 90 km/hr:8.8 1; 120 km/hr:10.4
Fuel tank capacity	80 liters (21 gallons)	80 liters (21 gallons)

The 500SL roadster, 1989

Prices and Production

The 500SL 32 sold in 1989 for . . . . DM 125,000
The 500SL sold in the United States in 1990 for $83,500

Production of the 500SL 32 [R129] (from June 1988)

was in	1988	31 units
	1989	3,413 units
	1990	10,649 units
	1991	15,053 units
	1992	9,483 units
	total	38,598 units

The 600SL sold in 1992 for . . . . DM 217,740

The 600 SL sold in the United States in 1992 for $119,500

Production of the 600SL [129] (from December 1991/January 1992)

was in	1991	3 units
	1992	2,107 units
SL600	1993	2,066 units
	1994	1,526 units

Model 500SL (1988–1992)
S = Sports, L = Light

The third version of the new SL body style model, introduced at the Geneva Auto Show in March 1989, was the 500SL, the top of the entire line.

This was the most desirable of the trio of the new SL models, was the most powerful, gave the best performance and, of course, was the most expensive as well. Basically, all three SL models were alike. The new 129 body style and many features were the same, but the 500 SL had the M119 V-8 engine of 4,973 cc with four valves per cylinder and four overhead camshafts, developing 326 hp at 5,500 rpm. It gave the 4,752 pound roadster a maximum speed of 250 km/hr (156 mph), and accelerated from 0-100 km/hr (62.4 mph) in 6.2 seconds. Unlike the other, six-cylinder models, the V-8 came only with the 4-speed automatic transmission.

The new KE 5 injection system was more exacting than the previous ones and the automatic camshaft adjustment made for smoother engine running, reduced pollutant emission and fuel consumption. The ABS anti-lock braking system was a standard feature on the cars.

The convertible was fitted with an electro-hydraulically operated top as well as a hard top. The soft top was activated by a push button and operated within 30 seconds. A roll bar was also provided, again controlled automatically and operating within 0.3 seconds when a critical situation registered.

The electrically adjustable seats were completely redesigned for comfort and increased passive safety. A three-point inertia-reel seat belt, belt tensioner, and a coordinated sash guide height adjustment and head restraint were provided. The car had shock absorber strut independent front suspension and multi-link independent rear suspension — a proven system — for sporty handling and riding comfort. An adaptive damping system (ADS) with automatic level adjustment and control was provided to insure improved driving in any road conditions. The emission control system had a new closed loop double fluted catalytic converter with two ceramic monoliths for high long-term stability.

Model 600SL (1991–   )
S = Sports, L = Light

The 600SL had the powerful, new V-12 cylinder, 48-valve, 6-liter engine of 389 horsepower and 420 ft/lb of torque and thus was the undisputed leader of maximum performance and elegance of this line. Nothing was left out; it was all here: ADS, ABS, ASR, fine leather, burl walnut, heated seats, CD changer, and cellular telephone.

Specifications

	500SL	500SL	600SL
Engine type	V-8 cyl four overhead camshafts (M119)		V-12 cyl four overhead camshafts (M120)
Bore and stroke	96.5 x 85 mm (3.80 x 3.35 in)		89.0 x 80.2 mm (3.50 x 3.16 cu in)
Displacement	4973 cc (303.5 cu in)		5987 cc (365.2 cu in)
Power output	326 hp (DIN) 240 Kw @ 5500 rpm	U.S.: 322 hp (SAE) 240 Kw @ 5500 rpm	394 hp (DIN) @ 5200 rpm U.S.: 389 hp (SAE)
Compression ratio	10.0:1		
Torque	450 Nm (332.0 ft/lb) @ 4000 rpm		570 Nm (420 lb/ft) @ 3800 rmp
Fuel injection	CIS-E5 mech. electronic KE 5		
Maximum engine speed	6000 rpm		
Gear ratios	I. 3.87 (automatic W4 A040) II. 2.27 III. 1.44 IV. 1.00		
Rear axle ratio	2.65		
Chassis	integral all steel body		
Suspension	shock absorber strut with anti-dive control, coil springs, anti-roll bar; multi-link independent rear, anti-dive, anti-squat control, coils, anti-roll bar		
Brakes and area	hydraulic, dual circuit, discs; ABS system		
Wheelbase	2515 mm (99.0 in)		
Track, front/rear	1532/1521 mm (60.3/59.9 in)		
Length	4465 mm (175.74 in)		
Width	1812 mm (71.3 in)		
Height	1286 mm (50.4 in)		
Tires	225/55 ZR 16		
Turning circle	10.75 meters (42.3 feet)		
Steering type and ratio	recirculating ball (3 turns); servo-assisted		
Weight	1770 kg (3894 lbs)	U.S.: 1880 kg (4145 lbs)	1980 kg (4356 lbs) U.S.: 2020 kg (4455 lbs)
Maximum speed	250 km/hr (156 mph)		
Acceleration	6.23 sec 0-100 km/hr		6.1 sec 0-60 mph
Fuel consumption	urban cycle: 16.6 liters; at 90 km/hr:10.1 l; 120 km/hr:12		20.2 liter urban; at 120 km/hr: 13.2 U.S.: 11/15 mpg
Fuel tank capacity	80 liters (21 gallons)		

The 300D 2.5 sedan, 1990, U.S. version

Prices and Production

The 300D 2.5 sedan sold in 1990 in the United States for $39,700

Production of the 300D 2.5 sedan [124D 25] (from October 1989 until August 1991)

was in 1989	6 units
1990	308 units
1991	209 units
total	523 units

The 350SDL sedan sold in 1990 in the United States for $56,800

Production of the 350SDL sedan [126d 35A] (from June 1989 until 1991)

was in 1989	18 units
1990	2,032 units
1991	875 units
total	2,925 units

The 350SDL sedan, 1990, U.S. version

Model 300D 2.5 (1989–1991)

D = Diesel

Two new diesel-powered models were introduced in early 1990 especially for the American market, where as many as 78.9% of sales were diesels at one time (1982). For two years no diesel models were offered because of some problems with the trap oxidizer units and ever more stringent and punitive emission controls. (The new engines did not use trap oxidizers.)

In fact, factory production of diesel-engined passenger cars decreased an alarming 36.7% (from a high of 209,999 units in 1986 to 132,830 in 1989) when total car production decreased only 8.7% (from 594,080 to 542,160 in the same period). It was imperative that a remedy was found to halt this appalling loss, and the two new remarkably cleaner and considerably quieter turbo-diesel powered models were the result.

The 300D 2.5 turbo diesel-engined model was similar to the 300E 2.6 gasoline powered model of the same year, using the W124 chassis. The five-cylinder diesel engine with 121 horse-power gave the car good acceleration, with 12.4 seconds for the 0-60 miles per hour. A four-speed transmission was fitted, and the torque was 165 lb/ft. With a fuel mileage of 33 miles per gallon, the new model was a most economical one.

Model 350SDL (1989–1991)

S = Super, D = Diesel, L = Lang (long wheelbase chassis)

The 350SDL diesel turbo shared the W126 body and as an S-Class model was opulently equipped. The six-cylinder engine was enlarged from the 3-liter unit to give 134 horsepower and 228 lb/ft torque as did the 420 V-8 gasoline unit. Acceleration was 11.4 seconds for the 0-60 miles per hour, and fuel mileage averaged 25 miles per gallon for the new model. It was a fine addition and would hopefully restore luxurious diesel models to their former prominence.

Specifications

	300D 2.5 turbo	350SDL Turbo
Engine type	5 cyl diesel, overhead camshaft, with turbo charger (OM602)	6 cyl diesel, overhead camshaft, with turbo charger (OM603)
Bore and stroke	87.0 x 84.0 mm (3.43 x 3.31 in)	89.0 x 92.4 mm (3.50 x 3.64 in)
Displacement	2497 cc (152.4 cu in)	3449 cc (210.5 cu in)
Power output	121 hp (SAE) 90 Kw @ 4600 rpm	134 hp (SAE) 100 Kw @ 4000 rpm
Compression ratio	21.5:1	22.2:1
Torque	165 ft/lb @ 2400 rpm	228 ft/lb @ 2000 rpm
Fuel injection	high pressure, mechanical Garrett T3 turbo	high pressure, mechanical Garrett T3 turbo
Maximum engine speed	4600 rpm	4600 rpm
Gear ratios	I. 4.25:1 (4-speed automatic) II. 2.41:1 III. 1.49:1 IV. 1.00:1	I. 3.87:1 (4-speed automatic) II. 2.25:1 III. 1.41:1 IV. 1.00:1
Rear axle ratio	2.65	2.82
Chassis	unit frame and body	unit frame and body
Suspension	shock absorber strut with anti-dive control, coil springs, anti-roll bar; multi-link independent rear, anti-dive, anti-squat control, coils, anti-roll bar	shock absorber strut with anti-dive control, coil springs, anti-roll bar; multi-link independent rear, anti-dive anti-squat control, coils, anti-roll bar
Brakes and area	hydraulic, dual circuit, discs; ABS system	hydraulic dual circuit, discs; ABS system
Wheelbase	110.2 in (2800 mm)	121.1 in (3075 mm)
Track, front/rear	59.1/58.7 in (1501/1491 mm)	61.5/60.4 in (1562/1534 mm)
Length	187.2 in (4755 mm)	208.1 in (3075 mm)
Width	68.5 in (1740 mm)	71.7 in (1820 mm)
Height	56.3 in (1431 mm)	56.7 in (1441 mm)
Tires	195/65 R15 91V	205/65 R15 94H
Turning circle	36.7 ft (11.2 meters)	40.6 ft (12.4 meters)
Steering type and ratio	recirculating ball (3 turns); servo-assisted, M-B power	recirculating ball (3 turns); servo-assisted, M-B power
Weight	3390 lbs (1535 kg)	3820 lbs (1730 kg)
Maximum speed	121 mph (195 km/hr)	109 mph (175 km/hr)
Acceleration	12.4 sec 0-60 mph	11.4 sec 0-60 mph
Fuel consumption	29 mpg, average (33 mpg highway)	24 mpg, average (25 mpg highway)
Fuel tank capacity	20.9 gallons (79 liters)	23.8 gallons (90 liters)

The 400E sedan, 1993

Model 400E (1991–   )

E (Einspritzung) = fuel injection

The 400E sedan was created in 1991 exclusively for the American Market. It was originally conceived in 1988, when several Japanese luxury cars were introduced and soon proved to be strong competitors in this country.

The 4.2-liter, twin overhead camshaft, 32 valve V-8 engine of 268 horsepower and 295 ft/lbs torque was installed in the regular W124 sedan body. It was somewhat less expensive than the more luxurious and faster 500E (with 322 hp). The projected price was $55,800, compared to the $79,200 for the 500E sedan.

The body had similar frame alterations to accommodate the larger engine, the wider drive shaft tunnel, the steering system and the front strut suspension and rear five-link suspension of the SL. Brakes were improved with four-piston front calipers and two rear, as in the 500E models. ABS was standard.

The 0-60 mph took 7.0 seconds with the four-speed automatic transmission. Weight was 3660 pounds (the six-cylinder car weighed 3315 lbs).

Prices and Production

The 500E sedan sold in 1992 for . . . . DM 134,520

The 500E sedan sold in the United States in 1992 for $79,200

Production of the 500E sedan [124] (from September 1990)

	was in 1990	46 units
	1991	2,566 units
	1992	4,416 units
E500	1993	1,596 units
	1994	1,735 units

The 400E sedan sold in 1992 for . . . . DM 92,340

The 400E sedan sold in the United States in 1992 for $55,800

Production of the 400E sedan [124] (from May 1991)

	was in 1991	1,155 units
	1992	7,655 units
E400	1993	7,577 units
	1994	4,867 units

Model 500E (1991–   )

E (Einspritzung) = fuel injection

The 500E model sedan was officially first shown at the 1990 Paris Automobile Salon in October. This limited production car had a slightly modified W124 body — modest fender flares and wider alloy wheels — and had the luxurious appointments of the CE and the S-class series, such as leather upholstery, automatic climate control, stereo casette and 10-speaker sound system with optional CD player, power front seats and steering column memory, airbags, knee bolster and tensioning seat belts.

The 500E was developed with the assistance of the Porsche engineers at Zuffenhausen, experts in sports car construction. The overall weight of the sedan was actually 400 pounds less than that of the 500SL sports car, and thus the performance with the same V-8 five-liter M119 engine of 326 horsepower, with double over head camshafts and four valves per cylinder and 332 lbs/ft of torque, was truly outstanding.

Specifications

	400E	500E
Engine type	V-8 cyl two overhead camshafts (M119)	V-8 cyl two overhead camshafts (M119)
Bore and stroke	92.0 x 78.9 mm (3.62 x 3.11 in)	96.5 x 85.0 mm (3.80 x 3.35 in)
Displacement	4196 cc (256.1 cu in)	4973 cc (303.5 cu in)
Power output	268 hp (SAE) 200 Kw @ 5700 rpm U.S.: 275 (SAE) hp	326 hp (DIN) 240 Kw @ 5700 rpm U.S.: 315 hp (SAE)
Compression ratio	10:1	10:1
Torque	295 ft/lb 400 Nm @ 3900 rpm	480 Nm (354.2 ft/lb) @ 3900 rpm U.S.: 347 ft/lb
Fuel injection	LH electronic	LH electronic
Maximum engine speed	6000 rpm	6000 rpm
Gear ratios	I. 3:87:1 (automatice) II. 2.25:1 III. 1.44:1 IV. 1.00:1	I. 3.87:1 (automatice) II. 2.25:1 III. 1.44:1 IV. 1.00:1
Rear axle ratio	2.24	2.82
Chassis	unit frame and body	unit frame and body
Suspension	double wishbones, anti-dive control, coil springs, anti-roll ball; multi-link independent, anti-squat and -lift control, coil springs, anti-roll bar	
Brakes and area		hydraulic; dual circuit discs; ABS system; 11.8/10.9 in
Wheelbase		110.2 in (2800 mm)
Track, front/rear		60.6/60.2 in (1538/1529 mm)
Length		187.0 in (4740 mm)
Width		68.5 in (1740 mm)
Height		56.9 in (1446 mm)
Tires	195/65 R-15 91 V	225/55 ZR-16
Turning Circle		44 feet (11.2 meters)
Steering type and ratio		recirculating ball; (3 turns); servo assisted
Weight	3660 lbs (1664 Kg) U.S. 1660 Kg (3652 lbs.) 1993: 3745 lbs	3745 lbs (1702 kg) U.S.: 3855 lbs (1750 kg)
Maximum speed	149 mph	260 km/hr (162 mph); special axle ratio: 177 mph (284 km/hr)
Acceleration	7.0 sec, 0-60 mph	6.1 sec 0-100 km/hr
Fuel consumption	U.S: city 16 mpg; highway 21 mpg	urban cycle: 17.5 liters; at 120 km/hr: 12.3 (U.S. 14/17 mpg)
Fuel tank capacity		90 liters (23.8 gallons)

The 350SD sedan, 1991

Prices and Production

The 350SD sedan sold in the United States in 1992 for $69,400

Production of the 350SD [140] (from September 1990/January 1991)

	was in 1990	3 units
	1991	615 units
	1992	1,314 units
S350	1993	6,784 units
	1994	5,541 units

The 300SE sedan sold in 1992 for . . . . DM 91,696

The 300SEL sedan sold in 1992 for . . . . DM 95,247

The 300SEL sedan sold in the United States in 1992 for $69,400

Production of the 300SE sedan [140] (from March 1990)

	was in 1990	29 units
	1991	17,340 units
	1992	24,099 units
S300	1993	10,644 units
	1994	9,901 units

Production of the 300SEL sedan [140] (from March 1990)

	was in 1990	27 units
	1991	3,657 units
	1992	9,412 units
	1993	12,529 units
	1994	13,485 units

Model 350SD (1990–   )

S = Super, D = Diesel

The 350SD diesel-engined sedan shared the new W140 body style with the other S-class gasoline models. As before, this powerful 6-cylinder 3.5 turbo-charged diesel engine of 150 horsepower at 4,100 rpm, with a torque of 229 lbs/ft (310 Nm) — the very same as the 300SE gasoline model, which also carried the same price tag — was sufficient to allow the 4,574 pounds sedan quite vigorous acceleration to do the 0-100 km/hr at 12.9 seconds and gave it a maximum cruising speed of 115 miles per hour. Never before had a diesel been so capable.

Built especially for the North American market, this model shared, of course, the sumptuous appointments of the entire luxury line of cars, and with the truly fabulous economical fuel mileage (23 mpg) was a most desirable alternative choice, particularily for long distance travel.

Model 300SE/SEL (1991–   )

S = Super, E (Einspritzung) = fuel injection, L = long wheelbase

The 300SE and 300SEL were the least expensive of the new S-class models, introduced at the Geneva Auto Show in 1991.

These new W140 body styles had undergone a subtle change over the previous W126 line, maintaining the traditional elegance of the upper-class Mercedes models. The newly designed grille was more slanted and flowing lines were smoother, making for a pleasing surfaced silhouette with the high windows.

Again, as in earlier years of body style changes, when the W126 style replaced the W116 S-class line, the drag coefficient was improved and now was C_d 0.30 against the former 0.37. The new models were also larger, allowing for the increased size in human beings — two inches since 1976 — over the years.

The interior headroom was increased by 1.9 inches and the cars were 2.3 inches taller. They were also 2.6 inches wider, allowing for an interior width increase of 5.5 inches. Door openings were about three inches wider.

The newly designed, modified M104.990 six-cylinder engine with 24 valves, based on the earlier one, was enlarged to displace 3,199 cc and produce 231 hp. It was adapted to the LH jetronic system. An adjustment mechanism on the drive of the intake camshaft was provided.

Three different transmissions were available. The five-speed manual was standard, with four- or five speed automatic an optional. The American version had only the four-speed automatic.

Specifications

	350SD	300SE	300SEL
Engine type	6 cyl diesel, overhead camshaft, with turbo charger (OM603)	6 cyl two overhead camshafts (M104)	
Bore and stroke	89.0 x 92.4 mm (3.50 x 3.64 in)	89.9 x 84.0 mm (3.55 x 3.32 in)	
Displacement	3449 cc (210.5 cu in)	3199 cc (195.2 cu in)	
Power output	150 hp (DIN) 110 Kw @ 4000 rpm U.S.: 148 hp (SAE) 110 Kw	231 hp (DIN) 170 Kw @ 5800 rpm U.S.: 228 hp (SAE)	
Compression ratio	22:1	10.0:1	
Torque	310 Nm U.S.: 229 ft/lb 229 NM = 2200 rpm	310 Nm (228.8 ft/lb) @ 4100 rpm	
Fuel injection	high pressure, mechanical Garret T3 turbo	LH electronic	
Maximum engine speed	4750 rpm U.S.: 4250 rpm	6700 rpm	
Gear ratios	I. 4:25:1 (4- speed automatice) II. 2.41:1 III. 1.49:1 IV. 1.00:1	I. 4.15:1 (manual) I. 3.87.1 (optional) II. 2.52:1 II. 2.25:1 III. 1.69:1 III. 1.44:1 IV. 1.24:1 IV. 1.00:1 V. 1.00:1	I. 3.87:1 (automatic) II. 2.25:1 III. 1.44:1 IV. 1.00:1 V. 0.75:1
Rear axle ratio	2.82	3.46 (standard) 3.46 (optional) 3.69 (five-speed automatic)	
Chassis	unit frame and body	unit frame and body	
Suspension	double wishbones, anti-dive control, coil springs, anti-roll ball; multi-link independent, anti-squat and -lift control, coil springs, anti-roll bar		
Brakes and area	hydraulic; dual circuit discs; ABS system	hydraulic; dual circuit discs; ABS system	
Wheelbase	3040 mm (119.7 in)	3040 mm (119.7 in)	3140 mm (123.6 in)
Track, front/rear	1603/1576 mm (63.1/63.0 in)	1602/1574 mm (63.1/62.0 in)	
Length	5113 mm (201.2 in)	5113 mm (201.2 in)	5213 mm (205.2 in)
Width	1886 mm (74.2 in)	1886 mm (74.2 in)	
Height	1485 mm (58.5 in)	1492 mm (58.7 in)	
Tires	235/60 R 16 U.S.: 225/60 R 16 97V	225/60 R 16 H2	
Turning Circle	12.18 meters	12.18 meters	12.51 meters
Steering type and ratio	recirculating ball; (3 turns); servo assisted, 14.02 ratio	recirculating ball; (3 turns); servo assisted, 14.02 ratio	
Weight	1940 kg (4268 lbs) U.S. 2075 Kg (4575 lbs)	1890 kg (4458 lbs) U.S.: 2050 kg (4520 lbs)	1900 kg (4180 lbs)
Maximum speed	185 km/hr (115 mph)	230 km/hr 5-speed, 225 km/hr 4-speed and automatic	
Acceleration	12.9 sec, 0-100 km/hr	8.9 sec, 8.6 sec 0-100 km/hr	
Fuel consumption	urban cycle: 11.7 liters; at 120 km/hr: 9.7 liters U.S.: city 20 mpg; highway 23mpg	urban cycle: 17.6 liters, automatic: 15.8 liters; at 120 km/hr: 12.2	U.S.: city 15 mpg; highway 19 mpg
Fuel tank capacity	100 liters (26.5 gallons)	100 liters (26.5 gallons)	

The 400SE sedan, 1993

Prices and Production

The 400SE sedan sold in 1992 for . . . . DM 116,377
The 400SE sedan sold in the United States in 1992 for $77,900
The 400SEL sedan sold in 1992 for . . . . DM 120,042

Production of the 400SE sedan [140] (from August 1990)

was in 1990		10 units
	1991	4,650 units
	1992	4,862 units
S420	1993	841 units
	1994	1,068 units

Production of the 400SEL sedan [140] (from June 1990)

was in 1990		11 units
	1991	831 units
	1992	5,177 units
S420	1993	5,140 units
	1994	5,410 units

The 500SE sedan sold in 1992 for . . . . DM 124,813
The 500SEL sedan sold in 1992 for . . . . DM 131,214
The 500SEL sedan sold in the United States in 1992 for $93,500

Production of the 500SE sedan [140] (from March 1990)

was in 1990		20 units
	1991	3,729 units
	1992	6,236 units
S500	1993	1,943 units
	1994	2,729 units

Production of the 500SEL sedan [140] (from March 1990)

was in 1990		40 units
	1991	8,196 units
	1992	12,662 units
S500	1993	8,774 units
	1994	8,627 units

Model 400SE/SEL (1991–   )

S = Super, E (Einspritzung) = fuel injection, L = long wheelbase

The 400SE and 400SEL models, also introduced at the Geneva Auto Show in 1991, had the smaller of the two available V-8 engines. The four-liter engine displaced actually 4,196 cc and developed 286 hp at 5,700 rpm.

The S-class body was, of course, the same as in the other models of that line, with exterior and interior features practically indistinguishable from each other. The cars were heavier than the ones they replaced. Considerably thicker steel was used in the panels for greater protection, and 69% of all panels were galvanized. The body work was protected from damage by self-generating bumpers and side moldings which could be finished in a dozen paint shades, with upper surfaces trimmed with steel and chrome.

The 400 line cars weighed 1990 kg and 2000 kg, respectively, but the acceleration of 7.6/7.7 seconds for the 0-60 mph (100 km) and a maximum speed of 153 mph (245 km/hr) were quite remarkable and appreciably better than the figures for the V-8 engined 218 hp 420SEC (9.0 seconds and 126 mph; and 1600 kg weight).

All cars for the American market were somewhat heavier still, because of the added features and required safety items. The 400SE model weighed here 330 pounds more, 4720 pounds, yet the acceleration figures remained the same.

Model 500SE/SEL (1991–   )

S = Super, E (Einspritzung) = fuel injection, L = long wheelbase

The 500SE and 500SEL sedans were another version of the S-class models, first publicly shown at the Geneva Auto Show in 1991.

Powered by a V-8 engine, based on the 400 unit, but with a longer stroke, bigger bore and shorter rods in the same block, it developed 326 horsepower. The intake manifold was refined and improved fuel injection gave it actually better torque, by 37 ft/lbs, than the engine of the 5.6 liter 560SL.

The 500SE and 500SEL weighed 2000 kg and 2010 kg respectively, and the acceleration was 6.6/6.7 seconds for the 0-100 km/hr (62 mph) with a top speed of 250 km/hr (156 mph).

Specifications

	400SE	400SEL	500SE	500SEL
Engine type	V-8 cyl four overhead camshafts (M119)		V-8 cyl four verhead camshafts (M119)	
Bore and stroke	92.0 x 78.9 mm (3.62 x 3.11 in)		96.5 x 85.0 mm (3.80 x 3.35 in)	
Displacement	4196 cc (256 cu in)		4973 cc (303.4 cu in)	
Power output	286 hp (DIN) 210 Kw @ 5700 rpm	1993. U.S. 275 (SEA) hp	326 hp (DIN) 240 Kw @ 5700 rpm	1993: U.S.: 315 hp (SAE) @ 5600 rpm
Compression ratio	10.0:1		10.0:1	
Torque	410 Nm (302.6 ft/lb) @ 3900 rpm	U.S.: 295 ft/lb	480 Nm (354.2 ft/lb) @ 3900 rpm	U.S.: 347 ft/lb
Fuel injection	LH electronic		LH electronic	
Maximum engine speed	6000 rpm		6000 rpm	
Gear ratios	I. 3.87:1 (automatic) II. 2.25:1 III. 1.44:1 IV. 1.00:1		I. 3.87:1 (automatic) II. 2.25:1 III. 1.44:1 IV. 1.00:1	
Rear axle ratio	2.82		2.65	
Chassis	unit frame and body		unit frame and body	
Suspension	double wishbones, anti-dive control, coil springs, anti-roll bar; multi-link independent, ant-squat and -lift control, coil springs, anti-roll bar			
Brakes and area	hydraulic, dual circuit discs; ABS system		hydraulic; dual circuit discs; ABS system	
Wheelbase	3040 mm (119.7 in)	3140 mm (123.6 in)	3040 mm (119.7 in)	3140 mm (123.6 in)
Track, front/rear	1602/1574 mm (63.1/62.0 in)		1602/1574 mm (63.1/62.0 in)	
Length	5113 mm (201.2 in)	5213 mm (205.2 in)	5113 mm (201.2 in)	5213 mm (205.2 in)
Width	1886 mm (74.2 in)		1886 mm (74.2 in)	
Height	1495 mm (58.8 in)		1495 mm (58.8 in)	
Tires	235/60 ZR 16		235/60 ZR 16	
Turning Circle	12.18 meters	12.51 meters	12.18 meters	12.51 meters
Steering type and ratio	recirculating ball (3 turns); servo assisted 14.02 ratio		recirculating ball; (3 turns); servo assiste	
Weight	1990 kg (4158 lbs) U.S.: 2140 kg (4720 lbs)	2000 kg (4400 lbs) U.S.: 4740 lbs	2000 kg (4400 lbs)	2010 kg (4422 lbs) U.S.: 2150 kg (4740 lbs)
Maximum speed	245 km/hr (153 mph)		250 km/hr (156 mph)	
Acceleration	7.6 sec 0-100 km/hr	7.7 sec 0-100 km/hr U.S.: 8.1 sec	6.6 sec 0-100 km/hr	6.7 sec 0-100 km/hr
Fuel consumption	urban cycle; 16.7 liters; at 120 km/hr: 12.3 U.S.: city 13 mpg; highway 17 mpg		urban cycle: 17.9 liters	U.S.: city 13 mpg; highway 16 mpg
Fuel tank capacity	100 liters (26.5 gallons)		100 liters (26.5 gallons)	

The 600SE sedan, 1991

Model 600SE/SEL (1991–   )

S = Super, E (Einspritzung) = fuel injection, L = long wheelbase

The 600SE and 600SEL models were the most prestigious of the S-class cars introduced at the Geneva Auto Show in 1991. As the "flagship" of the current Mercedes automobiles, these cars were in the tradition of the 600 Grand Mercedes of some years back.

Powered by the new 12 cylinder V type engine which developed 408 horsepower and torque of 428 ft/lbs, the cars had ADS (adaptive damping system) and hydropneumatic springing, the ABS (anti-lock braking system).

Powered by the new V-12 cylinder engine with four overhead camshafts and four valves per cylinder, and variable intake valve timing, it develops 408 horsepower at 5200 rpm. Torque is 428 lbs/ft at 3800 rpm. A two-chamber self-adjustable oil pump was fitted to conserve power. Newly developed LH jetronic fuel injection was used. The highly sophisticated computer controlling six electronic control units make for optimum operation.

The interior was, of course, the most elegant of the S-class models, with such features as twelve-way, three memory, power front seats, driver and front passenger air bags, anti-theft alarm, and an improved automatic climate control using a charcoal filter to eliminate irritating particles from entering.

Performance of the rather heavy (2,190 kg or 4,818 lbs) 600SEL sedan was quite outstanding with acceleration of 0-100 km/hr (62 mph) at 6.1 seconds and a maximum speed at a controlled 250 km/hr (156 mph).

The 600 models were superior automobiles in every way of the highest technological art with superb performance, and were prestige cars in the best tradition of the Grand Mercedes.

The 600SE sedan sold in 1992 for . . . . DM 201,364

The 600SEL sedan sold in 1992 for . . . . DM 204,231

The 600SEL sedan sold in the United States in 1992 for $127,800

Production of the 600 SE sedan [140] (from October 1990)

was in	1990	3 units
	1991	1,590 units
	1992	835 units
S600	1993	221 units
	1994	285 units

Production of the 600SEL sedan [140] (from May 1990)

was in	1990	25 units
	1991	7,852 units
	1992	7,497 units
S600	1993	3,165 units
	1994	3,615 units

Specifications

	600SE	600SEL
Engine type	V-12 cyl four overhead camshafts (M120)	
Bore and stroke	89.0 x 80.2 mm (3.50 x 3.16 in)	
Displacement	5987 cc (365.2 cu in)	
Power output	408 hp (DIN) 300 Kw @ 5200 rpm	1993. U.S. 389 (SEA) hp
Compression ratio	10.0:1	
Torque	580 Nm (428.0 ft/lb) @ 3800 rpm	U.S.: 420 ft/lb
Fuel injection	LH electronic	
Maximum engine speed	6000 rpm	
Gear ratios	I. 3.87:1 (automatic) II. 2.25:1 III. 1.44:1 IV. 1.00:1	
Rear axle ratio	2.65	U.S.: 2.64
Chassis	unit frame and body	
Suspension	double wishbones, anti-dive control, coil springs, anti-roll bar, multi-link independent, anti-squat and -lift control, coil springs, anti-roll bar	
Brakes and area	hydraulic, dual circuit discs; ABS system	
Wheelbase	3040 mm (119.7 in)	3140 mm (123.6 in)
Track, front/rear	1602/1574 mm (63.1/62.0 in)	
Length	5113 mm (201.2 in)	5213 mm (205.2 in)
Width	1886 mm (74.2 in)	
Height	1490 mm (58.6 in)	
Tires	235/60 ZR 16	
Turning Circle	12.18 meters	12.51 meters
Steering type and ratio	recirculating ball (3 turns); servo assisted, 14.02 ratio	
Weight	2180 kg (4796 lbs)	2190 kg (4818 lbs) U.S. 2260 kg (4985 lbs)
Maximum speed	250 km/hr (156 mph)	
Acceleration	6.0 sec 0-60 mph	6.1 sec. 0-60 mph U.S.: 6.3 sec
Fuel consumption	urban cycle; 20.7 liters; at 120 km/hr: 13.7	U.S.: city 11 mpg; highway 15 mpg
Fuel tank capacity	100 liters (26.5 gallons)	

The 600SEC coupe, 1992

Model 500SEC (1992–)

S = Super, E (Einspritzung) = fuel injection, C = Coupe

The 500SEC was the smaller engined version of the similar model introduced at the North American International Auto Show (Detroit) in January 1992 and at the Geneva Show in March. It had the very same styling as the more powerful model, but was equipped with the 5-liter V-8 engine with four camshafts and four valves per cylinder. There was but slightly less performance with the 0-60 acceleration, 6.7 seconds, and the same maximum electronically limited 250 km/hr. Practically all other features and equipment were the same superb quality as those in the more powerful model.

Model 600SEC (1992–)

S = Super, E (Einspritzung) = fuel injection, C = Coupe

The 600SEC was introduced to the New World at the 1992 Auto Show in Detroit. It was again based on the S-class models of the previous year and probably even more luxurious. The body style was new, yet the grille was the same as the earlier W126 coupe, but the headlights were more advantageously styled. The powerful V-12 engine with four camshafts and four valves per cylinder gives the coupe truly outstanding performance, with 6.1 seconds for the 0-60 mph acceleration.

The car is equipped with the ASR (automatic slip control), ADS (adaptive damping system), and ABS (anti-lock braking system). As in the past, in technical specifications the 600SEC shares practically all interior features with the largest S-class sedans. The coupe is a splendid and worthy flagship of the line of Mercedes automobiles.

Prices and Production

The 600SEC coupe sold in 1992 for . . . . DM 220,020

The 600SEC coupe sold in the United States in 1992 for $132,000

Production of the 600SEC coupe [126] (from January 1992)

was in 1992	307 units
S600C 1993	2,915 units
1994	1,585 units

The 500SEC coupe sold in 1992 for . . . . DM 157,548

Production of the 500SEC coupe [126] (from January 1992)

was in 1992	189 units
S500C 1993	3,743 units
1994	2,656 units

Specifications

	500SEC	600SEC
Engine type	V-8 cyl two overhead camshafts (M119)	V-12 cyl four overhead camshafts (M120)
Bore and stroke	96.5 x 85.0 mm (3.80 x 3.35 in)	89.0 x 80.2 mm (3.50 x 3.16 in)
Displacement	4973 cc (303.5 cu in)	5987 cc (365.2 cu in)
Power output	326 hp (DIN) 240Kw @ 5700 rpm U.S.: 315 hp @ 5600 rpm	408 hp (DIN) 3000 Kw @ 5200 rpm U.S.: 389 hp
Compression ratio	10.0:1	10.0:1
Torque	480 Nm (354.2 ft/lb) @ 3900 rpm U.S.: 347 ft/lb	580 Nm (428.0 ft/lb) @ 3800 rpm U.S.: 420 ft/lb
Fuel injection	LH electronic	LH electronic
Maximum engine speed	6000 rpm	6000 rpm
Gear ratios	I. 3.87:1 II. 2.25:1 III. 1.44:1 IV. 1.00:1	I. 3.87:1 II. 2.25:1 III. 1.44:1 IV. 1:00:1
Rear axle ratio	2.82 U.S.: 2.65	2.65
Chassis	unit frame and body	unit frame and body
Suspension	double wishbones, anti-dive control, coil springs, anti-roll bar; multi-link independent, anti-squat and -lift control, coil springs, anti-roll bar	
Brakes and area	hydraulic, dual circuit discs; ABS system; 11.8/10.9 in.	
Wheelbase	2945 mm (115.9 in)	
Track, front/rear	1603/1576 mm (63.1/62.0 in)	
Length	5067 mm (199.4 in)	
Width	1912 mm (75.3 in)	
Height	1455 mm (57.3 in)	
Tires	235/60 ZR 16	
Turning circle	11.89 meters (47 feet)	
Steering type and ratio	recirculating ball (3.3 turns); servo assisted	
Weight	4785 lb/(2170 kg)	5075 lb/(2300 kg)
Maximum speed	250 km/hr (156 mph) electronically controlled	
Acceleration	6.7 sec 0-100 km/hr U.S.: 7.2 sec	6.1 sec 0-100 km/hr U.S.: 6.3 sec
Fuel consumption	urban cycle: 17;.9 liters; U.S.: 13/16 mpg	city: 11 mpg; highway 15 mpg
Fuel tank capacity	100 liters (26.5 gallons)	

The 220E sedan, 1993

Prices and Production

The 220E sedan sold in 1992 for . . . . DM 52,041

Production of the 220E sedan [124] (from July 1991/January 1992)

was in 1991	1 unit
1992	11,753 units
E220 1993	41,735 units
1994	33,746 units

Production of the 200E sedan from January 1992

was in 1992	12,251 units
E200 1993	32,836 units
1994	23,428 units
E200 Cabrio 1993	231 units
1994	2,214 units

Model 200E (1992–)

E (Einspritzung) = fuel injection

The 200E sedan was one of several new models which were offered to fill the specific demand of a smaller engined car with the popular 124 body. This, the smaller of the two newly designed four cylinder engines (of 1,998 cc) with four valves per cylinder, developed 136 horsepower and 190 Nm torque and gave the 1,410 kg car a maximum speed of 200 km/hr (125 mph) and an economical fuel consumption of 9.6 liter average for the 100 kilometers distance.

The designation remained as that of the earlier 200E model, introduced in 1985, but now got the newer and more powerful engine.

New page

Model 220E (1992–)

E (Einspritzung) = fuel injection

The 220E sedan had a slightly larger four cylinder engine (2,199 cc) than the 200E, and consequently more power. The unit produced 150 horsepower and 210 Nm torque. Performance was somewhat better than that of the 2-liter engined sedan, and the maximum speed was 210 km/hr (131 mph), with still excellent fuel economy of 10.1 liter for the 100 km distance (23.5 mpg).

The 220E was made available to give customers a wider choice of this tremendously popular 124 bodied sedan, now with the new 4-valve per cylinder four cylinder engines and two new six-cylinder, all with four valves per cylinder and consequently more power than the earlier engines.

Specifications

	220E	200E
Engine type	4 cyl overhead camshaft (M102)-4V	
Bore and stroke	87.0 x 92.4 mm (3.43 x 3.64 in)	89.9 x 86.6 mm (3.5 x 3.16 in)
Displacement	2199 cc 110 Kw	1997 cc (121.9 cu in)
Power output	150 hp (DIN) 142 Kw @ 5500 rpm	136 hp (DIN) 100 Kw @ 5500 rpm
Compression ratio	10.0:1	
Torque	210 Nm @ 4000 rpm	190 Nm @ 4000 rpm
Fuel injection	microprocess HFM	
Maximum engine speed	6200 rpm	
Gear ratios	I. 3.91:1 manual I. 4.25:1 automatic II. 2.17:1 II. 2.41:1 III. 1.37:1 III. 1.49:1 IV. 1.00:1 IV. 1:00:1 V. 0.81:1	
Rear axle ratio	3.67 3.07 automatic	
Chassis	unit frame and body	
Suspension	shock absorber strut with anti-dive control, coil springs, anti-roll bar; multi-link independent rear, anti-dive, anti-squat control, coils, anti-roll bar	
Brakes and area	hydraulic dual circuit discs; 262/258 mm	
Wheelbase	2800 mm	
Track, front/rear	1501/1491 mm	
Length	4740 mm	
Width	1740 mm	
Height	1431 mm	
Tires	195/65 R 15 91 V	
Turning circle	11.27 meters	
Steering type and ratio	recirculating ball (3.3 turns) servo assisted	
Weight	1370 kg	
Maximum speed	210 km/hr manual; 205 km/hr automatic	200 km/hr (125 mph)
Acceleration	10.6 sec 0-100 km/hr	0-100 km/hr: 12.2 sec
Fuel consumption	city: 11.7 liters; highway: 8.2; automatic: 11.2/8.6	9.6 liter average
Fuel tank capacity	70 liters	

The 320E sedan, 1993

Model 280E (1992–   )

E (Einspritzung) = fuel injection

The 280E sedan was one of the two models which had the newly developed six-cylinder engines. This model had the highly popular 124 body style and was offered to augment the middle class line.

With the four valves per cylinder the 2.8-liter engine of 197 hp gave the 280E a fine performance, doing the 0-100 km/hr acceleration in 9.1 seconds and giving a maximum speed of 230 km/hr (144 mph).

Model 320E (1992–   )

E (Einspritzung) = fuel injection

The 320E was the other 124 body style with the new six cylinder engine. Developed from the 300E-24 unit, the 3.2 liter engine was then reduced to 2.8 liters for the other model. Special features were the engine management system for ignition and injection, direct ignition as well as a variable inlet manifold which increases torque in the lower and middle engine speed ranges, combined with the reliable four-valve technology and variable inlet camshaft control.

The 124 body style, first introduced in 1985, proved to be one of the most popular offerings and, in 1993, the factory produced 13 different size engines for the sedans and 9 for the station wagons, a considerably wider range than the compact or S-class lines. (A total of 79 models and 8 new ones were built in 1992.)

The new engines showed a substantial increase in power and torque in the low and medium range of engine speeds, and subsequently gave greater dynamic performance, increase in cruising speeds and favorable fuel economy as well as an appreciable reduction in emission, by ingenious engineering refinements.

Prices and Production

The 280E sedan sold in 1992 for . . . . DM 60,477

Production of the 280E sedan [124] (from January 1992)

was in 1992	7,327 units, long 35 units, chassis 24 units
E280 1993	26,192 units, long 216 units, chassis 113 units
1994	16,342 units, long 128 units, chassis 104 units

The 320E sedan sold in 1992 for . . . . DM 69,483

Production of the 320E sedan [124] (from January 1992)

was in 1992	7,446 units
E320 1993	20,945 units
1994	24,567 units

Specifications

	280E		320E	
Engine type	6 cyl overhead camshaft (M103) -4V			
Bore and stroke	89.9 x 73.5mm		89.9 x 84.0mm	
Displacement	2799 cc		3199 cc	
Power output	193 hp (DIN) 142 Kw @ 5500 rpm		220 hp (DIN) 162 Kw @ 5500 rpm	
Compression ratio	10:1			
Torque	270 Nm @ 3750 rpm		310 Nm @ 3750 rpm	
Fuel injection	microprocess HFM			
Maximum engine speed	6400 rpm			
Gear ratios	I. 3.86:1 manual II. 2.18:1 III. 1.38:1 IV. 1.00:1 V. 0.80:1	I. 3.87:1 automatic II. 2.25:1 III. 1.44:1 IV. 1:00:1	I. 4.15:1 manual II. 2.52:1 III. 1.69:1 IV. 1.24:1 V. 1.00:1	I. 3.87:1 automatic II. 2.25:1 III. 1.44:1 IV. 1.00:1 V. 0.75:1
Rear axle ratio	3.69 3.06 automatic			
Chassis	unit frame and body			
Suspension	shock absorber strut with anti-dive control, coil springs, anti-roll bar; multi-link independent rear, anti-dive, anti-squat control, coils, anti-roll bar			
Brakes and area	hydraulic dual circuit discs; ABS			
Wheelbase	2800 mm			
Track, front/rear	1501/1491 mm			
Length	4740 mm			
Width	1740 mm			
Height	1431 mm			
Tires	195/65 R 15 91V		195/65 ZR 15	
Turning circle	11.27 meters			
Steering type and ratio	recirculating ball; servo assisted			
Weight	1490 kg			
Maximum speed	230 km/hr; 225 km/hr automatic		235 km/hr; 230 km/hr automatic	
Acceleration	9.1 sec 0-100 km/hr; 8.8 sec automatic		8.3 sec; 7.9 sec automatic	
Fuel consumption	city: 14.6 liters; highway: 9.6 13.3 liters; 10.3 automatic		14.7 liters; 10 liters; 14.6 liters; 10.1 liters automatic	
Fuel tank capacity	70 liters			

The 280TE station wagon, 1992

Model 280TE (1992–)

T = Station wagon, E (Einspritzung) = fuel injection

The 280TE station wagon was a natural to have the new 2.8-liter engine installed. This entire line, with already seven different power units available, was a good selling development, going back to 1977 with the introduction of the 123 body style.

The engine was identical to that of the 280E sedan and gave the hundred kilograms heavier wagon still good performance, with 9.4 seconds for the 0-100 km/hr (9.1 for the sedan) and a maximum speed of 218 km/hr (230 for the sedan).

Model 320TE (1992–)

T = Station wagon, E (Einspritzung) = fuel injection

The 320TE station wagon was powered by the other of the two new engines, the larger 3.2-liter unit. Here, again, it seemed only natural that this engine would be made available in the fast selling station wagon, as it was in the sedan line.

And as in the sedans, performance was somewhat better than that of the 2.8 wagon. Acceleration was a bit more brisk, 9.2 seconds for the 0-100 km/hr time, than the 9.4 seconds, and maximum speed was slightly better, too, with 225 km/hr (235 for the sedan).

It was another example of the company offering the widest range in power in their vehicles, sedans as well as station wagons.

Prices and Production

The 280TE stationwagon sold in 1992 for . . . . DM 67,659

Production of the 280TE stationwagon [124] (from 1992)

was in 1992	729 units
E280T 1993	3,465 units
1994	3,768 units

The 320TE stationwagon sold in 1992 for . . . . DM 76,323

Production of the 320TE stationwagon [124] (from 1992)

was in 1992	1,709 units
E320T 1993	4,798 units
1994	6,439 units

Specifications

	280TE	320TE
Engine type	6 cyl overhead camshaft (M103) -4V	
Bore and stroke	89.9 x 73.5mm	89.9 x 84.0mm
Displacement	2799 cc	3199 cc
Power output	193 hp (DIN) 142 Kw @ 5500 rpm	220 hp (DIN) 162 Kw @ 5500 rpm
Compression ratio	10:1	
Torque	270 Nm @ 3750 rpm	310 Nm @ 3750 rpm
Fuel injection	microprocess HFM	
Maximum engine speed	6400 rpm	
Gear ratios	I. 3.86:1 man. / I. 4.25:1 man. / I. 3.87.1 auto. II. 2.18:1 / II. 2.41:1 / II. 2.25:1 III. 1.38:1 / III. 1.49:1 / III. 1.44:1 IV. 1.00:1 / IV. 1:00:1 / IV. 1.00:1 V. 0.88:1	I. 4.15:1 man. / I. 3.87:1 man. / I. 3.87:1 auto. II. 2.25:1 / II. 2.25:1 / II. 2.25:1 III. 1.69:1 / III. 1.44:1 / III. 1.44:1 IV. 1.24:1 / IV. 1.00:1 / IV. 1.00:1 V. 1.00:1 / V. 0.75:1
Rear axle ratio	3.69 3.09 automatic	
Chassis	unit frame and body	
Suspension	shock absorber strut with anti-dive control, coil springs, anti-roll bar; multi-link independent rear, anti-dive, anti-squat control, coils, anti-roll bar	
Brakes and area	hydraulic dual circuit discs; ABS	
Wheelbase	2800 mm	
Track, front/rear	1497/1485 mm	1497/1488 mm
Length	4740 mm	
Width	1740 mm	
Height	1490 mm	
Tires	195/65 R 15 91V	195/65 ZR 15
Turning circle	11.27 meters	
Steering type and ratio	recirculating ball; servo assisted	
Weight	1590 kg	
Maximum speed	218 km/hr; 213 km/hr automatic	225 km/hr; 220 km/hr automatic
Acceleration	9.4 sec 0-100 km/hr	9.2 sec 0-100 km/hr; 9.3 automatic
Fuel consumption	city: 14.8 liters; highway: 10.3; 13.6/10.9 automatic	city: 15.1 liters; highway: 10.9; 14.6/11.4 automatic
Fuel tank capacity	70 liters	

The SL320 roadster, U.S. version, 1994

Model SL280 (1992–   )

S = Sports, L (Leicht) = Light

Introduced in early 1993, the SL280 was another variation in the highly popular sports car line. This model was the smallest-engined version of the SLs, giving the buyer a wide choice and a wide price range in the SLs.

The new, modern high torque, four valve technology six-cylinder engine with a variable intake manifold, an electro hydraulically adjustable intake camshaft and a microprocessor-controlled injection and ignition system, was especially designed to produce high torque at low revolutions, and with the lowest possible level of emissions.

This straight six-cylinder four valve 2,799 cubic centimeter engine developed 193 hp and 270 Nm of torque, and gave the car a maximum speed of 230 km/hr (144 mph). Fuel consumption (the average of all three speed cycles) was merely 11 liters per 100 km (62 miles) or 21.5 miles per gallon.

Prices and Production

Production of the SL280 coupe [R129]
was in	1992	3 units
	1993	1,927 units
	1994	2,961 units

The SL320 sold in the United States for $85,200

Production of the SL320 coupe [R129]
was in	1992	3 units
	1993	4,688 units
	1994	6,795 units

Model SL320 (1992–   )

S = Sports, L = Light

The SL320 had a slightly larger six-cylinder engine, displacing 3,199 cc and developing 231 hp and 315 Nm torque. The power unit was quite similar to the smaller one, had the modern four-valve and high torque technology and gave this SL model a somewhat better all-around performance. Fuel consumption was nearly identical, 8.5 liters for the 100 km at 90 km/hr, against the 8.2 liters. A 5-speed automatic transmission was fitted.

The SL320 was available in this country, and along with the eight-cylinder SL500 and the twelve-cylinder SL600 offered an excellent choice to the buyer of one of these fine sports cars.

Compared with the 300SL, which it replaced, this car had about the same horse-power but at a much lower engine speed (5600 to 6300 rpm) and a higher torque (315 Nm to the former 272 Nm) also at a lower rpm (3,750 to 4,600). Fuel consumption was also improved (14.4 liters to 16.2; or 16.2 mpg to 14.5).

Specifications

	SL 280	SL 320
Engine type	6 cyl overhead camshaft (M103) 4V	
Bore and stroke	89.9 x 73.5 mm	89.9 x 84.0 mm
Displacement	2799 cc	3199 cc
Power output	193 hp (DIN) 142 Kw @ 5500 rpm	231 hp (DIN) 170 Kw @ 5600 rpm U.S.: 228 hp
Compression ratio	10.0:1	
Torque	270 Nm @ 3750 rpm	315 Nm @ 3750 rpm U.S.: 232 ft/lbs
Fuel injection	Microprocess HFM	
Maximum engine speed	6400 rpm	
Gear ratios	I. 3.86:1 manual I. 3.87 automatic II. 2.18:1 II. 2.25:1 III. 1.38:1 III. 1.44:1 IV. 1.00:1 IV. 1:00:1 V. 0.80:1 V. 0.75:1	
Rear axle ratio	3.92	3.69
Chassis	unit frame and body	
Suspension	shock absorber strut with anti-dive control, coil spring, anti-roll bar; multi-link independent rear, anti-dive, anti-squat control, coils	
Brakes and area	hydraulic dual circuit disks; ABS	
Wheelbase	2515 mm	
Track, front/rear	1535/1523 mm	
Length	4470 mm	
Width	1812 mm	
Height	1293 mm	
Tires	225/55 ZR 16	
Turning circle	10.75 meters	
Steering type and ratio	recirculating ball: servo assisted	
Weight	1760 kg	1780 kg (3916 lbs)
Maximum speed	225 km/hr; 230 km/hr automatic	240 km/hr (150 mph)
Acceleration	9.3 sec 0-100 km/hr; 9.5 sec automatic	8.4 sec 0-100 km/hr
Fuel consumption	city: 15.0 liters; highway: 9.9; 13.8 liters automatic	city: 14.4 liters; highway 10 liters
Fuel tank capacity	80 liters	

The 300SE 2.8 sedan, 1993

Prices and Production

The 300SE 2.8 sedan sold in 1993 for . . . . DM 79,002

Production of the 300SE 2.8 sedan [140] (from December 1992)

was in 1992	9 units
S280 1993	3,675 units
1994	6,058 units

The C36 sedan sold in 1994 for . . . . DM 97,348

The C36 sedan sold in the United States in 1995 for $49,800

The C36 sedan U.S. version, 1995

Model 300SE 2.8 (1992–　　)

S = Super, E (Einspritzung) = fuel injection

The 300SE 2.8 sedan was introduced at the March 1993 Geneva Auto Show as an expansion of the S-class range for customers who preferred an economical car, yet an elegant model.

The new engine, displacing 2.8 liters, had 193 horsepower at only 5500 rpm and a torque of 270 Nm at only 3750 rpm. The engine developed power rapidly and was quite economical. Maximum speed of the car was 215 km/hr and acceleration of the 0-100 km/hr was 10.8 seconds with the rather heavy (1890 kg) S-class car, and fuel consumption as low as 10.6 liters for the 0-100 km of highway driving.

During the year 1991 a total of 48,500 S-class cars were produced. In 1992 the figure was over 72,000. Of its predecessor in 1987, 70,900 S-class cars were built during the same period in time, thus clearly showing that this newest model, despite the criticism that it was the wrong car at this economically depressed time, was actually a better seller than the previous S-class models.

Model C36 AMG (1994–　　)

AMG = Aufrecht, Melcher, Grossapach

The C36 high performance, limited production model was the basic C280, but with the enlarged M104 engine of 3603 cc and 268 hp.

Many other engine and body modifications by AMG at Affalterbach made this special model equal in performance to the superb 500E sedan.

Transmission was as that of the E420 and E500, front brakes as the V-12 SL600, rear ones as the V-8 E420 models for the 17-inch wheels.

A vast number of features are standard on this C36 sedan, and only a few items, such as ASR, alarm, glass sunroof, cellular phone, etc., are optional, extra cost features.

The car carried the usual 50,000 mile, 4-year factory warranty.

Specifications

	300SE 2.8	C36 AMG
Engine type	6 cyl two overhead camshafts (M104)	6 cyl, overhead camshafts, 4 valve (M104)
Bore and stroke	89.9 x 73.5 mm	91 x 92.4 mm
Displacement	2799 cc	3606 cc
Power output	193 hp (DIN) 142Kw @ 5500 rpm	206 Kw 280 hp (DIN) @ 5750 rpm U.S.: 268 hp (SAE)
Compression ratio	10.0:1	10:5 U.S.: 10.5:1
Torque	270 Nm @ 3750 rpm	385 Nm @ 4000 rpm
Fuel injection	microprocess HFM	Microprocess HFM
Maximum engine speed	6400 rpm	6400 rpm
Gear ratios	I. 3.86:1 manual I. 4.25:1 I. 3.87:1 automatic :1 automatic II. 2.18:1 II. 2.41:1 II. 2.25:1 :1 III. 1.38:1 III. 1.49:1 III. 1.44:1 :1 IV. 1.00:1 IV. 1:00:1 IV. 1.00:1 :1 V. 0.80:1 V. 0.75:1 :1	I. 3.86:1 I. 3.87:1 (automatic) II. 2.18:1 II. 2.25:1 III. 1.38:1 III. 1.44:1 IV. 1.00:1 IV. 1.00:1 V. 0.80:1 V.
Rear axle ratio	3.92 3.46 (4) 3.69 (5)	2.85 U.S. 2.87
Chassis	unit frame and body	
Suspension	double wishbones, anti-dive control, coil springs, anti-roll bar; multi-link independent, anti-squat and -lift control, coil springs, anti-roll bar	
Brakes and area	hydraulic; dual circuit discs; ABS system	
Wheelbase	3040 mm	2690 mm
Track, front/rear	1603/1576 mm	1497/1468 mm
Length	5113 mm	4487 mm
Width	1886 mm	1720 mm
Height	1485 mm	1399 mm
Tires	235/60 R 16 100 V	225/45 ZR front; 225/40 ZR rear
Turning circle	12.18 meters	10.74 meters
Steering type and ratio	recirculating ball; servo assisted	recirculating ball
Weight	1890 kg	1560 Kg
Maximum speed	215 km/hr; 210 km/hr automatic	250 km/hr (156 mph)
Acceleration	10.8 sec, 10.6 sec 0-100 km/hr	6.9 sec 0-100 km/hr
Fuel consumption	urban cycle: 15.6 liters; highway: 10.6 liters; 14.1/11.6; 14.5/10.7	13.7 liters urban cycle
Fuel tank capacity	100 liters	62 liters

The C200 sedan, 1993

Model C180 (1993–   )

C = Compact class

The C180 model (conforming to the new method of designation) was officially shown to the general public at the Frankfurt Auto Show in September 1993. These new W202-bodied C-class models replaced the W201 of the 190 line of which over 1.9 million units had been sold during their ten years of production. However, the new cars had been shown to the general media at Lämmersbuckel in June and were then widely publicized.

With a slightly longer wheelbase and larger body, and somewhat rounder lines, these models afforded more inside space. And all new engines now had four valves per cylinder and double overhead camshafts with computer controlled variable valve timing, resulting in more power and greater mid-range torque. They also had improved fuel efficiency and lower emission than those they replaced. An improved front end suspension geometry made for improved handling.

The C180 model had the smallest of the three gasoline engines, a 1799 cc power unit of 122 horsepower at 5500 rpm and 125 ft/lbs of torque at 4200 rpm and excellent fuel economy.

Prices and Production
The C180 sedan sold in 1993 for . . . . DM 40,825

Production of the C180 model [202] (from late 1992/
February 1993)

was in	1992	11 units
	1993	54,532 units
	1994	122,101 units

Prices and Production
The C200 sedan sold in 1993 for . . . . DM 46,460

Production of the C200 model [202] (from 1993)

was in	1993	224 units
	1994	33,149 units

Model C200 (1993–   )

C = Compact class

The C200 was similar in practically all respects to the C180, but the 1998 cc four cylinder engine developed 136 horsepower and 140 ft/lbs of torque. Fuel consumption was only slightly more than that of the smaller-engined model, and performance was naturally somewhat better. This model was, however, not available until early 1994.

Specifications

	C180	C200
Engine type	4 cyl double overhead camshaft (M111)	4 cyl double overhead camshaft (M104)
Bore and stroke	85.3 x 78.7 mm (3.35 x 31.0 in)	89.9 x 78.7mm (35.4 x 31.0 in)
Displacement	1799 cc (109.8 cu in)	1998 cc (122.0 cu in)
Power output	122 hp (DIN) 90 Kw @ 5500 rpm	136 hp (DIN) 100 Kw @ 5500 rpm
Compression ratio	9.8:1	9.6:1
Torque	170 Nm @ 4200 rpm	190 Nm @ 4000 rpm
Fuel injection	Bosch P Motronic	Bosch P Motronic
Maximum engine speed	6200 rpm	6200 rpm
Gear ratios	I. 3.91:1 (5-speed manual) 4.25:1 (4-speed automatic) II. 2.17:1 2.41:1 III. 1.37:1 1.49:1 IV. 1.00:1 1:00:1 V. 0.81:1	
Rear axle ratio	3.91; automatic: 3.23	3.67; automatic: 3.07
Chassis	unit frame and body	
Suspension	upper and lower control arms, coil springs, stabilizer bar, anti-dive geometry, negative offset steering; multi-link design, coil springs, stabilizer bar, anti-lift and anti-squat geometry	
Brakes and area	hydraulic dual circuit, discs; 11.2/10.2 in; ABS	
Wheelbase	2690 mm (105.9 in)	
Track, front/rear	1505/1476 mm (58.8/57.6 in)	
Length	4487 mm (177.4 in)	
Width	1720 mm (67.7 in)	
Height	1414 mm (55.7 in)	1418 mm (55.8 in)
Tires	185/65 R 15 88 T	
Turning circle	10.74 meters (35.2 ft)	
Steering type and ratio	recirculating ball (3.5 turns); servo assisted	
Weight	1350 kg (2970 lbs)	1365 kg (3003 lbs)
Maximum speed	193 km/hr; automatic: 190km/hr	198 km/hr; automatic: 195km/hr
Acceleration	12.2 sec 0-60 mph; automatic: 13.0	10.8 sec; automatic: 11.4 sec
Fuel consumption	11.0/8.1 liters; auto: 10.6/8.5	11.2/8.0 liters; auto: 10.8/8.5
Fuel tank capacity	62 liters (16.4 gallons)	

The C280 sedan, 1993

Prices and Production

The C220 sedan sold in 1993 for . . . . DM 50,255
The C220 sold in the United States in 1993 for $29,900

Production of the C220 model [202] (from late 1992/
February 1993)

was in	1992	49 units
	1993	21,515 units
	1994	49,383 units

The C280 sedan sold in 1993 for . . . . DM 57,845
The C280 sold in the United State in 1993 for $34,900

Production of the C280 model [202] from late 1992/
February 1993)

was in	1992	51 units
	1993	11,387 units
	1994	36,974 units

Model C220 (1993–   )

C = Compact class

The C220 model had the largest of the three four-cylinder gasoline engines (150 horsepower) in this line of cars. Essentially, it was the same as the other models in appearance and body specifications.

The C220 was the only four cylinder gasoline engined model available in this country. The engine developed 147 horse-power and had 155 lbs/ft of torque, giving the car a very good performance rating, quite superior to that of the 190 E 2.3 which it replaced. Acceleration was for the 0-60 mph 10.2 seconds against the 10.8 for the 190, and fuel consumption was 20/26 miles per gallon against the 21/28.

For the American market, a great many formerly optional items became standard equipment in this model. And the price was about the same as that for the 190 model it replaced.

Model C280 (1993–   )

C = Compact class

The C280 model had the six cylinder gasoline engine of 193 horsepower, thus becoming the most powerful model of the C-class cars. Also available in the American market, but with the engine developing 194 (SAE) horsepower and a torque of 199 lbs/ft.

The performance was outstanding with this powerful engine which was also used in the medium E-class cars and even in one of the special S-class models. Compared with the 190E 2.6, which the C280 replaced, horsepower was 194 against 158, torque 199 against 162, and acceleration figures were 8.3 sec to 9.6 sec for the 0-60 mph.

As above, cars in this country had a vast number of formerly optional items as standard equipment, and with the same price the C280 was a strong centender against formidable competition.

Specifications

	C220	C280
Engine type	4 cyl double overhead camshaft (M111)	6 cyl double overhead camshaft (M104)
Bore and stroke	89.9 x 86.6 mm (3.54 x 3.41 in)	89.9 x 73.5mm (3.54 x 2.89 in)
Displacement	2199 cc (134.2 cu in)	2799 cc (170.9 cu in)
Power output	**150 hp (DIN) 110 Kw** @ 5500 rpm U.S.: 147 hp (SAE)	193 hp (DIN) 142Kw @ 5500 rpm U.S.: 194 hp (SAE)
Compression ratio	**10:1**	**10:1**
Torque	**210 Nm** @ 4000 rpm U.S.: 155 ft/lbs	270 Nm @ 3750 rpm U.S.: 199 ft/lbs
Fuel injection	**Bosch fully electronic, HFM**	**Bosch fully electronic, HFM**
Maximum engine speed	**6200 rpm**	**6400 rpm**
Gear ratios	I. 3.91:1 (5-speed manual) 4.25:1 (4-speed automatic) II. 2.17:1 2.41:1 III. 1.37:1 1.49:1 IV. 1.00:1 1:00:1 V. 0.81:1	3.86:1 (5-speed manual) 4.25:1 (4-speed automatic) 2.18:1 2.41:1 1.38:1 1.49:1 1.00:1 1.00:1 0.80:1
Rear axle ratio	3.67; automatic: 3.07	3.67; automatic: 2.87
Chassis	unit frame and body	
Suspension	upper and lower control arms, coil springs, stabilizer bar, anti-dive geometry, negative offset steering; multi-link design, coil springs, stabilizer bar, anti-lift and anti-squat geometry	
Brakes and area	hydraulic dual circuit, discs; 11.2/10.2 in; ABS	
Wheelbase	2690 mm (105.9 in)	
Track, front/rear	1505/1476 mm (58.8/57.6 in)	
Length	4487 mm (177.4 in)	
Width	1487 mm (177.4 in)	
Height	1424 mm (56.1 in)	
Tires	195/65 R 15 91 V U.S.: 195/65 R 15	
Turning circle	10.74 meters (35.2 ft)	
Steering type and ratio	recirculating ball (3.5 turns); servo assisted	
Weight	1410 kg (3102 lbs) U.S.: 3173 lbs	1490 kg (3278 lbs) U.S.: 3293 lbs
Maximum speed	210 km/hr; automatic: 207 km/hr (131/129 mph)	230 km/hr; automatic: 227 km/hr (144/142 mph)
Acceleration	0.4 sec 0-60 mph; automatic: 10.5	8.8 sec; automatic: 8.5 U.S.: 8.4 sec
Fuel consumption	1.5/8.1 liters; auto: 11.0/8.5 (21/28 mpg)	14.4/9.5 liters; auto: 12.9/9.8 (20/25 mpg)
Fuel tank capacity	2 liters (16.4 gallons	

The C250 Diesel sedan, 1993

Model C200 Diesel (1993–   )

C = Compact Class

The C200 Diesel was one of three diesel-engined models with the W202 body style shown at the Frankfurt Auto Show in 1993. The car had the tried and tested, but further refined (two valve per cylinder), four-cylinder engine of 1997 cc developing 75 horsepower at 4600 rpm and maximum torque of 130 Nm at 2000 to 3600 rpm. Fuel consumption was a meager 5 liters at 90 km/hr and 8.2 liters for the urban cycle.

Now, all diesel engines were fitted with an oxidation catalyst and exhaust gas recirculation as standard equipment.

Model C220 Diesel (1993–   )

C = Compact class

The C220 Diesel had one of the first diesel engines fitted with the four valves per cylinder technology, which was not only environmentally compatible, but also boosted performance and reduced fuel consumption appreciably. The 2155 cc four-cylinder engine developed 95 horsepower and 150 Nm torque. Fuel consumption was 5.3 liters at 90 km/hr (56 mph) and 8.5 liters for the urban cycle.

Model C250 Diesel (1993–   )

C = Compact class

The C250 Diesel was the most powerful of the three versions. It had the five cylinder diesel engine of 2497 cc which developed 113 horsepower and 170 Nm torque. Fuel consumption was an incredible 5.4 liters at 90 km/hr and 8.7 liters for the urban cycle.

All the new diesel C-class models compared most favorably with the previous 190 line of cars. All of them had larger bodies with more space and the engines had more power and significantly increased torque ratings, better performance and lower fuel consumption.

Prices and Production

The C200 Diesel sedan sold in 1993 for . . . . DM 42,435

Production of the C200 Diesel model [202] (from late 1992/February 1993)

	was in	1992	29 units
		1993	12,764 units
		1994	17,336 units

The C220 Diesel sedan sold in 1993 for . . . . DM 44,275

Production of the C220 Diesel model [202] (from late 1992/February 1993)

	was in	1992	7 units
		1993	6,570 units
		1994	35,997 units

The C250 Diesel sedan sold in 1993 for . . . . DM 49,565

Production of the C250 Diesel model [202] (from late 1992/February 1993)

	was in	1992	8 units
		1993	10,878 units
		1994	19,729 units

Specifications

	C200 Diesel	C220 Diesel	C250 Diesel
Engine type	4 cyl diesel, overhead camshaft	4 cyl diesel, overhead camshaft	5 cyl diesel, overhead camshaft
Bore and stroke	87.0 x 84.0 mm	89.0 x 86.6 mm	87.0 x 84.0 mm
Displacement	1997 cc (121.9 cu in)	2155 cc (131.5 cu in)	2497 cc (152.4 cu in)
Power output	75 hp (DIN) 55 Kw @ 4600 rpm	95 hp (DIN) 70 Kw @ 5000 rpm	113 hp (DIN) 83 Kw @ 5000 rpm
Compression ratio	22:1	22:1	22:1
Torque	130 Nm @ 2000-3600 rpm	150 Nm @ 3100-4500 rpm	170 Nm @ 2800-4600 rpm
Fuel injection	Bosch four plunger pump	Bosch distributor plunger EDC	Bosch five plunger EDC
Maximum engine speed	5150 rpm	5450 rpm	5450 rpm
Gear ratios	I. 3.91:1 5-speed manual II. 2.17:1 III. 1.37:1 IV. 1.00:1 V. 0.81:1	4.25:1 4-speed automatic 2.41:1 1.49:1 1:00:1	
Rear axle ratio	3.91; automatic: 3.23	3.64; automatic: 3.07	
Chassis	unit frame and body		
Suspension	upper and lower control arms, coil springs, stabilizer bar, anti-dive geometry, negative offset steering; multi-link design, coil springs, stabilizer bar, anti-lift and anti-squat geometry		
Brakes and area	hydraulic dual circuit, discs; 11.2/10.2in; ABS		
Wheelbase	2690 mm (105.9 in)		
Track, front/rear	1505/1476 mm (58.8/57.6 in)		
Length	4487 mm (177.4 in)		
Width	1720 mm (67.7 in)		
Height	1414 mm (55.7 in)	1418 mm (55.8 in)	1418 mm (55.8 in)
Tires	185/60 R 15 88 T	185/60 R 15 88 T	185/65 R 15 88 H
Turning circle	10.74 meters (35.2 ft)		
Steering type and ratio	recirculating ball (3.5 turns); servo assisted		
Weight	1380 kg (3036 lbs)	1400 kg (3080 lbs)	1450 kg (3190 lbs)
Maximum speed	160 km/hr; automatic: 157 km/hr (100/99 mph)	175 km/hr; automatic 172 km/hr	190 km/hr; automatic: 187 km/hr
Acceleration	18.4 sec 0-60 mph; automatic: 19.9 sec	16.3 sec; automatic: 17.4 sec	14.8 sec; automatic: 15.6 sec
Fuel consumption	8.2/6.8 liters; auto: 7.6/7.3	8.5/6.9 liters; auto: 8.2/7.5	8.7/6.9 liters; auto: 8.4/7.5
Fuel tank capacity	62 liters (16.4 gallons)		

Model Offerings

These random offerings are given merely to emphasize the fact that only carefully selected models of the large variety available from the factory were sold in the United States. For example, in 1976 only 10 models were marketed here while the factory offered a total of 27 models (actually 41 were listed, counting the 2 styles 115/114 and 123 of the smaller cars, the longer wheelbase versions, and three versions of the 600 limousine).

For 1966 Daimler-Benz offered for sale:

200	2.0 liter gasoline	4 cyl	95 hp DIN
200D	2.0 liter diesel	4 cyl	55 hp DIN
230	2.3 liter gasoline	6 cyl	105 hp DIN
230S	2.3 liter gasoline	6 cyl	120 hp DIN
250S	2.5 liter gasoline	6 cyl	130 hp DIN
250SE	2.5 liter gasoline	6 cyl	150 hp DIN
220SE coupe and convertible	2.2 liter gasoline	6 cyl	120 hp DIN
250SE coupe and convertible	2.5 liter gasoline	6 cyl	150 hp DIN
300SEb	3.0 liter gasoline	6 cyl	170 hp DIN
300SEL	3.0 liter gasoline	6 cyl	170 hp DIN
300SE coupe and convertible	3.0 liter gasoline	6 cyl	170 hp DIN
230SL	2.3 liter gasoline	6 cyl	150 hp DIN
600	6.3 liter gasoline	8 cyl	250 hp DIN
600 pullman	6.3 liter gasoline	8 cyl	250 hp DIN

For 1970 the following models were sold in the U.S.

220	2.2 liter gasoline	4 cyl	116 hp SAE
220D	2.2 liter diesel	4 cyl	65 hp SAE
250	2.5 liter gasoline	6 cyl	146 hp SAE
250C	2.8 liter gasoline	6 cyl	157 hp SAE
280S	2.8 liter gasoline	6 cyl	157 hp SAE
280SE	2.8 liter gasoline	6 cyl	180 hp SAE
280SEL	2.8 liter gasoline	6 cyl	180 hp SAE
280SE coupe and convertible	2.8 liter gasoline	6 cyl	180 hp SAE
280SL	2.8 liter gasoline	6 cyl	180 hp SAE
300SEL	2.8 liter gasoline	6 cyl	180 hp SAE
300SEL 6.3	6.3 liter gasoline	8 cyl	300 hp SAE
600 5 passenger	6.3 liter gasoline	8 cyl	300 hp SAE
600 7 passenger	6.3 liter gasoline	8 cyl	300 hp SAE

For 1976 Daimler-Benz offered for sale:

200D	2.0 liter diesel	4 cyl	55 hp DIN
220D	2.2 liter diesel	4 cyl	60 hp DIN
240D	2.4 liter diesel	4 cyl	65 hp DIN
240D 3.0	3.0 liter diesel	5 cyl	80 hp DIN
200	2.0 liter gasoline	4 cyl	95 hp DIN
230.4	2.3 liter gasoline	4 cyl	110 hp DIN
230.6	2.3 liter gasoline	6 cyl	120 hp DIN
250	2.8 liter gasoline	6 cyl	130 hp DIN
280	2.8 liter gasoline	6 cyl	160 hp DIN
280E	2.8 liter gasoline	6 cyl	185 hp DIN
250C	2.8 liter gasoline	6 cyl	130 hp DIN
280C	2.8 liter gasoline	6 cyl	160 hp DIN
280CE	2.8 liter gasoline	6 cyl	185 hp DIN
280S	2.8 liter gasoline	6 cyl	160 hp DIN
280SE	2.8 liter gasoline	6 cyl	185 hp DIN
280SEL	2.8 liter gasoline	6 cyl	185 hp DIN
350SE	3.5 liter gasoline	8 cyl	200 hp DIN
350SEL	3.5 liter gasoline	8 cyl	200 hp DIN
450SE	4.5 liter gasoline	8 cyl	225 hp DIN
450SEL	4.5 liter gasoline	8 cyl	225 hp DIN
450SEL 6.9	6.9 liter gasoline	8 cyl	286 hp DIN
280SL	2.8 liter gasoline	6 cyl	185 hp DIN
350SL	3.5 liter gasoline	8 cyl	200 hp DIN
450SL	4.5 liter gasoline	8 cyl	225 hp DIN
280SLC	2.8 liter gasoline	6 cyl	185 hp DIN
350SLC	3.5 liter gasoline	8 cyl	200 hp DIN
450SLC	4.5 liter gasoline	8 cyl	225 hp DIN

For 1976 the following models were sold in the U.S.

240D	2.4 liter diesel	4 cyl	62 hp SAE
300D	3.0 liter diesel	5 cyl	77 hp SAE
230	2.3 liter gasoline	4 cyl	93 hp SAE (Cal. 85)
280	2.8 liter gasoline	6 cyl	120 hp SAE
280C	2.8 liter gasoline	6 cyl	120 hp SAE
280S	2.8 liter gasoline	6 cyl	120 hp SAE
450SE	4.5 liter gasoline	8 cyl	180 hp SAE
450SEL	4.5 liter gasoline	8 cyl	180 hp SAE
450SL	4.5 liter gasoline	8 cyl	180 hp SAE
450SLC	4.5 liter gasoline	8 cyl	180 hp SAE

Production Totals
and United States Sales

Year	MB Pass. Car Production	MB Pass. Car Sales in U.S.	% of MB Sales of Total Imp. Car Sales	Total Imp. Car Sales in U.S.	Year	MB Pass. Car Production	MB Pass. Car Sales in U.S.	% of MB Sales of Total Imp. Car Sales	Total Imp. Car Sales in U.S.
1946	214				1985	541,039	86,903	3.27	2,837,573
1947	1,045				1986	594,080	99,314	3.27	3,244,621
1948	5,116	1			1987	598,079	89,918	3.55	3,195,701
1949	17,417	2			1988	559,713	83,727	3.70	3,099,467
1950	33,906	13			1989	542,160	75,714	3.73	2,825,165
1951	42,222	18			1990	574,227	78,375	4.07	3,192,347
1952	36,824	253			1991	577,990	58,868	4.98	2,930,892
1953	34,975	421			1992	529,428	63,312	4.61	2,916,975
1954	48,816	636			1993	480,571	61,899	4.66	2,887,387
1955	63,683	2,041			1994	594,366	73,002	4.28	3,125,725
1956	69,601	3,101							
1957	80,899	6,039							
1958	99,209	7,404							
1959	108,440	12,071							
1960	122,684	12,254							
1961	137,431	12,625							
1962	146,393	12,947		339,160					
1963	153,182	11,688	3.03	385,624					
1964	165,532	11,867	2.45	484,131					
1965	174,007	12,117	2.13	569,415					
1966	191,625	16,162	2.46	658,123					
1967	200,470	20,691	2.66	779,220					
1968	216,284	24,553	2.49	985,767					
1969	256,713	26,193	2.47	1,061,617					
1970	280,419	29,108	2.36	1,230,961					
1971	284,230	35,192	2.36	1,487,613					
1972	323,878	41,556	2.72	1,529,402					
1973	331,682	41,865	2.43	1,719,913					
1974	340,006	38,170	2.79	1,369,148					
1975	350,098	45,159	2.87	1,571,472					
1976	370,348	43,205	2.88	1,498,745					
1977	401,255	48,872	2.36	2,074,390					
1978	393,203	46,695	2.33	2,002,413					
1979	422,159	52,820	2.26	2,332,296					
1980	429,078	53,790	2.24	2,397,887					
1981	440,778	63,059	2.71	2,327,106					
1982	458,345	65,963	2.97	2,222,214					
1983	476,183	73,692	3.24	2,385,734					
1984	478,349	79,222	3.08	2,441,713					

Model Designations

Times past were not as complicated as the years are now, and things were not as confusing as they sometimes get in this electronic and computerized age.

Gottlieb Daimler called his first motorized vehicle (1889), which did not resemble a horse carriage, simply the Stahlradwagen, and a steel-wheel car it was. His earlier carriages (1885-1886) were a Motorkutsche, a motorized coach.

Karl Benz named his first four-wheeled car (1893) Viktoria, and subsequent styles were all carriages and had those designations, Landauer, Phaeton, etc. The name Velo was derived from velociped (bicycle), and it looked not like a carriage any more.

To indicate the performance of the vehicles, the horsepower was added to the name and from about 1902 on, the calculated rated output, called nominal output, and the brake horsepower were also given along with the designation, as in 14/18 h.p. Phaeton. After the rating formula was introduced, the first number referred to the taxable horsepower and the second to the effective output, as in 10/30 Benz touring car. Vehicles with superchargers had three numbers: the taxable horsepower, the effective output, and the maximum output with the supercharger engaged.

After the merger of Daimler and Benz in 1926, some models were given specific names, usually the plant where they were manufactured, as Stuttgart and Mannheim. Soon, the designation of the model signified the displacement of the engine, as in 180, which meant a 1.8-liter engine. This nomenclature went on for a long time and is still in effect, at least to some extent. Difficulties were soon encountered, however, and even greater difficulties were experienced with the letters.

The D stood for Diesel. Rear-engined models had the H for Heck, rear end. V indicated front-engined, Vorn. Fuel injection engines had the E for Einspritzung, injection. But the letter S stood for several things, but generally for Super.

The S designation in the 300SL stands for Sport and the L for Leicht, or light. In the 190SL it stood for the same, but that was neither a sports car nor was it light. Weight was 2,596 pounds against the 300SL's 2,849 and half the engine power. However, in sedans the L stands for Lang, or long wheelbase chassis, as in 280SEL.

In the elegant 300S line, the S stood for Super. It was the superior version of the 300 sedan model. But when another S was added, the first S did not stand for Sport, but Super, and the second S was Sport, as in the SS models (1927-1935). The added K meant Kurz, or short chassis, and the L was the model with holes drilled almost everywhere to save weight. The S, incidentally, never stood for supercharger — that was a K, for Kompressor, as in 500K, etc. They were not short wheelbase cars, but large sedans for special bodied roadsters or coupes.

Later C stood for coupe, as in the SLC line, or the 250C, which was actually a 280 in this country, with the 2.8-liter engine instead of the 2,496 cubic centimeter power unit, as elsewhere. Other misnamed cars were the 280 line in 1969, with 3.5-liter engines, as 280SE 3.5, later 4.5. The 300SEL had the same problem, as a 300SEL 4.5, etc. This confusion went on to the 6.3- and 6.9-liter cars, and the 450SLC 5.0, or even the first 300 diesels in Europe, which were the 240D 3.0; here the 300D. The 350SL was actually a 450 in this country, but a 3.5-liter engined car elsewhere, and the 280 or 450 SLs were correctly identified.

Occasionally, a slight difference is made for reasons of simplicity. The 633 Grosser sounded perhaps better as a 600, but the engine was, of course, of 6,332 cc capacity. There were 600, 620, 630, 660 and 680 models, some with K or S from 1924 to 1942, incidentally.

After having built so many different types of cars over the years, a shortage of designations was probably only natural. Thus, when the turbo-charged diesel engined models appeared, the T had already been appropriated elsewhere. That was the T for Touristik and Transport in the station wagon line of cars, as in 230T to 300TD. (On the factory production sheets this turbo station wagon model was shown as TDT, but then the sporty SL line was SLR; for roadster, not Racing, as in former years for the factory 300SLR machines.) Here the station wagon was merely the 300TD turbo.

The first turbo-charged diesel sedan, at least, got the S designation to differentiate this model from the regularly aspirated diesel sedan, and became the 300SD. When the regular line of five-cylinder diesel models got the turbo-charged engine, nothing but the extra power was added. They simply remained the 300D. This generation, of course, does not remember that an SD sedan in 1953 to 1955 was a diesel version of the 170V series (S for Special) and that a year before that there was a 170DS. That time the S designated really a Special model of the 170V series, because the car incorporated the components of several others, such as the engine and front axle from the V, the chassis from the Sb, and the body from the S model. The smaller letters are sometimes used in the subdivisions of a certain model and they indicate merely a further development, usually in the engine only, as 200, 200b, 200c, etc.

Designations were drastically altered, and greatly simplified, with the 1994 model year. The smaller sized cars, the Kompaktklasse, became the C (for Compact) class, as in C200. The intermediate body style cars, (sedans, station wagons and coupes), the Mittelere Klasse, became the E (for Executive) class, as in E300. The larger Sonderklasse models remained the S class (for Super) cars, as previously, as in S600. The sports cars kept their SL designations, as in SL300. These identification letters now preceded the engine size numbers, and the word Diesel appeared, as before, on the trunk lid for cars with such engines.

Production Eras (continued from page 9)

The 190 line of small cars was well accepted by the buying public and the basic 2.0 liter gasoline (90 hp) and 2.0 liter diesel engined (72 hp) models — for the U.S. 2.3-liter gasoline and 2.2-liter diesel — sold a total of 109,832 units the first full year (1983) after introduction.

However, Mercedes drivers demanded more powerful cars, even in this rather compact class. The gasoline models of 2.3 liter were added, and the diesels eventually received 2.5 liter engines of 90 hp. For the sports minded driver, the 2.3 gasoline engine was modified to have four valves per cylinder and this 2.3-16 model developed 185 horsepower (167 in the U.S.) and had a maximum speed of 230 kilometers (143.5 miles) per hour. To illustrate the superb performance of this model, twenty meticulously prepared such cars, driven in a 34-mile race by the elite of international Grand Prix drivers, performed in May 1934 at the dedication ceremonies of the new Nürburgring circuit to the enjoyment of some 120,000 enthusiastic spectators. Another set 3 world records at the Nardo track.

Eventually, the 190 line proliferated to include nine models, the most powerful sedan being the 2.6-liter engined of 166 horsepower in 1986. (The 16 valve version had actually 185 hp.) Sales of the models had quickly accelerated after the introduction and by 1985, production of the nine variants of the compact W201 bodied models exceeded those of the middle class (W124) sedan lines, 117,811 to 114,721.

With the sudden death in 1983 of the chairman of the board of management Gerhard Prinz, Werner Breitschwerdt was elected to that position and Rudolf Hörnig became the chief engineer of the company. His distinguishing contribution was the development of the straight six cylinder diesel engine and the further adaption of the four valve-per-cylinder configuration to other gasoline engined models. Hörnig chose this system over that of turbocharging as many other car manufacturers preferred.

With the acquisition by Daimler-Benz of three very important German manufacturing concerns — The Dornier, MTU, and AEG — a vast reorganization took place. The automotive manufacturing part (one-half of the entire marks volume) became the Mercedes-Benz group of factories. Wolfgang Peter was the new head of development in the passenger car division.

The first notable event was the introduction of the R-129 body style of SL cars to replace the 18-year old 107 line. The 300SL came also with four valves per cylinder and 228 horsepower, while the 500SL V-8 engine developed 322 horsepower. New S-class models were in the offering, and one new model per year was proposed.

Conversions of Power   SAE?

Engine output is not only given in horsepower but is also listed as Kw (kilowatt). And torque is not only mkg (meter/kilogram) or lb/ft (pounds/feet), but also Nm (Newton meter). [Conversion factors: 1 hp = 0.736 Kw; 1 mkg = 9.81 Nm].

Herewith are a few examples of the later model 1980 cars (in European trim).

200D/TD	60 hp (DIN)	44 Kw	113 Nm	11.5 mkg
240D/TD	72	53	137	14.0
300D/TD	88	65	172	17.5
300SD/TD turbo	125	92	250	25.5
200/T	109	80	170	17.3
230E/CE/TE	136	100	205	20.9
250	140	103	200	20.4
280/S/SL/SLC	156	115	223	22.7
280E/CE/TE/SE/SEL	185	136	240	24.5
380SE/SEL/SL/SLC	218	160	305	31.1
500SE/SEL/SL/SLC	240	177	404	41.2

and earlier (1975 models had these figures:

200D	55 hp (DIN	40 Kw	113 Nm	11.5 mkg
220D	60	44	126	12.8
240D	65	48	137	14.0
240D 3.0	80	59	172	17.5
200	95	70	156	15.9
230.4	110	81	186	19.0
230.6	120	88	179	18.2
250/C	130	96	216	22.0
280/C/S	160	118	226	23.0
280/E/CE/SE/SEL/SL/SLC	185	136	238	24.3
350SE/SEL/SL/SLC	200	147	286	29.2
450SE/SEL/SL/SLC	225	165	378	38.5
450SEL 6.9	286	210	550	56.0

Engine and Chassis Codes

To recognize the chassis or the engine numbers is simple because in the chassis numbers the fourth digit always is 0 or 1, while in the engine numbers it is always a 9.

The chassis as well as the engine numbers from 1946 to 1950 always had eleven digits consisting of the basic type, model style, and serial number.

In 1951 and 1952 the production year was added to the serial number, and from 1953 through 1959, while the numbers still consisted of 13 digits, code letters were added for clutch and transmission, and the production year digits were reversed.

From 1960 on, there were 14 digits to the identification numbers. The code letters had been changed to numbers and the production year was eliminated. Each model, regardless of year of manufacture, was numbered consecutively, making for a six-digit serial number.

As an example, a car has the following numbers (my 300CD coupe, 1980):

12315012005611 and 61791212098083

Chassis type 123, model 150, left-hand drive 1, automatic transmission 2, and serial number 005611. Engine type 617, model 912, left-hand drive 1, automatic transmission 2, and serial number 098083.

In 1980 a new 17 digit Vehicle Identification System was introduced. It started with the Manufacturer's code (WDB), that gave the model type, restraint system, year and place of manufacture (Sindelfinger or Bremen). To identify the chassis number from the engine number: the 4th chassis number is always 0 or 1, while the fourth engine number is always 9.

My 1988 300CE coupe has the following number:
WDBEA50D8JA781721
which reveals all of the essential destails of the car.

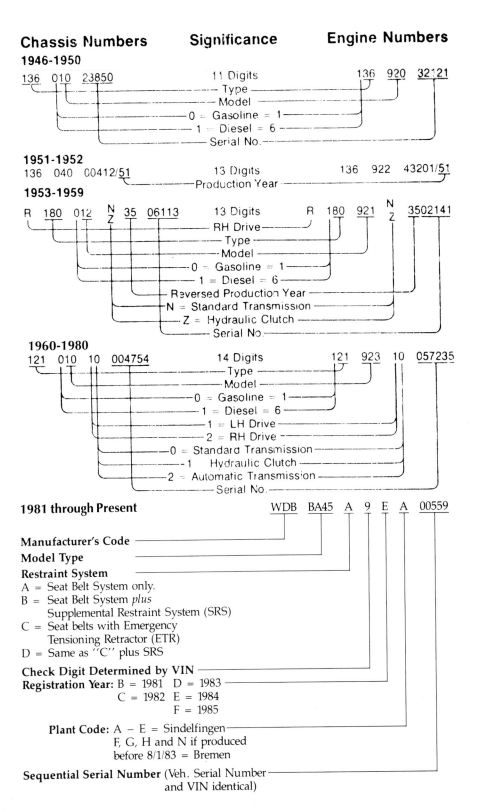